Politics of the Middle East

Cultures and Conflicts

SECOND EDITION

Michael G. Roskin
Lycoming College

James J. Coyle
Chapman University

PEARSON

Prentice
Hall

UPPER SADDLE RIVER, NEW JERSEY 07458

Library of Congress Cataloging-in-Publication Data

Roskin, Michael
    Politics of the Middle East: cultures and conflicts/Michael G. Roskin, James J. Coyle.—2nd ed.
        p. cm.
    Includes bibliographical references and index.
    ISBN 978-0-13-159424-1
    1. Middle East.   I. Coyle, James J.   II. Title.
    DS44.R745   2008
    956—dc22   2007013458

Editorial Director: Charlyce Jones Owen
Executive Editor: Dickson Musslewhite
Associate Editor: Rob DeGeorge
Editorial Assistant: Synamin Ballatt
Senior Marketing Manager: Kate Mitchell
Marketing Assistant: Jennifer Lang
Director of Operations: Barbara Kittle
Senior Operations Supervisor: Mary Ann Gloriande
Senior Managing Editor: Lisa Iarkowski
Production Liaison: Jean Lapidus
Production Assistant: Marlene Gassler
Cover Art Director: Jayne Conte
Cover Design: Bruce Kenselaar
Cover Photo: Andrew Parsons/Getty Images, Inc.–Agence France Presse
Interior Design: John P. Mazzola
Composition/Full-Service Project Management: Kari Callaghan Mazzola and John P. Mazzola
Printer/Binder: RR Donnelley & Sons Company
Cover Printer: RR Donnelley & Sons Company

This book was set in 10/12 Meridien.

Pearson Education LTD.
Pearson Education Singapore, Pte. Ltd
Pearson Education, Canada, Ltd
Pearson Education–Japan
Pearson Education Australia PTY, Limited

Pearson Education North Asia Ltd
Pearson Educación de Mexico, S.A. de C.V.
Pearson Education Malaysia, Pte. Ltd
Pearson Education, Upper Saddle River, NJ

10 9 8 7 6 5 4 3 2 1
ISBN 13: 978-0-13-159424-1
ISBN 10:   0-13-159424-9

Contents

CHAPTER 3
THE OTTOMAN EMPIRE   42

PART II   ARAB-ISRAELI CONFLICTS   57

CHAPTER 4
ORIGINS OF THE ISRAEL-PALESTINE WAR   57

CHAPTER 5

THE VERY LONG WAR   79

CHAPTER 6

IS PEACE POSSIBLE?   102

PART IV   THE RISE OF THE OIL KINGDOMS   167

CHAPTER 9
IRAN   167

CHAPTER 10
SAUDI ARABIA   186

CHAPTER 13

THE FIRST GULF WAR   241

CHAPTER 17

THE UNITED STATES AND THE MIDDLE EAST   315

Feature Boxes

CHAPTER 9

CHAPTER 10

CHAPTER 11

CHAPTER 12

CHAPTER 13

CHAPTER 14

CHAPTER 15

Preface

It is gratifying to see our introductory book appear in a second edition. Students are starting to take an interest in the Middle East, although few of them have the historical or geographic background to make much sense of the region. They know from brief television newsclips that there is much tumult in the Middle East but do not know why or what the United States has to do with it. As in the first edition, we aim to remedy this.

Our starting point is that many scholarly works on the Middle East are too specialized for a first undergraduate course in the area. With years of experience in college teaching on the region, government service, and journalism, we saw the need for a textbook covering Middle Eastern history, geography, and conflicts, including the 2003 Iraq War and its chaotic aftermath. That war illustrates the interrelated complexity of the Middle East. To understand Iraq now, one must delve into the past—religions, ethnic groups, and regimes—not only of Iraq but also of the entire region. How many young Americans know the difference between Sunni and Shi'a and why that difference became an American problem? Two areas especially shortchanged in most textbooks, Turkey and the Kurds, are here given their own chapters. (One of the authors did his doctoral dissertation on Kurdish nationalism.)

To remedy the geography gap, we include "bounding" exercises throughout the book. This old-fashioned exercise requires the student to recite, from forced recall, countries' boundaries, moving clockwise around the points of the compass. Students will thus be able to locate every country of the Middle East.

The news media still tend to use "Middle East" as synonymous with the Israeli-Arab struggle. When they talk about Iraq, Iran, or Saudi Arabia, they use "Persian Gulf." Actually, the two are both Middle East and, although a few hundred miles apart, interconnected. Israel angers the Muslim world and serves as fodder for radical Islamists who would like to take over the Gulf oil states, which already encourage and subsidize Palestinian movements, some of them violent.

As before, we interweave much general material in our chapters, everything from praetorianism to bureaucratic politics in Washington. All apply to the Middle East but have wider applicability as well. This is part of our purpose, to build what the French call *culture générale*. Topics in the abstract often become real when introduced in a relevant context. Accordingly, students will learn a great deal beyond the Middle East from this book.

The Middle East is full of controversies, and we are aware that our accounts and analyses may not please all. We are likely to be accused of being hostile or being supportive of certain causes. We are neither; we are simply realists. Our purpose is not to take sides but to tell several fascinating, complex stories in an accurate and balanced way.

The second edition, in addition to being updated, is smoother and better organized. We still stress basic concepts, vocabulary, and case studies. We continue with running glossaries for boldfaced terms and feature boxes for "Conflicts," "Cultures," "Geography," "Key Concepts," "Peace," "Personalities," "Religions," and "The United States in the Middle East." In response to reviewers' comments, we have added feature boxes on "Domestic Structures" for many Middle Eastern countries, recognizing that domestic structures influence foreign policy and international relations. Also in response to reviewers, we have integrated the first edition's Chapter 2, "The Ancients and Their Conflicts," into the first chapter, so now the book is one chapter shorter.

The authors thank Cullen Chandler, Mehrdad Madresehee, Robin Knauth, and Steven Johnson of Lycoming College for their valuable comments and corrections. We also thank the following outside reviewers: James M. Lutz, Indiana University–Purdue University at Fort Wayne; Husam A. Mohamad, University of Central Oklahoma; Jay C. Mumford, Pennsylvania State University at Harrisburg; James A. Piazza, University of North Carolina at Charlotte; and Yury Polsky, West Chester University.

Michael G. Roskin
roskin@lycoming.edu

James J. Coyle
coyle@chapman.edu

1   *Civilization and Its Cradle*

Points to Ponder

- What countries does the Middle East include?
- How does water determine much of the Middle East?
- What is a religion?
- Is it valid to characterize whole peoples by culture?
- What is "oral tradition" and why is it still important?
- Typically, how do Middle Easterners identify themselves?
- Do political units tend to expand their territory?
- What have ancient empires contributed to today's Middle East?
- What was Thucydides' explanation of war?

Markers on our Y chromosomes indicate that our distant ancestors moved north from their original home in Africa into the Middle East a mere 50,000 years ago. Some stayed in the Middle East while others moved on to populate Asia, Europe, and the Americas.

The Middle East is particularly interesting because here, according to most archaeologists, began **civilization**. This process started in the **Neolithic** period when the Ice Age ended, about 10,000 years ago. Humans, after millennia as hunter-gatherers, began staying in one area and cultivating crops they found growing naturally. Mesopotamia, scholars claim, was the first area cultivated because it contained grains and animals—especially wheat and sheep—that could be easily domesticated. Farmers and herders could produce more food than they needed to feed their families, enabling more humans to live in a given area than could hunter-gatherers, and populations grew.

---

civilization   Highly evolved culture featuring cities, writing, social classes, and complex economies and politics.

Neolithic   New Stone Age, transition to settled agriculture and dawn of civilization.

G : *Geography*

THE GREAT RIFT

One fascinating geological feature of the Middle East is the Great Rift Valley, a giant, jagged crack in the earth's surface where two of the earth's tectonic plates moved apart. It extends nearly straight southward from above the Sea of Galilee, down the Jordan River through the Dead Sea, Wadi Araba, and Gulf of Aqaba. Archaeologists believe early humans moved up the Rift Valley through the Middle East and then outward into Asia and Europe. At the Red Sea the rift takes a jog eastward, then another jog southward deep into Africa.

The Jordan Valley contains the lowest spots on earth. The Sea of Galilee is 680 feet below sea level. The Jordan River, entirely below sea level, flows south from Galilee until it empties into the Dead Sea, the lowest place on earth, nearly 1,300 feet below sea level, which explains why it is dead. Water flows in but cannot flow out, because there is nothing lower.

Water leaves the Dead Sea only by evaporation, which is rapid in the hot, dry air of the area. Evaporation used to balance inflow, leaving the Dead Sea's level relatively constant. Recently, however, with heavy usage of the Jordan's water, the level of the Dead Sea has been slowly dropping. Left behind in the Sea are the salts and minerals that make bathers extremely buoyant. Sodom and Gomorrah are still sought by archaeologists working by the Dead Sea. They could have drawn their water from small, sweet water streams that flow into the Dead Sea to this day. Lot's wife, turned into a pillar of salt as she fled Sodom, might teach today's Middle East peace negotiators something: Don't look back.

Israeli soldiers overlook the harsh landscape of the Dead Sea in the very gully where David hid from Saul. (*Michael G. Roskin*)

With this, came the "specialization of labor" and social classes. Very early, farmers fought herders over who was to use the land. Genesis 4:1–16 tells us how Cain, the cultivator, slew Abel, the shepherd—an example of this conflict. Labor became more specialized. An artisan class made shoes, clothing, and implements to be traded for the farmers' and herders' food. To facilitate production and selling, they clustered in towns. Market places are likely the origin of towns, which became tempting targets for marauding bands. Towns needed protection and thus began to be built on hilltops and walled. They also needed rudimentary political organization; chiefs turned themselves into petty kings. Jericho, the oldest town yet uncovered, was walled some 8,000 years ago, even before pottery was invented.

With the **Bronze Age** came an "urban revolution." Some towns grew into cities, the cores of ancient kingdoms, which increased complexity. They developed rules and professional magistrates to enforce them—the origins of legal systems. And cities needed to be defended, producing the first professional rulers and their helpers, males who were neither farmers nor artisans but warriors, first to defend their own turf and wherever possible to take someone else's. These rulers became kings, and their helpers became nobles, most hereditary, with new lines arising based on wealth and military victories. Nobles, scribes, treasury keepers,

Traditional Arab villages of sun-dried bricks have changed little over the millennia. (*Michael G. Roskin*)

Bronze Age   Beginnings of metal-working about 5,500 years ago.

G Geography

WHAT IS THE MIDDLE EAST?

The term *Middle East* is recent and controversial, a label that came out of Europe, not from the region itself. The simplest geographical definition is the region where Asia, Africa, and Europe meet, the "hub of the World Island."

Definitions of what it includes get arbitrary. All agree that Iran, which is Muslim but not Arab, is part of the Middle East, but until recently few included the "-stans" (meaning "place of," such as Pakistan, Afghanistan, Uzbekistan, and so on). They are also Muslim but not Arab and generally classified as Southwest or Central Asia even though they are culturally and geographically close to the Middle East. For example, Uzbekistan's Islamic past, architecture, and folkways give it a strong Middle Eastern feel. We will touch on Afghanistan in Chapter 14 because it has great bearing on current problems.

Turkey, considered Middle Eastern for the past century, was the core of the Ottoman Empire, which—in addition to its control over the Balkans—dominated the region for several centuries. But many Turks now insist that they are Europeans and ought to be admitted into the European Union. Many Europeans feel that, as part of the Islamic cultural area, Turkey does not belong in Europe. Israel is physically in the Middle East but culturally and politically is largely European.

The British used the term "Near East" for the eastern Mediterranean countries closest to Europe, including Turkey, Egypt, and the Fertile Crescent, which the French and Spanish call the "Levant." The British used "Middle East" for the region farther east, around the Persian Gulf, now sometimes called Southwest Asia. During World War II, however, Cairo was the headquarters of the British Middle Eastern Command, and soon the entire region was usually called the Middle East. You still see some older references to Near East. Any name you give a region is arbitrary and changeable.

Definitions of the Middle East have changed over time and according to circumstances. In the early 1990s, after the collapse of the Soviet Union and the emergence of independent states in Central Asia, the Middle East Institute in Washington announced that these new states were culturally more attuned to the Middle East than to Russia—and that henceforth they would report on these countries in their *Middle East Journal.*

When the U.S. Defense Department created the Central Command (CENTCOM) to monitor events in the Middle East, it included Lebanon, Jordan, Syria, and Egypt; Israel, however, was left under the European Command. Today CENTCOM's area of operations has expanded to cover the Central Asian republics of the former Soviet Union and the Horn of Africa but does not include most of North Africa. Until 1974, the State Department included Greece and Cyprus within its European division; Turkey belonged to the Near East and South Asia division. After Turkey invaded Cyprus, however, Washington bureaucrats found it too difficult to coordinate messages between two divisions on the same issue, so they transferred Turkey to the European division. With the stroke of a pen, Washington put Turkey in Europe.

We consider the Arab countries of North Africa, the Levant, and the Arabian Peninsula, as well as the non-Arab countries of Turkey, Israel, and Iran, to be the Middle East. Due to space constraints, we have not concentrated on North Africa.

architects, and poets together formed courts to serve the king. In times of war, commoners could be conscripted and armed under the guidance of the nobles, who were either skilled in the arts of combat or they lost to those who were. Agriculture, civilization, and warfare were likely born triplets.

THE LAY OF THE LAND

The prehistoric Middle East that was settled millennia ago must have been a nice region. With ice still blanketing much of Europe, the Middle East enjoyed a moderate climate. In places the soil was good, especially in the great river valleys of the Nile in Egypt and the Tigris and Euphrates in Mesopotamia. Rainfall was more abundant than now, and much of the region was woods and grasslands. Most deserts came later, partly the work of climate change and partly that of humans who too eagerly cut the trees and plowed the grasslands.

Rains come when moisture-rich clouds, formed over the seas, blow over land and cool. With lower temperatures, the air cannot hold its moisture and precipitates it out as rain. Clouds cool as they rise into the upper levels of the atmosphere, which are colder than the lower levels. Mountains can do this: Winds push the clouds into mountains, forcing them upward. The coastal range that runs down the eastern end of the Mediterranean can thus generate good rainfall. Much of the Middle East is not so lucky, and people had to become clever and redirect some of the water from their great rivers by canals and sluice gates to irrigate many acres. This seems to have begun in Mesopotamia around 6000 B.C. and is one highly plausible explanation of why civilization arose so early in the Mesopotamian and Nile river valleys (and in China's Yangzi valley): They produced more food, but only if kingdoms could build and maintain the irrigation systems. To do this they had to mobilize and direct masses of labor under centralized government. The management of water produced the earliest civilizations. Karl Wittfogel advanced a theory of "oriental despotism": The need to manage water resources led to one-man rule.

Rain clouds also cool when they blow over green lands, which absorb sunlight rather than reflect it back, as deserts do. Green is literally a cool color. When the forests and grasslands have been denuded by shoddy agricultural practices, the land loses this cooling ability and dries out. Once it turns into a desert, it stays that way until elaborately restored by expensive projects. Environmentalists should take note. In the classic comedy routine of the Five-Thousand-Year-Old Man, Mel Brooks mentions the "Sahara Forest." His interviewer asks if he means the Sahara Desert. Brooks replies, "Sure, *now* it's a desert." That line may describe what took place in much of the Middle East: man-made deserts. Irrigation in ancient Mesopotamia slowly built up salinity in the soil, turning it into desert and dooming ancient Sumer.

One great constant of the Middle East is the importance of water. Nomads flocked to it. Civilizations arose by controlling it. Kings conquered for it. In times of sparse rainfall, herders lost their pasture and had to intrude onto farmland, creating terrible conflict. When springs and rivers dried up, as they do periodically, whole peoples had to migrate to new lands, one explanation for the coming of ancient Israelites to Egypt. Even today, control of the aquifer under the hills of Judea and Samaria hampers agreement between Israel and the Palestinians. The states along the southern shore of the Persian Gulf have exploding populations in part because they can desalinate seawater with their abundant natural gas.

G Geography

KEY FEATURES OF THE MIDDLE EAST

Arabia   Large, mostly desert peninsula between Persian Gulf and Red Sea.

Asia Minor   Large peninsula bordered by Black and Mediterranean seas; also known as Anatolia or Turkey. Designated Asia Minor by ancient Greeks to distinguish it from main body of Asia.

Fertile Crescent   Curved swath of arable land from *Mesopotamia* through Syria and into Palestine. Sometimes includes Egypt.

Levant   Countries of the Eastern Mediterranean.

Mesopotamia   (Greek for "between the rivers") Valley formed by Tigris and Euphrates Rivers. Present-day Iraq.

Nile Valley   Thin band of arable land along Nile River.

Sinai Peninsula   Desert between *Fertile Crescent* and *Nile Valley*.

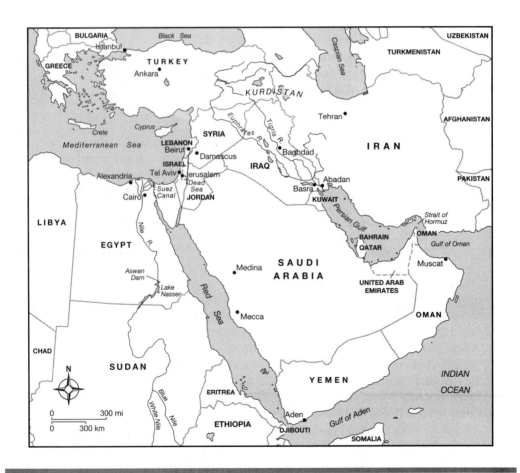

C Cultures

LANGUAGE GROUPS

Language is not the same as race or biological inheritance. Whole peoples have, after exposure through conquest or migration, learned to speak new languages. Do not confuse language groups with racial groups, a dreadful and deliberate error perpetrated by the Nazis. The Middle East is home to three of the world's several language groups:

Semitic, named after Noah's son Shem, are likely the oldest languages of the region and include Hebrew and Arabic plus Ethiopia's Amharic and Tigrinya. Swahili, the *lingua franca* (common tongue) that originated with Arab slave traders on Africa's east coast, is a Semitic language. Defunct Semitic languages include Akkadian, Assyrian, and Aramaic, the language spoken by Jesus of Nazareth.

Indo-European is a broad swath of languages stretching across Europe into India. Slavic, Italic, Celtic, and Germanic are the European branches of Indo-European. Although they may not sound or look like it, Hindi and Iranian are also Indo-European. The base of English is Germanic (with some Celtic remnants) topped by a thick layer of French (which is from Latin, an Italic language). Finnish and Hungarian are from another language group, Finno-Ugric, and Basque is related to no other language. Although Turkey was for centuries occupied by Indo-European speakers (Greek and Latin), now Iran is the only country in the region that uses an Indo-European language, Persian (*Farsi*), which is written in Arabic characters. Some Kurdish dialects are an archaic form of Persian.

Turkic languages are spoken in a band from present-day Turkey deep into Central Asia, its place of origin. Turkish was the administrative language of the Ottoman Empire and was thus used throughout the Middle East and the Balkans. Turkic languages include Turkish, Tatar, Azeri, Uzbek, and Khazakh. Originally all were written in Arabic letters, but Atatürk moved Turkish to Latin letters while Soviet Turkic languages were written in Cyrillic. More recently, several of them have opted for the Latin alphabet.

The archaeological record does not support the old view that civilization enjoyed **unilinear** growth. The ancient civilizations of the Middle East show spurts of consolidation and growth punctuated by periods of fragmentation and decline. Unified kingdoms expanded their territories; built cities, temples, and palaces; created writing and religion; and provided security for their subjects. Their subjects often suffered, however, from taxes and mandatory labor. Some theorize that most of the time peasants lived less well under unified kingdoms and disliked their tax-hungry kings. This is one explanation why all the ancient kingdoms sooner or later broke apart. After some decades of near-anarchy and cultural decline, strong new rulers would conquer the area and set up new kingdoms. Even ancient Egypt shows strong kingdoms followed by chaotic periods of weak governance and then new strong kingdoms. Like many Americans today, not all ancient Middle Easterners liked cities or taxes. The Tower of Babel and how it failed can be interpreted as criticism of government in general.

unilinear Progressing evenly and always upward.

Religions

WHAT IS RELIGION?

A **religion** is a belief system focused on ultimate questions that cannot be empirically verified. Death, for example, is an ultimate question that kept our primitive ancestors in awe and still leaves us uneasy. What happens to you after you die? No one has ever sent back a post card. Is there a soul that continues after death? Looking at the stars poses ultimate questions: What are they? God's handiwork?

Religion appears with the first humans, and some of the earliest artifacts unearthed in the Middle East are religious figurines, such as pregnant fertility goddesses. Until recently, sex and birth were indeed mysteries. Much of the evolution of human civilization is the development of religious beliefs from primitive nature worship, to divine kings and statues (ancient Egypt), to immortal but human-like gods (ancient Greece), to a single invisible tribal deity (ancient Israel), to a universal being laying down moral commandments (the modern **Abrahamic** faiths). Religion does not explain all of history—often there are important physical factors at work—but it is a major channel of human choices. We cannot make sense of the broad sweep of Middle Eastern history without paying attention to religions.

Some claim there is no clear border between religion and superstition. Superstition, however, is concerned with small things and luck, such as winning the lottery or avoiding trouble, and generally requires only small gestures, such as playing your birthday or bride and groom not seeing each other before the wedding. Superstitions do not ask ultimate questions.

A belief system that can be empirically verified—you can get evidence proving or disproving its tenets—is probably not a religion but a science, discipline, or area of rational discourse. Economics is a social science, for example, although its practitioners hedge their predictions so much ("on the other hand") that they almost ask you to have faith. They typically concern themselves with questions of here and now—how to get the economy to grow or control inflation—rather than ultimate questions.

Secular belief systems—ideologies such as Marxism or nationalism—may argue that they are empirically grounded, but they often fail in practice and do not focus on ultimate questions. Marxists swore they were following "scientific socialism." These -isms, however, mimic religions in requiring the faith and loyalty of adherents. Persons strongly caught up in an ideology often exhibit religious-like beliefs. Marxists, for example, whose faith explained everything, had no patience for religion and were devout atheists. Communist parties tried to prohibit members from practicing any religion.

THE IMPORTANCE OF THE SPOKEN WORD

Oral tradition is especially important in the Middle East. Many speak Arabic as their mother tongue; others use numerous Arabic words. Arabic speakers have a real affection for the language. In pre-Islamic times, Arabs developed an advanced form of poetry, and traveling poets were welcomed. Later, as the **Qur'an**

---

religion   Unverifiable belief system concerned with ultimate questions.

Abrahamic   The three religions that trace back to Abraham: Judaism, Christianity, and Islam.

secular   Nonreligious.

Qur'an or **Koran**   Islamic scriptures. Muslims believe it is the Word of God, given to mankind by an angel through the prophet Muhammad. The word Qur'an literally means recitation, because God's word was and is recited.

C : *Cultures*

PERCEPTION VERSUS REALITY

Those raised on television often picture the Middle East as rolling hills of sand, fierce desert winds, emptiness to the horizon. The men are either camel-riding **Bedouin** or bearded terrorists; the women are covered modestly but move with a delicate sensuality.

Some of the images are true, but most have faded into the past. Lose them. The Sahara desert and the Saudi peninsula's Empty Quarter resemble Hollywood's images, except where they are crossed by pipelines, refineries, petrochemical plants, and modern cities. In truth, the Middle East includes rugged Atlantic coastline, deserts, semi-tropical Mediterranean beaches, snow-peaked mountains, overcrowded cities, and modern high-tech industrial parks. The people of the Middle East—male and female—are now mostly urban and include highly educated professionals. Some wear traditional clothing, but they also wear business suits, sports uniforms, and Parisian haute couture.

Keep this in mind when studying the **political culture** of this or any other region. Do not confuse **archetypes** with **stereotypes**.

Some political scientists pay little attention to culture, but anthropologists are wedded to the concept, and psychologists have joined them. Since at least 1991, the American Psychological Association instructs practitioners to take into account the ethnic and cultural differences of their patients. In the Middle East, attempts to ignore the strength and depth of local culture end badly.

(see box on page 10) spread across the region, the language gained respect as the medium through which God spoke to his chosen people.

Today, the historical respect for the spoken language combines with widespread illiteracy so that the spoken word has a powerful effect in the Middle East. Rumors spread quickly and are believed, a problem compounded by government censorship in many countries. Citizens know the official news is often doctored and are more inclined to accept what they hear "on the street."

SHARED CULTURAL CHARACTERISTICS

The Middle East shares many cultural characteristics. Arabs, Turks, and Iranians share the concept of hospitality, where a host acquires merit by providing for a guest. This came out of the desert tradition where, if a host refused to help a visitor, the traveler might die of hunger or thirst before finding another benefactor.

Bedouin Arabic-speaking desert nomads.

political culture The psychology of a nation in regard to politics.

archetype The perfect embodiment of the characteristics of a particular group. All people diverge from an archetype.

stereotype The characterization of an individual based on the erroneous assumption that all members of a particular group are alike.

C Cultures

THE ARABIC LANGUAGE

Arabic is a *lingua franca* for much of the Middle East. In its classical form as written in the Qur'an, Arabic is revered but not so easily understood. *Beowulf,* the first literary work written in English, needs a glossary of terms to translate Old English into modern English. The Qur'an is the same way. Qur'anic scholars learn classical Arabic as a separate language from the Arabic spoken in the street. A Muslim scholar once told one of the authors that the reason Qur'anic Arabic is so different is because the human language was crushed under the weight of God's word.

Modern written Arabic is the same throughout the Middle East, although some words have different meanings in different areas. The common, written form is of little use to the hundreds of thousands of illiterate residents of the Middle East, who rely on the spoken word for communication. The common form of Arabic known as Modern Standard Arabic is taught in schools, but most Arabs speak local dialects. American diplomats learn Modern Standard, and most Middle Easterners can understand it but may have difficulty replying in the same tongue. Some diplomatic conversations are comically one-sided: The American speaks in modern standard but cannot understand the response in the local dialect. (Given their cultural differences, they might not understand each other even if they used the same language.)

Local dialects of Arabic vary considerably. A Moroccan has a hard time understanding a Syrian or Iraqi. As satellite television, with its popular Egyptian soap operas, takes over the Middle East, a common dialect is emerging: Egyptian Arabic that pronounces a "J" as a hard "G." The popular (and anti-U.S.) Al-Jazeera (or is it al-Gazira?) news channel, based in Qatar, on the other hand, uses Gulf Arabic. It will be interesting to see which dialect, Egyptian or Gulf, becomes standard pronunciation.

Hospitality thus became a self-survival mechanism: It was expected that the host would receive equal treatment if he became a traveler. In more recent times, tribal chieftains increased their prestige within the tribe by holding elaborate feasts for their followers. Today, hereditary rulers cement the allegiance of their political allies by including them at feasts on major holidays at the palace.

Despite the tradition of hospitality, the Middle East also holds a distrust of the foreigner and a reliance on family. This also arose from the desert tradition, where the traveler seeking shelter from the elements could be a noble merchant or a brigand intent on stealing the host's possessions. Mistrust of people outside the family leads to in-group marriages; family honor is often protected from outside pollution by marrying the children to their first cousins. This practice is on the wane but by no means extinct today. Understanding of genetic problems that come from first-cousin marriage is penetrating most countries.

Distrust of foreigners was deepened by attacks of Christian armies during the Crusades of the eleventh century and by the European imperialists of the nineteenth and early twentieth centuries. Politically, these cultural traits have resulted in an increased desire to embrace "authentic" movements such as fundamentalist Islamist movements, various nationalisms, and the expropriation of externally owned or controlled assets such as oil companies.

 *Cultures*

MIDDLE EASTERN LAYERS OF IDENTITY

1. Family
2. Religion
3. Ethnicity
4. Individuality
5. Nationality
6. Profession

There are, of course, numerous exceptions to this identity schema. With their long histories, Egyptians and Iranians have a stronger sense of nationality than many others. Similarly, Palestinians and Israelis have nationalisms born in part out of their struggles against each other. Many educated Middle Easterners now take great pride in their individual accomplishments, and many of the non-educated share that respect, either because of practical considerations (one respects a doctor who cures a sick child regardless of who his father is), or because of a respect for education that comes from the previously described respect for language.

The archetypical Middle Easterner derives his identity from the groups to which he belongs. These groups include family, clan, tribe, religion, ethnic group, and region. There has been less loyalty to the nation-state because Islam stresses the unity of all Muslims and sees countries as artificial constructs imposed by European imperialists less than a century ago. Thus, people may identify themselves as being from Damascus or Aleppo but pay little attention to the fact that they are Syrian.

Westerners, Americans especially, highly value individualism. Hollywood glorifies John Wayne, Chuck Norris, Sylvester Stallone—individuals who do it their own way—which is quite different from the Middle East (and Japan), where people prize their group identities.

A similar gap comes with professions. To Americans, their job is a large part of their identity; it is not just what they do but who they are. In the Middle East, by contrast, employment is merely a means to provide for one's family, not a measure of one's worth, which is calculated by lineage from noble blood. (Almost half the people in the Middle East claim the prophet Muhammad as their ancestor). There is a cultural disconnect when an American ambassador proudly announces that he started with nothing and pulled himself up by entrepreneurial skills. The Americans think they are sending over their best, because the envoy showed initiative and earned a lot of money; Middle Easterners welcome him out of hospitality but judge him as beneath them because of his self-admitted lack of noble lineage.

Unwelcome offshoots of the Middle Eastern reliance on the in-group and suspicion of the out-group are blood feuds and vendettas. Killing any member—including innocent women and children—of the group that has harmed your

K : Key Concepts

COMMUNALISM

One of the enduring features of the Middle East is **communalism**. Nations are new and weak; religious and linguistic communities are old and strong. Middle Easterners do not shed their **primordial** ties; you stay in the group into which you are born. Few Iraqi Shi'a, for example, convert to Sunni Islam and vice-versa. In Sunni-Shi'a marriages, most spouses keep their original religion. Some Iraqi Shi'a claim to be secular, but they still favor their coreligionists. The American style of freely choosing your religion is incomprehensible.

Every Middle Eastern country has important communities that do not easily blend into the overall nation. Some cause permanent tension and even violence. The biggest and most dangerous split is between mainstream Sunni Islam and minority Shi'a Islam (see page 31), who actually form a majority in Iran, Iraq, and Bahrain. But there are other communities.

The Berbers, the original inhabitants of North Africa, had been Christians before the Arab conquest (St. Augustine was of Berber origin) and resisted it, but finally converted to Islam. Many kept their Berber language, especially those who live in the mountains of Algeria and Morocco, where they are a large minority of the total population. Their language, which is not related to Arabic, and their culture are discriminated against. Some Berbers have formed resistance movements against Arab-dominated governments.

The original Christians of Egypt, the **Copts**, kept their distinctive religion but speak Arabic. They number about 10 percent of Egypt's population (some say higher) and have been discriminated against and persecuted by the Sunni majority. There are several branches of Christianity in Lebanon. The Maronites, tied to Rome but with distinct rituals, have long wielded power despite their minority status. Some claim to be descended from the original Phoenicians. Lebanon also has a Greek Orthodox community.

Mountains provide hiding places for other minority communities, most notably the Kurds, but also the strange Druze and Alawite faiths of the coastal range of Syria and Lebanon, which began as offshoots of Islam but added other elements and are not considered Muslim. Neither of these sects reveal many of the tenets of their religion to outsiders. Some Druze also live in the north of Israel. The Alawites are an offshoot of Shi'a Islam but deified Ali. Hafez al-Assad, one of the 12 percent of Syria's Alawites, gained power in Syria through the military in 1970 and ruled with an iron hand until his death in 2000. His son is now in power. The majority Sunnis of Syria do not like being ruled by Alawites. When the Muslim Brotherhood (see page 294) staged an uprising in the northern Syrian city of Hama in 1982, Assad leveled it with artillery fire, killing an estimated 20,000.

Every analysis of a Middle Eastern country must include the number and size of religious and linguistic communities, how much they feel discriminated against, and how strong a sense of group solidarity they show. Communalism works against the establishment of stable democracies, as the several communities distrust each other. In elections, citizens vote their communal identification, rather than for the good of the whole country. The United States hoped that the late-2005 Iraqi elections would allow secular parties to form a government that would calm the Sunni-Shi'a split, but the secular parties did poorly.

---

communalism   Identifying chiefly with subgroup (usually religion) rather than with nation.

primordial   Groups you are born into.

Coptic   Old branch of Christianity in Egypt and Ethiopia.

Conflicts

IS THE MIDDLE EAST ESPECIALLY WARLIKE?

Conflict is not, of course, a phenomenon limited to the Middle East. Although West Europeans have adopted a pacifist stance as a result of their own history and political culture (specifically, a reaction to the destruction of World Wars I and II), the history of Europe and the United States is also a history of recurring conflicts. Mostly, Westerners got their conflicts over with. In the past, however, the Middle East enjoyed long periods of peace—whenever a strong empire ran things—while the West was wracked with centuries of bloody conflicts. In this book we emphasize the causes and effects of conflict in the Middle East because that is the region under study, not because ancient empires, Arabs, or Turks are more inclined to violence than other peoples.

group is seen as justifiable retaliation, maybe even preferable to killing the actual perpetrator, because it inflicts more grief and pain. Thus for many Muslims, killing innocent Americans on 9/11 is sweet revenge for U.S. policy. Palestinians feel that bombing Israeli civilians is fit retaliation for what Israel has done. In Iraq today, Sunni and Shi'a kill each other at random to avenge the previous outrage. Europe had vendettas too—witness Romeo and Juliet—but they died out. Blood feuds are very hard to stop: One more retaliation is always called for.

Outsiders are not necessarily granted the same rights and protections as members of the in-group. Outsiders are fair game, and their goods are forfeit if they lose a fight. On the Arabian peninsula at the time of the Prophet (A.D. 570–632), Arab tribes would raid caravans belonging to other tribes to steal their goods. Further historical precedence for this unequal treatment is the role of the **dhimmi** in Islamic empires: A non-Muslim could live in peace provided he accepted a second-class status, did not participate in certain occupations, did not build a house larger than a Muslim neighbor's, did not join the military, but did pay a higher tax.

THE ANCIENTS AND THEIR CONFLICTS

There are few direct connections between the ancient empires and today's politics, but there are some indirect ones. Notice how the earliest civilizations, specifically those of Egypt and Mesopotamia, were based on water. The two civilizations were great rivals then, constantly striving for regional predominance, which included control of the coastal caravan route and farming belt of present-day Israel and Palestine. Egypt and Iraq in recent times have been rivals for leadership of the Arab world. Notice how no civilization lasts forever. Notice also how they fought

dhimmi   Protected person; non-Muslim living under an Islamic government, required to pay a special tax.

R Religions

THE FIRST MONOTHEISM

Some claim Egypt invented **monotheism**. Well, sort of. In 1375 B.C., Amenhotep IV assumed the throne and decreed that the sun god, symbolized by a disk, was superior to the other Egyptian gods. This was not really the worship of one god. It was also a way of resolving an economic disaster. His predecessors on the throne had emptied the royal treasury. By elevating the sun god, Amenhotep, who renamed himself Akhenaton, refilled the royal coffers with the riches of the priests loyal to the lesser gods, whom most Egyptians went on worshiping anyway. When the old gods were restored by Amenhotep's successor, the money was not returned to the priests.

each other, sometimes in the same places as today. Were (are?) these peoples especially warlike, or not more so than others? In some cases, their long fights so weakened these empires that they were easy prey for outsiders. The Byzantines and Persians bashed each other silly for centuries, making Muslim conquest easy.

At least three modern countries have inherited a proud nationalism from the ancient past: Egypt, Iran, and Israel. In ancient times the small Hebrew kingdoms were simply places to be conquered on an alternating basis by Egypt and Mesopotamia, but by nurturing a monotheistic religion, ancient Judah and Israel put their stamp on humankind. (We will have more to say about ancient Israel in Chapter 4.) These ancient empires were like tides sweeping over a beach, each leaving residues.

The Egyptians arose as a self-contained people about 3100 B.C. Protected by vast deserts on either side, the Upper and Lower kingdoms developed in their narrow Nile River valley without the competition of neighboring city-states seeking to invade. It was not until 1750 B.C. that the valley experienced its first invaders, the Hyksos, from Asia. Egyptian civilization was highly developed, with a royal court, and ruling and slave classes. They built one of the earliest high cultures, kept accounts on papyrus, sent out colonies, and irrigated farmland. King Zozer began building the pyramids around 2800 B.C., which, among other things, demonstrate a religion with emphasis on the afterlife. Egypt was conquered by the Assyrians in 670 B.C., and was to be ruled by foreign dynasties and colonial powers until the revolt of the Free Officers in A.D. 1952, which brought Abdul Gamal Nasser into power.

The Babylonians originated in Mesopotamia, northwest of the Persian Gulf, in the city of Ur (the scriptural birthplace of Abraham). The inhabitants of the area developed the city-state of Sumer and moved by fits and starts to Babylon—just north of the modern city of Baghdad. About 2270 B.C., Sargon the Great expanded Babylonian rule from a small fiefdom to all of the Fertile Crescent (and even Cyprus); this kingdom ruled for almost a thousand years. Like the Egyptians, the Babylonians had a ruling class, military nobility, and slave class. They also left the

---

monotheism   Worship of one god.

Cultures

CONQUERING THE CONQUERORS

Alexander left a series of generals to run the newly conquered lands, but they had to rely on the administrators they inherited from the defeated Persian Empire. Within a short time, the conquerors had been culturally assimilated into Asian ways. Persians have a long tradition of eventually coming out on top whenever they are defeated militarily. The Greeks burned Persepolis in 330 B.C., but within a few years the Greeks of Asia were speaking Persian, wearing Persian robes, and writing Persian poetry.

The Arabs defeated the Persians in A.D. 641, but within a few years the Muslim armies in Persia were reading poetry by the great Persian poet Ferdowsi. The Turks defeated the Persians in A.D. 1503, but had to import Persian courtiers to run the Ottoman Empire. Persian culture put a strong imprint onto the Middle East and, beneath a layer of Islamic culture, still lives in today's Iran.

first recorded legal system, the code of Hammurabi, written about 1700 B.C. They gave us the mathematical legacy of dividing a minute into 60 seconds, an hour into 60 minutes, and a circle into 360 degrees. In arts and letters, Babylon produced one of the world's first epic poems, the Epic of Gilgamesh. It also produced a religion that included stories of creation and world-destroying floods, similar to the accounts in Genesis. Invading marauders first weakened Babylon's greatness when they swept out of the surrounding mountains in 1677 B.C. and split the kingdom into three. The Hittites, the least known of the ancient superpowers, invaded and destroyed Babylon in 1595 B.C., although it survived in one form or another for another four hundred years.

The Hittites arrived about 1900 B.C. but by 1600 B.C. controlled all of Asia Minor and pushed down the Mediterranean coast. In 1595 B.C., the Hittites sacked the city of Babylon; and in 1294 B.C. they defeated the forces of Egyptian Pharaoh Ramses II at the battle of Kadesh. The two kingdoms then divided Syria between them in a peace treaty signed in 1278 B.C. Although a powerful warrior culture, the Hittites left little behind.

The Assyrians, another warrior kingdom, expanded from the mountains of northern Mesopotamia about 1100 B.C. as the **Iron Age** replaced bronze with iron for making stronger and sharper weapons. Assyria introduced the first standing army in history, the battering ram, and the siege tower. They became the largest empire in the ancient world but left little else behind. The kingdom was torn apart by revolt around 728 B.C. until a combined army from the kingdoms of Chaldea and Medea captured and destroyed its capital, Nineveh. The Chaldeans then held sway over the area for the next two hundred years, building the famous "Hanging Gardens of Babylon."

Iron Age   Followed *Bronze Age,* starting about 1000 B.C. in Middle East. These "ages" are named after weapons. Iron was a major advance.

G Geography

TURKISH STRAITS

From ancient times, control over shipping channels has meant life and death to the kingdoms that vied for power in the Middle East. While the nature of warfare may have changed significantly, the strategic role of waterways has not. To pass between the Black Sea and the Mediterranean Sea, all military and commercial shipping must pass through the **Turkish Straits**, namely, the **Bosporus** and Dardanelles, known in ancient times as the Hellespont. No shipping from the Danube River basin or from the countries surrounding the Black Sea (including successor states to the former Soviet Union) can reach the open sea without passing through these waters. As a result, the straits have been considered strategic prizes throughout the centuries. In the twentieth century alone, desire to control the straits led to the Allied invasion of Gallipoli in World War I and strong Soviet pressure to control the straits after World War II.

Today, thanks to the 1936 **Montreux Convention**, shipping through the straits is internationalized. This uneasy accord is threatened, however, by the prospect of oil tankers bringing millions of barrels of Central Asian oil to market through the crowded Straits, passing the heart of the Turkish city of Istanbul (estimated population 13 million) that straddles the Bosporus.

The Phoenicians, fisherman and traders who lived in what is today Lebanon, established trading posts and colonies throughout the Mediterranean. Phoenician merchants likely introduced writing—picked up from earlier Middle Eastern cultures—to the Greeks and thence to all of Europe. About 900 B.C., the Phoenicians passed through the Straits of Gibraltar and on the Atlantic side established a trading colony at the site of modern Cadiz, Spain. About 800 B.C., they established Carthage, in what is today Tunisia, a colony that soon surpassed the mother kingdom and became a great empire.

The Persians appear as the Iron Age came to a close, as a group of **Aryan** tribes that had migrated from Central Asia onto the Iranian plateau 1500 years earlier formed the **Persian** Empire. This last of the ancient empires held sway over the eastern reaches of the known world until they were defeated briefly by Alexander the Great in the fourth century B.C. and by the Arabs in the seventh century A.D.

The Persians had been a subkingdom under the Medes until 550 B.C. when Cyrus the Great overthrew them and conquered most of the Middle East. His son annexed Egypt in 525 B.C., and his nephew Darius invaded both India to the East and Europe to the West. Darius built a remarkable wooden pontoon bridge across the **Dardanelles** to march an army of 100,000 soldiers into Europe in 513 B.C.

Turkish Straits   Strategic waterway that connects Mediterranean and Black Seas.

Bosporus   Northern part of Turkish Straits; Istanbul is on its banks.

Montreux Convention   1936 treaty opening Turkish Straits to world shipping under Turkish control.

Aryan   Indo-European-speaking tribes who settled ancient Iran and northern India.

Persia   Old name for Iran.

Dardanelles   Southern part of the *Turkish Straits.*

P: *Personalities*

ALEXANDER THE GREAT

Alexander the Great (356–323 B.C.) brought the first European presence into the Middle East. Alexander and his father, Philip of Macedon, were not considered Greek by the mainland Greeks but of a tribe of northern barbarians. Philip united the mainland Greeks by the sword. Alexander received a Greek education—in part tutored by Aristotle—and became more Hellenic than the Hellenes. As is often the case with people marginal to a culture, Alexander passionately embraced Greek culture and vowed to spread it as he conquered with no clear limits.

Alexander, headstrong and clever, took a united Greek army into Asia Minor in 334 B.C. and in three months freed the Aegean coast of Persian rule. He then took Syria, Palestine, and Egypt, where he was crowned pharaoh and founded a city on the Mediterranean, Alexandria. He conquered the Persian Empire and burned its capital, Persepolis, which convinced Persians of his barbarity. On the Indus River in present-day Pakistan, he was ready to take India but died in 323 B.C. at the age of thirty-three. Although Alexander's reign was brief, Greek influence continued in the Middle East through the *Seleucids* and *Byzantium.*

This army was defeated by wild **Scythian** cavalrymen in what is today Romania. The Greeks of Ionia revolted and destroyed Darius's bridge. Darius later made an amphibious landing near Marathon in Greece, where the badly outnumbered Athenians annihilated 40,000 Persians. Darius's son Xerxes tried a third time to conquer Greece. His army crossed the Hellespont on two pontoon bridges to face the vastly outnumbered Greeks at Thermopylae, a mountain pass, where the Spartan soldiers died to the last man. Defeated in 479 B.C., the Persians never tried to conquer the Greeks again.

THE EUROPEAN EMPIRES

The Greeks for centuries lived in numerous squabbling city-states and their colonies. Greeks settled on the coasts of Asia Minor in the seventh century B.C., in what was called **Ionia**, but they were long under Persian control. Athenian expansionism led to the horrific **Peloponnesian War** against a Sparta-led alliance. One of the best statements on the cause of war in general was penned by a cashiered Athenian general, Thucydides, in his history of the war: "War became inevitable with the growth of Athenian power and the fear this caused in Sparta." Many later Middle Eastern wars can be explained by a similar formulation.

Scythia   Ancient kingdom in present-day Ukraine.
Ionia   Ancient Greek-inhabited area in present-day southwest Turkey.
Peloponnesian War   Long (431–404 B.C.) conflict between Athens and Sparta; marked end of Athenian greatness.

Alexander conquered most of the Middle East, but his descendants immediately fought over his empire and after fifty years divided it into three: Europe, Egypt and North Africa, and Asia. The Greek general Ptolemy was crowned king of Egypt, and his successors would rule that ancient kingdom until 30 B.C., when they were conquered by the Romans. They turned their capital, Alexandria, into a Greek city. General Seleucus was given the lands of Asia, and he established a dynasty at Antioch, in northern Syria. The Ptolemies and **Seleucids** developed **Hellenistic** culture, which brought Greek architecture and philosophy into the Middle East, with major repercussions. The more religious Jews of Judea, the **Maccabees**, from 168 to 164 B.C. led a bloody revolt against the enforced hellenism of the Seleucids—plural gods and Greek philosophy—which they regarded as pagan. Many scholars argue that the confluence of Greek philosophy and Jewish faith produced many of the ideas found in Christian theology.

The Romans took over the Mediterranean world well after Alexander. By 300 B.C., Rome collided with Carthage in three **Punic Wars**. In 146 B.C. Rome leveled Carthage and repopulated Carthaginian holdings in North Africa and Spain with Romans. Having defeated the Seleucids in 189 B.C., the Romans now controlled most of the Mediterranean, which they called *mare nostrum*, "our sea." Rome took over Asia Minor. In 133 B.C. the king of Pergamon (see photo on page 19) deeded the city to Rome. Swiftly defeating a challenge from the Greek kingdom of Pontus, along the Black Sea, in 47 B.C., Julius Caesar reported, *Veni, Vedi, Vici* (I came, I saw, I conquered). Rome seized Syria and Egypt, leaving Palestine to be ruled by a descendent of the Maccabees who was friendly to Rome. Rome thus ruled the East to the Euphrates River, imposing the **Pax Romana** over the region.

Byzantium grew out of Rome's imperial overstretch. Continually fighting the Persian Sassanians and putting down rebellions, the empire was stretched too thin for its Legions to control. Around A.D. 300 the emperor Diocletian split administration into East and West. In A.D. 305 Constantine took over and in 323 founded a magnificent new capital at the Greek town of Byzantium on the Bosporus, which he named after himself. Although he was not baptized until his death in 337, he favored Christianity and presided over the first Church Council in 325, which yielded the Nicene Creed. Over the centuries, eastern and western Christianity split into, respectively, Roman Catholic and Eastern Orthodox, the former using Latin, the latter Greek.

Seleucid   Hellenistic kingdom that dominated Middle East 312–64 B.C.

Hellenistic   Greek culture transplanted into the Middle East by Alexander.

Maccabees   Jewish priestly family who rebelled against Seleucids in second century B.C.

Punic Wars   Third-century B.C. struggle in which Rome destroyed Carthage.

Pax Romana   "Roman Peace"; Roman vision of the benefits of their empire; connotes peace imposed by armed strength.

Byzantium   Short name for *Eastern Roman* or *Byzantine Empire*.

The Altar of ancient Pergamon, a Hellenistic city-state in present-day Turkey, shows the beauty of this late-Greek culture. German archaeologists shipped the altar to Berlin, where it is now displayed (*Michael G. Roskin*)

The Byzantine Empire lasted a millennium, but it was so stultifying that the term "Byzantine" came to mean a complex and corrupt bureaucracy full of petty schemers. It contributed little to philosophy and destroyed the writings of "pagan" philosophers such as Plato and Aristotle. Were it not for some Arab philosophers in Damascus who had taken up the study of Greek philosophy, all trace of Western civilization's intellectual predecessors would have been lost. The Emperor Justinian (483–565), however, left two major Byzantine accomplishments, the *Corpus Juris Civilis,* a compendium of the laws of the empire, and the Aya Sophia Cathedral—the largest church in Christendom for a thousand years, later converted into a mosque, and today Istanbul's oldest museum.

Constantinople was strategic and impregnable. It controlled all transit to and from the Black Sea and much of the land trade between Europe and Asia Minor. It was surrounded by water on three sides and had a stout wall on the fourth. But it could not defend its giant empire. The Byzantine and Persian empires fought for centuries over Syria, so weakening themselves that both were easy prey in the seventh century for the Arab conquest that seized two-thirds of Byzantium's territory.

The Turks finally destroyed Byzantium. In 1071 the Seljuk Turks—nomadic Muslim tribes from Central Asia who had moved into Asia Minor—defeated the imperial army, and Byzantium shrank over the next few centuries to just Constantinople and some suburbs. Western Christians helped finish off Byzantium. In 1096, the Catholics of the First Crusade, regarding the Eastern Orthodox faith as heretical, robbed and sacked its lands. The Fourth Crusade conquered and looted Constantinople and took much of its art and treasures to Venice. Fatally wounded by brother Christians, Byzantium could not resist the successors to the Seljuk dynasty, the Ottomans. On May 29, 1453, Mehmet the Conqueror breached the walls of Constantinople with cannons, and extinguished the last vestiges of European rule in the Middle East. They renamed the city Istanbul and made it their capital.

CONCLUSIONS

The simplest definition of the Middle East is the hub of the World Island that connects Asia, Europe, and Africa. Most of it shares a common culture, which arose from the confluence of the history of the region with the cultural mores and religion of most of the area's inhabitants. The region has also experienced a series of conflicts that stretch back into antiquity. For 3,500 years, Middle Eastern empires rose and fell: Egyptian, Assyrian, Hittite, Persian, Babylonian, Phoenician, Greek, Roman, and Byzantine. Some empires made great cultural contributions and laid the foundation of Western civilization. Others left no legacy at all. Islam, to which we now turn, inherited previous civilizations and gave the region its distinctive culture.

KEY TERMS

Abrahamic (p. 8)

archetype (p. 9)

Aryan (p. 16)

Bedouin (p. 9)

Bosporus (p. 16)

Bronze Age (p. 3)

Byzantium (p. 18)

civilization (p. 1)

communalism (p. 12)

Coptic (p. 12)

Dardanelles (p. 16)

dhimmi (p. 13)

Hellenistic (p. 18)

Ionia (p. 17)

Iron Age (p. 15)

Maccabees (p. 18)

monotheism (p. 14)

Montreux Convention (p. 16)

Neolithic (p. 1)

Pax Romana (p. 18)

Peloponnesian War (p. 17)

Persia (p. 16)

political culture (p. 9)

primordial (p. 12)

Punic Wars (p. 18)

Qur'an or Koran (p. 8)

religion (p. 8)

Scythia (p. 17)

secular (p. 8)

Seleucid (p. 18)

stereotype (p. 9)

Turkish Straits (p. 16)

unilinear (p. 7)

FURTHER REFERENCE

Andersen, Roy R., Robert F. Seibert, and Jon G. Wagner. *Politics and Change in the Middle East: Sources of Conflict and Accommodation,* 8th ed. Upper Saddle River, NJ: Prentice Hall, 2006.

Bill, James, Carl Leiden, and Robert Springbord. *Politics in the Middle East,* 6th ed. Boston, MA: Addison-Wesley Longman, 2003.

Brown, Peter. *The World of Late Antiquity, A.D. 15–750.* New York: Norton, 1989.

Diamond, Jared. *Guns, Germs, and Steel: The Fates of Human Societies.* New York: Norton, 1999.

Feiler, Bruce. *Abraham: A Journey to the Heart of Three Faiths.* New York: Harper Perennial, 2004.

Fromkin, David, Zahi Hawass, Yossi Klein Halevi, Sandra Mackey, Charles M. Sennott, Milton Viorst, and Andrew Wheatcroft. *Cradle & Crucible: History and Faith in the Middle East.* Washington, D.C.: National Geographic, 2004.

Gabriel, Richard. *The Great Armies of Antiquity.* Westport, CT: Praeger, 2002.

Goldschmidt, Arthur, Jr., and Lawrence Davidson. *A Concise History of the Middle East,* 8th ed. Boulder, CO: Westview, 2005.

Held, Colbert C. *Middle East Patterns: Places, Peoples, and Politics.* Boulder, CO: Westview, 1989.

Khoury, Philp S., and Joseph Kostiner, eds. *Tribes and State Formation in the Middle East.* Berkeley, CA: University of California Press, 1990.

Lewis, Bernard. *The Multiple Identities of the Middle East.* New York: Random House, 1998.

Long, David E., and Bernard Reich. *The Government and Politics of the Middle East and North Africa,* 4th ed. Boulder, CO: Westview, 2002.

Norwich, John Julius. *A Short History of Byzantium.* New York: Alfred A. Knopf, 1997.

Said, Edward W. *Orientalism.* New York: Random House, 1978.

2 The Birth of Islam

Points to Ponder

- What are the similarities and differences among Islam and the religions that preceded it?
- What was the Hijra and what does it signify?
- How was the early Muslim community governed?
- How does Islam say a state should be governed?
- What, when, and where were the two great Arab caliphates?
- Does the development of Islamic thought show progress or innovation?
- What is Shi'a and how is it different from Sunni Islam?
- Does Allah demand that Muslims kill Westerners?

MUHAMMAD

Probably more has been written about Muhammad than any man who ever lived. From the beginning, Islamic scholars studied and documented his life as an exemplar for those to follow. European scholars, on the other hand, immediately wrote attacks against Muhammad as the devil incarnate, leading people away from the True Faith to eternal damnation. It therefore becomes difficult after thirteen centuries to get a true and fair picture of him. It is an important exercise, however, in that he is the central human figure in a religion that now has 1.2 billion adherents. It is also important because there is only one goal shared by all Muslims: to follow Muhammad's example. This goal is shared by liberals who claim Islam can serve as the ideological basis for freedom and democracy, by conservatives who pray for the world's conversion from sin, and by bearded fanatics who, in the name of God, fly airplanes full of innocent people into office buildings filled with other innocent people.

Not much is known about Muhammad's youth. What is known and agreed upon by all is that Muhammad ibn Abdullah was a city dweller, born into a minor branch of a major tribe in Mecca, the Quraysh, in about A.D. 570. His parents died

R⋮ *Religions*

BIRTHPLACE OF RELIGIONS

Most people know that the Middle East is the birthplace of the three great world monotheistic religions: Judaism, Christianity, and Islam. In fact, many religions have been born in the Middle East. Once established, it seems almost impossible for a religion to last long without splintering.

Ancient Persia was the birthplace of Mithra and of Mani. Mithra became the cult god of the Roman legions. Many Roman victories were won in his name (even when the empire was nominally Christian) through the fifth century. Mani brought us Manichaeism, a defunct religion that divided the world into good and evil and whose philosophical influence continues to be felt in the West today. The ancient religion of the Persian kings was Zoroastrianism: The leaders of their church were known as Mages, or Magi in Latin. The Three Wise Men whose visit to Bethlehem is celebrated on the feast of the Epiphany were Zoroastrian high priests. Zoroastrians continue to practice their religion in Iran and in India; indeed, Zoroastrianism is a protected religion under the Iranian Islamic constitution. Its followers get a seat in parliament.

Judaism splintered early into those who followed the Pharisees and the Samaritans who were left in Palestine during the Babylonian captivity. All the early Christian schisms took place in the Middle East, and followers of many of the schismatic churches can still be found in northern Syria and Iraq. Islam preaches adherence to "towhid," Arabic for unity. In reality, Islam is divided between the **Sunni** and the **Shi'a**, and each of these movements are subdivided into numerous smaller groupings. Each of these divisions leads to new identities for the faithful.

when he was a child, and Muhammad was raised by his uncle, Abu Talib. Arabia at that time was a mix of religions—Jewish, Christian, and pagan. Muhammad may have frequented synagogues and churches as a young man where he would have heard many bible stories that later appear, slightly altered, in the Qur'an.

Some Western sources report that as a child Muhammad had uncontrollable fits and passed out. These episodes caused Muhammad to focus on larger questions than daily living; he became deeply spiritual and began to go into the desert for periods of meditation. It was during one of these periods that he heard the angel Gabriel. Over the years, Gabriel returned many times, seen only by Muhammad, to reveal to him God's words. A modern psychologist might interpret these events as youthful episodes of epilepsy followed by psychotic episodes. A Christian or Jew might dismiss the whole history as a fantasy, since they hold that they already possess God's revelation. To a believing Muslim, however, the words that Gabriel revealed became the Holy Qur'an, the complete revelation of God, unadulterated by man's intervention. In this regard, all Muslims are automatically fundamentalists, because they take the Qur'an literally.

Sunni   Mainstream and majority branch of Islam.

Shi'a   Minority branch of Islam that claims Ali was rightful caliph.

R⋮ *Religions*

COMPETING REVELATIONS

Based on the Qur'an, Muslims accept that God gave his revelation to other peoples, including Christians and Jews. "I have sent messengers to all peoples, each speaking in a language to be understood." This is the same revelation that Gabriel carried to Muhammad. For this reason, Muslims accept that Abraham, Moses, Elijah, John the Baptist, and Jesus were all prophets who delivered God's word to the people. Muslims believe that the Old and New Testaments are based on true revelation, but these revelations have been corrupted through human intervention. Either by purposeful fraud, or merely by faulty memory, Christians changed the revelation before recording it. Thus, there are several stories found in both the Qur'an and the Bible, but with subtle differences. Muslims contend that the Qur'anic version is the correct one, unchanged by human intervention.

In both books, the Old Testament and Qur'an, Abraham took his son up the mountain to sacrifice him to God. In the Bible, the child was Isaac, son of Sarah. In the Qur'an, the child was Ishmael, son of Hagar. Both books report that the Virgin Mary married and bore a son named Jesus. In the Bible, Jesus' father was God; in the Qur'an, Jesus' father was human.

Muhammad and his cousin Ali were raised as brothers. For a long time, Mecca had been a pilgrimage center for all the inhabitants of the Arabian peninsula. They came to venerate the **Kaaba**, and Meccans made money from the adherents of all sects. Muhammad preached, however, that there was only one true God, and it was Him to whom he prayed.

There was a wealthy widow in the town, Khadije, who made her money as a merchant. She hired Muhammad to run the business, and the two eventually married. Westerners point to Muhammad's business acumen as evidence of education and sophistication, suggesting that he was not just a simple prophet. The Islamic tradition holds that Muhammad was illiterate and incapable of devising a complex new religion by himself. He simply recited God's words. The first word the angel said to him was "Recite," not "Write this down." But, non-Muslims ask, if Muhammad could neither read nor write, how could he manage an important trading business?

Khadije supported Muhammad financially for many years and through many difficulties. When the angel Gabriel first appeared to Muhammad, he rushed home and told Khadije. She accepted that her husband had received a divine revelation. Khadije holds an important place in Islam, as the first person to whom Muhammad revealed God's word, and the first person to accept his mission of prophecy.

Muhammad began to draw disciples around him. At first his followers were limited to close friends and family. His cousin Ali was an early convert. Later, he began to attract the Meccan underclass: slaves, tribal clients, and second sons. The upper

---

Kaaba   Ancient meteorite long venerated in Mecca, now focal point of Muslim faith.

Cultures

UNDER THE SPELL OF ARABIC

There is no single way to transliterate Arabic into Western languages. If you simply try to record the sounds, some hear them one way, some another. Some sounds in Arabic (and Chinese) are hard to render in English. Some academic disciplines try for a standard **transliteration**, but not all disciplines accept the same one. In America, the most common standard is that of the Associated Press, because it appears in almost all newspapers. The *New York Times,* however, has its own style.

Take something as basic as "the Base," Osama bin Ladin's name for his terrorist organization. The AP calls it Al-Qaida, the *Times* al Qaeda. The actual pronunciation sounds like "ul GUYduh." The Arab proper name originally meaning "lord" or "sir" is Said, spelled variously Saed, Sayid, Sayyid, Sayyed, and Saeed. Spaniards are likely to recognize it as the name of their medieval hero El Cid, a Christian knight who served both Moorish and Catholic princes. More than a dozen variations have been counted in the spelling of the ruler of Libya: Kaddafi, Qadafi, Kadaffy, Gadhafi, and so on. The Muslim holy book is rendered Qur'an, Quran, or Koran.

We will try to use the spelling Muhammad throughout, but if a Pakistani writing in English spells his name Mohammed, who are we to correct him? Scholars may spell the name Husayn, but most recognize it as Hussein. The media spells it Osama; some scholars spell it Usama. A leader can be a shaykh or a sheik. Under the spell of Arabic, one cannot be totally consistent. Even the coauthors cannot agree. We're doing you a favor, because you will face these spelling variations all your life. Get used to them and learn to recognize the variations.

---

classes feared that Muhammad's teachings of only one God had become a threat to the lucrative pilgrimage trade that was the lifeblood of the city. Upon the death of Muhammad's protector, Abu Talib, the leaders of Mecca decided to kill Muhammad.

At the same time, the city of Yathrib, about 200 miles north of Mecca, was in turmoil. Yathrib's inhabitants heard that Muhammad was a fair man and invited him to move to Yathrib to become a judge to hear the complaints of the various tribes. Muhammad accepted. At great risk to his own life, cousin Ali posed as Muhammad and slept in the Prophet's bed as the murderers descended on the house. When the attackers discovered the ruse, they fled leaving Ali unharmed. Muhammad and many of his followers, meanwhile, slipped out of the city and moved north. The year was 622, and this event—the **hijra**—marks the beginning of the Islamic calendar. Muhammad and his disciples established the first Islamic city-state, and Yathrib changed its name to **Medina**, meaning it was the "city of the Prophet."

---

transliteration   Rendering a word from one writing system into another.

hijra   Rendered in English as hegira;flight or migration; specifically, Muhammad's move to Medina in 622, the start of the Islamic calendar.

Medina   "City"; specifically, Islam's second holiest city.

 *Cultures*

ARABIC NAMES

Names are important in the Arab world, as a good name is often synonymous with family honor. For most of their history, Arabs did not use family names but were known as sons of their father, **ibn**, such as Ibn Khaldun. Arabs still sometimes do not use their given names but refer to themselves as the father of their son, **abu**. If a man named Ibrahim has a son named Hassan, he will often be known informally as the father of Hassan, or Abu Hassan. Women are sometimes called mother of their son, **umm**.

Muhammad made a treaty that governed relations between the various tribes. The tribes accepted the Muslims as another tribe, even though it was not organized on the basis of blood ties. The tribes agreed to maintain their separate identities, but to unite into a single polity that renounced traditional blood vengeance in favor of justice administered by Muhammad. The early Muslims accepted Jews as full partners. Later, when some Jewish tribes were expelled from Medina, it was for the crimes of cooperating with the enemy or for disobedience to the Prophet—not because of their religious beliefs. For most of history, Jews and Muslims got along.

MUHAMMAD'S ROLE

As judge, Muhammad was the head of the judiciary; later, as the Medinan tribes converted, he also became head of the executive. There was no legislature, however, because Muslims believed that God had already handed them the only law they needed. Muhammad's practices were recorded as **sunna**, which are also important in Islamic legal and social reasoning. The Medinans gave Muhammad special honor as the medium through whom they learned God's word. They did not consider Muhammad infallible, however. There are several **hadith** in which Muhammad makes a decision and is challenged as to whether he was functioning as prophet or executive. When told that Muhammad was making decisions based on his own logic, the people sometimes made him reverse those decisions.

ibn Arabic for "son of."
abu "Father of."
umm "Mother of."
sunna Traditions concerning the actions of the Prophet; origin of Sunni, mainstream Islam.
hadith Sayings of the Prophet.

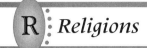

Religions

THE ISLAMIC CALENDAR

In the Middle East, history is judged as taking place either before Muhammad established the Muslim state, or after. The Muslim calendar dates from the Hijra of A.D. 622, when Muhammad and his followers fled Mecca and established the Islamic city-state in Medina. The Middle East of today therefore begins in many ways in the seventh century and not in the two millennium of civilization that preceded it. In the West, the years of the Islamic calendar are sometimes given as A.H. (anno hegirae, "year of the hijra"). For example, 1000 A.H. would be A.D. 1592 because each Muslim year is eleven days shorter than a Christian year.

Over the next decade, Muhammad fought many battles with the Meccans— winning some and losing others. Muhammad was the only founder of a major religion who was also a successful military commander. Islam was always closely connected to the sword. By 629, however, Muhammad signed a truce with the rulers of Mecca, known as the Treaty of Hudaybiya. He entered the city on pilgrimage and announced that the Kaaba was a site holy to the one true God. By his words and actions, the pilgrimage trade was saved, albeit transformed into service of the new religion. The following year, Mecca surrendered to the Muslims. Muhammad died in 632, just as his followers were seizing control of the Arabian peninsula.

BIRTH OF SHI'ISM

Muhammad's death immediately split the young Muslim community. Abu Bakr, the father of Muhammad's favorite wife Aisha, emerged from the death chamber to tell the assembled multitudes: "Those of you who followed Muhammad, Muhammad is dead. Those of you who follow God, God lives." The elders of the community elected Abu Bakr to be their new leader, or **caliph**, the one who replaced Muhammad in a temporal role as leader of the community. No one replaced him in his role as prophet. Muslims believe that since the Qur'an recorded God's revelation whole and intact, there is no need for any future prophet. Muhammad was thus the "Seal of Prophecy." A minority, however, believed that no one could lead the community unless he was related to Muhammad. They turned their allegiance to cousin Ali, who by now was married to the Prophet's daughter, Fatima.

---

caliph   Successor, specifically of Muhammad. (Root of *California*.)

Religions

THE CONSTITUTION OF MEDINA

The constitution Muhammad devised for Medina was incorporated into Islam, where much persists to this day. There was to be no clear separation between mosque and state, as all believers and their families form a single community, the **umma**. The tradition of family responsibility for violence and harm to others is enshrined in the provision that extended families must provide **blood money** and ransoms for its members. Revenge for the death of a family member was then and is now a prominent motive, as the Israelis have discovered on the West Bank. All members of the umma are expected to fight crime, even if the criminal is a relative.

In a practice that did not play much of a role in the 1991 First Gulf War but appeared strongly with the 2003 Second Gulf War, Muhammad's constitution required the entire umma to stick together against infidels who threaten any members of the umma. In trying to gain Arab allies against Saddam, we were working against Muhammad's intentions. Interestingly, Jews at that time (a large part of the population) were to be treated as members of the community but allowed to keep their religion. Jews and Muslims were to help each other, even with military assistance. This last point held up pretty well until the twentieth century. For most of history, Muslim-Jewish relations were good. Much of Tariq's army that invaded Spain in 711 were Jews.

There are even some hadith in which, before his death, the Prophet tells his followers that Ali is his successor. Those who accepted Ali as their leader became known as "Ali's Partisans," which in Arabic is *Shi'aat Ali*. From this term comes the word Shi'a, and it is this first succession conflict that marks the great schism in Islam between the Sunni and the Shi'a.

THE CHOICE OF THE CALIPHS

The first caliph, Abu Bakr, was chosen by the elders of the community and accepted by the community who swore allegiance to him. After consulting with the learned in the community, Abu Bakr designated his successor, Umar (sometimes spelled Omar), in a political will. The people, likewise, swore allegiance to him. Umar appointed a council of six men who chose his successor, the third caliph, Uthman. When Uthman died, the people of Medina acclaimed Ali as the fourth caliph.

Note the commonalities in the succession: The first three caliphs were chosen by the community's elders, acting in consultation. This provided the precedent of relying on the learned to decide right and wrong for the community. All four caliphs were then approved by the acclamation of the people, along the lines of

---

umma   Community or a people; specifically, the community of Islam.

blood money   Payment for injury done to member of one family by member of another.

Religions

HUDAYBIYA

Within the contemporary Muslim community, the 628 treaty of Hudaybiya is a controversial matter. The Qur'an gave Muslims a strict order to "command what is good, and forbid what is evil." Dealing with unbelievers was considered an evil act, yet here was the Prophet of God signing an armistice with them. Today, some use this example to justify a gentle form of Islam that can coexist with other religions. Others use it as an example that makes it permissible to hide your ultimate goal (conquest of the unbelievers) as a means to attain that goal. Deciding which interpretation is correct is an urgent matter on the current world scene.

the hadith, "My people will never agree on error." The people swore an oath of allegiance, or **bay'a**.

The second caliph, Umar, performed a valuable service. It was he who gathered together all the fragments upon which Muhammad's utterances had been written. Under Umar's guiding hand, the fragments that were identified as being true revelations were compiled into the Qur'an. Umar, and not Muhammad, organized the Qur'an as we know it today. Similarly, Umar discarded those fragments that he and his advisors considered specious.

Ali's predecessor, Uthman, was from another branch of the Quraysh, Muhammad's tribe. He was a descendent of the Prophet's great uncle Abu Sufyan, and thus was from the Meccan aristocracy from whom the early Muslims had fled in 622. Many of the early Companions of the Prophet had difficulty accepting him as leader. Eventually, insurgents killed Uthman at the door to his house. When Ali became caliph, he vowed to prosecute his predecessor's murderers, but he never found the assailants. Uthman's family, the **Umayyads**, launched a full-scale civil war against Ali. The Umayyads enlisted a number of allies, including Muhammad's favorite wife, Aisha. Eventually, Ali was assassinated and the Umayyad governor of Syria, Mu'awiyya, claimed the caliphate.

The early caliphs, known as the Rashidun or "Rightly Guided," and the Umayyads presided over the incredible expansion of Islam through the Middle East and beyond. In A.D. 638 Muslim armies took Jerusalem, in 641 Egypt, in 642 Iran and Libya, and in 711 gained a foothold in India. The Arab general Tarik crossed from Morocco to Spain in 711 and gave his name to Gibraltar, *Gebel al Tarik*, the "Mountain of Tarik." The Muslim advance was halted in Europe in 732 at Poitiers and Tours, only about a hundred miles south of Paris. Muslims controlled all of the Sassanid Iranian Empire and much of the ancient Roman Empire.

---

bay'a   Oath of allegiance, binding an individual to obey all the lawful commands of the leader.
Umayyad   First Muslim dynasty, centered in Damascus, 661–749.

Cultures

FAMILY HONOR

Remember our discussion in Chapter 1 about group identities in the Middle East? The primary group from which Middle Easterners derive their identity—and to whom they give their loyalty—is their family. The honor of the family needs to be protected above all else. This can mean that women must be carefully guarded and kept from any contact with males outside the family. In some countries, women rarely leave the house and then only when escorted by a male relative. Often they must be covered from head to toe lest they tempt lust. Some Muslims will not shake hands with a woman, as that can be seen as a form of sexual contact. Girls go to their own schools, if they are allowed schooling. Sexuality is tightly controlled and restrained. Adultery may be punished by stoning to death. Forget the image of belly dancers; they are remnants of a pre-Islamic culture now found chiefly in Egypt but forbidden in stricter Muslim countries.

As children reach marriageable age, however, how can a family be certain that the child will choose a partner from a good family? After all, if the spouse is from a family whose honor has been sullied, then the offspring (who are carrying the family name) will not be as honorable. The solution in more traditional societies: Marry partners from the one family you know to be truly honorable—your own. Arabs traditionally married their first cousins; this protected the purity of the bloodlines. (In ancient Egypt, the Pharaoh often married his sister for the same reason.) Today, cousin-marriage is still practiced in the area but is fading with the spread of knowledge of genetics.

THE UMAYYADS

The Umayyads ruled the Islamic world for less than a hundred years (661–749). They lacked legitimacy on several levels. They had obtained power through a civil war against the Prophet's son-in-law, alienating many who had supported Ali's cause.

Mu'awiyyah's son Yazid earned the eternal enmity of the Shi'a by ordering war against the Prophet's grandson, the third Shi'a Imam, Husayn. In fairness to Yazid, Husayn had raised the banner of rebellion against the central government. He gathered his followers into a small army, and moved on the town of Kufa. The Kufans had promised to aid Husayn. Unfortunately for the Imam, however, Yazid had dispatched an army of his own into the area, under General Ubayd. When the residents of Kufa heard the news of the caliph's superior force descending on the area, they barred the gates of the city and refused to allow Husayn to enter. He had to camp on the plain of Karbala, where he was killed in battle in 680.

Many who were not Shi'a, however, also found the method by which the Umayyads came to power distasteful. To escape the plots and machinations surrounding the old capital of Medina, Mu'awiyyah moved the capital to Damascus—the seat of his power. But Damascus derived its economic power from its connections to the Byzantine Empire; now, as an Islamic rival to the Greeks,

R : *Religions*

SHI'A LEADERSHIP PHILOSOPHY

The Sunni are followers of the sunna, or "customs," of the Prophet. They are over 80 percent of the world's Muslims. They believe that the first four caliphs were the rightful rulers of the Islamic state. The Shi'a, or partisans, accepted only the fourth caliph, Ali, as legitimate. The Shi'a became a religion of protest, whose leaders became a focal point of opposition to the caliphs. The Shi'a leaders, or imams, usually did not press their claims to the throne, arguing that an illegitimate ruler should still be obeyed rather than risk division and chaos in the community.

Most Shi'a, but not all, claim that the right to rule descended from Ali and Fatima to eleven other direct descendants of Muhammad. Ali and his descendants are known as the Twelve Imams; the Twelfth Imam disappeared as an infant in the tenth century. The Sunni claim that either the Imam died or possibly was never even born. The Shi'a claim that God would never leave his people without a legitimate leader; thus, the Twelfth Imam was born and then placed into hiding. The Shi'a say that he is still alive today, in this world but not in this time. He will return to restore justice to the world before the Last Judgment Day.

Since the Twelfth Imam is the rightful ruler, and he is still alive, Shi'a religious leaders have traditionally held that any other ruler on earth—including Muslim rulers—are, in a sense, usurpers of the Twelfth Imam's rightful place. This theory was accepted for a thousand years, until Ayatollah Khomeini assumed power in Iran in 1979.

Damascus was cut off from the trade flows that had been its lifeblood. Mu'awiyyah also tried to win the support of Muslims by initiating a mosque-building program, a strategy that would be pursued any number of times over the next 1,400 years by rulers whose claims were shaky. The Umayyads were responsible for building the Umayyad mosque in Damascus, the oldest Friday Mosque in Islam, and the Dome of the Rock in Jerusalem.

The Kharijites, Islam's first fundamentalists, also challenged the Umayyads. This group first formed in opposition to Ali, who had tried to compromise with his opponents. The Kharijites took the extreme position that the caliph was charged with executing the law of God—and there could be no compromise over God's law. The Kharijites formed their own community, in which any member could claim to be its leader. As the Umayyads were not members of the breakaway sect, the Kharijites would not recognize the Umayyad claim to the throne. They labeled Umayyad followers as heretics who had strayed from the true faith.

Finally, the Arab conquest of the Persian Sassanids did not sit easily on the Iranian population. While most converted from Zoroastrianism to Islam, that did not mean they accepted the overlordship of Arabs—whom the cosmopolitan Iranians considered ill-mannered louts from the desert with no culture to speak of. Soldiers from the far northeast of the empire, under the leadership of a general named Abu Muslim, rebelled against the impious rulers in Damascus.

THE ABBASIDS

All these groups opposed to the Umayyads united into a single movement, raised black banners as their standard, and marched on the caliph. Cleverly, the leaders of the opposition told their supporters that they were restoring the caliphate to the family of the Prophet but never identified which member was their choice. It was only after the armies had triumphed that they announced the new ruler: Abu Abbas. The new caliph was a descendent of the Prophet's uncle Abbas, not of the Prophet himself. Although technically entitled to be called a member of the family since he was a distant relative, the Shi'a felt they were shortchanged and continued to support the claims of their imams.

Following the fall of the Umayyads from power in the East, an Umayyad relative established himself as caliph in Spain. The people of Spain believed that this Umayyad survivor, Abd al-Rahman I, had escaped the fall of their house by swimming the length of the Mediterranean. This second Umayyad caliphate ruled only the Iberian peninsula, but its rule lasted from 756 to 1031, longer than their cousins' reign in Damascus. Spain under the Moors enjoyed a golden age of science and culture. Muslims, Christians, and Jews lived together unmolested. Moorish learning in Spain eventually returned the ancient Greek classics to the knowledge of the West.

THE ABBASID CALIPHATE

The **Abbasid** caliphate survived in one form or another from 750 until its destruction by the Mongols in 1258. The fact that it survived did not mean that it thrived. Its caliphal title was challenged by the Umayyads in Spain and by the Fatimids, another Muslim dynasty, in Egypt. Further, its control over the central Arab lands weakened in the ninth century when the caliphs came under the control of their military guards. In 945, the Buyids from Iran seized the capital and took over all temporal power. They were succeeded in 1055 by the latest wave of migrants from Central Asia, the Seljuk Turks. In Islamic theory, there is no separation between church and state; from 945 on, however, this separation became a reality regardless of the teachings of the theologians. The caliph was technically the ruler of the realm, and he held some religious authority. The true rulers, however, were the military commanders who took the title **sultan**.

Things began well enough for the Abbasids. Abu Abbas seized the throne, and promptly turned on those who had helped him to power but who might challenge him in the future. Abu Muslim and his forces were among the first to die. Using similar logic as their Umayyad predecessors, the Abbasids moved the capital from Damascus to avoid the political scheming of the inhabitants. They moved

---

Abbasid   Second major Muslim dynasty, centered in Baghdad, 750–1258.
sultan   Holder of power.

R ⦂ *Religions*

HUSAYN: MARTYR OR SUICIDE?

As Muslims accept God as the Creator of all things, including all living beings, they look upon suicide as a grave sin whereby the individual elevates his own choice to destroy God's creation over God's divine plan. By contrast, if a Muslim dies struggling in the way of God, he is a martyr and is promised numerous rewards in Paradise.

Was Husayn a martyr, or did he commit suicide? According to Shi'a teachings, the night before the battle of Karbala, Husayn called his army together. He told them that there would be a major battle the next day, that they were hopelessly outnumbered, and that any who took to the field would probably be killed. Husayn then dismissed all members of his army who had wives, children, or other responsibilities. He ordered the campfires doused so none would see the soldiers who had to leave the camp. When the fires were relit, only Husayn and seventy-two followers remained. Facing impossible odds, Husayn the next day fought to the death.

Shi'a faithful throughout the world remember this occasion every year with passion plays produced in every Shi'a community where public displays of their religion are allowed. Did Husayn remain true to God's plan by fighting against impossible odds, or did he commit suicide by placing himself in a position where it would be impossible to survive?

---

to the new city of Baghdad in central Iraq between the Tigris and Euphrates rivers. The city was designed to be a fortress, and the new caliphate was soon isolated from the population.

Under the Abbasids, there was a great flowering of Islamic culture. Following the Islamic edict to seek knowledge wherever it is found, Muslim philosophers founded the House of Wisdom in Baghdad. This school housed the only copies of ancient Greek writings.

During this time period, the great Islamic jurists codified Islamic law into the four schools of Sunnism: Hanbali, Hanafi, Maliki, and Shafi. In a Shi'a parallel, the Sixth Imam, Ja'afar al-Sadiq, organized the Shi'a school of law, the Ja'afari. Sunni jurists proclaimed that by the tenth century all questions had been answered (or at least the principles for deciding the questions had been answered). They declared the gate of independent reasoning, the Bab al-**ijtihad**, to be closed. Now there was only one, standard interpretation, **taqlid.** Shari'a law was now complete. Thenceforth, jurists would study the **Shari'a** and make rulings on questions before them based on the logic of the tenth century. Some scholars think this closing off of independent reasoning and interpretation of the Qur'an led to intellectual stagnation in Islamic culture.

---

ijtihad   Independent reasoning to interpret the Qur'an.

taqlid   Literally, "emulation"; single, orthodox interpretation of the Qur'an.

Shari'a   Codification of Islamic law.

Jerusalem's Dome of the Rock is one of Islam's holiest sites. (*Michael G. Roskin*)

CHALLENGES TO ORTHODOXY

The Abbasids also faced a major schism within Sunnism. One of the Abbasid caliphs, al-Ma'mun, embraced a rationalist interpretation of Islam. This view, known as Mu'tazilism, held that much of the religion could be understood through the use of human reason. It also argued that God created the Qur'an, meaning his revelation was not coeternal with him. Al-Ma'mun tried to unite the Sunni and Shi'a by endorsing the Eighth Imam, Ali al-Rida, as his successor. In the backlash against Mu'tazilism, however, theologians and their followers quickly overlooked al-Ma'mun's choice of successor. Instead, he was succeeded by one who repudiated his predecessor's dalliance with Aristotelian rationalism.

The Abbasids also had to deal with the rise of Sufism, which they frequently persecuted as a heresy. **Sufis** were mystics who sought a personal relationship with God and argued that God hid the true meaning of the Qur'an to all but the initiated. Probably the most famous incident of persecution involved the Sufi mystic Mansur al-Hallaj, whom the Caliph al-Mutaqdir ordered killed in 932. Filled with mystical delight at the union he felt with the divine presence within him, al-Hallaj exclaimed "Ana al-Haq," or "I am the Truth." As truth is a divine attribute, al-Hallaj was accused of blasphemy for calling himself God. Despite persecution, however, Sufism spread throughout the Middle East and Muslim world.

Sufi   Muslim mystic sect.

 *Religions*

FRIDAY MOSQUE

In Islam, the day of worship goes from sunset Thursday to sunset Friday. The major prayer service in each city is held at a large, central mosque known as the Friday Mosque. The leading religious figure in the city usually leads the prayers, and offers the prayers of the faithful in the name of the caliph. In modern times, in Iran, the role of the Friday mosque has been taken over by Tehran University because it can hold more worshippers than the principal mosque. The prayer ceremony is used to provide guidance to the faithful on the latest political positions of the rulers of the republic.

THE END OF THE ARAB EMPIRE

In 1258 Mongol invaders under Hulegu, grandson of Genghis Khan, conquered Baghdad and brutally ended the Abbasid dynasty. He made a pyramid of Arab skulls and ruined the irrigation systems of the region. To this day, Muslims bemoan the Mongol conquest; although the Mongols later converted to Islam they were always suspected of hypocrisy. The center of Arab cultural life was shattered just as Europe began to stir in the late Middle Ages. The Seljuks, who had been ruling the empire for two centuries as sultans—and who had reunited the Iranian, Arab, and Anatolian lands under one crown—also went into decline everywhere except in Anatolia, where they continued to press the Byzantine empire. Many believe that the caliphate died in Baghdad with the Mongol invasion; others believe it passed to the Ottomans through the Fatimids.

THE FATIMIDS

The Fatimids were Ismaili Shi'a and the founders of a dynasty that claimed direct descent from the Prophet through his daughter Fatima and husband Ali. For this reason, when the Abbasids began to lose their power in the eighth century, the Fatimids claimed that they were the rightful caliphs of Islam. The Fatimids ruled from Cairo, and they reigned over the ancient lands of Egypt. They built numerous mosques in Cairo, and presided over a major merchant kingdom.

THE MAMLUKS

In 1171 Saladin, liberator of Jerusalem, conquered the Fatimids in Cairo. He founded the Ayyubid dynasty that ruled in Egypt and the former Crusader lands until the mid-thirteenth century. To keep power in a hostile territory, the Ayyubids imported

Conflicts

THE CRUSADES

The Crusades represented a short interruption in Islam's dominance of the Middle East. They consisted of a series of military campaigns over almost two centuries, from 1095 to 1291. They were Christendom's counteroffensive against the Muslim armies that had dislodged Christianity from its birthplace.

The first crusade was the only successful one. The French Pope Urban II called it into existence at a council of bishops in the French town of Clermont in 1095. Most of the participants were French or spoke French, so Middle Easterners called them Franks. Today throughout the Middle East the term for foreigner is a derivative of the term Frank: *frangi* or *ferangi*.

The First Crusade took almost five years to reach and conquer Fatimid-controlled Jerusalem, its main target. In 1099, after a five-week siege, the Crusaders took Jerusalem and slaughtered its Muslim and Jewish inhabitants. In those days, Muslims and Jews were united against the barbaric Christians. The Crusaders also took most of Anatolia from the Seljuk Turks who had conquered it from the Byzantines. They spent the next twenty-five years establishing Crusader kingdoms throughout modern Israel, Lebanon, Syria, northern Iraq, and southeastern Turkey. Salah-al-Din, better known as Saladin, a chivalrous Kurdish general, later demolished the Crusaders at the decisive Battle of Hattin in present-day northern Israel in 1187 and quickly retook most Crusader lands, including Jerusalem. The Christian control of Jerusalem lasted less than a hundred years.

The Second Crusade, led by the crowned heads of Europe, was an unmitigated disaster. Most of the army was defeated in Anatolia long before reaching Jerusalem. The Third Crusade included England's Richard the Lionheart and France's King Phillip. While it failed to liberate Jerusalem, the Third Crusade reclaimed Cyprus for Christianity.

The Fourth Crusade degenerated into a sordid fight among Christians. The Doge of Venice agreed to provide the Crusaders with naval transport. When the Crusaders reached Venice they did not have money to pay the Venetians, so they agreed to support Venice in regaining a rebellious vassal Christian city, Zara (now Zadar on the Croatian coast), which had sought Hungarian protection. Already deflected from the goal of reclaiming Jerusalem, the Crusaders sailed to Constantinople to insure the succession of the Western-supported candidate for emperor, Alexius III. For the first time in 900 years, Constantinople was conquered and sacked—not by invading Muslims, but by Crusaders with crosses on their chests. Byzantium was irreparably weakened, and the Crusaders stole most of the treasures of Constantinople. (The horses atop St. Mark's Cathedral in Venice are from Constantinople, as are the relics of the Holy Cross in Rome.)

The Fifth Crusade passed without result, mainly because the Crusade's titular leader, Frederick II, stayed home. When the crusade failed, the pope excommunicated him. Frederick then sailed for the Holy Land, but without papal support. His Sixth Crusade managed to regain Jerusalem through diplomatic negotiations with the ruler of Egypt, the late Salah-al-Din's brother, al-'Adil. Because Frederick achieved this victory while still excommunicated, it led to internecine rivalry among the Christians between supporters of the Church and supporters of Frederick. Jerusalem remained in Christian hands for ten years, as specified by the truce; it then reverted to the Muslims.

The Seventh Crusade, led by King Louis IX of France, aimed at Cairo instead of Jerusalem. Muslim armies captured the French king, queen, and entire court and held them for ransom. The crusader army was either defeated on the battlefield or executed in captivity. The Eighth and final Crusade did not even head for the Levant but wasted its effort in North Africa.

Left to their own devices and divided by foolish rivalries, the Crusader states in the Levant fell one by one. The Mamluks captured Tyre (present-day Lebanon) in 1291 and drove the last crusaders from Asia. Once again the Holy Land was wholly Muslim.

What can be said of the Crusades? In the West, the movement soon passed into mythology and history books and was largely forgotten. Today in the West, a crusade means to fight for a noble cause, such as a crusade for literacy or to eliminate polio. President George W. Bush called for a "crusade" against terrorism.

Most of the Middle East was horrified at that word; they have not forgotten their two-hundred-year war with Christians. Muslims had learned several lessons from the Crusades: that Christendom in its ignorance opposed the true faith (Islam); that Christians sought to steal Muslim lands and establish military bases on them (never mind that the lands were those which Muslims earlier stole from Christians); and that, contrary to Muslim teachings of tolerance toward other religions, when the Christian armies captured a city they put all Muslims and Jews to the sword. To support this latter point, they often point to Salah-al-Din's behavior when he reconquered Jerusalem: Instead of killing the Christians, he merely sold them into slavery. With these lessons, and with the Arab compression of history into the recent past, the president's words provoked demonstrations in the Middle East. Muslims did not hear an invitation to join a noble cause; they heard a declaration of war on Islam—a war that would result in the occupation of Muslim lands and the death of the Muslim inhabitants.

Ruins of a crusader castle, one of many, could be close to a thousand years old. A nearby kibbutz listed small farm animals in the center as "bears." Secular kibbutzniks cared nothing for the Jewish ban on pork. (*Michael G. Roskin*)

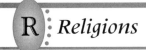

Religions

THE VARIETIES OF SHI'ISM

Throughout this volume we use the term Shi'a to refer to the branch of Islam that is in the majority in Iran, Iraq, Bahrain, and in Southern Lebanon. This movement is actually more properly referred to as Ithna'ashari Shi'a, or Twelver Shi'ism. The adherents of this religious interpretation claim that Muhammad was succeeded by twelve leaders, or imams. In fact, there have been several Shi'a movements. They are differentiated by how many imams the believers accept. Two groups that still have adherents today are the Zaydis and the Ismailis.

The Zaydis follow the teachings of the son of the Fourth Imam, Zayd bin Ali Zayn al-Abadin. Zayd preached that any descendent of the Prophet, provided he has the ability to rule, is entitled to be the imam of the people. There are few Zaydis left, and they are found predominantly in the highlands of Yemen.

Twelver Shi'a believe that the Sixth Imam, Ja'afar al-Sadiq, had two children: Ismail and Musa al-Kazim. Since Ismail died before Ja'afar, they accept that the younger one, Musa, became the Seventh Imam. The Ismailis disagree, and hold that since Ismail was the eldest son, the Imamate passed through him to his son Muhammad, whom they also identify as the **Mahdi**. There are still a number of Ismailis today, in India. Their head is the international philanthropist and playboy, the Agha Khan.

military slaves that would be loyal to the dynasty and that would have no local ties. These military slaves, or **Mamluks**, eventually overthrew the Ayyubids and ruled in Egypt from 1250–1517.

In many ways, the Mamluks saved civilization. After the Mongols destroyed Baghdad, their armies continued to rape and pillage deep into the Arab heartland. The Mamluks sent an army to meet the Mongols in Syria and blunted the Mongol advance. Three centuries later the Ottomans defeated the Mamluks and claimed the caliphate for their own chief.

IRANIAN DYNASTIES

Iran's history throughout this period was one of foreign conquest. The pre-Islamic Sassanids fought Byzantium to a standstill, but the battles drained Iranian strength. So, when the Arab armies invaded Iran in 636, the Sassanid armies fell. The last battle was in 641, the empire crumbled, and Iran became part of the Islamic caliphate.

Mahdi   The Rightly Guided One; missing imam some Muslims, especially Shi'a, believe will return at the end of the world.

Mamluk   Arabic for "slave"; Muslim Egyptian dynasty that originated in the army's corps of converted Caucasian slaves.

R Religions
================

IBN TAYMIYAH

The wars against the Mongols gave rise to one of the most influential political thinkers among Islamic fundamentalists today, ibn Taymiyah. An Iraqi scholar from the conservative Hanbali school of Islam, ibn Taymiyah lived in Damascus as a refugee from the Mongol invasions. When the Mongols caught up with him there, he led the resistance from 1299 to 1304. By this time, Mongols had been in Islamic lands for decades and had converted to Islam. Ibn Taymiyah was faced with the problem of justifying fighting a defensive war against these Muslim invaders, given Qur'anic prohibitions against a Muslim killing another Muslim.

He devised a theory that, even though they said they were Muslims, the Mongols were not true Muslims because their goal was to rule with Mongol law instead of with the Shari'a. Since it was the desire of all Muslims to implement Shari'a, and the Mongols did not implement Shari'a, then the Mongols were hypocrites and could be killed as unbelievers. Any fundamentalist group that advocates killing heads of Islamic states uses the same logic today.

When followers of the blind Shaykh Omar Abdul Rahman assassinated Egyptian President Anwar Sadat in October 1981, they left behind a manifesto justifying their actions entitled "The Forgotten Duty" in which they quoted the writings of ibn Taymiyah at length. Almost a decade later, one of the authors visited Algeria, when it appeared that the local Islamic political party was about to take power. The number-one, best-selling author in every bookstore was ibn Taymiyah. Religion has staying power.

When the Abbasids moved their capital to nearby Baghdad, Iran acquired considerable influence. The palace was built along Iranian lines, and Iranian courtiers staffed it. Abbasid strength came from the Persian lands to the east rather than the Arab lands of the west. It was a Persian tribe, the Buyids, who deposed the Abbasid caliph of temporal authority in the tenth century. Iran, like the Abbasids, was next invaded by the Seljuk Turks. Between 1055 and 1501, Iran was divided between Turkish, Mongol, and native families who ruled various parts of the territory.

CONCLUSIONS

In one form or another, Muslim rulers have held sway in the Middle East from the death of Muhammad until today. According to theologians, the goal of a Muslim ruler is to guide the people under his care to salvation, through his administration of Shari'a law. The most perfect manifestations of this law are the practices of Muhammad as ruler of Medina and later of Mecca.

Despite the myth that the Four Rightly Guided Caliphs ruled over a united Islamic kingdom guided by the Prophet's teachings, in reality the caliphate has been wracked with division from the very beginning. Eventually, the umma divided into several Muslim kingdoms, all claiming to follow the rightful successor to the Prophet. After the dreadful Mongol invasions, the lands of Islam were thrown into chaos. Only a slave army staved off total disaster.

Cultures

FERDOWSI: NATIONALIST POET

Illustrating the sense of Iranian difference was a new, literary form of Persian that replaced the language of the Zoroastrian Magi. The preeminent scholar of tenth-century Persia, Ferdowsi, composed the Shahnameh, a compilation of Persian history and mythology stretching back to the dawn of time. In sixty thousand couplets, Ferdowsi supposedly used less than one hundred Arabic words as he sought to use the new Persian language to the fullest. For a thousand years, Ferdowsi's poem has been an inspiration to Persian nationalists. Using the Persian language to describe Persian themes three hundred years after the Arab invasion, Ferdowsi is seen as a symbol of Iran's ability to persevere despite being conquered by foreigners.

Less well known is the early role Ferdowsi played as a symbol of protest after the 1979 Iranian Revolution. Because he had not used Arabic, the language of the Qur'an, monarchists and anti-clerics embraced Ferdowsi as a symbol of secularism.

KEY TERMS

Abbasid (p. 32)   Medina (p. 25)

abu (p. 26)   Shari'a (p. 33)

bay'a (p. 29)   Shi'a (p. 23)

blood money (p. 28)   Sufi (p. 34)

caliph (p. 27)   sultan (p. 32)

hadith (p. 26)   sunna (p. 26)

hijra (p. 25)   Sunni (p. 23)

ibn (p. 26)   taqlid (p. 33)

ijtihad (p. 33)   transliteration (p. 25)

Kaaba (p. 24)   Umayyad (p. 29)

Mahdi (p. 38)   umm (p. 26)

Mamluk (p. 38)   umma (p. 28)

FURTHER REFERENCE

Armstrong, Karen. *Muhammad: A Biography of the Prophet.* New York: Harper, 2001.

Aslan, Reza. *No God but God: The Origins, Evolution, and Future of Islam.* New York: Random House, 2006.

Berkey, Jonathan P. *The Formation of Islam: Religion and Society in the Near East, 600–1800.* New York: Cambridge University Press, 2003.

Black, Antony. *The History of Islamic Political Thought.* New York: Routledge, 2001.

Eaton, Charles Le Gai. *Islam and the Destiny of Man.* Albany, NY: SUNY Press, 1985.

Hourani, Albert. *A History of the Arab Peoples.* Cambridge, MA: Harvard University Press, 1991.

Jansen, Johannes J. G. *The Neglected Duty.* New York: MacMillan, 1986.

McAuliffe, Jane Dammen, ed. *The Cambridge Companion to the Qur'an.* New York: Cambridge University Press, 2005.

Nafziger, George F., and Mark W. Walton. *Islam at War: A History.* Westport, CT: Praeger, 2003.

Patai, Raphael. *The Arab Mind,* rev. ed. New York: Hatherleigh, 2005.

Saunders, J. J. *A History of Medieval Islam.* New York: Routledge, 1996.

Smith, Huston. *Islam: A Concise Introduction.* New York: Harper, 2001.

Tyerman, Christopher. *God's War: A New History of the Crusades.* Cambridge, MA: Harvard University Press, 2006.

Waines, David. *An Introduction to Islam,* 2nd ed. New York: Cambridge University Press, 2004.

Watt, W. Montgomery. *Islamic Political Thought.* Edinburgh: Edinburgh University Press, 1987.

3 The Ottoman Empire

Points to Ponder

- Can Muslims and non-Muslims live in peace under a single government?
- Why is the culture of the Middle East so similar across national boundaries?
- What are the causes of the fall of the Ottoman Empire?
- What impeded reform of the Ottoman Empire?
- Why did an Ottoman nationalism not develop?
- Are there parallels between the Ottoman decline and today's Middle East?

THE OTTOMANS

The Ottoman Empire was the last Islamic empire and caliphate. Unlike the Arab Umayyads and Abbasids, the Ottomans were Turks. When the caliphate was abolished (by Atatürk in 1924), Muslims as far away as India felt despair and humiliation. Some, such as Osama bin Laden, still vow to restore an Islamic empire and caliphate. Accordingly, although little-studied in American schools, the Ottoman Empire is important both for what it did and for what it left behind.

At the same time the Moors were slowly being pushed out of Iberia, two Mediterranean peninsulas to the east, a new Muslim force was pushing into Europe, the **Ottomans**, a subtribe of the Oguz Turks, the same Turkish tribe that was the progenitor of the Seljuks. Originally, the Seljuks were rulers while the Ottomans were the warriors who protected the land of Islam from the remnants of the Byzantine Empire. The Mongols destroyed the Seljuks as a ruling force in 1293.

Ottoman   Turkish tribe and later empire in Balkans and Middle East.

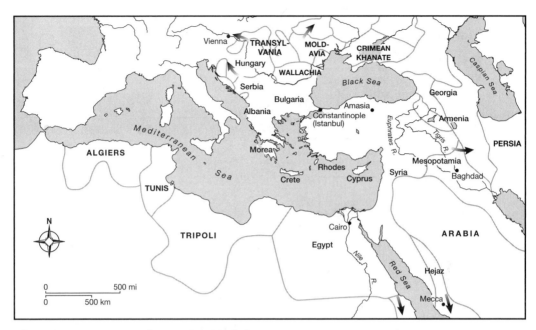

The Ottoman Empire at Its Height, 1683

After their victory, elements of the Mongols took over most of Iran and ruled it as the Ilkhanid dynasty. Small pockets of Turks remained free of the Mongol yoke. One of these pockets of resistance was in and around the town of Bursa, across the **Marmara** Sea from Constantinople. Freed of Seljuk overlordship by the Mongols, Osman and his family ruled Bursa as a small, independent principality. (Osman, from whom the dynasty derives its name, is the father of the dynasty. It became known as Ottoman in the West due to a mispronunciation of Osman's name.)

Osman and his successors initially bypassed Constantinople and conquered the **Balkans**. The Ottomans beat the Bulgars in 1361 and then beat the Serbian army at Kosovo Polje ("Field of Blackbirds") in 1389, a battle that killed both commanders. This opened the way for the Turks to surge into Hungary's rich Pannonian basin and even on to Vienna, which they besieged twice, in 1529 and again in 1683. All Europe trembled until Polish cavalry under Jan Sobieski drove the Turks back from Vienna in 1683. That was the high-water mark for the Turks in Europe. Thereafter, they were slowly pushed back. It is important to remember that the Ottomans were a Balkan empire before they expanded over the Middle East in the early sixteenth century.

Marmara Sea between Bosporus and Dardanelles separating Europe from Asia Minor.

Balkan Turkish for "mountain"; large peninsula of Southeast Europe that includes Greece, Bulgaria, and Serbia.

Worshippers in the Blue Mosque (also known as the Sultan Ahmet Mosque) of Istanbul, a beautiful early-seventeenth-century edifice in use today (*Michael G. Roskin*)

Before they tried Vienna, with all the Balkans as their empire, the Ottomans had returned to crack open the walls of Constantinople in 1453 with cannon, enabling Mehmet the Conqueror's triumphal entry into the city they renamed Istanbul. Over the next four and a half centuries, the Ottoman Empire rose to world power but then sunk so low that in 1853 the Russian tsar called it the "sick man of Europe." At its height, the empire stretched from the gates of Vienna in Europe to Azerbaijan in Asia; it controlled the entire coast of North Africa and all the Arab lands, including the east and west coasts of the Arabian peninsula (but not the untamed center).

The main impact of the Ottoman Empire was probably the protection of the Islamic, Middle Eastern culture that is today spread so uniformly from Morocco to Persia. Before the Ottomans recaptured the Arab lands, they had started to drift apart. There were multiple claims to the caliphate, multiple local rulers, and multiple accommodations with local conditions. The umma had never been so weak. Within fifty years of the Ottoman capture of Constantinople, specifically in 1492, Muslims were ejected from the Iberian peninsula. Today, while there are Arab influences on Spanish culture, Ottoman culture is very much alive in the foods, clothing, cultural artifacts, and manners of every corner of the Middle East and, to a lesser extent, of the Balkans.

The Ottomans were relatively tolerant of Christians and Jews, who were accorded dhimmi status and protection as "People of the Book." The Turks allowed each religious and ethnic group to rule themselves. Thus, there were Muslim courts, Christian courts, and Jewish courts. Unlike modern America, in the Middle East you stay in whatever ethnic and religious group you are born into. Bloodlines, not free choice, define who you are. Accordingly, under the Ottomans you had to obey the laws of your people and be judged in their law courts. A Muslim could be found guilty of a crime for an action that would be lawful for a Christian, or vice versa. This was known as the **millet** system.

THE JANISSARIES

The center of Mehmet the Conqueror's army was the **Janissary** corps. The Janissaries were mostly Christian boys collected as "blood tax" every few years from the Balkans to serve as slaves in the Sultan's service. Converted to Islam, they were trained from youth to be fighters. This is one reason there is a great deal of Balkan blood among today's Turks. Atatürk himself was of Balkan descent. For centuries, the Sultans used the Janissaries as an all-purpose paramilitary police to run the vast empire. As property of the Sultan, they had no rights. To prevent corruption and nepotism, they could not even marry, as Janissaries might then give legitimate wives and children official and monetary favors. When they were too old to fight, they were released from their service, but new boys were always acquired for the Janissaries from the latest Christian territory the Ottomans captured.

From an early time, the Janissaries wielded significant power at the court, since they controlled much of the weaponry of the empire. Janissaries frequently threw their weight behind competing claimants to the throne, a pattern called **praetorianism**. Some rose to become the Sultan's **viziers**, the day-to-day administrators of the empire. Later, the Janissaries received permission to marry and have legitimate children, who could then inherit their fathers' lands and titles. Sure enough, corruption immediately set in. The Janissaries ceased being a true fighting force and became just another part of the ramshackle Ottoman regime.

When Mehmet died, the Janissaries decided which of his children and grandchildren became Sultan. In 1520, Mehmet's great grandson assumed the throne. Crowned Sulayman (often spelled Suleiman) I, his subjects called him Sulayman the Lawgiver because he codified the laws and imperial proclamations that were enforced in the empire. As these laws were written in Arabic script, his lawgiving stature was relatively unknown in the West, where he was known as Sulayman the Magnificent. His reign was the height of the Ottoman Empire.

---

millet In Ottoman times an ethnic community; in modern Turkish a nation.

Janissary From Turkish *yeniceri,* "new soldier"; elite military units of the Ottoman Empire.

praetorianism After Rome's Praetorian Guard; military takeover of or influence in government.

vizier Ottoman Sultan's appointed minister.

K · Key Concepts

PRAETORIANISM

As Rome turned from republic to empire, its emperors appointed a special corps as imperial bodyguards, the Praetorian Guard, which soon became so powerful it could make or break emperors. The guardians took over what they were supposed to be guarding. In modern usage, praetorianism indicates a situation of political breakdown in which no one plays by the rules and all manner of political forces try to grab power by rigged elections, student demonstrations, and nationwide strikes. In this chaos, the military become convinced that they are the only ones who can save the country, so they seize power by military coup. Other groups can sometimes pull coups—radical parties such as Mussolini's Fascists or Muslim fundamentalists as in Iran—but usually the military is the best organized and armed to take over. Praetorianism does not necessarily indicate headstrong or power-mad generals but rather the collapse of political institutions.

Praetorianism became common in Latin America, where weak institutions could not handle social and political stress, so the army stepped in repeatedly. Twentieth-century Europe saw coups in Spain, Portugal, Poland, Greece, and an attempt in France in 1958. Praetorianism arrived in the Middle East with the Ottoman Empire and the military influences on its politics, earlier the Janissaries and later the Young Turks. The Turkish Republic after World War II experienced two outright coups and two additional episodes of strong military influence on the civilian government. Pakistan has had several coups—all designed to save the country from foolish or corrupt elected politicians—and is now ruled by a general. Egypt had one coup in 1952 and power stayed in the hands of a succession of generals. Syria had several coups; its current ruler is the son of an officer who led a coup. The simplest way to explain a coup—perhaps too simple—is that when chaos breaks out, the generals take over.

Sulayman expanded the empire to the west, besieging Vienna in 1529. His desire to increase his holdings derived from several factors: to spread the Muslim faith, to emulate the conquerors of old, and—most of all—to appease the Janissaries with booty from military campaigns. The Viennese withstood a Turkish siege for almost three weeks, after which Sulayman withdrew his forces and returned to Istanbul.

THE REIGN OF SULAYMAN

Although stopped at Vienna from entering the heart of Europe, Sulayman ruled over a kingdom that included the Balkans and most of the Middle East and made the Mediterranean a Turkish lake. Through a series of naval victories, he eliminated Venice's merchant power that had dominated the sea for hundreds of years. His great rival was Charles, the Holy Roman Emperor of Spain and Austria. To hold Charles at bay, he allied himself with the French king, Ferdinand I. It was in making the alliance that Sulayman made his greatest mistake: He granted the French the equivalent of "most favored nation" status. French merchants paid the same taxes on their goods as their Muslim counterparts, while other European

K Key Concepts

CAPITULATIONS

The Ottoman government first capitulated to French demands and then to those of other Europeans. The capitulations were signs of growing European strength and Ottoman weakness. No government gives foreigners so many advantages if it can help it. The capitulations did not cause a great burden to the Ottoman government in the sixteenth century, but other European powers used the French precedent to demand similar treatment in the seventeenth to nineteenth centuries. By the time of the fall of the Ottoman Empire, foreigners paid little or no taxes, had immunity from prosecution, and received trade terms from the government that were more favorable than the terms a typical Ottoman subject could get.

The capitulations also stipulated that Ottoman subjects who worked for foreign consulates and trading companies as translators received the same rights as foreigners. This became known as the **dragoman** system, a corruption of the Turkish word for "translator," *turcoman*. Being a translator thus was a road to great wealth and power, and the inequalities in treatment between translators— usually Greek Christians—and the common Muslim Ottoman caused great resentment.

merchants paid much higher rates. The treaty of alliance also recognized the jurisdiction of French consular courts over French citizens. Sulayman was the first Middle Eastern ruler to grant **capitulations** to European powers.

In the East, Sulayman's forces fought three campaigns against the Persians, liberating Baghdad from Shi'a control. Finally, in 1555, he signed a peace treaty with the Persians that established the Iranian western border basically where it is today. Sulayman died in 1566, preparing to fight his enemies on a Hungarian battlefield.

OTTOMAN SUCCESSION

Ottoman forces continued to consolidate their hold on the Mediterranean, conquering the island of Cyprus in the years 1570–1572. This caused Venice, Spain, and the Papal States to join forces and launch a combined naval force against the Turks. The two navies met off Greece near the Gulf of Lepanto in late 1571, and the European forces ultimately triumphed. Sulayman had been stopped on land at Vienna; his son was stopped on the sea at Lepanto. Europe remained Christian and outside of Ottoman control. Some peg Lepanto as the turning point for Ottoman power, although Istanbul dismissed it as a minor setback.

dragoman   Privileged translator in Ottoman Empire.

capitulation   From Latin *capitula,* chapters; granting of special rights and privileges to Europeans, usually including extraterritoriality (the right to be tried in the courts of one's own country).

P : *Personalities*

HURREN

Hurren, known in the West as Roxelana, daughter of a Ukrainian priest, became a concubine to Sulayman. She so entranced the monarch that he married her—something no Ottoman Sultan had ever done with a concubine. As Sulayman aged, he turned to his **Grand Vizier** for guidance. This gentleman was Sulayman's son-in-law, married to his daughter by Hurren. It was Hurren who had convinced Sulayman to appoint the man to the post, and Hurren controlled much of the empire through the Grand Vizier. She then convinced Sulayman that his eldest son, borne by another concubine, was plotting to take the throne from the Emperor. Sulayman killed the young man, clearing the path for Hurren's son, Selim the Drunkard, to be crowned emperor on Sulayman's death. For all her scheming, Hurren died before Sulayman, so she did not live to see her son's victory. She is buried next to Sulayman behind his memorial mosque, the Sulaymaniyeh, on the banks of the Golden Horn in Istanbul.

The Ottoman Sultans long practiced fratricide to eliminate claimants to the throne. Usually within twenty-four hours of a coronation, the new Sultan would order all his brothers killed. But in 1595, the newly crowned Mehmet III exceeded all bounds. He had his nineteen brothers strangled to death, and he threw six pregnant girls from his father's harem into the Bosporus. The people were outraged at the abuse; from that time on, princes were confined to a "golden cage." Prisoners for life within the harem, they lived a life of unsurpassed luxury.

While more humane on the individual level, it ultimately weakened the Ottoman Empire by leaving a steady supply of rivals for the throne to be manipulated by the Janissaries. And by the time one of these caged princes were placed on the throne, they often knew nothing of the outside world and wanted nothing except to continue the debauched life they had led in the harem. They were easy to manipulate for anyone who wanted to be the power behind the throne, and they were unable to lead or defend Ottoman territories when they came under attack. The following centuries witnessed much bloodshed in the palace, not by command of the Sultan, but by command of the Grand Vizier and/or the Janissaries of various sultans.

ECONOMIC DECLINE

As the Ottoman Empire's growth stagnated and the royal house grew increasingly enfeebled, European merchants discovered America and pioneered routes to the Orient around Africa. This allowed the great trading empires of England and

Grand Vizier   Sultan's prime minister.

K ⋮ *Key Concepts*

LOGISTICS

Why could the Ottomans not expand beyond Vienna? Or Napoleon not conquer Russia? The answer: **logistics**. In the Ottoman case, the army was bivouacked in Adrianople, modern Edirne, on the border of modern Bulgaria. The infantry could not carry enough food with them for their own needs, and the cavalry had the added burden of providing feed for the horses. The army could only march in the summer months, when it could forage for food among the peasants and the horses could find grass. They could only conquer lands as far away as they could travel and return to barracks before the end of the growing season. Thus, when Vienna's walls remained standing on October 14, 1529, Sulayman ordered a withdrawal so his army could return to safety before they exhausted their supplies. Logistics play a decisive role in war.

Holland to bypass the ancient, land-based trade routes of the Middle East, precipitating a long economic decline throughout the Ottoman Empire. Europeans mastered the new techniques of war while their countries' economies boomed. Unknown to the Turks, their empire had already entered into a long eclipse.

THE SICK MAN OF EUROPE

The Ottomans suffered a series of military defeats, beginning at the end of the seventeenth century. Beaten by the Austrian Habsburgs, the Ottomans signed the Treaty of Karlowitz in 1699 and surrendered Slavonia, Transylvania, and a large section of Hungary to the Habsburgs. Then the Ottomans lost at the hands of the Russians. Peter the Great and Catherine the Great were determined to expand southward until Russia had a warm water port—one that did not freeze over in winter—and the Ottoman Empire was in the way. These wars continued in one form or another for two centuries (see box on page 50). Russia's great power designs were usually thwarted through the intervention of France, Great Britain, and/or the Austro-Hungarian Empire. In the great game of international politics, however, each time Russia's ambitions were thwarted, it was usually at the expense of the Ottoman Empire.

MILITARY REFORM

In 1805 Sultan Selim III reviewed the military record of the Janissaries and found it lacking. The Janissaries had considerable power because of their control of the arms of the Empire. In addition, they were allied with the Bektasi Sufi order, a

---

logistics   The supplying of an army.

C Conflicts

VENDETTA ON THE BLACK SEA

In Chapter 5 we will consider the long series of Arab-Israeli wars. But another series of "vendetta wars" happened much earlier: the long struggle between Russians and Turks over mastery of the Black Sea. For two centuries (1678 to 1878), Tsarist Russia and Ottoman Turkey fought each other in ten wars. By 1566 the Turks nearly surrounded the Black Sea, but by 1812 they had lost its whole northern coast to Russia. They fought for one last time in World War I. There were several underlying causes of these Russo-Turkish wars, and they help us understand the depth and durability of the Arab-Israeli wars.

Religion played a role, although it was rarely the whole cause. When the Turks conquered Constantinople in 1453 and renamed it Istanbul, they also ended the city's importance as the center of Eastern Orthodox Christianity. While Constantinople never had the status that Rome did in Western Christianity, it was still the seat of Eastern Christendom and the center of its religious scholarship. The monks Cyril and Methodius from Constantinople first converted the Slavic peoples to Christianity in the sixth century A.D. Operating out of churches and monasteries on the shores of Lake Ohrid in present-day Macedonia, they taught the newly arriving (from the north) Slavic tribes Scripture, using the Greek alphabet to transcribe it into Old Church Slavonic. This is why the Cyrillic alphabet is used today in Orthodox Slavic countries such as Russia, Ukraine, Bulgaria, and Serbia. Aiding their millions of coreligionists still under Ottoman rule and recovering Constantinople gave Russians a sort of crusader mentality.

Culturally, the Eastern Orthodox peoples conquered by the Turks disliked being ruled—sometimes harshly—by strange people who spoke a strange language. Many Turkish words made their way into Serbian, especially in Bosnia, where heretical Christians known as Bogomils converted to Islam under the Turks. Their descendants are today's Bosnian Muslims and explain the blond, blue-eyed Muslims in Bosnia today. The Orthodox Serbs, on the other hand, through five centuries of Ottoman rule, always dreamed of getting rid of their Turkish overseers. To rob Turks as a *haiduk* (bandit) was a respected profession in Montenegro, which boasted that the Ottomans had never conquered it. Economically, the Ottomans misruled the Balkans, squeezing them for taxes, stifling industry, and generally keeping them impoverished.

Geography was an important reason for the long feud. Great rivers—the Danube, Volga, and Don—flow into the Black Sea but could not become commercial highways like West Europe's Rhine because for centuries the Black Sea was a Turkish lake. Whoever controls the Turkish Straits controls the Black Sea. That is why Roman Emperor Constantine chose the site for the city of his name, literally, "Constantine's city." With the Ottomans on both sides of the straits, Russian sea traffic could come and go only as the Turks wished; they could tax the traffic or block it altogether. Russian warships could be bottled up in the Black Sea, but friendly warships (such as British and French during the Crimean War of the 1850s) could be let in to attack Russia's soft underbelly. Tsars dreamed of taking Istanbul and the straits to give Russia this vital maritime outlet to the world, although they often cloaked their campaigns with religious goals. After the Communists took over Russia, they had the same dream, for, as Stalin's Foreign Minister Vyacheslav Molotov laconically noted, "A ship passing from the Mediterranean to the Black Sea must traverse the Straits whether the flag on its stern is tsarist or Soviet."

And not to be underrated as a cause is sheer human cussedness, the profound desire to beat the enemy. Sometimes the original or underlying causes are forgotten; all the participants remember is that the enemy is still out there, gloating, and attempting to crush you. Get him or he'll get you. Whatever the causes of the long Russo-Turkish fight, they do not give one grounds for optimism in the Arab-Israeli fight. They teach us, rather, that wars can last for centuries. And each of the Russo-Turkish wars ended in a peace treaty.

powerful and wealthy religious group with direct lines into the palace. The Sultan tried to replace the Janissaries with a "New Army" of infantry and artillery organized along European lines. He also drafted members of the Janissaries into this new army. Fearing a threat to their position, the Janissaries allied with provincial notables and clerical leaders and revolted. They destroyed the New Army and replaced Selim III with his cousin, Mustafa IV.

Mahmut II replaced Mustafa IV in 1807 and, alarmed at the decline in the Janissaries' fighting abilities, asked the units to send a handful of men for Western training. Confident in their position, the Janissaries pursued their usual strategy of ignoring the Sultan's commands. Mahmut had anticipated this reaction, however, and he ordered his artillery units to fire on the Janissaries' barracks, killing many. By 1826, Mahmut abolished the Janissaries, freeing the Sultanate from their grasp.

THE TANZIMAT

The reforms of the Turkish government known as the **Tanzimat** began in 1839. The Sultan reorganized the army and gave it more modern equipment. Troops organized in the provinces reported to Istanbul instead of to provincial governors. A reserve force and gendarmerie for keeping peace in the countryside were created. The Sultan introduced (from the Code Napoléon) European family, commercial, and maritime law, reducing the importance of the Shari'a and its clerical protectors. For the first time, non-Muslims had equal status with Muslims. Christians could now serve in the army, own land, and petition the judiciary on the same terms as a Muslim adversary. These rights were granted in the Noble Edict of Gulhane in 1839, and confirmed by the Imperial Edict of 1856.

Many opposed such reforms. In 1859, midlevel officers led their troops into the Kuleli incident, an attempted coup. When this failed, a group of Istanbul-based intellectuals calling themselves the Young Ottomans proposed the establishment of a parliament as a way of reuniting the empire and reestablishing Muslim law. In 1876, Sultan Abdul Aziz attempted to curry British favor by announcing an Ottoman constitution. Conservative theology students rioted, and Abdul Aziz stepped down. Later in the same year, Abdul Hamid II assumed the throne, and asserted his claim to the caliphate of all Islam. Such a conservative move endeared the new Sultan to those who had opposed the Tanzimat, because their position had been threatened by the improved status of Christians. To meet the demands for a parliament, Abdul Hamid II convened the institution in 1877, but dissolved it in 1878, using war with Russia as an excuse.

Meanwhile, the Ottoman Empire went bankrupt. The Sultans traditionally had relied on tax revenues for money, but in 1854 they began borrowing from Europe. At first they were able to pay back the loans on schedule, but in 1873, amidst a world financial crisis, the Sultan's tax revenues dropped, and by 1881 the

---

Tanzimat   Turkish "reorganization"; 1839–1876 Turkish reforms.

K ⋮ Key Concepts

A CHRONOLOGY OF OTTOMAN PUSHBACK

Europe overlaps with the Middle East in the Balkans. The connecting link: the Ottoman Empire, which occupied much of the Balkans for five centuries, giving the colorful region some of the Middle East's foods, architecture, culture, attitudes, and corruption. Since the second siege of Vienna in 1683, the Ottoman Empire steadily lost territory in the Balkans. In a series of wars, the Habsburgs, who ruled Austria from 1278 to 1918 (and Spain from 1516 to 1700) pushed back the Turks in Hungary (including Transylvania), Slovenia, Croatia, and Bosnia. Meanwhile, the Russians pushed the Turks out of Ukraine, Crimea, Romania, and Bulgaria. Key dates are as follows:

1774—Treaty of Kucuk Kaynarci (sometimes spelled Kuchuk Kainarji) gives Crimea and Bessarabia independence and Russia a port on the Black Sea. Russia also gets the right to intervene in the affairs of the Empire to protect Christians. Russia then annexes the Crimea in 1783.

1798—Napoleon invades Egypt.

1799—Napoleon invades Palestine and Syria.

1802—Napoleon driven out of Egypt by a Turkish-English force led by the Albanian general Muhammad Ali. The Sultan agrees to let him rule Egypt.

1803—Britain begins making treaties with Persian Gulf states.

1829—Treaty of Edirne. Russia gains the mouth of the Danube.

1830—Serbia granted autonomy. France invades the *beylik* (Ottoman province) of Algeria, nominally part of the Ottoman Empire. At first the French merely want to crush piracy but stay and turn Algeria into a French colony.

1831—Muhammad Ali, Pasha of Egypt and titular vassal of the Empire, invades Syria.

---

empire was bankrupt. In December of that year, in order to receive permission to continue borrowing, he turned over his treasury to the Ottoman Public Debt Authority, a new government department that was staffed and controlled by the European creditors. Ottoman subjects were outraged at the latest humiliation. They had always been taught to judge the Europeans as inferiors, but now they had equal rights. The Empire was always at war and losing territory to culturally inferior alien powers. Now representatives of these same powers collected taxes. The Ottoman Empire, in both its internal and external weakness, was paying the price for centuries of cultural, intellectual, and economic stagnation.

THE COMMITTEE OF UNION AND PROGRESS

Abdul Hamid II did not trust the military, several of whose leaders were trained in the West. He refused to allow the military to modernize, to hold live-fire exercises, or the navy to leave port. He quickly lost any support he may have had in the officers' corps.

1832—Greece recognized as independent.

1840—Treaty of London. Syria is restored to the Empire, but Muhammad Ali and his heirs are recognized as hereditary rulers of Egypt.

1853–1856—Crimean War. No net gain or loss for the Empire.

1861—Mount Lebanon obtains autonomy.

1878—Russian forces push to the gates of Istanbul and force the Treaty of San Stefano on the Ottoman Empire. In it, Romania, Serbia, and Montenegro obtain their independence. An enlarged Bulgaria under a Russian prince is awarded autonomy, as is Bosnia and Herzegovina. Some eastern Anatolian cities are ceded to the Russians.

1878—Treaty of Berlin tones down some of the Russian gains of the Treaty of San Stefano. Romania, Serbia, and Montenegro retain their independence. The Austrian-Hungarian Empire occupies Bosnia and Herzegovina. Greece obtains some border adjustments. Bulgaria is reduced in size, divided into two provinces, ruled by princes appointed by the Sultan.

1881—France invades the *beylik* of Tunisia.

1897—Greece aids an uprising on Crete. The Ottomans suppress it but grant the island autonomy.

1908—Austria-Hungary annexes Bosnia and Herzegovina over Serb protests. This plants the seed that started World War I.

1912—Treaty of Ouchy. Italy invades Libya, and the Ottoman Empire cedes it to Italy.

1912–1913—First and Second Balkan Wars. The empire loses, retaining only eastern Thrace in Europe.

By the time World War I started in 1914, the Ottoman Empire retained of its formerly vast holdings only the Fertile Crescent and would soon lose that.

In 1889, students of the Imperial Military Medical School formed a secret revolutionary society, the Ottoman Union Society. In 1896, this group planned a coup d'etat, but it was cut short when one of the plotters drunkenly revealed the plans to a senior officer the night before the coup. To escape arrest, many of the society escaped to Paris where they formed the Committee of Union and Progress (CUP), popularly known as the **Young Turks**. In 1907, dissident members of the military in the province of Salonika made contact with Paris, and assumed the CUP mantle. This new group was led by a postal clerk (Mehmet Talat), a major (Ahmet Cemal), and a captain (Enver). In power in 1915, the three ordered the Ottoman army's murderous expulsion of Armenians. In the 1920s, all three were assassinated outside Turkey by vengeful Armenians.

The CUP staged an armed rebellion in 1908 known as the Young Turk Revolution, which called for a restoration of the Constitution of 1906. To maintain the peace, the Sultan agreed to their demands. The CUP then established itself as a

Young Turks   Turn-of-twentieth-century reform movement of Ottoman officers.

Conflicts

THE ARMENIAN MASSACRES

With the start of World War I, Russian troops invaded Eastern Anatolia and enlisted the support of the local inhabitants, Russia's Christian coreligionists, the Armenians, who for years had been restless under Ottoman rule. In 1894–1896, irregular local forces massacred thousands of Armenians. Under orders of the CUP, the Ottoman army in 1915 rounded up Armenians and marched them at gunpoint into the Syrian desert with little food or water. The Armenians were murdered with impunity along the way; as many as 1.5 million died between 1914 and 1923.

American diplomats sent back dozens of horrified reports, and U.S. newspapers carried many stories of the massacres. Armenians who could fled for their lives or fought to the end. Armenians disappeared as a people from Anatolia, contributing to the Armenian diaspora, much of which came to America. Many Armenian-Americans—easily identifiable by family names ending in -ian—are both proud of and troubled by their tragic past.

Turkish historians still claim the 1915 march was a precautionary move to protect Turkey's eastern flank from Russian sympathizers and the massive deaths were unintended. Armenian historians say it was part of an intentional genocide, the twentieth century's first genocide. (As Hitler planned the extermination of Europe's Jews, he cackled, "Who remembers the Armenians?") A few Turkish intellectuals are willing to face up to the truth. Turkish writers are arrested and tried for "insulting Turkish identity" for discussing the massacres. Turkey's denial hinders its acceptance into the European Union.

guardian council to oversee the actions of the Sultan and his ministers. The CUP won a majority of seats in the new parliament, and the military leadership of the movement used its parliamentary base to control the government. Within nine months, a countermovement in the military tried to seize power. Calling themselves the Muhammadan Union, a group of officers allied with minor clerics and Sufi shaykhs organized a march on parliament to demand the constitution be abrogated and to return Christians to their status as *dhimmi*. CUP legislators went into hiding. The real leadership of the CUP, however, was not in Istanbul but in Salonika. They dispatched a relief force that freed the capital. Suspecting that the Sultan instigated the rebellion, the parliament deposed Abdul Hamid in favor of his brother, Mehmet V. The CUP regained power and in 1914 led the Empire into the Great War on the side of their ally, Germany.

WORLD WAR I

World War I in the Middle East was chiefly a British affair. (The United States never declared war on the Ottoman Empire and took no role in the region until much later.) Britain, seeking to guard its "imperial lifeline" and aware of Iraq's oil potential, sent troops from India to fight up the Tigris and Euphrates and sent Australian and New Zealand forces to Egypt. Britain suffered some reverses, but overall things went badly for the Ottomans, with every general but one suffering military defeats. That one exception was Mustafa Kemal, an Ottoman general who prevented British and Anzac troops from seizing the Gallipoli peninsula, Winston Churchill's bright idea that turned into a catastrophe. The British, pinned down under withering fire, never made it more than a few miles inland. True, if Britain had succeeded in taking this strategic finger of land, it would have strangled commerce between Istanbul and the Mediterranean and possibly knocked Turkey out of the war early.

Another British effort, more successful, encouraged Arabs to free themselves from Ottoman rule. To this end, Britain's Sir Henry McMahon promised Sharif Hussein of Mecca an Arab kingdom (see pages 68–69). British intelligence officer T. E. Lawrence ("Lawrence of Arabia") delivered the offer and rode with Arabs loyal to the Sharif in their revolt of 1916. Arab irregulars took out Ottoman forces in northern Arabia, Palestine, and Syria, paving the way for the British conquest of Palestine in 1917.

The Ottomans withdrew from World War I on October 31, 1918, eleven days before the Armistice went into effect on the Western Front. The Turkish armistice stipulated the victors had the right to occupy any part of the empire if they considered their security to be under threat. The CUP leadership fled the country in a German submarine. Soon five hundred years of Ottoman history would come to an end.

CONCLUSIONS

A traveler passing through the lands from Morocco to Afghanistan finds the intervening countries remarkably alike. The laws are similar, the culture the same, and the food identical (except for variations in local spices). All the countries were part of the Ottoman Empire. Some of this holds true for the Balkans as well.

The Ottomans ruled a multiethnic empire and allowed Christians and Jews to live in peace, albeit in an inferior social position. As the empire grew, it expanded as far as logistics would allow it. Istanbul paid little attention to technological or economic innovation or Western advances in weaponry and changes in trade patterns. In effect, it fell asleep.

By the end of the eighteenth century, it was too late to reverse Ottoman decline, and the Empire suffered a series of military defeats and loss of its provinces either to independence or to European colonialists. Finally, in World War I the Ottomans were shorn of all their lands except Thrace and the Anatolian peninsula.

Elements within the Empire tried to reform and modernize in order to survive in the new age. The Tanzimat promised liberty to the people of the Empire, but at the price of granting equality to Christians and Jews. The Young Turks tried to push reform on a reluctant society. Ultimately, the Empire failed because it had never created a distinctly Ottoman identity in the minds of its subjects, as Europe had. It was an **anachronism.**

---

anachronism   Something from the wrong time, from a bygone age.

KEY TERMS

anachronism (p. 55)   Marmara (p. 43)
Balkan (p. 43)   millet (p. 45)
capitulation (p. 47)   Ottoman (p. 42)
dragoman (p. 47)   praetorianism (p. 45)
Grand Vizier (p. 48)   Tanzimat (p. 51)
Janissary (p. 45)   vizier (p. 45)
logistics (p. 49)   Young Turks (p. 53)

FURTHER REFERENCE

Goffman, Daniel. *The Ottoman Empire and Early Modern Europe.* New York: Cambridge University Press, 2002.

Goltz, Thomson, ed. *Turkey,* 3rd ed. Boston, MA: Houghton Mifflin, 1993.

Kinross, John Patrick Douglas Balfour (Lord). *Ottoman Centuries: The Rise and Fall of the Turkish Empire.* New York: Perennial, 1979.

Lewis, Bernard. *What Went Wrong? Western Impact and Middle Eastern Response.* New York: Oxford, 2002.

Merdin, Serif. "Freedom in an Ottoman Perspective," in Heper, Metin, and Ahmet Evin, eds. *State, Democracy, and the Military: Turkey in the 1980s.* New York: de Gruter, 1988.

Quataert, Donald. *The Ottoman Empire, 1700–1922,* 2nd ed. New York: Cambridge University Press, 2005.

Wheatcroft, Andrew. *The Ottomans: Dissolving Images.* New York: Penguin, 1996.

CHAPTER

4 Origins of the Israel-Palestine War

According to Genesis, the Hebrew faith and the land of Israel originated simultaneously in God's command to Abraham to leave his native Ur of the Chaldees in southern Mesopotamia, then part of ancient Sumer, and move far to the west, to a land God promised to Abraham's descendants for evermore. A more prosaic explanation looks at the ancient pattern of nomadic peoples, who have to lead their flocks to green pastures. Tribes have been traversing the Fertile Crescent for millennia, fleeing drought. Abraham was likely the leader of one such band about 2000 B.C.

Ancient Egyptian records indicate periodic influxes of peoples from the north, also fleeing drought. Among them, according to Scripture, was Abraham's great-grandson Joseph, along with many other Hebrews, as they were by then known (after the town of Hebron, home and tomb of Judaism's founding patriarchs). As described in Exodus, after some generations in slavery, in the thirteenth century B.C. Moses led the Hebrews out of Egypt and through forty years of wandering in the desert, which some take as a metaphor for having to replace the old slave generation by a new free generation that was fit to return to the Promised Land, then called Canaan. In a parallel metaphor, God did not allow Moses to enter Canaan but only to glimpse it across the Jordan River.

G Geography

PALESTINE

This small land has had many names: Canaan, Israel, Judah, Judea, and Palestine. This last term originates from what the Greeks named Philistia, a kingdom on the southern coast between present-day Tel Aviv and the Gaza strip. The Philistines were sea traders whose name became synonymous with narrow commercialism. Goliath was a Philistine giant whom David slew with a slingshot.

Fed up with Jewish revolts against them, the Romans in the second century A.D. used the Latin name Palaestina (from the old Greek Philistia) and tried to erase memory of Judea by calling it Syria Palaestina, suggesting it was just the southernmost province of Syria. The name Palestine stuck, and the British made it official when they took the area from Ottoman Turkey in World War I. Its Arab inhabitants call it *Filistin*.

The Book of Joshua says they conquered Canaan, a mountainous area shielded from the powerful Philistines on the coastal plain. Archaeologists find mixed evidence for a conquest but point to great continuity between Canaanite and Hebrew culture. The pottery is the same, and the Hebrew language is a branch of Canaanite. Some theorize that the Hebrews originated as Canaanites who invented a monotheistic faith and converted most of the other Canaanites. The "exodus" may have consisted of a few hundred runaway slaves from Egypt who joined them in setting up a small kingdom with capital and temple high in the mountains, in Jerusalem.

KINGDOMS AND CONQUESTS

Scripture calls these people Israelites, after the Hebrew *Yiz-ra-el*, contends with God, suggesting a contentious people. Israel's most famous kings were Saul, David, and his son Solomon in the eleventh and tenth centuries B.C. Ever contentious, the kingdom split into Israel in the north and Judah (origin of "Jew") in the south. Thus weakened, the northern kingdom was conquered by the warlike Assyrians in the eighth century B.C. Judah continued to exist in a weakened condition until Babylonia's Nebuchadnezzar conquered it in 597 B.C. and exiled its nobles and priests to Babylon. A majority of the Jews stayed in Canaan but were subject to assimilation into the conqueror's culture and religion.

In Babylonian exile, Jews struggled to keep their distinctive faith alive. To do so, they gave Judaism a written narrative that included emphasis on a Promised Land (see box on page 59), and it has been with the Jewish people ever since. The first **Zionists** were those who followed Ezra back from Babylon in 397 B.C.

Zionism   From Mt. Zion in Jerusalem; movement to return to Israel.

R ⋮ *Religions*

THE BIBLE'S "PROMISED LAND"

The early books of the Old Testament are replete with references to God granting the Hebrews the Land of Israel in perpetuity. In Genesis 11, God commands Abraham to leave his home in Mesopotamia for "a land that I shall show thee." From Egypt, Moses led the Hebrew slaves back to their Promised Land. There are many other such references. Do they prove that Jews have a valid claim to Israel, superseding all other claims?

Some, including Orthodox Jews and Fundamentalist Christians, think the Bible gives Israel to the Jews. Those who believe in the inerrancy of Scripture accept that what God said needs to be carried out today. Others, who think the Bible was written by humans, note that the first five books of the Bible, what Jews call the Torah, were redacted in Babylonian exile from earlier Hebrew religious usages and legends that had likely not been written down in finished form. The redactors aimed to make sure Jews would not forget their religion or their homeland, so they inserted numerous references to "chosen people" with a God-given attachment to the land of Israel. Around 400 B.C. an advance party of Babylonian Jews—the first Zionists—did return to Israel (although many stayed in Babylon) to reclaim it.

Seen in this light, biblical references to a perpetual Jewish right to Israel are a product of time and place, a powerful man-made narrative to persuade Jews to stay attached to the Land of Israel. Fundamentalists do not like the man-made theory of Zionism any more than they like evolution: The Bible says so, and that takes care of that.

Either way—word of God or man-made—the concept of a people bound to a special land stirs strong emotions that can push people to leave their old homes, set up a new state, and fight for it. Rationalists may dismiss founding narratives of nations and religions as "mytho-poetic legends," but they underrate the power of such stories in motivating humans, who are only partly rational. They also have a great need to believe in things that cannot be empirically verified.

to reclaim Israel and revive its religion. Ezra may have brought the first Torah scrolls to Israel and thus started a gradual shift from the old religion that focused on the Temple in Jerusalem to the new Rabbinic Judaism that focused on Scripture (see box on page 60).

In 332 B.C. Alexander the Great and his Greek army fought their way through the Middle East. Although his empire quickly decayed, it implanted a *Hellenistic* overlay on the region in language, architecture, and religion. Under the *Seleucids,* everyone was supposed to act Greek. Many Jews, however, despised Hellenistic culture as immoral, especially its worship of idols and human rulers and its celebration of the body, such as male nude wrestling. One Jewish priestly clan, the Maccabees, led a revolt in 165 B.C. against the Seleucids and liberated the Temple in Jerusalem. To rededicate the Temple they needed a special, consecrated olive oil for the sacred lamps, but there was only one day's supply of it. Miraculously, it burned eight days and nights. Thus when Christians celebrate Christmas, Jews still celebrate Hanukkah, the Festival of Lights, with the mother lighting one more candle each night until eight are burning.

Jesus bar Roman into roles — Ceasar Augustus

R : *Religions*

Judaism spread up to Roman empire

THE BIRTH OF TWO RELIGIONS

Two faiths were born out of the Roman occupation of Judea, a time of great religious ferment. Taxation and war had impoverished Judea, and people were eager for spiritual uplift. Judaism was changing rapidly, with new sects and self-proclaimed messiahs springing up. The old faith, centered on the Temple in Jerusalem—rebuilt and enlarged by Herod the Great (a descendant of the Maccabees) under the Romans—drew fewer believers. Some turned to mysticism and withdrawal, such as the Essenes, who left behind the Dead Sea scrolls in caves. Some turned to baptism to mark a new spiritual life.

In this atmosphere, two religions emerged, Rabbinic Judaism and Christianity. The early **rabbis** turned away from the hereditary Jewish priesthood, the *Kohanim* (present-day Cohens), who ran the Temple, and instead embraced the Torah as the true faith. Discussion and commentaries on the Torah became the bulwark of the new Rabbinic Judaism, which had one big advantage over the old one: Based on books, it was portable and teachable. The great rabbi of this transition was Hillel, who was born in Babylonia. By A.D. 70, as the Romans crushed Jerusalem during a Jewish revolt, the rabbis were carrying Judaism with them throughout the Roman Empire. The Judaism of today is Rabbinic Judaism and made Jews "people of the Book."

Jesus of Nazareth was not the only religious figure in Roman Judea preaching a new creed, but he had **charisma** and faithful disciples to spread his word. Jesus never claimed to be anything but Jewish and his teachings are a development of Judaism, but one with a simple, universal message, one much easier to understand and accept than the complexity of Rabbinic Judaism. Jews rarely sought converts; Christians always did. The standard Roman punishment for troublemakers, crucifixion, gave Christianity the indelible symbol it used to slowly and quietly take over the Roman Empire from within.

In 64 B.C. the Romans took over what they called Judea from the decaying Seleucid empire. The Mediterranean became a Roman lake, *mare nostrum,* Rome's far-flung legions constantly fought barbarians and expanded Roman rule, and Rome turned from a republic into an empire. It was just too big and diverse to be ruled by a handful of Roman nobles in the Senatus. Julius Caesar started turning himself into an emperor but was assassinated; his great-nephew Octavian became the first Roman emperor under the name Augustus. Jesus of Nazareth was born twenty-seven years into the reign of Augustus.

Many subject peoples disliked Roman rule, and the empire was nearly constantly plagued by revolts, in Spain, Germany, and Judea, as the Romans now called it. In Judea the cause was again religious. Some Jews, the **Zealots**, hated the Romans and insisted on their own state and a purified religion. The Zealots—some

---

rabbi   Teacher of the Jewish faith, not a priest.

charisma   Greek for gift; spiritual drawing power, such as that of Jesus.

Zealot   Jewish sect opposed to Roman rule of Judea.

R : *Religions*

FIRST OR SECOND COMING OF THE MESSIAH?

Ancient Israel's priests anointed a new king by pouring olive oil on his head, which became a symbol of elect status. The use of the word **messiah** as a savior from God did not appear in Judaism until the Babylonian exile. There the Jewish tradition developed (but was not clearly stated in the Old Testament) that a descendant of David will come to lead the Jews back to the Promised Land.

For Jews, the messiah is yet to come, and his coming will be closely linked to the recovery of Israel. It is focused on this world, not the next. For Christians, the messiah came two thousand years ago and leads us to eternal peace in the next world. For some fundamentalist Christians, the founding of the modern state of Israel indicates that the messiah's second coming is nigh. A few Ultra-Orthodox Hasidic Jews argue that Israel should not have been reestablished *until* the messiah appeared; the proclamation of Israel in 1948 was pushing things. Muslims (see Chapter 2) also await a sort of messiah, the *Mahdi*, the last true heir of Muhammad, who will return and save Muslims at the end of time.

of the earliest terrorists—killed all who disagreed with them, including more moderate Jews, many of whom did not mind Roman rule. Even then, fighting among Jews weakened and ultimately brought down the Jewish cause. Rome was tolerant on religion, and many Roman soldiers came back from the East with new religions, including Judaism, which was spreading within the Roman Empire.

Jewish fundamentalists, including Zealots, revolted against Rome from A.D. 66 to 70. Their remnants fell back to a fortified mesa overlooking the Dead Sea, Masada, where they held out for three years, finally committing suicide rather than be taken prisoner. To celebrate their victory after a long, hard fight, the Romans issued a coin proclaiming *Judea Capta* ("Judea is captured"). Masada is now a major tourist attraction and symbol of Israeli toughness.

Jewish revolt reignited with the Bar Kochba rebellion of A.D. 132–135, crushed by the Tenth Roman Legion, whose motto was "Let them hate me so long as they fear me." This time, Rome leveled Jerusalem and exiled Jews from Judea to distant parts of the Roman Empire. By the second century Jews were already in Spain, France, Germany, Italy, North Africa, and elsewhere as traders and merchants. Thus began the Jewish **diaspora**, which saw Jewish communities throughout Europe, the Arab world, India, and even China. By intermarriage (and other means), Jews took on the appearance and much of the culture of the peoples they dwelt among. Today one finds Jews who look just like Germans, Russians, Spaniards, Arabs, and Indians. Jews are united more by belief than by blood.

---

messiah   From the Hebrew *mashiah;* "anointed one," divine savior.

diaspora   Scattering, a dispersed people without their own country.

G *Geography*

EVERYONE IS FROM SOMEWHERE ELSE

Is any territorial claim rooted in history or religion valid? What makes a land "ours"? One people may have lived there a very long time, but no one has lived there forever. Go back far enough—in some cases, not so far back—and everyone came from somewhere else, and when they got there they usually found other humans already living there. Sometimes they assimilated them, but often they conquered them.

England, for example, has been conquered by successive waves of Celts, Romans, Angles and Saxons, and Normans. Tribes of wandering Ostrogoths, Visigoths, Vandals, and others washed over Europe, each bumping out previous inhabitants. Americans might not wish to look too closely at the origins of the United States, previously inhabited entirely by tribes of Indians. Does anyone seriously propose giving it back?

If the ancient Israelites really wandered forty years in the desert and then conquered Canaan (the source of "Joshua Fit the Battle of Jericho"), does that mean they own it forevermore? (Actually, the theory that the Israelites were really just Canaanites gives them a longer heritage in Palestine.) Then Assyrians, Babylonians, Egyptians, Greeks, and Romans conquered ancient Israel. Do any of them have a claim to it? In 639, Arabs spreading their new faith of Islam conquered what had been a Byzantine province, and until the twentieth century their language and culture dominated Palestine, except for the Crusaders' interlude in the twelfth century. In 1516 the Ottoman Turks expanded their empire to include Palestine. In 1917 in World War I, the British took it from the Turks and ran it until 1948. Then Zionists proclaimed the modern state of Israel.

So to whom exactly does history give the title deed? Neither history nor religion gives title deeds to any land. Invoking either or both of them simply makes people more adamant and unwilling to compromise and hence prolongs the bloodshed. When it comes to settling claims for sovereignty, history, in the words of Henry Ford, really is bunk.

THE LONG DIASPORA

The Jews' long exile did not erase their hope of eventually returning to the Promised Land, a hope renewed almost every time they read the Torah. The Babylonian redactors of the Torah had done their job well. Jews raised their glasses to toast "Next year in Jerusalem." Keeping this feeling alive was intermittent mistreatment at the hands of their Christian neighbors. There were Jews throughout the Roman Empire centuries before the various Germanic tribes arrived. But these newcomers soon turned Christian and despised Jews as misguided and dangerous because most refused to convert. (Thousands of Jews did convert to Christianity over the centuries.) At the beginning of the Middle Ages, a fair percentage of Europe's population was Jewish, a percentage that shrank over the centuries. In Medieval Europe, Jews were not rare.

During the Middle Ages, Jewish life in Muslim lands was generally better than in Christian Europe. The Qur'an teaches that Jews and Christians are also "people of the book" and should be treated as *dhimmis,* "protected people," who had to pay a special tax but were otherwise unmolested. Under the Arabs, Spain reached a cultural high point in which Jews fully participated. While Europe north

C   *Cultures*

SEPHARDIC AND ASHKENAZIC JEWS

In Europe, Jews formed two cultural traditions. Those in Spain (*Sefarad* in Hebrew) spoke Spanish but were expelled from Spain in 1492 and scattered around the Mediterranean, including the Ottoman Empire. They continued to speak a fairly good Spanish called Ladino that until recently could be heard in cities such as Istanbul and Sarajevo. They became known as Sephardim.

Jews who settled at first in the Rhine Valley were called the Ashkenazim, from *Ashkenaz,* Hebrew for Germany. They spoke Middle High German and later moved into Central and East Europe. On top of their German they added Hebrew and Slavic words, producing **Yiddish.** Most American Jews are of Ashkenazic origin, and most of their ancestors spoke Yiddish, which can still be heard in various cities around the world. I. B. Singer, winner of the 1978 Nobel Prize for literature, was born in Poland but lived in New York and wrote in Yiddish, which uses Hebrew characters.

The two branches, although based firmly on Torah, also developed different religious traditions and pronunciations of Hebrew. The founders of Modern Hebrew a century ago chose a mostly Sephardic pronunciation as closer to ancient spoken Hebrew, a language that had been liturgical rather than spoken since the third century B.C. At the time of Jesus, Judeans spoke Aramaic, a related Semitic language. Israel today has two chief rabbis, one Ashkenazic and one Sephardic (now called Mizrahim, from the Hebrew for "east.")

---

of the Pyrenees was a backward area, Moorish Spain created great architecture (the Alhambra), literature, philosophy, and medical care. Moses Maimonides, born in Córdoba in 1135, wrote (in Arabic) his famous *Guide for the Perplexed,* a philosophical defense of religion in general. In Egypt, Maimonides later became court physician to the famed Saladin, who beat the Crusaders.

During the late Middle Ages, many Jews were expelled from West Europe and went eastward. Jewish cultures that had thrived for a millennium in Spain and the Rhine Valley were destroyed, often violently. The causes were several. The Crusades and Reconquest of Iberia created religious hatred against non-Catholics, including Muslims and Eastern Orthodox Christians. Jews were under constant pressure to convert, and many did. Religious anti-Semitism grew, leading to the first ghettoes, established in Northern Italy in the late sixteenth century.

Another factor was that Jews were often unable to own land but could loan money at interest, which was (technically) prohibited to Catholics. (The Qur'an prohibits Muslims from charging or paying interest.) Jews came under economic and political pressure in the Late Middle Ages as Italian banking houses sought to displace Jewish moneylenders. Christian kings often ran up major debts to Jews and took to expelling them rather than paying them. This was the beginning of Yiddish (see box above) and of the concentration of Jews in Central Europe. The biggest single Jewish community was in Poland.

Yiddish   Judeo-German language written in Hebrew letters.

Meanwhile, when Spanish kings reconquered Spain from the Moors (the *Reconquista,* completed in 1492) they ordered all Muslims and Jews to either embrace Catholicism or leave. Portuguese kings did likewise. Some Jewish converts (*Marranos*) continued to secretly practice Judaism in their homes. Those suspected of insincere conversion were tried for heresy, blasphemy, and much else by the Spanish Inquisition, which used torture and burning at the stake, what the Inquisitors called the *auto da fé* (act of faith). The Inquisition even pursued suspect families to Peru, Mexico, and New Mexico, where Marrano families exist to this day. Some families very quietly retained a Jewish identity for centuries, and one can meet Spanish and Portuguese Jews who only recently "came out of the closet."

Most of the Spanish Jews who left sailed to the eastern Mediterranean, where the Ottoman Turks, who were tolerant on religion, recognized the economic benefit of skilled Jewish settlers. "Spain's loss is our gain," was the Ottoman phrase. Thus Sephardic Jews found a home in the Ottoman Empire, which included the Balkans and soon enveloped most of the Middle East.

THE RISE OF MODERN ZIONISM

Jewish life in Central and East Europe, where most of the world's Jews lived, was precarious but possible until the late nineteenth century. Restricted as to residence and profession and suffering occasional violence, Jews built a vibrant cultural life based on Yiddish and traditional religion. They found their niche in the economy as shopkeepers and artisans, seldom as farmers. More educated than most of their neighbors, they could read Hebrew for religious purposes. They were classic "marginal men," everywhere a minority at the mercy of forces beyond their control. As long as Central and East Europe stayed relatively static and backward (compared to West Europe), Jews could survive. But when the region awoke in the nineteenth century, their situation worsened, and this laid the foundation for **modern Zionism**.

The belated arrival of capitalism in Central and East Europe brought local Christians into economic competition with Jews, who lost their "niche" status. Napoleon's legions awoke **nationalism** in the region. Having to live under and fight the French taught nationalism to most of Europe. In struggling to free themselves from French rule, Spaniards, Germans, Russians, and others became nationalistic. Nationalism spread, and by the middle of the nineteenth century Central Europeans rejected rule by empires and longed for their own nation. In the Habsburg Empire (known as Austria-Hungary from 1867 to 1918), Czechs, Hungarians, and others wished to be rid of the Habsburgs. Poland, partitioned between Germany, Austria, and Russia since the 1790s, never died in the hearts of Poles, whose Catholicism was a kind of nationalism. During the nineteenth century, nationalism grew until it covered Europe.

---

modern Zionism Jewish *nationalism,* founded in late nineteenth century to recover Israel as a Jewish state, secular and socialistic rather than religious.

nationalism Desire to cast off foreign rule in favor of own state.

P : *Personalities*

DREYFUS AND HERZL

What galvanized modern Zionism was the trial of Captain Alfred Dreyfus, a Jewish French officer accused in 1894 of selling war-ministry secrets to Germany. On flimsy evidence (some of it forged), he was convicted and sent for life to the infamous Devil's Island penal colony. The Dreyfus Affair, which dragged on twelve years, revealed that France was still split into two camps by the 1789 Revolution. On one side liberals accused the French army of using Dreyfus as a handy scapegoat because he was Jewish. French conservatives and Catholics rallied to the army and denounced all Jews. The two sides battled in print and in the street, and anti-Semitism came into the open. Emile Zola's famous *J'accuse* ("I accuse") was penned to support Dreyfus and accuse the generals of a cover-up.

An assimilated Hungarian Jewish journalist, Theodore Herzl, covering the trial for a Vienna newspaper, was horrified at the outburst of anti-Semitism in the most civilized country of Europe. If it could happen in France, he reasoned, it could happen elsewhere. Herzl detected the danger of extreme anti-Semitic nationalism just under the surface in Europe and concluded that Jews would not be safe until they had their own country. In 1897 he organized the first Zionist congress, which began to raise funds to buy land and send Jewish pioneers to Palestine. At that time Herzl predicted that his dream of a Jewish state would be a reality in fifty years. He was off by only one year; Israel was born in 1948.

Nationalism can be a progressive force, awakening peoples to unity, independence, modernization, economic growth, and democracy. But it can also be highly destructive, leading to racism, intolerance, expansionism, and war. One of the major components of nationalism is hatred of the Other, those who are not like us, who misrule us, exploit us, or rob us. The Jews in much of Europe, perceived as eternal foreigners, were natural targets for these feelings. Thus, racial (as opposed to the earlier religious) anti-Semitism appeared in much of Europe during the nineteenth century. Both Jews and Christians started posing the **Jewish question**, which some Jews answered with their own nationalism, one focused on Palestine. By the 1860s, Jewish writers were proposing a return to Palestine, and in 1882 the first **aliyah** brought a few Zionist immigrants to Palestine, then under Ottoman rule as a series of *vilayets* (provinces) and *sanjaks* (districts), not as a single entity. Only the British mandate made it a single entity after World War I.

Zionism started as a minority and romantic movement. Many Jews in Central and East Europe, where conditions were worsening, immigrated to the United States, only a few to Palestine. Tsarist Russia (which at that time held eastern Poland) contained the largest Jewish population and deflected domestic discontent onto Jews. The people are unhappy? Blame the Jews. The tsarist police encouraged **pogroms** and forged *The Protocols of the Elders of Zion,* a book purporting

---

Jewish question   Nineteenth and twentieth century; what should become of Europe's Jews?

aliyah   Hebrew for "ascent" (implying uplift); a wave of Jewish immigration to Israel.

pogrom   Russian for "devastation"; murderous anti-Jewish riots encouraged by tsarist police.

R : Religions

ISRAEL'S SECULAR FOUNDERS

Many suppose modern Israel was founded on a religious basis, but nearly the opposite is true; Israel's founders and early leaders were **secular** and paid little attention to Judaism. Many were committed to socialism, which in the early twentieth century was riding high in Europe. Their idea was to build not only a Jewish homeland but a socialist one where people would live in equality and sufficiency in a co-operative rather than capitalist economy. This was the foundation of the kibbutz movement and of "Labor Zionism," its strongest branch until the 1970s.

Few early Zionists had religious feelings; most saw themselves as Jewish pioneers establishing a safe haven for Jews from the growing anti-Semitism of Europe. They focused on agriculture, arguing that getting Jews back to the land—and there had been few Jewish farmers for two millennia—was a form of worship far more authentic than prayer and synagogues. Some leftist *kibbutzim* even raised pigs as a tasty and economical source of protein. Most Israelis are still secular, but religion has grown with the influx of new immigrants and recovery of the Old City of Jerusalem, with its religious significance, in the 1967 war. In Israel, religious Jews are the newcomers.

to reveal a Jewish plot to take over the world (which keeps turning up, most recently in Egypt).

A few religious Jews had long lived in Jerusalem, but at the turn of the twentieth century modern Zionist pioneers arrived in Palestine, whose Turkish governors saw the Jews as a boost to the economy of the poor and thinly populated area. The early Zionists used to say, "A people without a land shall have a land without people," a mistaken perception that ignored the roughly 446,000 Arab Palestinians of the late nineteenth century. The number of Jewish immigrants was not large, and many soon left the inhospitable conditions for the United States. Few saw the trouble coming from two peoples claiming the same land. Around 1900 Hebrew was revived as a spoken language and displaced Yiddish among the Jewish pioneers. Tel Aviv and the first **kibbutz**, Deganya, were founded by early Zionists in 1909. On the eve of World War I, Jews were a small minority in an otherwise Arab Palestine.

Absentee Arab and Turkish *effendis* (landlords), who lived in Beirut and Damascus, owned much of the land of Palestine, which they rented to Arab *fellahin* (peasants), often for so many generations that the farmers felt the land was theirs. Starting in 1901, the Jewish National Fund purchased land (often at exorbitant prices) from the legal owners and set up Jewish farms and towns, displacing the traditional Arab tenants. The Arab farmers were often not legal owners but felt the transfers of land robbed them of what they had long tilled.

secular   nonreligious; government and daily life little influenced by religion.
kibbutz   Jewish collective farm founded by Zionist pioneers in Palestine.

Religions

SEPARATE ARAB STATES?

Islam, in its intertwining of state and religion, presents a permanent problem to Muslim nationalists. The nationalism of the Europeans is built on and vows to strengthen separate states, but Muslims in general and Arabs in particular were never comfortable with the concept of separate nations. Believers should live in one big Islamic community, the *umma,* not divided into nations, which are European concepts, argued strict Muslims. Even in the twenty-first century, Osama bin Ladin and his followers hold that nationalism soon turns into the worship of nation, which is a form of idolatry. (American Jehovah's Witnesses argue along similar lines.) Perhaps the *hajj* is the purest expression of this feeling, for in Mecca all Muslims are brothers and equal, and nationality is unimportant.

Accordingly, every Egyptian or Iraqi or any other Arab nationalist movement meets resistance from devout Muslims who denounce it in favor of a single pan-Muslim entity, a new caliphate. Arab secularists embrace the related concept of a **pan-Arab** entity. Both agree they should cast off foreign domination but disagree over which is more important, nation or Islam? It is for this reason that ambitious Arab leaders cast themselves not just as national saviors but as pan-Arab heroes, destined to unite and lead a new Arab empire. It's not good enough to just head your nation; you must pose as liberator of all Arabs too. Examples: Nasser of Egypt and Saddam Hussein of Iraq.

Muslim extremists sometimes ally with Arab nationalists on a temporary and opportunistic basis, but ultimately they are at odds. Nasser kept thousands of members of the Muslim Brotherhood in prison and executed some of its top people. Egyptian Islamists, long suppressed by secular Cairo governments, still smolder in hatred that bursts out in such horrors as the 1981 assassination of President Sadat and 1996 massacre of foreign tourists. The struggle between nation and religion, long solved in Christian countries, still destabilizes Muslim lands.

THE RISE OF ARAB NATIONALISM

At about the same time Jews were undergoing a national awakening, so were Arabs. Nationalism, once out of the bottle, spread over the globe. The entire Fertile Crescent had been in Ottoman hands since the sixteenth century, and most Arabs did not mind. The Turks were also Muslims who swore the Arabs were their brothers. The Ottoman sultan in Istanbul was also the caliph of the Islamic faith, so he enjoyed a double legitimacy. There were Christian revolts against Turkish rule in the Balkans, but no Arab revolts against it until World War I.

When Napoleon invaded Egypt in 1798, his army brought a printing press and scholars of Arabic with them in order to win over the local people. There had been some printing in the Ottoman Empire, but only in Turkish; now Arabs could read newspapers in their own language. The French interlude in Egypt awakened Arab thoughts that a better, freer life awaited them outside of Turkish rule. Although soon ousted from Egypt by Britain in 1801, France, as in Europe, triggered nationalism in the Middle East.

---

pan-Arab   All Arab lands in one political entity.

Later in the nineteenth century, Arab Christians in Lebanon began a literary revival of Arabic—including a dictionary and encyclopedia—which quickly led to an Arab cultural revival. The nationalistic Young Turk movement to reform and centralize the Ottoman Empire prompted Arab resentment and nationalism. Arab civilian and military officers in the Ottoman structure saw they were not promoted as high as Turkish officers and started plotting eventual Arab independence from the Ottoman Empire. Just before World War I broke out, the first Arab Congress met in Paris in 1913 and called for Arab autonomy within the Ottoman Empire; Istanbul ignored the demand.

THE IMPACT OF WORLD WAR I

The Great War of 1914–1918 was the seminal event of the twentieth century, the point where it went off the tracks. The war destroyed four empires—the German, Russian, Austro-Hungarian, and Ottoman. From their ruins flowered the twin evils of Communism and Fascism, both aimed at remaking society by coercive means into controlled hierarchies. One offshoot of World War I, little noticed at the time, was what it did to the Middle East.

Ottoman Turkey, in decay, was courted by Imperial Germany, which had plans to rival Britain in various parts of the world, including the Middle East. One such plan was a Berlin-to-Basra railway that would bring German power into the Persian Gulf. Istanbul, fearing (accurately) dismemberment by Russia, France, Britain, Italy, and Greece, allied with Berlin. The Turkish army had German weapons and advisors during World War I.

The British, aware of German designs, felt they had to protect their **imperial lifeline**, which ran through the Middle East. They were also aware of the oil in the Turkish province of Mosul, which later became northern Iraq. In the **Sykes-Picot** agreement, Britain and France along with Russia and later Italy, planned to carve up the Ottoman Empire after the war. The new Bolshevik government in Russia published its details as a way to discredit the "capitalist war," and Sykes-Picot was never formally carried out, but Britain after the war got Mesopotamia and Palestine, while France got Syria and Lebanon.

Turkey put up a good fight, inflicting setbacks on British-led colonial forces from India in Mesopotamia and from Australia and New Zealand at **Gallipoli**, until Gen. Edmund Allenby, with help from an Arab uprising, pushed the Turks out of Palestine, taking Jerusalem in December 1917. Paving the way for this uprising were the **McMahon-Hussein letters** exchanged by Britain's Sir Henry McMahon,

---

imperial lifeline   Britain's sea route to India, through the Mediterranean, Suez Canal, Red Sea, and Indian Ocean.

Sykes-Picot   Secret 1916 British-French agreement to carve up Ottoman Empire.

Gallipoli   Ill-fated 1915 Allied landing south of Istanbul.

McMahon-Hussein letters   1915–1916 British pledge to set up Arab states for Arab help to oust Turks.

who ran Egypt during the war, and Sherif Hussein of Mecca. If Hussein would help Britain defeat the Turks—whom many Arabs disliked—the Arabs would get their own independent states, the borders of which were left vague. Britain's liaison and advisor to Hussein was T. E. Lawrence, who had earlier done archeology in the region and whose exploits were turned into the legend of Lawrence of Arabia. The British never told their Arab allies that they had already made the Sykes-Picot deal with France to take the Fertile Crescent for themselves.

British policy also boosted the Zionist movement. The British cabinet, desperate for allies and aware that many Jews lived in Russia (which was dropping out of the war) and America (which was just entering the war), tried to rally Jewish opinion to its cause by issuing the 1917 **Balfour Declaration**:

> His Majesty's Government view with favour the establishment in Palestine of a national home for the Jewish people, and will use their best endeavours to facilitate the achievement of this object, it being clearly understood that nothing shall be done which may prejudice the civil and religious rights of existing non-Jewish communities in Palestine, or the rights and political status enjoyed by Jews in any other country.

Although carefully hedged—it promised no Jewish state and vowed to protect Arab rights—Zionists took it as a charter for their dream. They too had not heard of Sykes-Picot. The next month, Allenby took Jerusalem, and the war ended with Britain in control of the Fertile Crescent. Britain, in effect, had promised the same land, which included Palestine, to three sets of claimants: the Arabs, the Jews, and themselves. Cynical manipulation was always part of imperialism. These incompatible promises laid the groundwork for much of the region's subsequent strife.

THE MANDATE

U.S. President Woodrow Wilson had pushed for the new **League of Nations** but could not persuade the Senate to ratify U.S. membership. Between the wars, the United States slouched into **isolationism**, leaving Britain and France, the other chief victors in World War I, to run the League and give themselves the **mandates** they wished. Under the mandate system, the League assigned former German colonies and Arab Ottoman lands to be supervised by the winners, chiefly Britain and France, until the colonies were ready for independence.

Balfour Declaration   1917 British support for a Jewish homeland in Palestine, then under Ottoman control.

League of Nations   Interwar precursor to UN.

isolationism   Interwar U.S. policy of no involvement in Europe.

mandate   *League of Nations* grant to World War I victors to run colonies of defeated German and Ottoman empires.

P : Personalities

GOLDA MEIR

As a child in Kiev, Ukraine, Golda Meir (1898–1978) remembered cowering during a pogrom. Her family immigrated to Milwaukee in 1906. She went to college there and became a local Labor Zionist youth leader. In 1921 she and her husband went to Palestine to join a kibbutz. By World War II Meir had become an important leader of the Palestine Jewish community, sometimes guiding underground activities in opposition to the British.

One of the signers of Israel's declaration of independence in 1948, Meir was elected to the Knesset in 1949. She was minister of labor from 1949 to 1956, then foreign minister from 1956 to 1966 when she helped set up the 1956 Sinai Campaign with Britain and France. Upon the death of Levi Eshkol in 1969, Golda Meir became Israel's prime minister. Accused of lack of preparedness for the 1973 war, she resigned in 1974.

An extremely tough lady, she impressed a wide variety of world leaders, including Henry Kissinger, with her intellect, determination, and get-to-the-point negotiating skills. She admitted that she sacrificed her private and family life to the Zionist cause but said it had to be that way.

In 1922 Britain created three new entities. It put together the three Ottoman provinces of Mesopotamia—Mosul in the north, Baghdad in the center, and Basra in the south—and called it by its Arab name (from the seventh century) Iraq (see Chapter 11). Britain did not rule Iraq as a mandate but invented a new kingdom and placed on its throne Faisal, one of the sons of Hussein, whom Britain owed for leading the Arab revolt against the Ottomans. In 1932, Britain granted Iraq independence but continued to quietly influence it through Iraq's royal family and ruling class.

At the same time, Britain split its Palestine mandate along the Jordan River and Wadi Araba. To the east, it created the Hashemite Kingdom of Transjordan and placed on its throne Abdullah, another of Hussein's sons. (Transjordan means on the other side of the Jordan River, a creek in U.S. terms.) In 1946, it took the name Jordan. To the west of the Jordan, Britain ran things directly in its Palestine mandate on a semi-colonial basis.

Why did Britain want Palestine? Its motives mixed idealism and realism, and it did not know that it would turn into an impossible problem area, one from which it would have to retreat amidst cries of betrayal from both Arab and Jewish sides. Idealistically, Britain had been fixated on the Holy Land since at least the Crusades, in which many English knights fought. To rule over Jerusalem and Bethlehem again in the twentieth century—for the good of all mankind, of course—seemed the fulfillment of English hymns and a sacred trust. Aiding the Zionist cause also appealed to British Protestantism, which read the Old Testament carefully. Britain would facilitate biblical prophecy. There was a bit of romanticism in British motives.

Idealism seldom lasts, however, without realistic backing. Control of Palestine, along with Egypt and Iraq, protected Britain's imperial lifeline and gave Britain control over the major oil fields around Mosul and Kirkuk. Under Sykes-Picot,

C Cultures

CULTURAL VERSUS MATERIAL

Perhaps the greatest issue in the social sciences is whether human behavior originates inside the heads of people or outside in the physical world in which they live. The first camp emphasizes culture—including psychology, religion, and ideology—as the underlying cause. The second emphasizes the material world—including geography, economics, and political structures—as the underlying cause. Max Weber was the great proponent of the cultural school, Karl Marx of the material school. An example of the latter is the great Arab historian Ibn Khaldun, who in the fourteenth century recognized the impact of climate on the formation of Arab character: The material caused the cultural.

The question is lively and important in the Middle East today. Is the Arab-Israeli struggle one of conflicting cultures—and their cultures are quite different—or conflicting material interests? Do they fight because they embody two different religious psychologies and see the world differently? Or is culture a secondary concern, less important than the fact that there is only one Palestine and both strive to possess it?

On a broader level, intellectuals ask if the current difficulties of Muslim countries stem from religious doctrines that became frozen centuries ago or from foreign conquest and exploitation over those same centuries. Princeton scholar Bernard Lewis spent a lifetime studying the decline of the Ottoman Empire and put most of the blame on a stagnant mentality, one that refused to adapt and modernize, an example of the cultural school. Does this explain the rise of Islamic fundamentalism? Is it the centuries-old fundamentalist doctrines of *salafiyya* that turn Muslims into fanatics? Or is it the enormous numbers of unemployed Muslim youths who find Islamism a convenient outlet for their frustrations? A complete analysis of the Middle East (or anywhere else) must take both cultural and material factors into account and examine how they feed into one another.

France had been promised an interest in the area, but Britain renegotiated the French demands. French Premier Georges Clemenceau alluded to the heavy French battle losses in the Great War with his famous phrase, "A drop of blood is worth a drop of oil." He was referring to the oilfields of northern Iraq that became so important during and after the 2003 Gulf War. One of Britain's projects was a small (12-inch) oil pipeline from northern Iraq through Jordan and across northern Palestine to exit at the port of Haifa (one of the best ports on the eastern Mediterranean), every foot of which ran through British-controlled territory. Britain aimed to control the world's most important petroleum corridor but could not keep it. Even the small pipeline and refinery at Haifa were of great help to Britain in World War II. In sum, British motives were religious, strategic, and economic.

THE FIRST ARAB-JEWISH CLASHES

Almost immediately Britain's Palestine mandate was trouble. The Balfour Declaration did not unleash great Jewish immigration to Palestine after World War I—for most of the 1920s it was a trickle—but it was enough to alarm some Palestinian Arabs, who perceived that Jewish land purchases and immigration could

G : *Geography*

POLITICS BY DEMOGRAPHIC MEANS

In 1914, when Palestine was still under the Ottomans, the 85,000 Jews there constituted 12 percent of the small total population of 690,000. In 1933, the Jewish population had grown to 238,000, then 20 percent of Palestine's overall population of 1.2 million. Just three years later, in 1936, the Jewish population had grown to 400,000, then 30 percent of Palestine's population of 1.33 million. Jewish population had increased nearly fivefold from 1914 to 1936, but Palestine's overall population had nearly doubled.

A **demographic** race was underway, fueled by both immigration and births, that continues to our day. Both Jews and Arabs encourage high birth rates and immigration of their kin with an eye to eventual power. In the late 1930s, when the British largely cut off Jewish immigration, Palestine's Jews practiced "internal immigration," making lots of babies. Now some 5 million Israeli Jews face nearly as many Palestinians (some citizens of Israel, some on the West Bank and Gaza Strip, and some in other countries). Ten million people now wish to live where two-thirds of a million had lived a hundred years earlier.

eventually turn Palestine into a Jewish state. The first Arab rioting against Jewish immigration flared in 1920 but got bloody in August 1929, when 133 Jews were killed while the British-officered Palestine Police killed 116 Arabs. Governing the Holy Land was no picnic for the British.

With the Nazi takeover of Germany in early 1933 and the takeover of Poland by anti-Semitic colonels in 1935, more Central European Jews turned to Palestine as a refuge. The U.S. Immigration Act of 1924 incorporated tight national-origin quotas and effectively closed America to large numbers of Jewish immigrants. In 1933, 30,000 Jews immigrated to Palestine, 42,000 in 1934, and 61,000 in 1935. By 1936, Jews were 30 percent of Palestine's population, and Arabs did not like it. Leading the Arabs was the **mufti** of Jerusalem, Hajj Amin al Husseini, appointed by the British high commissioner of Palestine in 1921. The mufti soon turned bitterly anti-Jewish and anti-British and was fired by the British in 1937. He spent much of World War II in Germany, urging Muslims worldwide to side with the Nazis.

In 1936 Palestinian Arabs revolted and civil war raged until 1939. Both Arabs and Jews armed themselves, and the British could barely keep a lid on the fighting. The mainstream Jewish self-defense force, the Haganah, later became the core of the Israeli army. A militant Jewish organization, the Irgun, rejected compromise in favor of the gun. An even more extreme group, Lehi, assassinated Arabs and British. Hundreds died on both sides. It was in effect the first Palestinian *intifada* (uprising, see page 106) against Israelis and a demonstration of the impossibility of Jews and

demography   Study of population growth.
mufti   Islamic legal authority; issues *fatwas.*

G : *Geography*

PARTITION

Everyone agrees that partitioning a country torn by ethnic strife seldom fixes things; usually the conflict continues. Still, when it seems that two communities, religious or ethnic, cannot live together in one state, partition may be the only solution halfway workable. The historical record, however, is grim.

> *Ireland,* 1922—Britain, after misruling Ireland for seven centuries and putting down several Irish uprisings, agreed to an "Irish Free State." But Northern Ireland, with its Protestant majority, stayed British. This did not satisfy the Irish Republican Army (illegal in both Ulster and Eire), which renewed terrorism in the late 1960s.

> *India,* 1947—Britain took India about the time of U.S. independence, but by the 1920s many Indians demanded their independence. Fearing that India would slide over to the Japanese in World War II (some Indians did), Britain promised Indian independence after the war, but some of India's Muslims refused to be ruled by the Hindu majority and demanded their own state. Pakistan split off, producing 12 million refugees and three wars over Kashmir and East Pakistan (now Bangladesh). The next India-Pakistan war could be nuclear; both have the bomb.

> *Cyprus,* 1961—Britain agreed to leave the eastern Mediterranean island, which it had taken from the Ottomans in 1878, but the Greek Cypriot majority wanted *enosis* ("union") with Greece while the Turkish Cypriot minority wanted *taksim* ("partition"). When Turkey feared a massacre of its kin in 1974, it invaded and partitioned Cyprus, its current condition.

> *Bosnia,* 1992—As Yugoslavia fell apart, Bosnian Muslims demanded their own state, something that never existed before. Bosnia's Serbs and Croats demanded their own ethnic areas and for a while fought a bloody three-sided civil war that was calmed only by a U.S.-led force in 1995. Bosnia is now effectively partitioned but poor, corrupt, and dependent.

Partition has no success stories. With many Palestinian refugees, five wars, two intifadas, and no solution in sight, it would be hard to call the partition of Palestine a success. Barring a Rodney King solution—"Why can't we all just get along?"—partition is an unhappy last resort.

Arabs living together in a single state, even one supervised by an outside power. A tiny political party, Ihud ("Unity"), supported by some Jewish intellectuals and leftists, urged a binational state but got essentially no Arab takers. Those who now propose a "one-state" solution should reflect on the 1936–1939 revolt.

With Palestine ungovernable, Britain sent the Peel Commission in 1936 to investigate and advise. They came back in 1937 with a **partition** plan to divide Palestine into a small Jewish territory and a larger Arab territory, with Jerusalem under international trusteeship. Some of the Peel ideas turned up in the 1947 UN partition plan, but at the time neither side was interested.

---

partition   Dividing a country to keep warring groups apart.

In 1939 World War II loomed, and Britain had extensive interests throughout the Arab world, which Nazi agents were attempting to subvert. To calm Arab anger, London issued a **white paper** that drastically restricted Jewish immigration to Palestine. Only 75,000 were to be allowed in over the next four years, allegedly to not overburden Palestine's very limited "absorptive capacity," a dubious argument. At the very moment Europe's Jews needed a place of refuge, the world closed its doors to most of them. No country wanted Jewish refugees in large numbers. (Actually, even today no country accepts large numbers of refugees.) The only open port to Europe's Jews was far-off Shanghai, which had a sizable Jewish colony during World War II.

The white paper temporarily mollified the Arabs but outraged the Jews, who saw it as a betrayal of the Balfour Declaration. A few Jews turned to terrorism directed against British immigration policy. Two of Israel's prime ministers, Menachem Begin and Yitzhak Shamir, began their political careers leading respectively the Irgun and Lehi, militant underground organizations with a British price on their heads. "The Germans kill us, and the British don't let us live," was their rationale for turning to the gun and bomb.

The mainstream Jewish community of Palestine, however, saw no choice but to cooperate with the British. Many joined the British army, which gave them the military skills they needed after the war. "We will fight the Germans as if there were no white paper," said Zionist leader David Ben Gurion, "and we will fight the British as if there were no Germans." Few Arabs joined the British army.

With World War II, the Zionist movement lost all patience. Meeting in New York's Biltmore Hotel in 1942, they demanded a Jewish state in Palestine. A mere "Jewish homeland" shared with Arabs would no longer suffice. The liberation of the Nazi death camps in the spring of 1945 confirmed what had been rumored: In what later was called the **Holocaust**, the Nazis had systematically murdered some 6 million Jews. Zionist agents organized concentration-camp survivors and smuggled them into Palestine. The British tried to stop the ships, but this just gave them more publicity. Irgun and Lehi terrorists in Palestine shot British police and blew up the British military headquarters in Jerusalem's King David Hotel.

Exhausted and exasperated, Britain threw the question to the new United Nations in 1947 and announced it would withdraw from Palestine the following spring. Meeting in Lake Success on Long Island (the UN building was not built yet), the UN Trusteeship Council, which inherited the League of Nations' mandates, devised a partition plan that pleased neither side but seemed to provide a way out of the mess.

The 1947 UN partition plan divided Palestine, checkerboard-style, into three Arab patches and three Jewish patches touching at their corners (see map on page 75). Jerusalem was to be an international city belonging to neither. The plan was imaginative but too complex to be carried out. On November 29, 1947, the UN

---

white paper   Major diplomatic statement of policy.

Holocaust   From the Greek "burnt sacrifice"; Nazi genocide of Europe's Jews in World War II. (Hebrew: *Shoa.*)

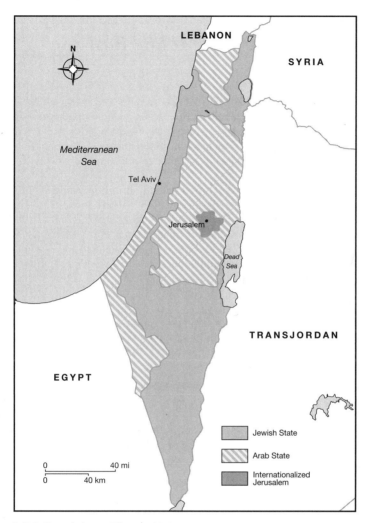

UN Partition Plan, 1947

General Assembly voted 33–13 in favor of the plan with ten abstentions. The United States led its European allies and Latin American client states to vote yes. The Soviet Union—seeing a way to oust Britain from the Middle East—led its satellites in East Europe to also vote yes. All Arab countries, Israel's immediate neighbors, voted no. Israel was born with world but not regional approval.

The Palestinian Jewish community was delighted, for this gave them a state, however odd its shape. The Arab community was totally against it. The way they saw it, Arabs should have to give up zero percent of Palestine; giving up half was outrageous, particularly since Jews were only 35 percent of the population and owned only 7 percent of the land. To Arabs, Israel looked like a continuation of Western imperialism, a colonial settler state imposed on an unwilling indigenous

⑤ *The United States in the Middle East*

TRUMAN RECOGNIZES ISRAEL

President Harry Truman extended U.S. **diplomatic recognition** to Israel within minutes of its proclamation, but it was not a sure thing in advance. Recognition, especially by the major powers, is a powerful signal that confirms the sovereignty of a new country and lends it legitimacy. To withhold or withdraw recognition means we wish to have nothing to do with the other country, and possibly wish its regime would disappear.

Leading State and Defense Department officials worried (like the British in World War II) that U.S. recognition of the new Jewish state would enrage Arabs, damage U.S. national interests, and expand Soviet influence in the region. State Department **Arabists** especially argued that the Arabs have the numbers, the territory, and the oil, and we should do nothing to anger them.

Truman pondered the issue but recognized Israel for both domestic political and personal reasons. American Jews, although only a few percent of the population, vote and give money (mostly to the Democrats). As the plain-spoken Truman put it in 1948: "There ain't many Arab voters in this country." (There are now.) And Truman was up for election that November, which he surprisingly won. Politicians strongly favor whatever gets them elected.

And Truman had an old Jewish friend and army buddy, Eddie Jacobson, with whom he briefly ran a haberdashery in Kansas City in the early 1920s. Jacobson visited President Truman in Washington and told him emotionally of the suffering of the Jewish people in World War II. Some think the personal connection is what ultimately decided Truman.

population. In the absence of compromise, only one thing could happen: war. The Arabs lost, and the Israelis took more land. This outraged the Arabs more, and they were even less willing to compromise. This led to another war, which again the Israelis won, taking even more land and outraging the Arabs still more. The two sides play into each other's hands.

Local Arab-Jewish fighting was underway many months before the last British forces pulled out of Palestine. David Ben Gurion proclaimed the State of Israel on May 14, 1948, and five armies from neighboring Arab states immediately invaded. Israel was born because of and amidst war.

CONCLUSIONS

Neither the Bible nor history gives a title deed to a land. Abraham, Moses, and the Jews in Babylonian exile claimed a New Jersey-sized "Promised Land" that has been called Canaan, Israel, Judea, and Palestine. Crushed and dispersed by the Romans,

---

diplomatic recognition   Establishment of official relations with another country.

Arabist   Presumably pro-Arab State Department official.

Jews carried their religion and thoughts of eventual return into nearly two millennia of exile. Jews fared better in Muslim lands than in Christian ones. Bad conditions in Central Europe and France's Dreyfus trial awoke modern Zionism, secular and socialist, by the turn of the twentieth century. Jewish pioneers trickled into the Ottoman province of Palestine, but the British interwar mandate over Palestine brought more, especially with the rise of the Nazis in Europe.

A parallel Arab nationalism grew in the Ottoman Empire, and the British—by promising Arabs their own big kingdom—encouraged an Arab revolt against the Turks in World War I. Jewish immigration to the British mandate of Palestine led to a series of Arab disturbances, culminating in an Arab revolt from 1936 to 1939. The British curbed Jewish immigration but after World War II threw the question to the new UN, which voted to partition Palestine into Jewish and Arab states. Jews accepted partition, but Arabs rejected it, leading to Israel's 1948 birth and the first Arab-Israeli war.

Patterns emerged early and persist. Two culturally different peoples claim the same small land. Outside powers help set up conflicts. Populations grow rapidly. Compromise is hard to find.

KEY TERMS

aliyah (p. 65)	McMahon-Hussein letters (p. 68)
Arabist (p. 76)	messiah (p. 61)
Balfour Declaration (p. 69)	modern Zionism (p. 64)
charisma (p. 60)	mufti (p. 72)
demography (p. 72)	nationalism (p. 64)
diaspora (p. 61)	pan-Arab (p. 67)
diplomatic recognition (p. 76)	partition (p. 73)
Gallipoli (p. 68)	pogrom (p. 65)
Holocaust (p. 74)	rabbi (p. 60)
imperial lifeline (p. 68)	secular (p. 66)
isolationism (p. 69)	Sykes-Picot (p. 68)
Jewish question (p. 65)	white paper (p. 74)
kibbutz (p. 66)	Yiddish (p. 63)
League of Nations (p. 69)	Zealot (p. 60)
mandate (p. 69)	Zionism (p. 58)

FURTHER REFERENCE

Fisk, Robert. *The Great War for Civilisation: The Conquest of the Middle East.* New York: Knopf, 2006.

Fromkin, David. *A Peace to End All Peace: Creating the Modern Middle East, 1914–1922.* New York: Holt, 1989.

Gelvin, James L. *The Israel-Palestine Conflict: One Hundred Years of War.* New York: Cambridge University Press, 2005.

Hilberg, Raul. *The Destruction of the European Jews,* rev. ed. New York: Holmes & Meier, 1985.

Khalidi, Rashid. *The Iron Cage: The Story of the Palestinian Struggle for Statehood.* Boston, MA: Beacon, 2006.

———. *Palestinian Identity: The Construction of Modern National Consciousness.* New York: Columbia University Press, 1997.

Laqueur, Walter. *A History of Zionism.* New York: Weidenfeld & Nicholson, 1974.

Sachar, Howard M. *A History of the Jews in the Modern World.* New York: Knopf, 2005.

Said, Edward. *The Question of Palestine.* New York: Times Books, 1979.

Segev, Tom. *One Palestine, Complete,* trans. Haim Watzman. New York: Metropolitan, 2000.

Shafir, Gershon. *Land, Labor, and the Origins of the Israeli-Palestinian Conflict, 1882–1914.* New York: Cambridge University Press, 1989.

Stein, Leslie. *The Hope Fulfilled: The Rise of Modern Israel.* Westport, CT: Praeger, 2003.

Tessler, Mark A. *A History of the Israeli-Palestinian Conflict.* Bloomington, IN: Indiana University Press, 1994.

5 The Very Long War

- Are we looking at separate wars or one long war?
- How does Israel bear out what Napoleon said about morale?
- Is there any way Israel could have been born peacefully?
- Has the UN prevented wars in the Middle East?
- Were Israel's 1949 borders indefensible?
- How do Arab and Israeli cultures differ?
- How was 1967 a big but incomplete Israeli victory?
- Could 1973 be considered a "necessary" war? Why?
- Are these wars any of our business?

There are two ways to look at the Arab-Israeli conflict, either as separate wars or as one long war punctuated by cease-fires. Either way, the conflict has no quick or simple solution, and good will among the contending parties is absent. Do not count on a big peace conference to settle things. The crux of the problem is that Israel wishes to exist, while Arabs, especially Palestinians, wish it had never existed. As we considered in the previous chapter, history or Scripture cannot settle these things. Reason and international law do not fare much better.

THE 1948 WAR

Israelis call it their War of Independence; Palestinians call it their Catastrophe. The worst could have been avoided if Palestinian leaders had accepted the 1947 UN Partition Plan and let half of Palestine become the new Jewish state of Israel. Few Palestinians gave this possibility a second thought: All of Palestine was theirs, and they were in no mood to share. Result: They lost even more territory, which Israel gained, a pattern that keeps reappearing. Inability to compromise has created a chronic and endemic Palestinian catastrophe.

G : *Geography*

ISRAEL'S BOUNDARIES AND FEATURES

An old technique will help you learn the region's geography. It is called a "bounding exercise" and requires you to recite from memory a country's adjoining neighbors, starting in the north and preceding clockwise. The directions need be only approximate.

Israel is bounded on the north by Lebanon and Syria;
on the east by Jordan (and the new state of Palestine, when it happens);
on the south by the Gulf of Aqaba and Egypt;
and on the west by the Mediterranean Sea.

Also learn the features of Israel/Palestine:

Galilee—the northernmost portion.
Golan Heights—Syrian ridge overlooking Upper Galilee, taken by Israel in 1967.
Kinneret—Hebrew for Sea of Galilee.
Plain of Sharon—coastal strip in center of country.
Negev—large southern desert.
Haifa Bay—natural harbor in north of country.
Mount Carmel—mountains around Haifa.
Samaria—in current usage, northern portion of West Bank.
Judea—in current usage, southern portion of West Bank that includes Jerusalem.
Jerusalem—ancient and current capital, high in Judean hills.
West Bank (of the Jordan River)—Judea and Samaria, home of many Palestinians.
Gaza Strip—area along Mediterranean around city of Gaza, also home of many Palestinians.
Jordan River—South-flowing stream from Kinneret to Dead Sea.
Dead Sea—large salty lake, lowest spot on earth.
Wadi Araba—(Valley of the Arabs) depression that continues southward from the Dead Sea.
Tel Aviv—Israel's largest city, on coast in center.
Eilat—Israel's seaport on Gulf of Aqaba.

The first Arab-Israeli war started as a bigger and worse resumption of the 1936–1939 Palestine civil war, one that the British mandate authorities could barely keep a lid on. After World War II, the lid blew off. Holocaust survivors demanded to be let into Palestine. Jews worldwide demanded a state. The Jewish community in Palestine formed battalions, many of them trained by the British army, and scrounged up weapons. Arabs, both Palestinian and infiltrators from neighboring lands, did the same but were poorly organized. The British, reduced in strength and already committed to withdrawal, mostly stood by as Jewish forces (the Haganah, Palmach, and Irgun) battled several groups of Arab fighters.

Local fighting had been underway for months in Palestine, but the war officially broke out upon Israel's declaration of independence on May 14, 1948, as five Arab

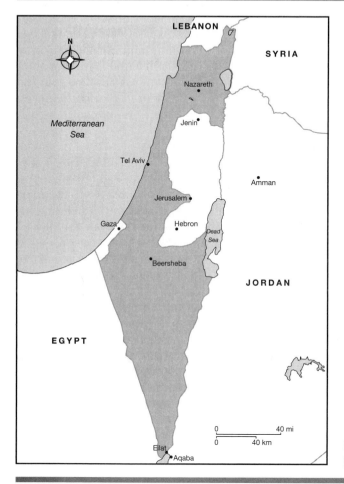

Israel's 1949–1967 Boundaries

states immediately invaded, aiming to make Israel disappear. This invasion masked the underlying Israel-Palestine struggle, turning it into a series of wars between Israel and its Arab neighbors with the fate of the Palestinians fading into the background. This was convenient for Israelis but horrible for Palestinians, who over the decades learned that they could not rely on Arab countries to "protect" them. All Israel's bordering neighbors—Egypt, Jordan, Syria, and Lebanon—invaded, plus a contingent from Iraq. The Egyptian army was by far the biggest and greatest threat to Israel, although it turned out that the small British-officered Arab Legion of Jordan achieved much more.

The Arab states emphatically rejected the 1947 UN partition plan (see the previous chapter) and felt it their duty to rescue their brother Arabs, the Palestinians.

At the same time, they wanted pieces of Palestine for themselves. As always, motives mixed a little generosity with a lot of self-interest. The Israeli motive was extremely simple: win or die. In Israeli eyes, the recent murder of six million of their kinfolk in Europe blended into Arab cries of "Drive the Jews into the sea!" For Israelis, the Arabs were a continuation of the Nazis. (A few German mercenaries fought for Arab armies, which Israelis claimed proved the fascistic-reactionary nature of Arabs. Israeli forces shot German prisoners out of hand.) Israel paid only negative attention to Palestinians. Some Israelis argued then and argue now that there is no distinct "Palestinian" nationality; they were simply Arabs who could be at home in other Arab countries. Few Israelis worried about Palestinian refugees; compared to Israel's survival the point seemed irrelevant. As we shall see, it is highly relevant for any peace settlement.

Informed opinion thought it was an unequal match that the Arabs would win. The Arab armies were professional and had trained and equipped for years. Many Israelis had been in the Haganah or British army (or both) but had few weapons. For years, the British had confiscated weapons in an effort to hold down the communal violence in Palestine. Even before the British left, however, Israelis manufactured and imported whatever they could. Some British rifles had been squirreled away. Mortars and Sten guns were machined in small shops. Trucks were armored with steel plates. U.S. war surplus was imported as "scrap metal" and reassembled. Czech rifles were purchased from Europe. Everything was done on a desperate basis.

For soldiers, Israel mobilized most men, welcomed foreign volunteers (many Americans), and quickly trained new immigrants from Europe. It was a strange mixture: "The air force spoke English, the tank corps Russian, and the infantry Yiddish," Israelis joked. Actually, the backbone of the Israeli army spoke Hebrew as many officers were born and raised on kibbutzim with a highly nationalist and egalitarian ethos. The Israeli shock troops, the Palmach, were largely Marxist kibbutzniks. The Hebrew language evolved so quickly, with different units developing their own new terms for weapons and tactics, that units had trouble cross-communicating. Holding them together was their high morale and ability to improvise. As Napoleon, himself a great improviser, noted, "In war the morale is to the physical as three is to one."

Arab armies, on the other hand, lacked a sense of desperation: If defeated they would simply go home. Officers were socially higher than soldiers, who were treated as inferiors. Officers were not trained to be daring and imaginative. What should have been a quick Arab victory ground to a halt and was pushed back. An Egyptian army was surrounded and cut off in the "Faluja Pocket" along the present Israel-Egypt border. One of those trapped was a young major, Abdul Gamal Nasser, who with his fellow officers swore revenge, first against the corrupt Egyptian regime that had got them into this and second against Israel. These formed the core of the Free Officers Movement that did overthrow King Farouk in 1952.

One Arab force did well: Jordan's Arab Legion, set up, trained, and officered by the British. As the mandate ended, the Arab Legion crossed from Jordan and captured most of the West Bank, including several kibbutzim (best known: the Etzion bloc south of Jerusalem, since reestablished) and the Old City of Jerusalem, the walled portion that contains most holy sites. The departing British turned over to the Arab Legion sturdy stone police stations built during the mandate. One of

G Geography

DIVIDED JERUSALEM

Israel claimed Jerusalem as its capital, but it was cleft by a no man's land (where tourists could be shot by Jordanian snipers). It stayed divided until Israel conquered the Old City in 1967. Israelis longed to recover the City of David. The only place diplomats and tourists could normally cross directly between Israel and an Arab country was at the so-called Mandelbaum Gate in Jerusalem, on the border of its Jordanian and Israeli halves. It was not one of the biblical gates into Jerusalem but simply the street by the house of an unfortunate Mr. Mandelbaum, who lost it in the 1948 fighting.

Tourists would arrange with their consulates a few days before they wanted to cross. It was normally a one-way trip; if you exited through the Mandelbaum Gate you were not allowed to return through it. An exception was made at Easter allowing Christians living in Israel to visit East Jerusalem, which contains the Via Dolorosa and Calvary, and then return.

No man's land split Jerusalem from 1948 to 1967. (*Michael G. Roskin*)

Mandelbaum Gate was the only crossing point from Israel into a neighboring country for Israel's first decades. (*Michael G. Roskin*)

Cultures

"ON WINGS OF EAGLES"

The semi-clandestine airlift of 45,000 Jews from Yemen to Israel in 1949 and 1950 illustrates the cultural differences of the Middle East. Living in medieval circumstances, Jews boarded airplanes to fly to Israel because Scripture promised that they would be born back to the Promised Land "on the wings of eagles." Some cut holes in the roofs of the aircraft for their cooking fires. Once landed in Israel, however, many refused to get into trucks, for there was nothing in the Bible about these lumbering ground creatures.

In a generation, the Yeminites modernized and Europeanized. Their education levels climbed, and they served in the military. Especially important was the emancipation of Yemenite women, allowed for the first time to go to schools and jobs. The rapid cultural change of Israel's Yemenite community illustrates what can be done if people are willing to modernize and the context is conducive.

these forts and an abandoned monastery on the Latrun Heights gave the Arab Legion command of the only road from the coast to Jerusalem, the Jewish parts of which they intended to starve out. With no artillery, Israeli infantry, many fresh off the boat, could not take Latrun, and repeated attacks came under withering fire. Some of Israel's top officers got blooded at Latrun. The Israelis managed, however, by fierce fighting and by building a new road up steep, rocky hills, to open a wedge-shaped corridor to western Jerusalem, the bigger and more modern part of the city, largely built and populated by Jews in the twentieth century.

By late summer of 1948 Israel had not only repelled the Arab armies but had taken more territory than the 1947 UN partition plan had mapped out. If the Arab states had accepted the UN partition plan, Palestinians would have had their own state in 1948, and it would be larger than anything they have been offered since. From an allotted 55 percent of Palestine, by the time the **cease-fire** took effect in 1949, Israel had 77 percent. Should they have given the additional lands back? Israel's answer was terse and negative: You Arabs rejected and violated the UN plan, so you have no claims under it. This left three-quarters of a million Palestinian refugees with nothing and laid the groundwork for the present impasse: What shall become of the Palestinians?

Israel immediately encouraged Jews from all over the world to immigrate, and by 1960 its population was 2.1 million. Soviet Jews were trapped until the 1980s, but some East European countries let their remaining Jews go. Poland, which once had a large and vibrant Jewish minority, saw most of the remaining Holocaust survivors leave. The biggest source of new Jewish immigrants, however, were Sephardim (see box above) in Muslim countries. Although they had lived in these lands for centuries, Arab governments turned hostile with the birth of Israel. Ancient Jewish communities in Morocco, Algeria, Tunisia, Egypt, Iraq, and Yemen nearly disappeared as their people went to Israel. Now around half of Israel's Jews are Sephardic.

---

cease-fire   Temporary halt in fighting; does not imply a settlement.

D Domestic Structures

Israel's Electoral System

Israel is a parliamentary democracy of a pure type that has died out in most of Europe. Its single, 120-member legislature, the **Knesset**, is elected by **proportional representation** (PR) with the country as one big electoral district. (Only the Netherlands shares this electoral system; other PR countries are divided into smaller districts, such as Germany's Länder and Sweden's counties.) An Israeli party needs to win only 2 percent of the vote to get seats in the Knesset.

This has led to extreme party fragmentation—the Knesset had twelve parties in 2006—and difficulty in forming coalition governments and choosing a prime minister. Israel's biggest parties are the centrist Kadima (Forward), which won twenty-nine seats in 2006; the center-left Labor, with nineteen seats; the right-wing Likud (Consolidation) and Sephardic-religious Shas, with twelve seats each; and the Russian-immigrant Our Home Israel party, with eleven seats. The 2007 cabinet was a strange coalition of Kadima, Labor, Shas, Our Home, and the small (seven-seat) Pensioners party. The more parties in a coalition, the more likely that one will defect, thus bringing down the cabinet. Then the parties must negotiate the formation of a new one, often by giving in on a policy that the defecting party has objected to. This can produce cabinet paralysis over big issues, such as how to end the impasse with the Palestinians.

New Israeli parties constantly spring up—religious, secular, leftist, liberal, you name it—because there is little incentive to form one big party. Likud was cobbled together from several smaller parties in the 1970s. In 2005, Likud Prime Minister Ariel Sharon defected from his own party and founded Kadima, now headed by Prime Minister Ehud Olmert.

In contrast, **majoritarian** systems, such as Britain and the United States, elect one member each from hundreds of districts by simple plurality. This system penalizes third parties (unless they are territorially concentrated) and generally produces two big, long-lasting parties, one of which commands a majority of legislative seats, making coalitions unnecessary. Such systems may be unfair—because they do not reflect all shades of opinion—but they make government policy more decisive and stable.

Israel's founding prime minister, David Ben Gurion, opined that Israel's electoral system, borrowed from interwar Europe, was the worst ever devised and should be scrapped in favor of an Anglo-American system that would produce fewer but bigger parties. Such a reform, however, would require Israel's small parties to vote themselves out of business. Israel's electoral system, ultrademocratic in theory, leads to too many parties, whose quarrels sometimes impede decision-making.

The Origin of Palestinian Refugees

The real losers of the first Arab-Israeli war were some 750,000 Palestinian refugees who fled Israeli-held territories. Arab leaders and broadcasts told them to temporarily clear out while Arab armies made short work of Israel, and they had a natural desire to get out of harm's way. Israel's standard explanation was that they

---

Knesset   Israel's parliament.

proportional representation   Electoral system that assigns parliamentary seats in proportion to party vote.

majoritarian   Electoral system that encourages dominance of one party in parliament.

G Geography

BOUND JORDAN AND LEBANON

Jordan is bounded on the north by Syria;
on the east by Iraq and Saudi Arabia;
on the south by the Gulf of Aqaba;
and on the west by Israel (and the new state of Palestine, when it happens).

Lebanon is bounded on the north and east by Syria;
on the south by Israel;
and on the west by the Mediterranean Sea.

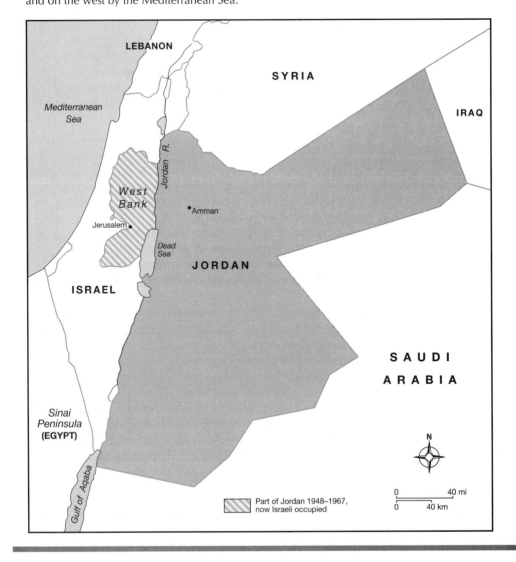

Part of Jordan 1948–1967, now Israeli occupied

left voluntarily and abandoned their properties. But the new Israeli leaders ordered many driven out by threats and gunfire; hundreds were shot. The way Israelis saw it, Palestinian Arabs hated Israel and would be a permanent **fifth column**, always trying to overthrow Israel.

The most shocking single incident came just before Israel's independence, when full-scale civil war already raged and the British could do nothing to stop it. Some 130 militants from Irgun and Lehi in the early morning attacked the Arab village of Deir Yassin on the western edge of Jerusalem, believing it harbored Palestinian irregular forces. The Irgun killed over 250 Arabs, including women and children. Then Israelis spread news of Deir Yassin, stampeding thousands of Palestinians into flight. The Haganah repudiated the Irgun and its bloody tactics but not its purpose of getting Arabs to leave. And once they left, even after the 1949 cease-fire, they were not allowed back. Israeli courts declared their property abandoned and sold or gave it to Israelis. Approximately 250,000 Arabs remained in Israel, mostly in remote villages; they were given Israeli citizenship but were under military rule for many years. They now number about 1.2 million.

Palestinians generally fled to the closest Arab country. Most went eastward into the Jordanian-controlled butterfly-shaped territory later known as the West Bank, which Jordan officially annexed in 1950. Most became Jordanian citizens, although many Palestinians disliked the king of Jordan and his mostly Bedouin army. Most of Jordan's population was Palestinian; 43 percent still is. Another sizeable group fled into the Egyptian-controlled Gaza Strip, which was never made part of Egypt. Gazans generally did not obtain Egyptian citizenship. The UN Relief and Works Agency (UNRWA) provided tents, food, and medical care to those clustered in sprawling refugee camps in several countries. Smaller numbers fled to Lebanon, which did not make them citizens, and Syria, which did.

Over the decades, two trends appeared among the Palestinians—one demographic, the other educational. With no jobs but adequate food, Palestinians had little to do but make babies. For many years the Gaza Strip had the world's highest **fertility rate**; an average woman there bore eight children (now down to six). Replacement rate, at which a population holds steady, is 2.1. With such large families, the Palestinian population soon doubled and doubled again, and now numbers some 5 million. (In 1900, it was around 0.5 million.) Many Palestinians think that this is good; it will enable them to destroy Israel and reclaim their land.

Even before 1948 Palestinians were some of the best-educated Arabs, and they moved rapidly into the twentieth century. Deprived of their farms and businesses, many saw education as the way up. They are now by far the most educated of all Arabs, and Palestinian doctors and engineers are found throughout the Arab world and even in the United States. Palestinians did much of the skilled work in the Persian Gulf oilfields. Yasser Arafat worked as an engineer in Kuwait before becoming leader of the Palestinian cause.

---

fifth column   From 1936–1939 Spanish Civil War; enemy sympathizers and agents inside one's territory.

fertility rate   Number of children an average woman bears.

P : *Personalities*

ABDUL GAMAL NASSER

Nasser was not simply an Egyptian nationalist; he was a **pan-Arabist**. Egypt, the core of the Arab world, would unite it under his leadership. The Arab world in turn was the core of what came to be called the Third World, and he would play a major role in leading it too. Permanent President Nasser saw himself as the new Saladin (all revolutionary Arab leaders see themselves as the new Saladin) and instituted an ambitious program to build a socialist, secular, militaristic Egypt and lead the entire Arab world. (Iraq's Saddam Hussein, born in Saladin province, copied Nasser in this aspiration.)

Nasser seized the estates of the rich and redistributed land to poor peasants. He kept almost all industry under state control. There was no democracy; elections were fake. Nasser brooked no opposition, neither by Islamic fundamentalists on the right nor Communists on the left. Egypt's large Muslim Brotherhood detested Nasser, who kept thousands of them in prison and executed their leaders. (For more on the Muslim Brotherhood, see Chapter 16.) Only in 2005 were Brotherhood members allowed to run (as independents, not as Brotherhood members) in imperfect elections for Egypt's parliament; they did well.

Nasser, responding to a Syrian overture, engineered a short-lived Egyptian-Syrian union (1958–1961), called the United Arab Republic (UAR). Several such Arab unions have been declared; Qaddafi of Libya was especially eager for them. In the name of Arab unity, Nasser sent Egyptian forces to put down tribal resistance in Yemen, where he used poison gas for the first time since Mussolini used it in Ethiopia in 1935. (Saddam Hussein also used poison gas in his war with Iran.)

For many years, Israel claimed that the crux of the problem was the hostility of Arab states to Israel. If only they could negotiate peace agreements, all would be well in the region. Without the backing of Arab states, Palestinians would soon also compromise with Israel, they argued. But state-to-state hostilities are only part of the problem. The underlying problem is the plight of the Palestinian refugees. Egypt and Jordan have signed peace agreements with Israel, but Palestinian unrest has grown. The several Arab-Israeli wars only masked the Palestinian problem.

THE RISE OF NASSER

In Cairo a 1952 military **coup** ousted King Farouk, whose corrupt rule was blamed for defeat in the war with Israel and for the continuing presence of British military bases in Egypt. The coup leader was Colonel Abdul Gamal Nasser, who took over the presidency in 1953 and kept it until his death in 1970.

His associates on the world scene were the leftist neutrals Tito of Yugoslavia and Sukarno of Indonesia. He was hostile to Britain and the United States. Although friendly to the Soviet Union, Nasser imprisoned Egyptian Communists.

---

pan-Arabism   Movement to draw together all Arab countries.

coup   From French *coup d'état,* strike at the state; an extra-legal seizure of power, usually by the military.

G : *Geography*

DAM FOOLISH

Environmentalists criticize big dams, as do some scientists and engineers and many archaeologists. The Aswan High Dam helps make their case. First, it created big but shallow Lake Nasser behind it. The best such lakes are narrow and deep, to minimize water loss through evaporation. In the hot, dry climate of the Upper Nile, some 30 percent of Lake Nasser's water is lost annually by evaporation. Egypt's ancient prosperity was based on the Nile flooding every year, depositing new, nutrient-rich silt. The Aswan dam retards this process. Species that used to migrate up and down the Nile are now blocked.

Invaluable archaeological treasures were either inundated by Lake Nasser or had to be disassembled and set up elsewhere. (A side benefit of this, however, is that New York, Madrid, and other cities now have ancient Egyptian temples.) Strategically, Egypt has given itself a great vulnerability. In the event of all-out war with Israel (or any country), the Aswan dam would be a tempting target. If it were burst when Lake Nasser was full, it would send a wall of water down the Nile. For a fraction of the enormous expense of the high dam, irrigation could be done by simply pumping water without a dam. But Nasser wanted a showcase project, and the Soviets were happy to oblige him, figuring they were winning an important client state in the Third World.

Nasser made an old engineering dream his own: a high dam at Aswan on the Upper Nile. The British had built a low dam at Aswan, but a high dam would harness the Nile to irrigate the desert and generate hydroelectricity. The project was terribly expensive. Nasser made an initial feeler for U.S. financing, but Eisenhower's Secretary of State John Foster Dulles, who had no patience with neutralism, turned him down after Egypt made a small purchase of Soviet arms (via a Czech cutout). So Nasser nationalized the Suez Canal Company, owned largely by British and French investors. As far as Nasser was concerned, the Suez Company was a last remnant of colonialism; it was built by Egyptian labor and should be run by and for Egyptians. Nasser would use the revenues from Suez transit fees to pay for the dam, and he would get Soviet aid and technical help to build it.

THE 1956 WAR

Palestinian refugees helped start the second Arab-Israeli war. Seething with hatred in refugee camps, some could glimpse their homes or fields across the cease-fire line. Some slipped across the lines to harvest their old orchards. By 1953 they organized bands of *fedayeen,* "self-sacrificers," who shot up Israeli homes and highway traffic, including a school bus. In 1953 fedayeen murdered an Israeli mother and her two children, and Israeli commandos retaliated by blowing up a Palestinian village in the West Bank, killing sixty-nine. The fedayeen attacks increased.

Israel retaliated against the fedayeen with cross-border raids. Many Israelis believe they can gain security only by "teaching the Arabs a lesson." (Israelis are not alone in this approach.) Unfortunately, this produces a never-ending spiral of lessons, what Clausewitz saw as a natural process of **escalation**. In a large retaliation in 1955, Israeli commandos attacked an Egyptian army headquarters in Khan Yunis in the Gaza Strip. (Egypt never annexed the Strip, which is crowded with Palestinian refugees, but did administer it.) The attack enraged Nasser, who immediately purchased the Soviet arms, which in turn ended any U.S. help for the Aswan dam. Nasser paid for the arms by mortgaging Egypt's cotton harvest for decades.

Nasser claimed to be neutral in the Cold War, but in 1955 the West believed Nasser was turning Egypt into a Soviet **client state**. Britain and France were furious at having the blue-chip Suez Canal Company taken from them and plotted to get it back. They found the perfect partner in **collusion**, Israel, which was alarmed by Nasser's buildup of his newly acquired Soviet weapons in the Sinai. The three countries agreed that Israel would invade Egypt, but just before it reached the canal British and French forces would land to "protect" the canal and keep both Israel and Egypt ten miles distant from it. It was phony as a three-dollar bill. Eisenhower warned London and Paris against it, but they ignored him. British Prime Minister Anthony Eden (who had studied Arabic at Oxford) thought Nasser was much like Hitler, a dangerous expansionist who had to be stopped early. The French hated Nasser for his help to the Algerian National Front, then fighting to expel France. Unlike today, France in the 1950s was very pro-Israel, seeing Israelis as comrades-in-arms against both Nazis and Algerian nationalists. Israel purchased its best jet fighter, the Mystère, from France.

The plan initially went like clockwork. Israel took Egyptian forces by surprise by knocking out Egyptian armor in the Sinai with air strikes, blocking the Sinai's mountain passes by paratroopers, and streaking across the peninsula with its own armored columns in 100 hours. Then British and French paratroopers and marines landed to "save" the canal. They had to fight their way in, and the effort bogged down as Nasser scuttled many ships in the canal to render it useless.

Eisenhower, although no friend of Nasser, feared the attack would alienate the entire Arab world. (Note the similarity of French criticism of U.S. actions against Iraq in 2003.) And at the same time the Soviet Union was crushing the 1956 Hungarian uprising. Eisenhower wanted the world's attention focused on this crime; the British and French Suez misadventure distracted the world from Soviet brutality. Eisenhower put pressure on Britain and France to withdraw, and they soon did, angry at the United States.

Eisenhower was much more even-handed in his approach to Israel and the Arab countries than later U.S. presidents. He pressured Israel to withdraw from Sinai, and Israel did in the spring of 1957, so the 1956 war netted Israel no territorial gains. Israel was unhappy at the lack of a peace settlement with Egypt but had accomplished some of its goals. It had destroyed much Egyptian equipment in

---

escalation   Tendency for conflicts to intensify, caused by each side trying to outdo the other.

client state   A weaker state depending on and attached to a major power; not as close as a Soviet satellite state in East Europe.

collusion   Connivance; a seemingly spontaneous activity that has been planned in advance.

the Sinai so that Egypt was not an immediate threat. Israel **spiked** Egyptian guns at Sharm el Sheik, opening the Strait of Tiran to Israeli shipping, crucial to its economy. Israel's southern port of Eilat became its maritime opening for commerce with Asia and Africa. Israel warned that closing the Strait would be a *casus belli*, a cause of war.

Israel also got some concessions from Washington: The Americans said they would keep the Strait of Tiran open and would support a UN Emergency Force (UNEF) composed of volunteers from several countries to supervise the truce and sound alarms in case of a military buildup. UNEF, however, was to be stationed only on the Egyptian side of the border. Israel thought it had gained something from the Sinai Campaign, but it was temporary.

THE SIX DAY WAR

The eleven years between the second (1956) and the third Arab-Israeli wars (1967) were arguably the happiest and most secure period in Israel's life. There were relatively few Palestinian Arabs within Israel's borders and almost no terrorist attacks or bombings. One could live and travel in Israel freely and safely. The 1949 borders continued, leaving Israel a funny shape. At one point, along the Plain of Sharon, Israel was only ten miles wide between the Jordanian-held West Bank and the Mediterranean. This bothered Israelis, who worried that Israel could be cut in two at this narrow neck by a force invading from the east. As it turned out, this was never a serious threat.

Numerous border clashes, some precipitated by Israeli military and agriculture encroachments, led up to the 1967 war. Syria, which held the commanding Golan Heights, a ridgeline overlooking Israel's Hula Valley, would react to these encroachments by shelling Israel, and Israel would fire back. On April 7, after one especially strong Syrian shelling, Israeli jets hit Syrian gun emplacements on the Golan Heights. Syria sent its Soviet-made MiGs into an aerial dogfight with Israel's French-made Mystères. Superior aircraft and pilot skills told the story: Syria lost six, Israel none. Damascus screamed in rage, accusing Israel of massing forces in the Galilee in preparation for an attack on Syria. Damascus also demanded that Nasser of Egypt, still billing himself as the leader of the Arab world, do something about it. Syria and Egypt were allies, and Nasser began mobilizing his forces.

The Soviet Union, patron of both Syria and Egypt, also accused Israel of massing its forces. Israel invited the Soviet ambassador to go to Galilee and see for himself that this was not true. Everything in the Hula Valley, only 12 miles long and 6 miles wide, can be seen from a hill on its west. The Soviet ambassador refused and repeated the charge. The Soviet Union, trying to enhance its power by manipulating tensions in the region, deserves much of the blame for the war that followed.

---

spike   To render an artillery piece useless.

G : *Geography*

TERRITORY AND SECURITY

Many people think territory equals security. That is, the more geographical features under your control, the more secure you are. Gaining land from the enemy means victory and safety. This is not always so, as Clausewitz realized early in the nineteenth century. What matters in war, he wrote, is seldom any particular territorial gains but destruction of the enemy's *center of gravity,* usually his main forces. Napoleon, whom Clausewitz briefly fought against and later studied, invaded Russia and captured Moscow in 1812. (He did better than Hitler in 1941.) But Napoleon was overextended, and much of the Russian army was still intact, waiting for the right time. Moscow burned down, and the Grande Armée had to retreat hundreds of miles through the snow, harassed by the Russian army that Napoleon had not broken. Napoleon's overextension deep into Russia led to his defeat and eventually to his downfall.

Additional territory can actually turn into a vulnerability. The United States took the Philippines from Spain in 1898, thinking the islands would give America a splendid presence in East Asia. Theodore Roosevelt, who helped engineer the move, later regretted it because the Philippines now had to be defended. They were easy pickings for Japan in 1942 (when U.S. forces in the Philippines outnumbered the Japanese invaders).

Israel's seizure of the West Bank in 1967 delighted most Israelis, as it removed the threat of the narrow neck left over from the 1949 borders and gave Israel "strategic depth." Now Israel's main line of defense was the Jordan River, much farther from Israel's population centers. It looked great on a map. But with the West Bank Israel also got some 1.5 million Palestinians, who grew more numerous and angrier over the decades. They launched uprisings and bombings, making life for Israelis far less secure than it had been prior to 1967. Now Israelis must worry about security constantly.

Furthermore, Israel's narrow neck from 1949 to 1967 was not especially vulnerable. All attacks require the massing of forces, and any massing of Arab troops and armor on the West Bank in preparation for an invasion was easily detectable—we're talking about a few miles here—making surprise impossible. Considering current difficulties, Israel's 1949 borders were not so bad.

On May 17, Nasser ordered the UNEF, in the Sinai as peace observers since 1957, to leave, and they did, perhaps too quickly. There were no UNEF observers on the Israeli side of the border, and UN Secretary General U Thant believed he had to accede to Cairo's demand. UNEF was never intended or able to impose peace, merely to serve as an alarm bell should either side start massing forces. With UNEF's departure, that function was over and signaled to Israel that Egyptian armor in the Sinai would soon be a threat, as it had been in 1956. Some speculate that U Thant could have stalled Nasser a few weeks—for example, by insisting that the UN Security Council debate withdrawing UNEF—to let things calm. Critics say the Burmese U Thant was too eager to please Nasser, a fellow Third World neutralist.

Next, on May 22, Nasser declared the Strait of Tiran closed to Israeli shipping—in the face of Israel's warning that it would constitute a *casus belli*. The ship channel passes through Egyptian territorial waters and is easily blocked by mines and shore batteries. Israeli Prime Minister Levi Eshkol asked Washington, which had promised to keep the Strait open in 1957, what it was going to do. President

Lyndon Johnson, trapped in the Vietnam War, could do nothing. This confirmed Israelis' longstanding conviction that they must look after their own security; outside powers are undependable.

For Israel, the final move came on May 30, when King Hussein of Jordan, hitherto extremely cautious, signed a three-country alliance with Egypt and Syria. Hussein may have wanted to stay out of the war but, with a majority-Palestinian population (many of whom wished to overthrow him), felt he had to show solidarity with the Arab cause. (Burdened by the same fears, Hussein, although personally pro-American, gave verbal and some material support to Iraq in the 1991 Gulf War.)

After days of agonizing debate, Israel's government decided to **pre-empt**. No one was sure it would work, but they were sure they could not wait for the enemy to strike first. On June 5, 1967, Israel launched a textbook-perfect three-front war that stunned the world and soon became known as the Six Day War. (In 1867 Bismarck beat Austria in the Six Week War.) American officers, then bogged down in Vietnam, complained in jealousy at the quick, decisive Israeli war. Israeli officers learned many of the tactics at the U.S. Army Command and General Staff College at Fort Leavenworth, Kansas.

First, Israeli jets came in low across the Mediterranean—at one point tailing a commercial jetliner to disguise their presence on Egyptian radar—and destroyed most Egyptian air power on the ground in the first hours of the war. Then Israeli jets knocked out Egyptian tanks in the Sinai, enabling Israeli armor to race to the Suez Canal in two days.

King Hussein of Jordan honored his pledge to enter the war, and Jordanian artillery in the West Bank began shelling Israel. This gave Israelis the excuse to do what they had longed for: seize the Old City of Jerusalem, which they did with three battalions of paratroopers, who surrounded East Jerusalem and stormed through it, pausing in awe at the Wailing Wall, the western wall of the last temple. Jordan was out of action, and with little resistance Israeli forces took the entire West Bank.

The third phase, on days five and six of the war, was the hardest and bloodiest: straight up the Golan Heights with tanks and infantry against entrenched and bunkered Syrian positions. Time was important, as Moscow promised to send troops to support its Arab client states. Washington passed word to Israel to wrap it up quickly. The dead from the Six Day War: 983 Israelis and 4,296 Arabs. Israel's victory was brilliant but did not lead to peace. The Arabs simply refused to negotiate (see box on page 94).

THE 1973 WAR

The Arabs call it the Ramadan War, for it came during the holy month of Ramadan, when Muslims fast during daylight hours. Israelis call it the Yom Kippur War, for it came when Jews observe the Day of Atonement, one of their holiest. Some call it the October War. We will call it simply the 1973 war. Several steps led up to it.

---

pre-empt   To strike first on the eve of war.

 *Peace*

WHY NO PEACE IN 1967

Rather naively, Israel expected that in the aftermath of the Six Day War the Arab countries would, in the parlance of bygone centuries, "sue for peace." They would say enough of war, agree to some compromises, and sign peace treaties. Instead, meeting in Khartoum, Sudan, on September 1, 1967, the Arab countries passed their famous triple rejection: no recognition of Israel, no peace, and no negotiations.

The problem was that the Six Day War—thanks to the Soviet threat to intervene—ended too soon and was not as decisive as many thought. Israel seized no Arab capitals—Cairo, Amman, and Damascus were far from the fronts at the war's end—or even vital territories. Jordan was hurt by the loss of the West Bank, but Egypt and Syria suffered only humiliation from their losses, respectively, of the Sinai and Golan Heights. Much of the Egyptian, Jordanian, and Syrian armies were still intact if bloodied and were quickly resupplied by the Soviets. The Arab countries did not sue for peace because they did not have to.

If the war had lasted longer and Israel had really crushed the enemy main forces and taken their capitals, then Egypt, Jordan, and Syria would have had to settle. Instead, the war was frozen in mid leap, *bellum interruptum*. Instead of peace settlements among the warring parties, the region got UN Security Council Resolution 242. Something similar happened with the 1991 Gulf War, which left Saddam Hussein in power and led directly to the 2003 Gulf War. As Edward Luttwak commented on such situations: "Give war a chance." War is horrible, but a series of incomplete wars is even worse.

In the aftermath of Egypt's defeat in 1967, Egyptian President Nasser took responsibility for the debacle and resigned, but cheering crowds implored him to stay, and he did. Nasser does indeed bear much responsibility; his decisions made the war inevitable. He had built himself up as the hero of the Arabs and then had to deliver on it. To hide Egyptian shame at having been beaten by the technologically superior Israeli air force, Nasser charged that actually U.S. jets had bombed Egypt during the war. In the face of this preposterous lie, Washington broke relations with Cairo; they were not restored until 1973. Arabs tend to be awfully loose with their words (see box on "Fighting Words" on page 95).

To restore Egyptian self-confidence and get the world to take Egypt seriously, Egypt had to recover the Sinai Peninsula, in Israeli hands since 1967. In holding this vast desert, Israel made what might be termed the "**Maginot Line** mistake": supposing that fixed fortifications, lightly manned, could repel an attack. After victory in 1967, Israel constructed on the east bank of the Suez Canal the Bar Lev Line, named after one of their generals. It consisted of bunkers for observers and weapons, and withstood Nasser's "war of attrition," artillery duels from 1969 to 1970. It required few troops, as any Egyptian attack could be detected in advance, giving Israel time to mobilize its forces. The Suez Canal would

Maginot Line   French fortifications against Germany before World War II.

C : *Cultures*

FIGHTING WORDS

Israel picks up Arab radio broadcasts, and many Israelis understand Arabic (many are from Arab countries). The air waves in 1967, especially from Egypt's Voice of the Arabs, were full of rage and promises to erase Israel and Israelis. Much of this was hyperbole; exaggerated rhetoric is part of Arab culture. Leaders especially are expected to use dire accusations and threats; it plays well with the home audience. (Notice how Saddam Hussein in 1991 and 2003 promised to fight to the bitter end.) Nonetheless, in 1967 Nasser swore on the radio that he was ready for war and welcomed it. Some suspect he was bluffing, but the Israelis took him literally and called his bluff. Never bluff.

Israelis, especially those of European origin, are more careful with words, using few of them and weighing their meanings. (Hebrew is a very concise language.) Further, the early Zionist pioneers were fed up with windy ideologues who talked a lot of theory but could not get off their duffs to do anything. They vowed to go heavy on deeds and light on words, building a tough, no-nonsense culture based on hard work and results. (Soviet Communists tried, less successfully, to build a similar culture.)

The very different use of words by the two cultures makes their clashes worse. Israelis take literally the fiery Arab words: "If they say it, they must mean it. When they scream they're going to kill us all, we must take them literally. When we say something, we mean it." Israel, using few words, then takes forceful military measures, which causes the Arabs to scream even more. Fighting words lead to more fights. In recent years, with the spread of education and modernity in the Arab world, some Arab intellectuals have become moderate and rational in their rhetoric, a hopeful sign of cultural change.

---

serve as Israel's moat. Actually, some Israelis, including General Ariel Sharon, warned against relying on the Bar Lev Line and urged using the mountains of Sinai to the east as Israel's main line of resistance. As noted earlier, having more territory does not necessarily make you more secure.

In 1973, the Egyptian army held a series of maneuvers to lull Israel into thinking the movement of troops and armor were just drills. Egyptian military communications were heavy, but they had been heavy for a long time, so Israel took no special note. The United States, however, did warn Israel about "increased Egyptian communications security," meaning more encrypted messages, a possible tip-off. An Israeli commission after the war admitted Israel was taken by surprise in 1973.

The Egyptian attack across the Suez Canal on October 6, 1973, was daring and well executed, something Israelis thought Egyptians could not carry out. Commandos paddled across the Canal at relatively weak spots so that military engineers could cut openings in the sand banks with fire hoses. Pontoon bridges then brought across trucks and armor, which fanned out behind the lightly held Bar Lev Line, capturing it the first day. On the same day in coordination with Egypt, Syrian (and some Iraqi) forces smashed into the Golan Heights with a huge armored force.

P : *Personalities*

ANWAR SADAT

After Nasser died of natural causes in 1970, another Egyptian revolutionary army officer, Anwar Sadat, took over. Sadat, from a poor village family, was a more subtle manipulator than Nasser and reversed some of his policies. Sadat recognized that Egypt had become much too dependent on the Soviet Union, both for the Aswan dam and for military advice and hardware. He also recognized that U.S. influence in the region, especially on Israel, was crucial to getting a peace settlement. "The United States holds 90 percent of the cards," he used to say, an exaggeration but a welcome corrective to Nasser's anti-Americanism.

Sadat therefore deliberately worsened Cairo's relations with Moscow and improved them with Washington. He found fault (deservedly) with Soviet engineering at Aswan and had European firms complete the project. He shopped elsewhere for arms, annoying Moscow. In 1971, he sent Soviet military advisors home, something Washington liked. Sadat put out feelers to President Nixon to get peace talks with Israel going. Unfortunately, neither Washington nor Jerusalem nor many Arab capitals took Sadat seriously. Some recalled Nasser's nickname for him: "Mr. Yes-Yes." Sadat solved this problem by going to war in 1973, after which he was taken very seriously. Israel invited him to visit in 1977 and signed a peace treaty with him in 1979 (see next chapter).

Sadat, perhaps the most appealing figure of the twentieth-century Middle East, had a vision larger than mere nationalism. Sadat was gunned down by Islamic extremists in 1981, and no one has taken his place in the region. His journey from warrior to peacemaker does not prove that good will alone can settle a terrible quarrel. It shows, rather, that the proper balances of power and psychologies may enable realistic statesmen to take steps to peace.

In the six years since 1967, the technological nature of warfare had changed, and Egyptians and Syrians showed they could master it. Microelectronics now enabled them to knock out Israeli aircraft and tanks, areas where previously Israel held a big advantage. Israeli losses were larger than before. Israel, of course, immediately mobilized. A large column under the bold General Sharon (later prime minister) crashed through Egyptian lines between the two Bitter Lakes at the southern end of the Suez Canal and crossed to the *west* side of the Canal, trapping the Egyptian Third Army on the east side. Meanwhile, on the Golan Heights Israel and Syria fought the biggest tank battle in history, bigger than Kursk in Russia in 1943. Israel prevailed and pushed the Syrian forces half-way back to Damascus. The losses in 1973 were heavier and narrower than in 1967: 2,838 Israelis killed to 8,528 Arabs. Israel saw that it might not always prevail.

Again, the war stalled, in part because Washington delivered enough munitions to Israel to keep it from losing but not enough to decisively triumph. Moscow again threatened to intervene, a threat nullified by President Nixon's firm warning and his placing of U.S. nuclear forces on alert. In 1973 Washington manipulated cleverly and constructively (see page 318), leading to a military and psychological balance of power between Israel and Egypt. Out of this came Sadat's historic visit to

C : *Cultures*

ISRAELI OVERCONFIDENCE

In the 1956 and 1967 wars a victorious Israel became convinced that it had the brains, daring, and skill to trounce its Arab opponents, who were deemed permanently backward in technology and inept and cowardly in war. The only time Arabs fight well is when they are cornered, Israelis used to say; just give them an escape route and they'll take it. Overconfidence in war, as in sport, can be disastrous, as Israel learned in the 1973 war.

What Israelis neglected is the fact that everyone has a learning curve, and that sooner or later Arabs would develop the high-tech skills and bravery under fire the Israelis thought they had a monopoly on. Victory is a wasting asset; it lulls you into thinking you will be permanently victorious.

Jerusalem in 1977 and the first Arab-Israeli peace settlement, between Egypt and Israel in 1979 (see pages 103–105). If you want peace, you must manipulate disputants until they see that they have more to gain by negotiating than by fighting. A hands-off approach does not work.

THE LEBANON INCURSION

Israel's 1982–2000 incursion into Lebanon was the fifth Arab-Israeli war. It was Israel's messiest and most frustrating military action and ultimately a failure. Israel had been able to beat enemy countries, but it could not fight chaos. At that time Lebanon as a country barely existed; it was more like a Hobbesian war of each against all. Israelis were arrogant to suppose they could fix this. (It was equally arrogant of the United States to suppose its "peacekeeping" forces in Beirut could bring peace; they were blown up by a suicide truck bomb. See Chapter 17.)

Lebanon's Muslim majority has grown increasingly discontented with Christian rule. In 1958, amidst civil strife, U.S. Marines landed briefly (see Chapter 17). But starting in 1971, things got much worse. Since 1967, the main headquarters of the Palestinian Liberation Organization had been in Amman, Jordan, where they increasingly acted like a state within a state. The Jordanian army, composed heavily of Bedouin, resented them. Palestinian terrorists tried to assassinate Jordan's King Hussein in September 1971. This sparked a bloody showdown between the **PLO** and the Jordanian army; the army won and forced the PLO to

PLO   Palestine Liberation Organization, formed in 1964, chaired by Yasser Arafat from 1969 to 2004; leads Palestine Authority; contains several factions, some violent.

D : *Domestic Structures*

LEBANON'S SHAKY MOSAIC

Lebanon epitomizes the **weak states** common in the developing areas. Its government does not near-ly control the country. Armed militias run their own turfs. Syria and Israel have occupied much of Lebanon. For better-off people, Lebanon had been a delight but is rent by major inequalities of wealth and power.

Lebanon's weak domestic structure is to blame. France gave Lebanon (and Syria) independence in 1943, and a National Pact whereby the elites of all major Lebanese religious groups—a total of eighteen are officially recognized—shared power in what is called **consociation**, a type of pluralism but not real democracy. In parliament, Christians and Muslims were represented in a constant 6:5 ratio. The presi-dent was always a Maronite Christian, the prime minister always a Sunni, and the speaker of parliament a Shi'a. Christians had the most power and wealth even though, over the years, they slipped into minority status. No census has been taken since 1932. Christians are now estimated at 35 percent, Shi'a at 35 per-cent, Sunni at 25 percent, and Druze at 5 percent.

The National Pact broke down because Muslims—especially Shi'a, who are also the poorest Lebanese—grew rapidly and demanded more power, which the Christians did not wish to relinquish. Start-ing in 1958, violence flared and got much worse in the 1970s. In 1989, Saudi Arabia mediated the Taif agreement that gave a 1:1 ratio to Christians and Muslims in parliament, still a fiction. To a certain ex-tent, the rise of Hezbollah is a Shi'a demand for domestic political power commensurate with their num-bers. Lebanon's 2005 elections under the 1:1 formula were not fully democratic.

move its headquarters to Beirut. (The Palestinian extremist Black September group took its name from this fight.) From the south of Lebanon, Palestinians fighters, most of them in Yasser Arafat's mainstream Al Fatah, launched raids and rocket attacks on northern Israel.

The PLO presence accelerated the internal collapse of Lebanon. Lebanese Christians tried to hang on to their old power and privilege, but Muslims turned increasingly radical and demanded a new political and economic deal. By 1975 Lebanon had fallen apart as a dozen politico-religious armies battled. Syria took advantage of the chaos to occupy the Bekaa Valley of eastern Lebanon, which it claimed was Syrian territory the French never should have included in Lebanon. Syrian agents still manipulate Lebanese politics and assassinate politi-cians hostile to Syria. A one-ton car bomb got former Prime Minister Rafik Hariri in 2005.

Some Lebanese Christians started seeing a tie to Israel as their solution and established contacts. Some Israelis started thinking that ousting the PLO and

---

weak state   National government unable to enforce its writ.

consociation   General agreement and power sharing among the leaders of all major groups.

 *Conflicts*

THE SIX WARS OF ISRAEL

War of Independence	1948–1949	Israel survives Arab invasions and ends up with most of Palestine.
Sinai Campaign	1956	Israel, in collusion with Britain and France, takes Sinai.
Six Day War	1967	Israel takes Sinai and Gaza from Egypt, West Bank and Jerusalem from Jordan, and Golan Heights from Syria.
October War	1973	Israel narrowly beats back Egypt and Syria.
Lebanon incursion	1982–2000	Israel holds southern Lebanon.
Hezbollah War	2006	Israel again in southern Lebanon.

returning Christians to power in Beirut would safeguard their northern border. Both oversimplified an extremely complex situation (as did Washington) and soon made the chaos even worse.

In 1982 Israel's ambassador was shot and wounded in London by an agent of Abu Nidal, an anti-PLO Palestinian nationalist (and a "suicide" in Baghdad in 2002, shot three times in the head). Israel used the shooting as a pretext to invade the south of Lebanon to clear it of Fatah fighters. Israel called it "Operation Peace for Galilee," and said that it would go only about 25 miles into Lebanon. At first Shi'a in the south of Lebanon, who never liked the Palestinians and their disruptions, welcomed the Israelis. Fatah simply pulled back further north, and Israel pursued, reaching Beirut and shelling its neighborhoods for two months. In August 1982, with help from the U.S. Navy, the PLO left Beirut, its headquarters since 1971, taking some 15,000 PLO fighters with it. Arafat later set up a new headquarters in Tunis. Israel celebrated briefly, but it had just opened a can of worms. Syria held back, not wishing to tangle with Israel. Besides, the more chaos Israel inflicted on Lebanon, the easier it would be for Syria to take it over.

In September 1982 a car bomb killed the leader of Lebanese Maronite Christians, Bashir Gemayel, head of the Phalange militia. The bomb was probably Syria's work, but the Phalange took out its wrath on Palestinians. Phalangists charged into the Sabra and Shatila Palestinian refugee camps in Beirut, killing over 1,000 civilians, including women and children. Israeli soldiers did not participate but watched and did nothing, figuring, "Why not let Christians take care of Palestinians for us?" An Israeli commission later found Defense Minister Ariel Sharon indirectly complicit in the massacre—he had met earlier with Phalange leaders and did nothing to prevent or stop the bloodshed. Israel pulled back but kept a 30-kilometer "security zone" (about 20 miles) in the south of Lebanon, staffed by Israeli soldiers and local Shi'a mercenaries.

Israel also got a formidable new foe in 1982, **Hezbollah**. In 1979 radical Islamists took over Iran (see pages 223–224) and encouraged Shi'a coreligionists throughout the Muslim world to rise up. The Shi'a in Lebanon are poor, discontent, and numerous. In 1982 they founded the militant Hezbollah with weapons, money, and guidance from Iran (funneled through Syria) and harassed Israeli forces in the south of Lebanon. Over eighteen years Israel lost scores of soldiers to ambushes, mines, and suicide bombings in Lebanon. Labor Prime Minister Ehud Barak, a former general and Israel's most-decorated soldier, in 2000 withdrew Israeli forces from Lebanon. Hezbollah boasted they were the only Arabs to defeat Israel and urged Palestinians to use the same tactics.

Hezbollah won twenty-three seats (out of 128) in Lebanon's 2005 parliamentary elections and took two cabinet posts. Some thought it would become moderate. Unlike Palestinians, Lebanese Shi'a have no territorial stake in fighting Israel. But Hezbollah echoes Iran's hatred of Israel, and in 2006 Hezbollah infiltrators seized two Israeli soldiers. Israel retaliated with air strikes on Shi'a neighborhoods and sent ground forces into southern Lebanon. Hezbollah, well trained and armed (by Iran and Syria), stood its ground and rained some of its 12,000 Iranian-supplied rockets onto Israeli towns. It lasted a month and looked like the sixth Arab-Israeli war. Israel had 159 killed, mostly soldiers; Lebanon some 1,200, mostly civilians. A shaky cease-fire depends on the willingness of the Lebanese army and UN peacekeepers to occupy southern Lebanon and disarm Hezbollah. Hezbollah chief Hassan Nasrallah claimed to have defeated Israel and became Lebanon's most powerful political figure.

CONCLUSIONS

The six Arab-Israeli wars—1948, 1956, 1967, 1973, and the Lebanon incursions of 1982–2000 and 2006—can be viewed as one long war that never gets settled. The vital national interests of the belligerents are hard to compromise, and the separate wars never reached definitive defeats or victories. Each war has specific causes, but the underlying cause is that Israel exists, and the Arabs, especially the Palestinians, wish it had never existed.

The real losers have been the Palestinian refugees, some three-quarters of a million in 1948 and roughly four million now. At least two wars, 1956 and 1982, were triggered in part by Palestinian attacks on Israel. Israel's wars with neighboring Arab states to some extent served to mask the Palestinian question, which is much harder to solve than wars between countries.

A common mistake is to equate territory with security. Israel occupied enemy territory, but the addition of the West Bank and Gaza, with its millions of angry Palestinians, did not make Israel more secure. In two wars, 1956 and 1967, Israel "preempted." When it failed to take preemptive action in 1973, Egypt breached the Bar Lev Line along the Suez Canal. We have likely not seen the last Arab-Israeli war.

Hezbollah   Also spelled Hisballah, Hizbullah, and other ways; "Party of God," armed, radical Shi'a movement, aided by Iran.

KEY TERMS

cease-fire (p. 84)	Knesset (p. 85)
client state (p. 90)	Maginot Line (p. 94)
collusion (p. 90)	majoritarian (p. 85)
consociation (p. 98)	pan-Arabism (p. 88)
coup (p. 88)	PLO (p. 97)
escalation (p. 90)	pre-empt (p. 93)
fertility rate (p. 87)	proportional representation (p. 85)
fifth column (p. 87)	spike (p. 91)
Hezbollah (p. 100)	weak state (p. 98)

FURTHER REFERENCE

Bar-On, Mordechai, ed. *A Never-Ending Conflict: A Guide to Israeli Military History.* Westport, CT: Praeger, 2004.

Bickerton, Ian J., and Carla L. Klausner. *A Concise History of the Arab-Israeli Conflict,* 5th ed. Upper Saddle River, NJ: Prentice Hall, 2006.

Herzog, Chaim. *The Arab-Israeli Wars: War and Peace in the Middle East.* New York: Vintage, 1984.

Milton-Edwards, Beverley, and Peter Hinchcliffe. *Conflicts in the Middle East since 1945,* 2nd ed. New York: Routledge, 2003.

Morris, Benny. *Making Israel.* London: I. B. Tauris, 2004.

Oren, Michael B. *Six Days of War: June 1967 and the Making of the Modern Middle East.* New York: Oxford University Press, 2002.

Pappe, Ilan. *A History of Modern Palestine: One Land, Two Peoples,* 2nd ed. New York: Cambridge University Press, 2006.

Pollack, Kenneth M. *Arabs at War: Military Effectiveness, 1948–1991.* Lincoln, NE: University of Nebraska Press, 2002.

Thomas, Baylis. *How Israel Was Won: A Concise History of the Arab-Israeli Conflict.* Lanham, MD: Lexington Books, 1999.

Westwood, John. *The History of the Middle East Wars.* North Dighton, MA: World Publications, 2002.

6 Is Peace Possible?

- Are Americans too optimistic to understand the Middle East?
- Have efforts for peace been insufficient?
- How has the UN worked for Middle East peace?
- Under what circumstances can diplomacy work?
- What do Israelis want from a peace agreement?
- What do Palestinians want from a peace agreement?
- Can the above two be compromised?
- Explain the "downward spiral."
- Do unilateral Israeli steps stabilize things?

We begin this chapter with the unhappy thought that peace may be impossible. Americans, products of an optimistic society, are uncomfortable with this notion. On the evidence, though, the conflicts and wars between Arabs and Israelis we reviewed in the previous two chapters do not point toward peace. We must put aside three common misconceptions: (1) that the UN has not tried hard enough to settle the Arab-Israeli conflict; (2) that Washington has not tried hard enough to settle the Arab-Israeli conflict; (3) that Arabs and Israelis could settle it if only they would meet together. There have been massive efforts in all three areas. Lack of peace is not from want of trying.

The United States has been involved in Middle East peace efforts from the beginning. U.S. involvement during and after the 1973 October War became especially deep. Secretary of State Kissinger practiced "shuttle diplomacy," flying tirelessly between Cairo, Jerusalem, and Damascus to arrange cease-fires. For years the State Department had a top diplomat with rank of ambassador and a staff working full-time on Arab-Israeli peace. U.S. presidents, especially Carter and Clinton, have hosted numerous meetings—often at Camp David, the president's personal retreat in the Maryland mountains—of Egyptian, Palestinian, and Israeli leaders.

 *Peace*

UN Efforts at Middle East Peace

1947—UN Partition Plan, General Assembly Resolution 181. See pages 74–75.

1948—UN General Assembly Resolution 194 established a "conciliation commission" to settle the first Arab-Israeli war.

1967—UN Security Council Resolution 242 called for Israel to withdraw from its conquests in the Six Day War in exchange for the Arabs making peace. This "land for peace" idea became the basis for all subsequent formulas for settlement.

1973—UN Security Council Resolution 338 called for a cease-fire during the October War and implementation of Resolution 242.

1978—UN Security Council Resolution 425 called for Israel to withdraw from southern Lebanon.

The UN passes resolutions on the Middle East nearly every year. After several iterations, one comes to doubt the effectiveness of UN resolutions. Much the same came of UN resolutions on Iraq and Iran: The UN passes lofty sentiments with no means of implementation; they are therefore ignored by strong-willed leaders who deem their countries and causes just. Threat of a veto by one of the Security Council's five permanent members—the United States, Britain, France, Russia, and China—often kills stronger resolutions.

And Israel has had numerous contacts with Arab countries—some official, some informal, most of them secret—since its founding. After Egypt's 1952 revolution, for example, Egyptian and Israeli diplomats met secretly in Paris. But a 1954 Israeli attempt to bomb the American library in Cairo (to worsen U.S.-Egyptian ties), the rise of Palestinian *fedayeen* attacks into Israel, and Israel's retaliatory raids killed this faint possibility. King Hussein of Jordan had repeated personal contacts with Israeli diplomats over the years. Even in the middle of a war, enemies maintain discreet contacts with each other, usually in the capitals of neutral third countries. Please do not say, "If only they could meet." They have met many times. It is not lack of personal chemistry (see the box on "atmospherics" on page 107) but inability to compromise what they deem their vital national interests that prevents peace settlements.

Sadat's Incredible Journey

Egyptian President Sadat won much in the October War of 1973. He vindicated his country by showing that Egyptians could fight. He got back part of the Sinai. The world now took him seriously. He reestablished diplomatic relations with the United States and hosted a visit by President Nixon. But he still did not have all of the Sinai, and he did not have peace.

 *Peace*

THE UN'S FIRST EFFORTS

From its founding in 1945, the United Nations has been deeply involved in the Palestine question, initially through the tireless efforts of Ralph Bunche, the first black American to earn a Ph.D. in political science (at Harvard). During World War II Bunche became a State Department official and worked on setting up the new United Nations. He saw the need for a UN committee to handle non-self-governing territories—in 1945, most of the great colonial empires were still intact—and how to decolonize them. The U.S. delegation was not interested, so Bunche took his idea to the Australian delegation, which was. Bunche built support for and got a UN Trusteeship Council, which inherited the mandates set up by the League of Nations, including Palestine. The 1947 UN partition plan aimed at ending the British mandate in a way that would allow Arabs and Jews to live in peace.

Many UN efforts do not lead to peace. The problem is generally not flawed plans or lack of enforcement mechanisms. The UN has no armed forces or even police; all are on temporary loan (at high salaries) from member countries that wish to participate. The conflict itself may be so deep and bitter that there is no peaceful solution. Debating the issue in the UN puts a diplomatic gloss on the violence but does essentially nothing to get the warring parties to compromise. When—and only when—the sides are ready to compromise, the UN can facilitate contacts, draft documents, and put in place stabilization measures, such as truce observers. The UN has no enforcement powers.

As soon as open war broke out in 1948, the UN, still trying to implement its partition plan, set up a Truce Commission and sent mediators to calm the fighting. By that time, with five Arab armies invading, the partition plan was road kill. The chief UN diplomat on the scene, Swedish Count Folke Bernadotte, arranged a **truce** in June that lasted a month, giving Israel time to buy Czech small arms and other weapons. He also recommended changes in the plan, giving all of Galilee to the Israelis and all the Negev to the Arabs. Jerusalem, as envisaged by the original plan, was to remain under international supervision. An Irgun member assassinated Bernadotte for allegedly selling out Israel (he had not). An angry Ben Gurion ordered the Irgun to disband, but none of its members were ever punished. Israel has not been good about cooperating with the UN, viewing it as hostile and pro-Arab.

By late 1948, when both sides were mutually exhausted, they agreed to **mediation** by Ralph Bunche, now a UN official, who invited delegations from Israel and the five Arab countries to the Greek island of Rhodes. The Arabs would not meet face-to-face with the Israelis, so Bunche put them on separate floors of the same hotel. He shuttled between floors in what are called **proximity talks**, adding suggestions of his own. He got a series of **armistices** between the Arab countries and Israel in early 1949 and won the 1950 Nobel Peace Prize. Unfortunately, the armistices could not turn into peace settlements, for an underlying problem remained; namely, the Palestinians' situation.

---

truce   A long cease-fire.

mediation   Neutral third party makes suggestions for compromise.

proximity talks   Close, but not in the same room.

armistice   Stable, longer-lasting *truces;* does not imply a peace settlement.

To gain that, Sadat delivered another surprise. In late 1977 Sadat stated that he would be willing to visit Israel. Actually, secret contacts probably began earlier. One story (unconfirmed) has it that Israel's Mossad intelligence service learned of a plot by Egyptian Muslim extremists to kill Sadat. (In 1981, they did.) Israel's new prime minister, Menachem Begin, former Irgun chief and a right-wing hawk, ordered the information to be passed on to Cairo, and this began a dialog. Sadat pushed matters along when CBS's Walter Cronkite, the dean of American newscasters, asked Sadat what would happen if Begin invited him to Jerusalem. (The question was likely planted in advance.) Sadat said he'd go. On November 17, 1977, Begin invited and Sadat accepted.

The world was astonished and delighted, for it seemed to herald the beginning of the end of a series of ghastly wars. Just two days later, on November 19, Sadat jetted a mere 40 minutes to Ben Gurion airport near Tel Aviv and motorcaded to Jerusalem for meetings with Begin and a speech to the Knesset. The meetings were awkward and chilly, but they got things rolling. U.S. President Jimmy Carter, a religious man who dreamed of peace in the Holy Land, in 1978 brought Sadat and Begin together at Camp David. Long negotiations led both sides to conclude they had more to gain by ending their war, and on the White House lawn on March 26, 1979, they signed the first Arab-Israeli peace treaty. Sadat and Begin jointly won the Nobel Peace Prize in 1978. Egypt got back the entire Sinai. Israel even demolished settlements in Sinai over the violent objections of Israeli settlers (a prelude to the 2005 withdrawal of Israelis from Gaza). Egypt did not get back the Gaza Strip, which it had never claimed as part of Egypt.

Many Israelis had assumed that as soon as Israel had a peace treaty with Egypt, its biggest and most dangerous foe, most of the other Arab countries would quickly follow suit, like a logjam giving way. This did not happen. Each Arab country has its own problems and interests, which may point away from peace with Israel. A second agreement signed in 1979 vowed to solve the Palestinian problem, but both Israel and Egypt forgot about it. Many Arabs reviled Sadat for selling out the Palestinians.

THE PROBLEM THAT WON'T GO AWAY

The Palestinian problem will not go away; the 1967 war brought it to the forefront. Palestinians, with one of the world's highest birth rates, saw their numbers soar to perhaps 5 million. Their status has been dangling since at least the 1967 war, which removed the last fiction that the neighboring Arab states would protect them. They were neither Jordanians, nor Egyptians, nor Israelis, and did not yet have their own country. In peace talks and accords, the Arab side always insisted on provisions for Palestinian statehood, but the Israelis viewed the clauses as nonbinding and implemented few of them. The Palestinian situation had to explode.

Geography

BOUND EGYPT

Egypt is bounded on the north by the Mediterranean Sea;
on the east by Israel, the Gulf of Aqaba, and the Red Sea;
on the south by Sudan;
and on the west by Libya.

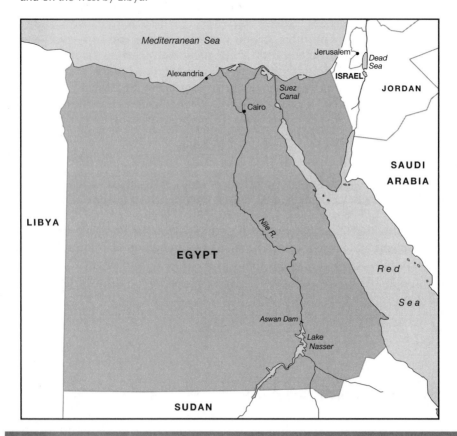

   The first **intifada**, 1987–1991, seems to have begun spontaneously as West
Bank Palestinians, seeing their lands eaten away by Israeli settlements, started throw-
ing rocks at Israeli police and soldiers. Arafat, in Tunisia, did not instigate the uprising; he reacted only afterward by supporting it. He was not even very aware of what
was going on in the West Bank and Gaza Strip, a continual problem with absentee

---

intifada   Literally, "shaking"; Arabic for uprising.

 *Peace*

THE DECEPTION OF "ATMOSPHERICS"

Henry Kissinger, national security advisor and secretary of state in the 1970s, was also a major scholar (Harvard) of diplomacy. He constantly warned against confusing **atmospherics** with the substance of negotiations. Statesmen deliberately cultivate atmospherics to build a psychology of acceptance and sway public opinion. Then if things go wrong it will be the other side's fault. The media especially like to note the superficial smiles and handshakes and read into them progress on the talks: "Look, they're getting along nicely!"

This can be terribly deceptive. The two sides are often miles apart and making little progress, usually the case in Middle East negotiations. One-sided statements released during talks may deliberately raise false hopes as a form of pressure. These negotiators are hard-headed people who have fought long for their cause and are not about to give anything away. They operate under orders from their home governments that allow them little room for on-the-spot compromises. To be sure, nice atmospherics are better than bad ones, but friendly photo-ops at the start of a conference predict nothing.

leaders. Palestinians came to view Arafat as aging, ineffectual, and corrupt, and turned to Hamas, which started as an Islamic charitable organization in 1987 but soon turned violent. Ironically, Israel had earlier approved of Hamas as a counterweight to the PLO, figuring that its religious fundamentalism was better than the secular PLO's political focus, an example of **blowback** (see page 261).

The first intifada ended after the 1991 Gulf War. Many Palestinians foolishly pinned their hopes on an Iraqi victory, expecting that Saddam Hussein would then liberate them. Some celebrated the Iraqi Scud missiles that hit Israel (just as some celebrated the 9/11 attacks on America). Iraq's quick defeat in 1991 showed there would be no help from Baghdad. Now American power and prestige were appreciated in the Middle East. Further, President George Bush 41 wisely included several Arab countries in his anti-Iraq coalition, but he had to promise them a conference on the Israel-Palestine problem after the war. The Gulf War thus opened a window of opportunity for negotiations.

Co-chaired by President Bush and Soviet President Gorbachev (who was barely clinging to power and was about to lose it), Arab and Israeli delegates met in Madrid in the fall of 1991 for two days and agreed on an ambitious agenda. Israel would not accept a separate PLO delegation, but it did accept Palestinians from Jerusalem as part of a "Jordanian-Palestinian" delegation. A major sticking point for Israel: The 1968 Palestine National Covenant called for the destruction of Israel (finally dropped in 1998). Many celebrated Madrid as an historic breakthrough because Arab and Israeli diplomats negotiated for the first time face-to-face. The atmospherics were good, but little of substance was achieved (see box above).

atmospherics   Pleasant settings and personalities presumed to make diplomatic meetings succeed.
blowback   Supporting a group that later turns against you.

G ⦂ *Geography*

THE ISRAELI SETTLEMENTS

For a few years after the Six Day War, the Labor government of Israel did little beyond the **green line** (that demarcated the West Bank and Gaza), thinking that they would soon have a peace treaty with the Arabs. A few Jewish settlements were started in the Jordan Valley for security reasons. After the 1973 war, which showed Israel's vulnerability, the Israeli government acquiesced to construction of more settlements in the West Bank. The hawkish **Likud** government took office in 1977 and encouraged Jewish "hillcrest settlements" closer to Israel's border. Likud in effect told the world that Israel was in the West Bank to stay, never mind that the Fourth Geneva Convention of 1949, which Israel signed, forbids settling on lands seized by military force. The UN continually condemns Israel for its settlements. The Labor party, initially more cautious, doubled the settler population in the West Bank during the seven years of the Oslo peace process (1993–2000), when Labor governed.

From 30,000 settlers in 1984, the Jewish population in the West Bank grew to over a quarter of a million in some 125 settlements, some of them pleasant towns with as many as 25,000 settlers. All together—with settlements, security zones, military areas, and settler-only bypass roads—Israel controls 40 percent of the West Bank, much of it seized from Palestinian owners. Gaza had seventeen Jewish settlements, abandoned unilaterally under Israeli government order in 2005.

An estimated quarter of the settlers are "ideological," that is, they have political and religious motives for setting up new towns. Typically, a group of settlers, often led by the Gush Emunim (Bloc of the Faithful), would claim a rocky hilltop of little economic value, arguing that they were "creating facts on the ground" that God had granted them as Judea and Samaria (they do not use the term "West Bank"). With government approval or without, they quickly set up house trailers for the first occupants. Then they swiftly build stone-and-concrete row houses, often employing local Arab labor, and sell the homes at bargain prices (starting at $60,000) to Jewish settlers, who get cheaper mortgage rates, lower taxes, and subsidized local government. A majority of the buyers simply want affordable housing. For jobs, they commute to nearby Israel by car, always running the risk of ambush. Settlement growth slowed in recent years because of the obvious danger of living in the West Bank.

Ariel Sharon, then a cabinet minister in charge of the West Bank, was the master architect for its Jewish settlement. First, the settlements are on hilltops to improve their security and keep watch on the surrounding terrain. Second, also for security purposes, they form two swaths, one of fewer settlers down the Jordan Valley, a second and much more populous one down the Samarian hills near the 1967 border. With scattered Jewish settlements elsewhere, patches of the land in between the two swaths—perhaps half the total of the West Bank—would be left to Palestinians, who would

---

green line   UN manner of marking cease-fire lines by green barrels; in Israel indicates 1949–1967 borders.

Likud   Israel's main right-wing party.

have local self-governance but not a state. Third, the settlements tap into the aquifer under the Samarian hills and tie it into Israel's water system. Sharon's map, if implemented, would prevent any territorially coherent Palestinian state on the West Bank; it would look like a Swiss cheese with many large holes, connected by roads and "security zones" controlled by Israel.

One can see religious, defensive, hydrological, and territorial purposes to Israeli settlement in the West Bank, but all seemed to aim at eventually incorporating it into Israel itself, in effect recreating Britain's Palestine mandate. This idea pleased rightwing Israelis, but the mandate was unworkable and roughly half the inhabitants of an enlarged Israel would be Palestinian Arabs. Any peace plan must take them into consideration.

Palestinians, seeing more of their lands and aquifers taken every year, turned violent. They murdered settlers and ambushed their road traffic. Settlers went armed and shot Palestinians they thought threatened them, including women and children. The Israeli army patrolled and controlled most of the West Bank. Many Israeli soldiers did not like this duty, as it meant shooting civilians. Elaborate and expensive security fences did cut the number of suicide bombings and made Israelis feel a little safer. The fences cut off thousands of Palestinians from fields, water, and roads, forcing them to leave. Some say the fence will eventually become a border. Several Israeli generals and much of the public favor removing the most outlying of the settlements as indefensible and a drain on military resources. The settlements, originally rationalized as security outposts, have made Israel terribly insecure.

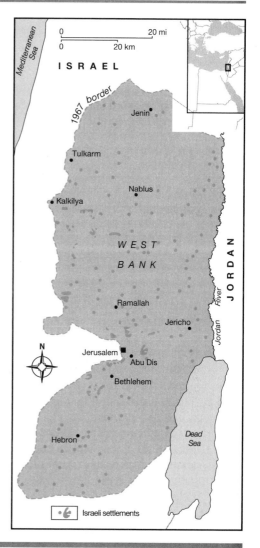

Another momentous event occurred at the very end of 1991: The Soviet Union ceased to exist. Moscow had been the main outside backer of the Arab cause, providing vast quantities of arms, especially to the radical Syrian and Iraqi regimes. Suddenly the Arabs had no major outside power to support them. Only the United States now mattered. Together, the two signal events of 1991—the Gulf War and the Soviet collapse—changed the power map of the region.

P : *Peace*

THE KILLING OF RABIN

Labor party Prime Minister Yitzhak Rabin, a career soldier, born and raised on a kibbutz, finally saw the futility of warfare and took a chance for peace in the early 1990s. After some diplomatic progress (the "Oslo process"), he shook hands with Arafat on the White House lawn in 1993. Departing from a peace rally in Tel Aviv in late 1995, he was gunned down by a fanatic Israeli law student who viewed any concessions to Palestinians as a sellout of Israel. (He was sentenced to life in prison; Israel currently does not have capital punishment.)

The tragedy extended beyond the death of one courageous leader, as more than a few right-wing Israelis sympathized with the assassin. Some Israelis, perhaps as many as one-quarter, oppose returning any land to Palestinians and want the entire West Bank. Although fewer in number and less lethal than Palestinian terrorists, Israeli terrorists are also capable of blocking and reversing attempts at peace. All subsequent prime ministers of Israel are thus on warning that they must not offer Palestinians too much.

Norwegian diplomats quietly arranged at least fourteen meetings near Oslo where Israeli and PLO representatives made some progress. As part of the "**Oslo** peace process," on September 13, 1993, on the White House lawn, PLO Chairman Yasser Arafat and Israeli Prime Minister Yitzhak Rabin signed a Declaration of Principles on Interim Self-Government for the Palestinians. With President Clinton enveloping both with his arms, the two adversaries shook hands. (As a photo opportunity, it looked much like the 1978 handshake between Begin and Sadat, blessed by President Carter.) Now the two sides halfway recognized each other, a first step.

But little came of Oslo; Arabs and Israelis alike were disappointed. U.S. President Bill Clinton sponsored several follow-up talks. The Palestinians got a new **Palestinian Authority** (PA) that controlled—well, was supposed to control—parts of the West Bank and Gaza. Many Israelis felt that Prime Minister Rabin gave the Palestinians too much, and in late 1995 an Israeli fanatic assassinated him (see box above). After terrorist bombings, **Shin Bet** would identify where they originated, and Israeli armor and helicopter gunships would retaliate into the PA-controlled Gaza Strip and West Bank towns—the biggest are Qalqilya, Tulkarm, Jenin, Nablus, Ramallah, and Bethlehem—to detain or shoot suspects, search for weapons, and bulldoze houses. Israeli strikes enrage more young Palestinians, who carry out more bombings.

Oslo   Shorthand for unsuccessful 1993–2000 Israel-Palestinian peace talks.

Palestinian Authority   Interim government of parts of the West Bank and Gaza, began in 1993.

Shin Bet   Israel's domestic security agency. (Mossad does foreign security and intelligence.)

P : *Personalities*

YASSER ARAFAT

Yasser Arafat (1929–2004), a sort of mirror image of Ariel Sharon (see box on page 114), dedicated his life to "redeeming Palestine." He held some grudging, tactical discussions with Israel for a Palestinian **rump** state, but only as a step to getting all of historical Palestine. Many saw Arafat as inflexible, but Palestinians followed him precisely because of his vision of a full-size, Arab Palestine. The problem is bigger than one person.

Arafat (his *nom de guerre*) was one of seven children of a prominent Jerusalem family. He grew up and studied civil engineering in Cairo, where he became a passionate Palestinian nationalist. Arafat went to Kuwait in 1956 to work as an engineer and contractor and to organize a new militant group, al Fatah, to fight for Palestine and collect funds from the many Palestinian oil workers.

Arab defeat in the 1967 war showed Palestinians they must not depend on other Arab countries. Fatah's ranks swelled. Arafat, in his *kaffiyeh* headcover, became the charismatic symbol of Palestinian resistance and in 1969 took over leadership of the umbrella Palestine Liberation Organization (PLO). In a bloody showdown over who was to control Jordan, King Hussein expelled the PLO in September 1970. The PLO relocated to Beirut, where it fought in Lebanon's long civil war until the Israeli incursion pushed it out in 1982. Arafat then set up in Tunisia, where he was the target of an Israeli air strike.

The 1991 first Gulf War—in which Arafat supported Iraq—opened peace possibilities, and Israel and the PLO recognized each other's right to exist as part of the Oslo process in 1993. This led to setting up the Palestinian Authority (PA), with Arafat as its leader and its headquarters in Ramallah, just north of Jerusalem. The PA was supposed to lead to Palestinian statehood, but the election of hard-line Israeli Prime Minister Benjamin Netanyahu in 1996 ended that. In the Camp David talks Arafat would not budge on key issues—borders, refugees, and Jerusalem. After that, neither Israel nor the United States would negotiate with Arafat.

In the meantime, the PA became a corrupt shambles, unable to provide security or order. Arafat appointed PLO cronies, and between $1 billion and $3 billion went missing. Arafat died in 2004 a very wealthy man. Many Palestinians turned away from the ineffective PLO leadership of the PA and to **rejectionist** groups such as Hamas, which won the PA legislative elections in 2006 and took over the Palestine government. Americans and Israelis saw Arafat as inflexible, but Hamas refused any meetings or negotiations with Israel, which Hamas vowed to destroy. Finding the right personality is only part of the problem. The underlying problem is that few Palestinians will settle for a rump state.

The long-held theory that Arab-Israeli peace should be based on small steps leading up to **final-status** talks must be reexamined. Oslo was a series of small steps aiming at peace, but in a few years the process hit a wall of uncompromisable demands. Oslo never got close to final-status talks, which became a euphemism for "the really hard parts," such as borders, Jerusalem, and the right of Palestinians to

---

rump   Small, leftover portions of a state.

rejectionist   Uncompromising demands that reject peace settlement.

final status   The difficult end goal of the peace process: a Palestinian state and Israeli security.

return to Israel. Some progress was made in the 1990s, but Palestinians and Israelis were still too far apart for a general settlement.

In a last-ditch effort, Clinton called Israeli Prime Minister Ehud Barak and Palestinian leader Arafat to Camp David in July 2000. Barak offered territorial concessions, possibly more than his parliament would ratify. Americans called it a good offer. Arafat saw it as a surrender of Palestinian rights—which include the right of Palestinians to return to their original homes and lands in Israel—and rejected it. The window of opportunity opened by the Gulf War closed, setting the stage for the next, much more dangerous intifada. Israel-Palestinian talks at Taba on the Red Sea in January, 2001, put forward hopeful ideas, but it was held as the second intifada raged and on the eve of Israeli elections. Sharon won and became prime minister, and he opposed compromise. The "Oslo peace process" was over.

THE SECOND PALESTINIAN INTIFADA

In September 2000, after the collapse of the Camp David talks, Ariel Sharon—head of the hard-line Likud party then in **opposition**—visited the Haram es Sharif (Noble Sanctuary) in Jerusalem, the plaza around the Dome of the Rock, Islam's third holiest shrine. This area, which Jews call the Temple Mount, overlooks the Western or Wailing Wall, last remnant of the Temple and sacred to Jews. Sharon wished to show that no part of Israel's capital city was off-limits to Israelis, so he ostentatiously strolled through the Haram with a large security detail. Muslims were outraged at this enemy walking on their hallowed site. Sharon's walk triggered—but by itself did not cause—the second intifada, which grew out of long-standing grievances and the collapse of the Oslo process. At this same time, Lebanese Hezbollahis, Shi'a militants supported by Iran, told radical Palestinians that if Hezbollah could harass Israel into withdrawing from Lebanon, Palestinians could harass Israel into withdrawing from the West Bank and Gaza.

About 2,100 Palestinians and 1,000 Israelis died in the second intifada, many by suicide bombings (Arabs prefer "martyr operations"). Many Palestinians, even young women, volunteered to die by taking several Israelis with them. Bombers have religious and political motives. Many have lost family, friends, and homes to Israeli bullets and bulldozers. Israelis, angry and fearful, voted out the Barak government and replaced it with a new Sharon government in early 2001. The 2003 Israeli elections confirmed the trend by boosting Likud and cutting Labor to its weakest showing ever. Like Americans, Israelis prefer hawks for leaders in time of peril.

INCOMPATIBLE DEMANDS

Peace deals between states are much easier than ending civil strife within a state. Two relative success stories illustrate the relatively simple problems of ending hostility between states. Thanks to the manipulations of Sadat—a surprise 1973 war

---

opposition   Political party in parliament that does not support the prime minister.

G Geography

JERUSALEM INTERNATIONALIZED?

An internationalized Jerusalem—part of both the 1937 Peel Commission and the 1947 UN partition plan—is not a bad idea. It would, unfortunately, require compromise on both the Israeli and Palestinian sides. Jerusalem—the City of David to Jews and *al Quds* (the holy) to Arabs—is sacred to all three Abrahamic religions; it contains their sites and shrines and should be open and welcoming to pilgrims of all faiths. Jerusalem is an extremely important archaeological site and thus a world cultural treasure. More important, putting Jerusalem under international supervision would remove one of the bones of contention between Palestinians and Israelis.

Neither side would accept such an idea; both claim Jerusalem as their own. And what kind of "international" government could supervise this complex, fascinating city? The UN is not equipped for anything like that. One possibility: Move the UN headquarters from Manhattan to Jerusalem, which would become a sort of world District of Columbia (not, to be sure, everyone's favorite model of city governance). An international solution for Jerusalem is intriguing but impractical.

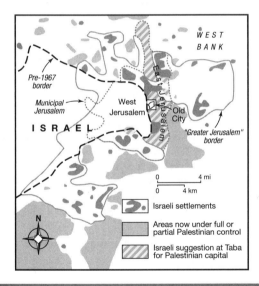

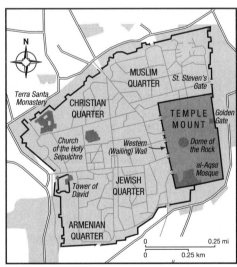

and an even more surprising 1977 visit to Jerusalem—plus arm-twisting by President Carter, Egypt and Israel signed the first Arab-Israeli peace treaty in 1979. Jordan followed in 1994. Their demands could be compromised. For example, when Israel gave back the Sinai to Egypt in 1979, it won Egypt's assurance that it would station no major forces there. This was backed up by UN (including U.S.) peace observers who dotted the desert with electronic listening devices to detect any troop movements. Israel could relax about attack from Egypt, use the Suez Canal, and even send tourists to see the pyramids (no longer advisable for Israelis). Israel and Egypt never developed warm relations—it was called a "cold peace"— but it was much better than war.

P :: *Personalities*

ARIEL SHARON

Ariel Sharon (1928–2007) spent his entire life fighting Arabs, until, near its end, he turned to trying for peace with them. His trajectory resembles that of Yitzhak Rabin, who also went from farmer to warrior to prime minister seeking peace. Israelis of that generation were imbued with the Zionist notion that founding and securing Israel was the only way to save the Jewish people from extermination. They were trained to be tough and decisive, but some, after a lifetime of war, discovered that revenge and reprisal led to a downward spiral that brought no security.

Sharon fought as an officer in five of Israel's wars (see box on page 99). He was born on a cooperative farm and joined the youth wing of the Haganah at age fourteen. In 1948, as a twenty-year-old lieutenant, Sharon was seriously wounded at Latrun, on the road to Jerusalem. In 1953 Colonel Sharon led an Israeli commando reprisal on a Palestinian village in which many women and children were killed. In 1956 he dropped with his paratrooper brigade on the Mitla Pass in Sinai and took it. In 1967 General Sharon's armored division crashed through Egyptian forces in Sinai. In 1973 his reserve armored division broke through to the west side of the Suez Canal and cut off the Third Egyptian army.

Patterns emerged in his military career. Sharon was bold, daring, and successful, but he also ignored orders and did not mind the deaths of Arab civilians. As defense minister in 1982, he sent the Israeli army into Lebanon to Beirut, where Lebanese Christians massacred Palestinian civilians. Sharon denied any role in it, but even some Israelis thought he was callous.

Sharon helped form Likud in the 1970s and joined its cabinet as agriculture minister after it won the 1977 elections. He immediately encouraged Israeli settlements in the West Bank and Gaza Strip, and in four years the number of settlers doubled. Sharon, who held several ministerial posts, and other hawks figured that "creating facts on the ground" would gradually make the territories part of Israel.

Sharon, now the leader of Likud, was elected prime minister in early 2001 and toughly put down the Palestinian intifada. With a life dedicated to Israel's security, Sharon realized that holding the West Bank and Gaza meant permanent insecurity. His solution: Unilaterally pull back Jewish settlements, build a security fence, and hand the Palestinians territory. Forget about negotiations; the Palestinians won't negotiate. Under criticism from hard-liners in his own party, in 2005 Sharon resigned from Likud and set up a new centrist party, Kadima (Forward). A stroke felled Sharon, however, and his follower Ehud Olmert took over as prime minister and Kadima chief with the same **unilateral** policies.

Jordan, a threat to Israel because the West Bank nearly choked Israel's narrow neck on the Plain of Sharon, became less of a threat when King Hussein in 1988 renounced any Jordanian claim to the West Bank, which his grandfather's army had taken in 1948. This move actually complicated any settlement. Giving the West Bank back to Jordan would have been relatively easy, and Israel could have lived with that. Setting up a Palestinian state on the West Bank is far more difficult, for many Israelis feel they cannot live with it. Hussein did not give the West Bank to Israel in 1988; rather he gave it to a future Palestinian state. At any rate,

---

unilateral   One side doing something on its own (opposite: bilateral).

G ⦂ *Geography*

MIDDLE EAST IRREDENTISM

When Italian patriots were kicking out foreign rulers and unifying Italy in the nineteenth century, they called the parts of Italy still outside their control "unredeemed Italy," *Italia irredenta,* which they aimed to recover. Foreigners had no right to rule any part of Italy, argued the irredentists. The term caught on especially in the Balkans, where the new little states that emerged from Ottoman rule all sought borders that included their ethnic kin or lands that they once ruled long ago. **Irredentism** is thus closely tied to nationalism. Efforts to build **Greater** Serbia sparked World War I and wars in Croatia and Bosnia in the 1990s. Efforts to regain Greater Romania led Bucharest to ally with Hitler in World War II. Irredentism is a dangerous force, as it makes exaggerated and unrealistic claims that bring it into conflict with other states that also claim those lands.

he was never going to get it back and from now on it would be an Israeli problem. With the West Bank approximating a deadly buffer zone between Israel and Jordan, a peace treaty was not difficult. This too is a "cold peace."

A Syria-Israel settlement is much tougher, as the Golan Heights is a serious security problem for both sides. Damascus demands the return of all the Golan Heights, and Israel is unlikely to give it. When Syria held the Golan Heights before 1967, it shelled Israeli farms. Taking the Heights in the Six Day War was costly, and Jerusalem swore to make them part of Israel. On the other hand, Israeli control of Golan means that its tanks can roll easily into Damascus, only some 40 miles distant. Furthermore, Golan is historically part of Syria, and most of its Arab inhabitants fled in 1967. Getting back Golan is a question of national honor about which no ruler of Damascus can show weakness.

The point is that some conflicts (as with Egypt and Jordan) are amenable to compromise, while others (as with Syria) are not. The Palestine-Israel situation is even tougher; demands tend to be uncompromisable because they concern the very right of two states (Israel and Palestine) to exist. Just because diplomacy worked in one case does not mean it will work in other cases.

Americans love to focus on personalities—an appetite fed by the media—and assume that war is caused by mean personalities and peace by nice ones. Yes, personalities matter, but as one factor among several. Sadat (see page 96) illustrates how personality can play a role, but even the "nice" Sadat went to war with Israel in 1973 to break the stalemate. It was his October War that changed the psychological balance of the region and made his subsequent visit to Jerusalem possible. It is not merely problem personalities that make compromise impossible;

irredentism   Desire to enlarge state to include all lands where it has ethnic or historical roots.
Greater   *Irredentist* end goal.

P : *Peace*

REJECTIONISTS ON BOTH SIDES

"If only Israelis and Palestinians could sit down and talk things through!" say many partisans of peace. Well, persons of good will and high intelligence on both sides have for years tried to talk things over. They sometimes make verbal progress toward settlement but are blocked by the many rejectionists (sometimes called maximalists) in both camps who demand all of historic Palestine. No compromise, no sharing: It's ours!

Graphically, the situation looks like two circles that overlap a bit. Where they overlap is the area where reasonable negotiators on both sides can sometimes compromise. Behind them is a portion of their publics (the white areas) that might go along with a compromise solution of two states, one Israeli and one Palestinian, living side by side in peace. Farther back in their publics, however, are the rejectionists who want the whole of Palestine. Public-opinion surveys—which vary with the latest outrage and the precise wording of the question—suggest that roughly half of Palestinians and a quarter of Israelis are rejectionists. Both exercise an ultimate veto over any peace process and easily reverse the process by bombings and retaliations. The 2006 electoral victory of Hamas put rejectionists in charge of the PA and further convinced Israelis to pursue their unilateral steps.

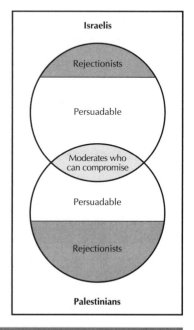

it is underlying strategic, geographic, and political realities. Events rather than personalities are usually in charge.

We must remember this in dealing with the most difficult problem, that of Israelis and Palestinians. Commentators often focused on the personalities of Israel's Sharon—described as a militarist Arab-hating right-winger—or of the PLO's Arafat—labeled as a rigid and corrupt control freak who quietly encouraged Palestinian violence. There is truth in both pictures, but these leaders were molded by the struggle of two peoples and by outside forces that led to the violent birth of Israel. They were not accidents but the products of history and circumstance. And their successors are not free agents; they face the same agonizing issues with many rejectionists in their respective camps.

If you ask any side in a war what they want, they will all say "peace." That would seem to make peace settlements easy to achieve. When you get them seated at the bargaining table, however, you soon learn that they have additional demands to go with peace. Their demands are always "peace plus." The devil is in the add-on elements, many of which are vital. By the time you elucidate them, you can understand why the two sides are at war. Such is the case with Israelis and Palestinians.

 *Peace*

THE FOUR GREAT ISSUES

1. *Borders:* What borders will a new Palestinian state have? Nearly the same as the pre-1967 borders of the West Bank and Gaza Strip, or considerably smaller?
2. *Jewish Settlements:* Which ones stay and which have to go? Palestinians will not accept a state fragmented by Israeli towns and roads, the present unstable situation.
3. *Jerusalem:* Will Palestinians be able to use even part of Jerusalem as their national capital? If so, which part?
4. *Palestinian Refugees:* How many can return to their ancestral homes inside Israel? Or can they be given material compensation?

As a first step, the Israelis want no more Palestinian violence, especially suicide bombings. Then they want (1) all of an enlarged Jerusalem and (2) dozens of Jewish settlements in the West Bank, especially those close to Israel's pre-1967 borders. Israel unilaterally pulled out of the Gaza strip in 2005. Many Israelis want to keep the Golan Heights, but it could be returned to Syria with guarantees it would stay forever demilitarized. To reach this, however, would require a climate of trust that is utterly lacking.

Most Israelis understand that settlements beyond the new security barrier, housing 35 to 40 percent of West Bank Jewish settlers, have to be given up. Militants insist, however, on keeping all settlements and building new ones. Their goal is to eventually turn these areas—minus most of their Arab inhabitants—into a Greater Israel, an unrealistic and dangerous vision. They want no Palestinian state at all, not even a small one, and propose "transfer" of Palestinians to other countries, a euphemism for expulsion and a prescription for a new war.

Palestinians want (1) a **sovereign** Palestinian state with (2) its capital in Jerusalem, (3) abandonment of most Israeli settlements in the West Bank, and (4) the right of Palestinians to return to their ancestral homes in Israel. This last point simply cannot happen unless Israel wants to commit suicide. The influx of a million or two Palestinians into Israel would severely destabilize and eventually destroy it. Property claims would be insoluble.

A large fraction of Palestinians openly want all of historic Palestine and the destruction of the state of Israel, a mirror image of Israeli maximalist demands. Many Palestinians see violence as the only way to accomplish this and vow to never give up their arms. For them, a peace deal would be simply a stepping stone to the total recovery of all of Palestine. Israeli hawks point to this as reason to give Palestinians little or nothing in peace talks. "They aim to destroy Israel, so why give them a base for attacking us?" they ask.

---

sovereign   Fully independent, boss on their own turf.

Hamas and Islamic Jihad are violent movements with the aim of recovering all of Palestine and with no interest in compromises. Said one young Hamas member, referring to possible borders: "We don't believe in '67 or '48—it's all our land." Hamas became more popular than the PLO and won the 2006 Palestinian parliamentary elections. Hamas wants the West Bank and Gaza integrated into Israel with citizenship for all Palestinians. Very soon, of course, Palestinians with a birth rate twice that of Israelis, would outnumber and outvote Jewish Israelis. They would set up "an Islamic state with Islamic law," said one Hamas leader. Needless to say, this is a prescription for civil war, a return to the 1936–1939 fighting on a much larger scale. Clearly **one-state solutions**—notice how they are proposed by both Israeli and Palestinian extremists—will not work.

THE WEST BANK

In hindsight, some Israelis say, it would have been better if the West Bank, with some border rectifications, had soon been given back to Jordan, with perhaps the Gaza Strip thrown in. In the flush of victory over the Six Day War, few could see what an Israeli occupation would lead to. Many expected peace with the Arabs soon, and then Israel would give back most of the West Bank. But peace never came, settlement building took off, and some Israelis started defining the West Bank as part of Israel. More than anything else, the growth of Jewish settlements in the West Bank fuels Palestinian rage and terrorism. If peace is to have any chance, settlement building has got to stop and be reversed. Many Israelis reject this notion.

Shortly after the 1967 war some Israelis (mostly on the left) concluded that Israel would have to choose between being a democracy and being Jewish. If Israel kept the West Bank and Gaza, it would come under pressure to grant Israeli citizenship to more than 3 million Arab Palestinians and with it the right to vote. If it did not, Israel would not be a democracy. If it did grant them citizenship, the rapidly growing Palestinian population would make Jews a minority by 2010. Most Israelis, however, ignored the dilemma. The results, decades later, were intifadas, terrorist bombings, and Israeli retaliations.

But for a while it worked, say defenders of the status quo. True, at certain times cheap Palestinian labor contributed to a booming Israeli economy that also gave Palestinians more pay and a higher standard of living than they had ever seen. Many built nice homes and sent their children to college, but this did not solve the political question of what was to become of Palestinians, who were neither Israelis nor Jordanians. No one offered a plausible plan for them, and they had no voice in their future. Their hilltops were increasingly Israeli building sites. It was a prescription for unrest.

Israeli occupation of the West Bank and Gaza was compared to South Africa's infamous **apartheid** that confined blacks to the lowliest jobs, forced them back to segregated "townships" by sundown, and sent others into rural poverty in

---

one-state solution   Making Israel and Palestine a single state with common citizenship.

apartheid   Literally, "apartness"; South Africa's system of strict racial segregation, ended in early 1990s.

D: *Domestic Structures*

THE PALESTINIAN AUTHORITY

The Palestinian Authority was supposed to be a democratic protogovernment, but Yasser Arafat controlled and corrupted it by one-man rule. Arafat headed Fatah; Fatah dominated the PLO; and the PLO ran the PA. After Arafat's death, in free and fair elections in early 2006, the fundamentalist Hamas (the Islamic Resistance Movement and Arabic for "zeal") won seventy-four out of 132 seats; secular Fatah got only forty-five. Hamas, related to the Muslim Brotherhood (see page 294), refuses to recognize or deal with Israel, which it swears to destroy. Hamas sponsors suicide bombers, lobs rockets from Gaza, and stages raids into Israel. The Bush administration, a big supporter of Middle Eastern democracy, now faced elected terrorists.

Unlike Israel, which uses straight proportional representation (PR) for its Knesset elections, the PA uses half PR and half direct election, a system called **mixed-member**. Each Palestinian voter gets two ballots, one for a party, which gets seats in proportion to its percent of votes. That accounts for sixty-six seats in the Palestinian Legislative Council (located in Ramallah, just north of Jerusalem). The other ballot is for individual candidates in sixteen electoral districts for the other sixty-six seats. An interesting twist: Each voter can cast as many votes for candidates as there are seats in that district. For example, a voter in the six-seat Nablus district, could cast six votes, either all for one candidate or spread around. The top six vote-getters win.

PA President Mahmoud Abbas, himself a Fatah man, had no choice but to name Hamas leader Ismail Haniya as prime minister, who in turn named a Hamas-dominated cabinet. Hamas ministers expressed support for suicide bombings against Israelis. Western countries denounced Hamas as terrorist and stopped discussions and aid until Hamas renounces violence. Financial help dried up, leaving the PA broke. Hamas and Fatah fought each other for power and came to near-civil war in 2006.

Some, however, detected a pragmatic streak in Hamas, which won largely on its effective social-aid programs and on PLO corruption. Hamas was in no position to take on Israel and spoke of continuing a vague *hudna* (truce) with Israel. Fatah had begun as armed rejectionists in the 1960s but was forced to become pragmatic over the years. Hamas too could grow moderate, but other militant groups, such as Islamic Jihad, would then become the new rejectionists and terrorists.

"bantustans," territorially fragmented fake little republics. Whatever truth there was to this, now Israel is cutting the number of Palestinian workers it allows in, aiming for zero in 2008. Sadly, Israel has the jobs that Palestinians badly need, but security concerns trump economic rationality. Israel would rather import Romanian laborers, who bring no bombs.

What can be done? First, a one-state solution is out. It was tried under the British mandate and blew up. It was tried informally under the Israelis and blew up. Persons of good will who still think it is possible are actually proposing permanent civil war. A **two-state solution** is the only one vaguely possible, and it would be difficult.

---

mixed-member   A split electoral system that uses both PR and individual candidates.

two-state solution   Making a separate Palestine on the West Bank and Gaza.

P Peace

A UNILATERAL SOLUTION?

Exasperated after years of getting nowhere in negotiations with the PLO, Israel imposed unilateral measures. From 2003 to 2006, Israel constructed a 450-mile security barrier—mostly electronic fencing but about 5 percent of it 30-foot-high concrete walls—to make it harder for Palestinian suicide bombers to enter Israel. Most of the barrier is near the 1967 border, but parts jut deep into the West Bank. Palestinians hate the barrier, which cuts off many from jobs, fields, and schools, but Israelis like the sharp decrease in terrorism. Several crossing points let Palestinians (with the proper ID) enter, but usually with a long wait. Palestinians say the fence is the unilateral imposition of a final border; Israelis say it is temporary until Palestinians get serious about negotiating a border.

In August 2005, after a year's warning, Sharon ordered 8,500 Israeli settlers out of the Gaza Strip, where they lived among 1.4 million Palestinians in an area just twice the size of Washington, D.C. Most Israelis recognized that security in Gaza was impossible and a drain on the Israeli army, but a militant minority had to be pried out of their Gaza homes. Much of Sharon's own Likud party denounced the Gaza eviction. An Israeli fence keeps Gaza isolated and impoverished. Vehicles in and out are carefully inspected, at great cost to shippers. The PA is supposed to run Gaza, but warlords and terrorists operate amid near-anarchy. Proclaimed Hamas banners: "Jerusalem and the West Bank after Gaza."

The purpose of both moves was to physically separate Israelis and Palestinians. This may not bring peace, say Israelis, but it cuts the violence. It also implies an Israeli offer to the Palestinians: "You don't like these barriers? Then negotiate a stable peace." American poet Robert Frost wrote that "good fences make good neighbors." But Palestinian militants have not given up and launch rockets into Israel, which retaliates with air and artillery strikes. Israel's unilateral steps leave the underlying problems untouched.

This would involve redrawing borders. Some of the largest Jewish settlements in the West Bank are close to the 1967 border and could be incorporated into Israel by moving the border only a few kilometers further east. Other Jewish settlements would have to be abandoned. Even the hard-line Sharon recognized in 2005 that Israeli settlements in crowded Gaza had to go. The portion of the aquifer in Palestine would have to be restored to Palestinian control, an important but often neglected point. Further, a land corridor about 25 miles long could connect the West Bank and Gaza Strip, under Israeli supervision but with Palestinian right of transit. This would give Israel some leverage over a Palestinian government: Curb violence or we cut the corridor to Gaza.

JERUSALEM

Jerusalem has always been one of the most difficult problems. Israel annexed East Jerusalem in 1967 and proclaimed the city its eternal capital. Municipal borders were enlarged in order to ring the city with Jewish neighborhoods. Now

200,000 Israelis live in East Jerusalem alone. Arab inhabitants of the Old City are encouraged to depart. Arab homes and apartment houses in the area of the Western or Wailing Wall were cleared away to make a broad plaza for worshippers and tourists. The municipal governance of Major Teddy Kollek did a fine job, transforming Jerusalem into a clean and attractive limestone city and a tourist magnet. (The legendary Kollek, after twenty-eight years as mayor, was defeated in 1993 by the right-wing Ehud Olmert, who became prime minister in 2006.) Since 1967, Jerusalem was transformed from Arab to Jewish in character, although 200,000 Arabs still live in Jerusalem.

One of the biggest sticking points for Palestinians is their demand to have their capital in Jerusalem. Yasser Arafat would not yield on this at the 2000 Camp David talks and neither will Hamas. The Palestine Authority's present administrative offices are in Ramallah, ten miles to the north, but most of them were destroyed by Israeli troops during the second intifada in the early 2000s. Jerusalem is an emotional symbol for both sides.

Could two separate countries have their capitals in one city? (Actually, Nicosia is the divided capital of partitioned Cyprus, but it is a poor model.) It goes against the notion that capitals should be in a nation's **core area**, surrounded by friendly territory. Most Israelis reject out of hand the notion of letting the Palestinians set up a capital in Jerusalem. Some suggested that an Arab suburb such as Abu Dis could be designated as part of Jerusalem and serve as a Palestinian capital. This satisfied few on either side. In late 2000 President Clinton suggested that Jewish sectors of Jerusalem be under Israeli sovereignty and Arab sectors under Palestinian sovereignty, not a bad idea if both sides would accept it. There could be an advantage in having two capitals in one city. Potential rioters and terrorists might not wish to harm their own capital city; they might be blowing up their own leaders.

RIGHT TO RETURN

The right of Palestinians to return to their parents' or grandparents' homes inside Israel also blocks a settlement. It, along with Jerusalem, was one of Arafat's rigid demands that wrecked the 2000 Camp David talks. Why did Arafat stick to a point he knew the Israelis had to reject? First, he believed passionately in it. Second, he feared (correctly) that if he gave in, he would be ousted by more radical Palestinian groups, such as Hamas. Aside from provisions for reuniting divided families—Taba suggested a total of 25,000 Palestinians might be let in—there is little wiggle room on this issue, as Israelis know they would soon be demographically swamped.

---

core area Territorial heart of a country, often where it originated historically and where it has its capital.

Peace

THE BLAME GAME

Do not play the blame game. It is worthless and just makes things worse. All sides have killed civilian noncombatants in what they see as a life-or-death struggle for their own people, one in which conventional morality can play no role. In such a situation it is impossible to accurately assign blame. The historical trail is too long, complex, and tangled to say "who started it," which is an irrelevant question. Should it include the Arab conquest of Spain? The Crusades? The European imperialists? And, if you do figure out who started it, how do you get the culprit to admit it? When you accuse someone, they just become more obdurate.

The tragedy of the Middle East (and the Balkans) is that everyone is the righteous victim of historical injustice and seeks **aggrieved entitlement**. On this basis, all sides rationalize their moves, even ones that prove self-destructive. In dealing with a problem like the Middle East, effective diplomats soon learn to exclude from their vocabulary words like "justice," "right," and "morality," as the contending parties thunder that they alone possess them. Peace marchers who carry placards proclaiming "No Justice, No Peace" might reflect that both sides pursuing justice makes wars.

Socrates, at the start of Plato's monumental *Republic,* famously asks "What is justice?" He finds the answer in *stability.* Chaos leads to horror, but Plato's imaginary Republic, by cleverly balancing several elements, would attain stability, and out of that would grow a just and orderly society. Without stability, peace and justice shrivel. Perhaps one day a philosophical peace marcher will carry a placard proclaiming "No Stability, No Hope."

THE DOWNWARD SPIRAL

If the Palestine Authority could guarantee an end to Palestinian violence, especially terrorist bombings, they could get many concessions from the Israelis. But the current Hamas government does not wish to curb violence, although some day it may. Hundreds of young Palestinians volunteer for suicide bombings. Several groups have either formed within or split away from the PLO because officially it condemned violence, as does PA President Mahmoud Abbas. Some Palestinian intellectuals notice that violence merely plays into the hands of Israeli hard liners. Ehud Barak, who offered concessions in 2000, was pushed out of office in 2001 elections in favor of hard-liner Ariel Sharon. Palestinian violence shrank the Israeli peace movement.

From the discussion above it is easy to conclude that peace has little chance. There is one factor that might save it: the realization on both sides that they are caught in a downward spiral that is killing and ruining both. Thousands of lives have been lost. The once-booming Israeli economy has slumped. The Palestinian economy has been ruined; many Palestinians live in poverty. For every Palestinian terrorist act there is an Israeli reprisal. Can the security barrier, mutual exhaustion, and the abandonment of irredentist dreams on both sides lead to peace?

---

aggrieved entitlement   We've been massively wronged, so we deserve whatever we want; leads to aggressive behavior.

CONCLUSIONS

Arab-Israeli peace may be impossible. Whenever you hear, "If only they got together and negotiated," remember that they have met off and on for years, at peace talks sponsored by the UN, Washington, and others. The UN's Ralph Bunche mediated the 1949 truce. UN Security Council Resolution 242 in 1967, calling on Israel to trade land for peace treaties with the Arabs, has been the basis for subsequent efforts.

Egyptian President Sadat visited Israel in 1977, paving the way for the first Arab-Israeli peace treaty in 1979, supervised by President Carter. Sadat was assassinated by Islamists in 1981. The 1979 treaty was a "cold peace" and did not tackle the Palestinian problem, which only grew worse. Israeli settlements in the West Bank, few at first, seemed aimed at incorporating it into Israel. In reaction, the first Palestinian intifada, 1987–1991, was relatively mild, but the second, 2000–2004, brought suicide bombings and harsh Israeli reprisals.

The 1991 Gulf War encouraged talks in Madrid, Oslo, and the United States, leading to the creation of a Palestine Authority over major West Bank and Gaza cities. At Camp David in 2000, Israel's Barak offered territorial concessions, but Yasser Arafat would not budge on key issues: (1) the borders of a Palestinian state, (2) withdrawal of Jewish settlements, (3) Jerusalem as Palestine's capital, and (4) right of Palestinians to return to homes and lands in Israel.

Many Palestinians see violence as their only path, and they do not lack for suicide bombers or guerrilla fighters. In turn, Israelis seek security by resorting to tough military retaliations and unilateral measures, such as the long security fence and Gaza withdrawal. These have calmed the violence somewhat but do not solve the problem of the Palestinians, which could easily produce another major war.

KEY TERMS

aggrieved entitlement (p. 122)

apartheid (p. 118)

armistice (p. 104)

atmospherics (p. 107)

blowback (p. 107)

core area (p. 121)

final status (p. 111)

Greater (p. 115)

green line (p. 108)

intifada (p. 106)

irredentism (p. 115)

Likud (p. 108)

mediation (p. 104)

mixed-member (p. 119)

one-state solution (p. 118)

opposition (p. 112)

Oslo (p. 110)

Palestinian Authority (p. 110)

proximity talks (p. 104)

rejectionist (p. 111)

rump (p. 111)

Shin Bet (p. 110)

sovereign (p. 117)

truce (p. 104)

two-state solution (p. 119)

unilateral (p. 114)

Further Reference

Aronson, Geoffrey. *Palestinian Refugees, Arab Host Countries, and the Right of Return.* Boulder, CO: Lynne Rienner, 2005.

Ben-Ami, Shlomo. *Scars of War, Wounds of Peace: The Israeli-Arab Tragedy.* New York: Oxford University Press, 2006.

Cordesman, Anthony H. *The Israeli-Palestinian War: Escalating to Nowhere.* Westport, CT: Praeger, 2005.

Creveld, Martin van. *Defending Israel: A Strategic Plan for Peace and Security.* New York: St. Martin's, 2005.

Dumper, Michael. *The Future for Palestinian Refugees: Toward Equity and Peace.* Boulder, CO: Lynne Rienner, 2007.

Gorenberg, Gershom. *The Accidental Empire: Israel and the Birth of the Settlements.* New York: Henry Holt, 2006.

Hefez, Nir, and Gadi Bloom. *Ariel Sharon: A Life.* New York: Random House, 2006.

Jamal, Amal. *The Palestinian National Movement: Politics of Contention, 1967–2005.* Bloomington, IN: Indiana University Press, 2006.

Kimmerling, Baruch, and Joel S. Migdal. *The Palestinian People: A History.* Cambridge, MA: Harvard University Press, 2003.

LeVine, Mark. *Impossible Peace: Israel/Palestine since 1989.* New York: Palgrave, 2007.

Meital, Yoram. *Peace in Tatters: Israel, Palestine, and the Middle East.* Boulder, CO: L. Rienner, 2006.

Miller, Jennifer. *Inheriting the Holy Land: An American's Search for Hope in the Middle East.* New York: Ballantine, 2006.

Mishal, Shaul, and Avraham Sela. *Palestinian Hamas: Vision, Violence, and Coexistence.* New York: Columbia University Press, 2006.

Nusseibeh, Sari. *Once Upon a Country: A Palestinian Life.* New York: Farrar, Straus and Giroux, 2007.

Reinhart, Tanya. *The Road Map to Nowhere: Israel/Palestine since 2003.* New York: Verso, 2006.

Ross, Dennis. *The Missing Peace: The Inside Story of the Fight for Middle East Peace.* New York: Farrar, Straus and Giroux, 2004.

Rotberg, Robert L., ed. *Israeli and Palestinian Narratives of Conflict.* Bloomington, IN: Indiana University Press, 2006.

Wasserstein, Bernard. *Israelis and Palestinians: Why Do They Fight? Can They Stop?* 2nd ed. New Haven, CT: Yale University Press, 2005.

———. *Divided Jerusalem: The Struggle for the Holy City.* New Haven, CT: Yale University Press, 2001.

Wittes, Tamara Cofman. *How Israelis and Palestinians Negotiate: A Cross-Cultural Analysis of the Oslo Peace Process.* Herndon, VA: U.S. Institute of Peace, 2005.

7   Turkey

**Points
to
Ponder**

- Can democracy flourish in a Muslim country?
- Is there something about an Islamic society that resists modernization?
- Can a traditional country modernize without a dictator?
- Why has Turkey been caught in praetorianism?
- Can a country where the military holds veto power be considered a democracy?
- Is Turkey a Middle Eastern country or a European one?
- Can a country with an Islamist government function as an American ally?

Twentieth-century Turkey was caught in a permanent tug-of-war between a secular elite, centered in the army and loyal to Atatürk's vision of a modern Turkey, and parties with considerable mass support that tried to pull Turkey back to Islam. The two streams seriously disliked each other, leaving Turkey, in Huntington's terms (see Chapter 15), a "torn" society: a Westernizing elite on top of a traditional Muslim society, the two continually pulling in opposite directions. The result was episodic military intervention directly in Turkey's politics either as coups or as strong warnings to not undo Atatürk's legacy. While it is too early to tell, there is evidence that this situation may have begun to change in the twenty-first century. Turkey is currently ruled by a moderate Islamist party that is dedicated to the same goal that the secular elites have supported for almost a century: moving Turkey into Europe.

FROM EMPIRE TO REPUBLIC

By the end of World War I, the Ottoman Empire crumbled like the Byzantine Empire before it. Having supported the losing side in the war (Germany), the Ottomans found themselves shorn of all their Arab possessions, all their European

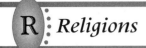

Religions

THE CALIPHATE AND SEPTEMBER 11

Many rumors surround Osama bin Ladin and the destruction of the World Trade Center in New York. One is that bin Ladin wants to see the caliphate restored and that he chose September 11 as the attack date because it was the anniversary of the Turkish abolition of the sultanate. Not so. The Congress of Sivas met on September 11, 1919, and ratified the National Pact originally approved in Erzerum. But no decision was taken on the caliphate until March 3, 1924, when the Republic of Turkey's parliament abolished the caliphate.

possessions except for a small corner of Europe, their capital occupied by the British, their Aegean coast occupied by the Greeks, their Mediterranean coast promised to the French and the Italians. Trying to keep his throne despite the occupation, the Sultan acquiesced to the victorious Allies' demands.

The remnants of the Committee for Union and Progress (CUP) organized guerrilla bands and Societies for the Defense of National Rights throughout Anatolia and Thrace. Sympathizers within Istanbul assisted by smuggling men and materiel through the Allied lines. Mustafa Kemal, the only undefeated general in the Turkish army, became a military inspector in the Ottoman Third Army, giving him a cover to leave the occupied capital and contact nationalist military leaders in the field. The British grew suspicious of him and forced the Sultan to recall Kemal to Istanbul or to resign his commission. At Erzerum, Kemal's resignation crossed the Sultan's edict that he be decommissioned. Despite Kemal's lack of military rank, Erzerum's military commander declared himself still under his command.

The Erzerum Congress, a gathering of **nationalist** leaders, elected Kemal president and formed a National Pact that called for the election of a provisional government within the borders of modern Turkey. The next meeting of the Nationalists was the Congress of Sivas in September 1919, which denounced the sultanate as illegal because its decisions were supervised by occupation forces. The Nationalists vowed to have no further contact with the Istanbul government.

INDEPENDENCE WAR

While most of the Allies and the Sultan himself limited their actions to condemnations of the Nationalists as rebels against lawful authority, the Italian army tried to seize Turkish territory. Reacting to Italian gains in what they perceived to be "their"

nationalist   Movement for unity and independence of nation; in Turkish case, also repudiation of empire and caliphate.

P : *Peace*

TURKEY'S TWO PEACE TREATIES

Turkey actually signed two peace treaties ending World War I. The first one did not take; the second one did. In August 1920, the helpless Sultan signed the lopsided Treaty of **Sèvres**, a document dictated by the victorious allies. It sheared off all of the Empire's lands outside of modern-day Turkey and divided most of today's Turkey into mandates supervised by the allies. It also promised a Kurdish autonomous region (see next chapter).

The Nationalists meeting in Ankara refused to recognize the treaty, using the same logic they used in Sivas to disavow the Sultan's sovereignty: No treaty could be valid when the signatory (the Sultan) was under military occupation. With the Nationalist victory against the Greeks, Sèvres became a moot point. It had never gone into effect.

On July 24, 1923, the **Lausanne** Peace Conference concluded with the signing of a treaty between the new Nationalist government of Turkey and the **Entente**. It established Turkey's borders ever since, allowed no foreign occupiers in Turkey, and said nothing about Kurdish autonomy.

sphere of influence, the Greeks landed troops to counter the Italians. Although the Italians abandoned their attempts to carve out an Aegean empire from the side of Turkey, the Greeks (with the blessing of the Allies, including the United States) decided to move inland against the Nationalists. The Turkish Nationalist strategy followed the same tactics used by George Washington and the Russians fighting Napoleon and Hitler: Avoid a conclusive battle as long as possible, keep the army in the field, and draw out the enemy until his supply lines are over-extended. The expanses of the Anatolian plateau became the Turks' greatest ally. Finally, in August 1921, the Greeks reached the Sakarya River, a mere fifty miles from the new Nationalist capital of Ankara. The Nationalist parliament made its president, Mustafa Kemal, commander of the Nationalist army, and it defeated the Greeks. The Nationalists were too exhausted to follow up and had to wait almost a year to regain enough of their strength to push the Greeks off the mainland, which they did on September 9, 1922. The Greeks set fire to Izmir (Greek: Smyrna) as they departed.

The Entente signed an armistice with Kemal one month after the Greeks were forced off the mainland. The Nationalists still did not control the old Ottoman capital of Istanbul. The rest of Anatolia answered to the new Grand National Assembly in Ankara, but Istanbul still answered to Sultan Vahit-ed-Din and the British occupation authorities.

Sèvres   (Paris suburb.) 1920 treaty to end World War I signed by Ottomans but repudiated by Turkish Nationalists.

Lausanne   (Swiss town.) 1923 treaty ending World War I with Turkey.

Entente   (French for "understanding.") World War I alliance of Britain, France, and others against Germany and its allies.

The Allies held a second peace conference, this one in Switzerland. The Nationalist representative to the peace conference, Refet Bey, traveled to Lausanne via Istanbul. Refet stopped by the palace, swore religious devotion to the caliph, and declared preservation of the caliphate a Nationalist goal. Refet said nothing about the Sultan's political claims. Sultan Vahit-ed-Din appealed to the British occupiers to support his demand that the Turkish delegation to the conference be composed of both Nationalists and monarchists. When the British announced they would remain neutral on questions of Turkish internal affairs, meaning they would not force the Nationalists to accept the Sultan's representatives, Vahit-ed-Din knew he had lost and left Istanbul on a British warship on November 17, 1922. The Grand National Assembly elected Vahit-ed-Din's cousin, Abdul Mejit, as caliph. The Assembly recognized the last of the Ottomans as the religious leader of Islam but reserved political power to itself.

The Treaty of Lausanne officially ended World War I between Turkey and the Entente. The Grand National Assembly, the governing body throughout the War of Independence, dissolved itself. The country held elections that were only partly free because many political opponents of the Nationalists were banned as candidates.

The Second Grand National Assembly was sworn in. The Allies withdrew from Istanbul as Turkish troops entered on October 2, 1923. Fearful of Ottoman palace intrigues and anxious to avoid having to deal with the Istanbul merchant classes and their allies in the old, imperial elite, Mustafa Kemal rewarded Ankara for supporting the Nationalists by declaring it the country's capital. Twenty days later, October 29, 1923, the Grand National Assembly declared Turkey a **republic**, and elected Mustafa Kemal as president.

In 1924, President Kemal announced—somewhat deceptively—the revival of a pure Islam untainted by politics. As a first step, he had the parliament abolish the caliphate, the office of the Shaykh al-Islam, and the Ministry of Religious Affairs. The caliph and his family were put on a train to Switzerland and forbidden to return. Kemal was clever at making his reforms look conservative. In a series of "reforms," he turned Turkey from empire to republic and, symbolically, moved its capital from Istanbul to Ankara.

The government closed the religious schools and confiscated the assets of the religious charitable foundations, the Awqaf. They then closed the Shari'a courts, declaring that secular law (the Swiss civil code) was to rule in questions of family law. These steps alienated the religious and conservative elements of society from the new republic, and they have been alienated ever since. Unlike America where secularism is separation of church and state, in Turkey (and many other lands) secularism means the subjugation of church to state. The Directorate of Religious Affairs, an arm of the central government, assumed control of all mosques, mausoleums, Sufi lodges, and other religious institutions.

Having deprived his religious-based rivals of their power base, Mustafa Kemal moved against his rivals in the army. He announced the discovery of a "generals' coup" and forced the "coup plotters" to resign. He also ordered his military aide and

---

republic   Government without a monarch; in Turkish case, also repudiation of Ottoman Empire.

G : *Geography*

THE POPULATION EXCHANGES

In a parallel to the difficulties of partition (see Chapter 5), population exchanges are another hellish solution in situations where ethnic groups cannot live together. In 1923 Greece and Turkey agreed to an exchange of populations. Greeks in Turkey (where they had lived for two and a half millennia) were to go "back" to Greece; Turks in Greece (where they had lived half a millennium) were to "return" to Turkey. In the months that followed, families who had lived on the same land for centuries were uprooted and moved to a country they did not know. Massive death and impoverishment resulted. One Smyrna Greek refugee who made good: Aristotle Onassis, who kept on going to Argentina.

The decision for expulsion was not based on bloodlines, where the family originated, or language; it was entirely religion. Christian Orthodox Turks (yes, there are some) were sent to Greece, and Muslim Greeks were sent to Turkey. Is religion and ethnicity the same thing in the Middle East?

army chief of staff to resign either from parliament or the army, establishing the precedent that active-duty military officers would not serve in parliament.

Kemal's supporters called themselves the Peoples' party and later the Republican Peoples' party. A group of his fellow Nationalists broke ranks in parliament over the population exchanges with Greece, in which thousands of people died. They formed an opposition party, the Progressives. They saw themselves as a loyal opposition, but it was inevitable that a group openly contesting the authority of the government became a magnet for all those members of the former elite who had been disenfranchised by the Nationalists: monarchists, tribal chieftains, religious leaders. The Istanbul newspapers flocked to the new party, calling for a restoration of the caliphate as the basis of traditional legitimacy for a new government.

INDEPENDENCE TRIBUNALS

Things turned nasty when the Kurds revolted, supposedly in support of the Progressives. The Turks, Republican and Progressive alike, were appalled and denounced the revolt. The Progressives even supported the government in declaring martial law. The government took advantage of the opening, however, by having parliament let the cabinet suppress any organization deemed **reactionary**. To enforce the law, the government established Independence Tribunals, who closed the opposition party. In 1926, in Ankara and Izmir, several members of the failed party were tried and executed for fomenting rebellion. Many of the Imperial generals in the opposition were spared, but they had learned their lesson. It would be many years before any military officer led an active opposition movement.

---

reactionary   Extremely conservative, trying to return to bygone ways.

Kemal continued his religious reforms. In November 1925, he issued an edict mandating the wearing of hats with brims and outlawing the fez that could be worn while praying. (A brim kept a pious Muslim from touching his forehead to the ground, part of the Muslim prayer.)

The Third Grand National Assembly (1927–1931) completed Kemal's religious program. The parliament **disestablished** Islam as the state religion, making Turkey a secular republic. The assembly also ordered use of the Latin alphabet in place of the Arabic/Ottoman script. This far-reaching change meant that within a generation few educated Turks could read four hundred years of Ottoman thought. For these changes, Kemal—better known as Atatürk—is considered the first great reformer of what we now call the Third World.

The Free Party Experiment

Mustafa Kemal, despite authoritarian tendencies, liked things to look democratic. He interpreted any attempts by others to create an independent opposition as hostile. To create a loyal opposition he set up a contrived Free Republican party. The experiment lasted three months. Kemal had anticipated a kind of debating society. Instead, the disenfranchised former elite and their followers flocked to the new party, which began as a parliamentary faction but quickly opened branches throughout the country. Whenever he traveled, the Free party leader was met with Islamic banners and demands for the repeal of many of Kemal's reforms. The party leader, loyal to the Republic, dissolved his party rather than allow the controversies to hurt the government. Then as now, not all Turks liked Kemal's reforms.

Six weeks later, a religious riot broke out in the town of Menemen. During a religious celebration, Sufi clerics called for a return to Islamic law and Arabic. One of the clerics killed a military officer, and the army opened fire on the rioters with machine guns. Newspapers blamed the Free party for the outburst, despite the fact that the party had already ceased to exist.

Ismet Inönü

Mustafa Kemal died in Istanbul on November 10, 1938. In death, he was given the name Atatürk, Father of the Turks. Ismet Inönü, a Nationalist general who had served many years as Atatürk's vice president, won support of the military's chief of staff and became president. Inönü kept Turkey neutral throughout most of World War II, but the defense ministry increased its share of the budget from 30 to 50 percent, and the size of the army ballooned from 120,000 to 1.5 million. The government tried to tame inflation through a series of price controls, devices that always fail. Rampant inflation, shortages, the black market—and the repressive measures to control them—made the Ankara government and the leading party unpopular. To ensure a place in the postwar United Nations, Turkey declared war on Germany only in February 1945.

---

disestablish   Breaking tie between state and official religion.

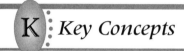

Key Concepts

THE SIX ARROWS OF ATATÜRKISM

In 1931, the Republican Peoples' party platform outlined the six principles that would eventually be incorporated into the Turkish constitution: republicanism, secularism, nationalism, populism, **statism**, and revolutionism. To some extent, each of these principles still guides the Turkish state elite. Turgut Özal introduced the free market into the Turkish economy in the 1980s, abandoning the statism that had retarded economic growth. Secularism is under siege by **Islamist** parties today, but is still zealously guarded by the military, the constitution, and the courts. Kurdish revolutionaries challenge Turkish nationalism. The Turkish military, defenders of Atatürk's legacy, still live by these six arrows.

Inönü, a democrat, announced in 1945 that Turkey needed an opposition party. He consulted with the military and got their approval to preserve the democratic order. Allowing an opposition may have been done to provide a safety valve for the frustrations of the Turkish people, built up during the siege economy of the war years. Turkey's democracy also strengthened its claim to join the new United Nations and to enlist Western support against Turkey's threatening neighbor, the Soviet Union. In 1947, as part of the Truman Doctrine, the United States did precisely that.

THE DEMOCRATIC PARTY

Like Inönü, Celal Bayar was a member of the Young Turks and Republican Peoples' party and a former vice president under Atatürk. Bayar combined forces with Adnan Menderes, a large landowner who opposed land reform. The Land Reform Bill, passed in January 1945 by Inönü's government, had driven a wedge between the rural-based landowners and state-centered bureaucrats.

The two registered the Democratic party (*Demokrat Parti,* DP) in early 1946 and quickly gathered support in the countryside, from those who blamed the Republicans for repression of Islam, from people hurt by inflation and shortages, and opponents of land reform. The Republicans tried to counter DP popularity, and in 1947 called for the repeal of the Land Reform bill.

The Republicans also competed with the Democrats for the religious vote and for the first time allowed foreign exchange for pilgrims for the hajj to Mecca. They allowed the teaching of Islam in public schools on a voluntary basis and allowed Ankara University to open a Faculty of Divinity, which graduated the first religious personnel trained in Turkey in over a decade. They authorized the reopening of Sufi tombs and shrines, and offered Turkish citizenship to displaced Muslims if they immigrated to the country.

---

statism   National government owns main industries and leads economy.
Islamism   Islam turned into a political ideology or party.

The public was convinced, however, that Republican rule meant secularism and Democratic rule a return to Islam. Actually, the Democratic leadership was as firmly committed to secularism as Atatürk's party. DP leaders ousted a group of Islamists from their party in the summer of 1946 and vowed that they would honor the secular basis of the state. To maintain their hold on power, the Republicans called for snap elections in 1946, so as not to give the Democrats time to organize. The Republicans captured 396 of 466 seats in parliament, holding off a Democratic victory for four years.

MILITARY SUSPICIONS

As the Democratic party gained, military officers in Ankara and Istanbul began organizing as early as 1946 to monitor the political situation. They suspected the DP would abandon Atatürk's path. In 1947, a political discussion group was organized at the Istanbul Staff College, which by 1949 sounded out generals about a future military coup if the Democrats should ever win the government. In public, the army vowed to respect election results.

At the funeral of the long-serving minister of defense in 1950, the Republican-led government arrested twenty-five mourners for reciting the Qur'an in Arabic. This created a voter backlash against the Republicans, and in the elections a month later the Democrats won 53.4 percent of the popular vote, giving them 408 of the 487 seats in parliament. Ismet Inönü was taken by surprise that the public had not rewarded his party for introducing democracy into the political system. For the first time in Turkish history, power passed peacefully to an opposition party.

DEMOCRATIC RULE

The Democrats did not trust the bureaucracy they inherited, particularly the military supporters of former general Ismet Inönü, who was now leader of the opposition. The Democrats purged the military by retiring senior officers, a move supported by junior officers trained in the United States, who believed their promotion prospects were being hindered by less well-trained superiors. Prime Minister Menderes's antipathy to the officer corps was legendary and mutual. In 1954, he said he could run the army with reserve officers, a blow to officers' already weakened morale. With high inflation and low wages, by 1956 one-third of all commissioned officers had resigned, citing inadequate income.

The DP got support from the religious public. They legalized the use of Arabic in the Muslim call to prayer, and within twenty-four hours the entire countryside returned to the practice banned by Atatürk twenty-five years before. A month later, the Democrats approved broadcasting the Qur'an over state radio. Religious education was made mandatory. During the Democrats' stay in office, an average of 1,500 new mosques a year opened. In December 1950, the Democrats reintroduced public piety in a ceremony to which the military could not object: The regime allowed the largest public prayer service in a quarter century on behalf of the Turkish troops in Korea, where they fought gallantly and took heavy casualties. Turkey was turning part way back to Islam.

Despite its reputation as the party of religion, the Democrats did not stray too far from the secularism of the Turkish constitution. In 1951, a group of Sufis from the Tijani order (Sufis are divided among various orders, the Tijaniyya being one of the larger ones in the world) went on a rampage, smashing statues of Atatürk. The new government was quick to respond, arresting the order's leader. Similarly, in January 1953, the government banned the Nation party (*Millet Parti*) for political use of religion. Followers of the banned party reorganized into the Republican Nation party and held onto five seats in parliament. To eliminate them, the Democrats gerrymandered the conservative district that had voted for the five candidates. The Democrats did allow one change that had a profound impact on the future of religion in Turkey, the opening of eleven additional Muslim seminaries. Designed to provide Turks with indigenous prayer leaders, these schools later fostered an Islamist challenge to the political center.

In 1955, the DP played the nationalist card by allowing a limited "spontaneous" student demonstration in Istanbul after a bomb exploded near the Turkish consulate in the Greek city of Salonika. As slum dwellers joined the students, however, it turned into unlimited attacks on Greeks and the wealthy. (In 1961, the courts acquitted DP officials of responsibility for the riots.) The police, who had been ordered not to intervene, took no action. To restore public order, the Democrats turned to the military and declared martial law in the major cities.

Once the military had been invited to participate in politics, it was hard to get them back to the barracks. Dissident military officers sought the views of Ismet Inönü about a coup. Most Turkish officers still admired and followed Inönü, but the DP government of Menderes feared him and tried to keep him isolated. Praetorianism (see box in Chapter 3 on page 46), the tendency for military takeovers, tends to become a chronic, self-reinfecting endemic illness. Catch it once and you'll get it again.

By 1957, with the Turkish economy again in recession, the bureaucracy and armed forces withdrew their support as their buying power declined. The Democrats also lost many intellectuals, who began to listen to Republican complaints that the Democratic party used religion for political purposes. The DP, born as an opposition movement, now attempted to silence opposition. As early as 1953, they ordered the government to confiscate most of the Republicans' assets, claiming they had been illegally acquired with public funds during the single-party period. In 1956, they passed laws allowing them to suspend newspapers for publishing "false" news, to approve all newspaper advertising in advance, to ration newspaper print, and to prohibit newspapers from covering subjects deemed to be "of an offensive nature." They amended the Law on Elections and forbade opposition parties from uniting by running a joint list.

THE 1961 MILITARY REVOLUTION

On the morning of May 27, 1961, Turkish radio told the nation a military coup had ended Democratic party rule to prevent civil strife. Thirty-eight junior officers, led by General Cemal Gürsel, formed a National Unity Committee (NUC) to lead the country. The **junta** abolished party structures and suspended party activities. A new constitution established a National Security Council of top generals to advise the government on security issues.

The NUC abolished the Democratic party and charged former government officials with treason. The trials that followed kept the party in the eyes of the public throughout the period of military rule and were a public relations disaster. Judges dismissed many of the charges against the Democrats for lack of evidence. The public perceived other charges as petty. The senior officers hanged Prime Minister Menderes and two colleagues.

To maintain and protect the military hierarchy from the junior officers in the NUC, the generals who were not involved in the coup organized the Armed Forces Union. Throughout 1961 and 1962, the Union warned politicians not to return to the pre-coup policies that had so disrupted the country. The Union lobbied in support of the death sentence for Adnan Menderes, fearful that if he lived he might regain power and put the junta on trial.

In June 1961, the Union reached the height of its influence. Fearing a NUC plan to purge the armed forces of Armed Forces Union members, the Union sent jet fighters to buzz Ankara and demanded their members be protected. The NUC caved in and established the independence of the traditional military hierarchy from the governing junta. The mixing of governing and military roles is always one of the weak points of military takeovers. Like the Brazilian generals a few years later, the Turkish generals had to decide whether to be an army or an administration.

Civilian political activity also began to pick up. A coalition of industrialists, shopkeepers, landowners, peasants, religious reactionaries, and Western-oriented liberals formed the Justice party in 1961. The party's platform called for "justice" for the imprisoned DP members. The junta allowed elections in October 1961, but only after forcing participants to sign a "National Declaration" supporting the legitimacy of the coup. The Republicans had survived the coup and received 36.7 percent of the vote. The upstart Justice party won 34.7 percent, with many of their successful candidates still in jail because of their previous DP activities. Inönü formed a coalition government that included members of the Justice party. The coalition collapsed after less than a year, and President Gürsel turned to Justice to form the new government.

One coup tends to lead to another. The head of Ankara's War College attempted another coup and came within minutes of arresting the government. He was forced to resign from the army, and the Armed Forces Union was broken. The same man tried again in 1963, but this time he was executed.

---

junta   Cabinet, usually dominated by military, that governs after a coup.

NEW POLITICAL FACES

Suleiman Demirel led the Justice party into the October 1965 elections, which it won, and for the first time a European-type left-right cleavage entered Turkish politics. The Republicans moved away from their role as party of the state toward a more radical platform. The Democratic party, now under another name, returned to power. Alpaslan Türkes, who was part of the 1961 military coup, took over the Republican Peasant's National party in 1963 and infused it with Turkish nationalism. In 1969 he changed the name to the Nationalist Action party. He declared that Islam was an integral part of Turkish nationalism and sponsored a paramilitary group known as the Gray Wolves. In 1969 Necmettin Erbakan's National Order party arrived. An avowed Islamist, Erbakan said the country could only reclaim its past glory by turning back to the Islam that it had abandoned over the previous half century.

THE "COUP BY MEMORANDUM"

Right and left clashed in the streets, with left-wing terrorists battling right-wing Gray Wolves. The government invaded campuses to crush student radicals. As violence grew, groups within the military began plans for a new military intervention. The General Staff handed the prime minister a memorandum demanding he halt violence or face military intervention. Demirel immediately resigned. Turks called it the "coup by memorandum."

Violence continued, and in 1971 the National Security Council declared martial law in eleven provinces. After a terrorist group, the Turkish People's Liberation Army, killed the Israeli consul in Istanbul, the military arrested over 5,000 alleged leftists. In the general anti-leftist mood of the era, the Workers party was closed but the Gray Wolves were allowed to operate more or less freely. Note that this was a time of radical leftism in many countries, including Germany and Italy. The military also closed Erbakan's National Order party for bringing religion back into politics. Erbakan opened a new party, the National Salvation party but did not call for an Islamic state, only one that furthered traditional Turkish culture and its Islamic components.

The new government changed the constitution to give the military an institutional method to voice its recommendation through the National Security Council. The 1971 intervention failed to resolve the conflicts in Turkish society because it did not convince a single major group or party that the military should have intervened. Civilian officials grew frustrated at operating under the implied veto of the generals.

RETURN TO ELECTIONS

In 1973, voters elected Bülent Ecevit and his Republican Peoples' party. This was not, however, the party of Atatürk. Ecevit had abandoned the statist perspective and converted it into a center-left party. Ecevit's party received 33.5 percent of the

C Conflicts

THE CYPRUS PROBLEM

Until 1960 Cyprus was a British colony with a Greek majority and Turkish minority. After years of guerrilla warfare by Greek Cypriots aiming at union with Greece, Britain granted the island independence provided it not join Greece. Greek Cypriot militants did not give up; some murdered ethnic Turks.

In 1967, Turkey threatened to intervene to protect the Turkish minority that lived mostly on the northern side of the island. President Johnson warned the Turks that NATO would not cover them if they did, and the Turkish military shelved their plans. Many Turks never forgot their abandonment by the Americans. In 1974, a Greek-inspired coup in Cyprus brought the Cypriot National Guard to power, and it proclaimed the island a part of Greece. Faced with this, Turkish Prime Minister Ecevit ordered Turkish intervention to protect Turkish Cypriots. They captured 40 percent of the island, which declared itself the Turkish Republic of Northern Cyprus. No government recognized the new republic except Ankara. Cyprus stays split today.

The United States kept the UN Security Council from passing a resolution demanding Turkey's immediate withdrawal, but the U.S. Congress suspended all military aid to Turkey. Turkish intellectuals, who already felt abandoned by the United States in 1967, concluded that the West was aligning against Muslim Turkey to support the Christian Greeks. This provided the psychological and cultural foundation on which Erbakan built his political movement.

In April 2003, the two sides reopened the border between the north and south of the island. Family members were able to visit and see each other for the first time in a generation. This hopeful sign was soon overshadowed, and the plan of UN General Secretary Kofi Annan to reunify the island failed.

The Annan plan of November 2002 (revised in February 2003) would have reunited the island but left both ethnic groups with significant autonomy. Under intense pressure from the United States and the European Union (EU), the governments of both Greece and Turkey supported the plan. Residents of the island voted in a referendum in April 2004. In the north, the Turkish Cypriots approved the plan, but it was decisively rejected by Greek Cypriots in the south for surrendering their rights to rule a united island. In an ironic twist, the Turks who followed the EU's wishes and endorsed the plan remain in diplomatic isolation, while the Greeks who ignored the EU's wishes acceded to the Union shortly after the vote.

This has set the stage for a further Cyprus problem. The Republic of Cyprus (the south) is now a full member of the European Union. Since the other EU governments recognize the Republic as sovereign over the entire island, Turkey remains an illegal occupier. This will block Turkey's own effort to join the EU, which requires unanimous approval—meaning the Republic of Cyprus could veto Turkey's admission.

vote, surpassing Demirel and the Justice party's 29.5 percent. Ecevit entered a governing alliance with Erbakan and the National Salvation party, whose Islamists demanded unsuccessfully to make Friday, the Muslim sabbath, part of the weekend, that the government forbid tourists from entering Turkey, and that female police officers and customs officials wear longer skirts. Islamism, however, was now part of Turkish politics and grew.

Capitalizing on his popularity following the Turkish invasion of Cyprus, Ecevit resigned as prime minister and called new elections. The president, however, deferred elections and asked Suleiman Demirel to organize a new coalition. The Justice party therefore formed the new government with the Nationalist Action party and Türkes' Nationalist Order party, which took advantage of their control of the interior ministry to infiltrate the security forces with Gray Wolves.

Over the next five years, weak coalition governments alternated, and they could do nothing to stop increasing left and right violence. Even the security forces divided into left and right factions, which arrested their ideological opponents. Prime Minister Ecevit, fierce opponent of the 1971 military intervention into politics, was forced to declare martial law "with a human face." From the military's view, this meant continued civilian interference in military activities that prevented them from carrying out their jobs. When Demirel again assumed power, he abolished the martial law, but it was too late to appease the military. When you have a mess, you get coups.

THE THIRD COUP

With an average of twenty Turks a day killed in political violence, on New Year's Day 1980 the general staff issued a 1971-style warning that Demirel worried over but basically ignored. On September 12, 1980, the military again took over, and much of the public was relieved. The National Security Council had a retired admiral form a government of nonpartisan **technocrats**, including six retired military officers, who took orders from the Council.

The generals blamed the politicians for the state's gridlock and arrested all of the country's senior politicians, disbanded the parties, and dismissed mayors and municipal councils. The Council ruled via regional and local commanders. To break the terrorists, the military conducted mass arrests, and military tribunals condemned 3,600 people to death (although only fifteen sentences were actually carried out). Action against the opposition was not limited to only the terrorists, however; the junta cracked down on anyone who disagreed: leftists, rightists, violent activists, non-violent dissidents, antinuclear and human rights activists, and others.

A constitutional assembly wrote a new constitution, in use today. To win support of religious Turks, it expanded compulsory religious education to primary as well as secondary schools. In March 1983, Ankara authorized the return to civilian rule, but pre-coup parties and politicians remained banned. The Council approved three parties for the scheduled elections. The party least associated with the military, the Motherland party under the former Deputy Prime Minister for Economic Affairs Turgut Özal, won 45 percent of the vote (and a majority of parliament) from a populace weary of taking orders from the army. The junta resigned on December 6, 1983, and the third military intervention in twenty years was over.

The new parliament called for a referendum that overturned the ban on pre-coup politicians and parties. In 1991, Suleiman Demirel was reelected as the head of his renamed party, the True Path party. When Demirel was elected president following Özal's death by heart attack in 1993, True Path had a new leader, Prime Minister Tansu Ciller (pronounced Chiller), a woman who had only two years of parliamentary experience.

---

technocrat   Nonparty official appointed on basis of technical, usually financial, skills.

P Personalities

TURKEY'S TANSU CILLER

Tansu Ciller was a female economics professor with limited government or party experience. After graduate school in the United States, she became the youngest professor in modern Turkish history. Intensely disliked by traditional faculty members for her imperious style, the chiefs of her True Path party united behind her because they thought they could control a woman.

The party elders misjudged her. She was tough. Through speculation in Turkish and American real estate, Ciller had amassed a fortune estimated at $50 million to $100 million. Unusually, Ciller did not assume her husband's last name. Instead, Ciller's father made the groom change his name, so that the Ciller family name would not die out (as Ciller has no brothers). Ciller bucked thousands of years of tradition, and her time in office marked a new stage in Turkish modernization.

THE RISE OF REFAH

While Turkey won praise for choosing a female prime minister, things were different at the local level. In 1994, Necmettin Erbakan's newest effort, the Refah (Welfare) party, captured city governments in Ankara and Istanbul, shocking the secular establishment. The lower-middle class, many of them rural villagers, had moved to the cities without changing their Islamic orientation. The party also captured twenty-nine other major cities, and 400 smaller towns. Two-thirds of the population of Turkey now lived under Islamist municipal governments.

The secularist military and Refah were on a collision course. Erbakan announced the inevitability of the "Just Order," code for an Islamic state. In 1995 the General Staff warned against "reactionary" trends, the term the military used for the Islamists. Refah captured 21 percent of the popular vote and a plurality of seats in parliament. Much of their vote came from southeastern Turkey, home of an armed Kurdish rebellion. The government had banned Kurdish political parties, and many voters supported Refah simply to protest the ban. Others protested the rampant corruption of the centrist parties. Secular parties formed a shaky coalition and kept Refah out of the government, despite its parliamentary plurality. Then Erbakan struck a deal with Ciller of the True Path party to form a new coalition with Erbakan as prime minister. Turkey now had an Islamist chief of government, and the army did not like it.

Erbakan was cautious toward the army. He wanted the United States out of the Middle East but let the U.S. Air Force continue to use the important Incirlik air base to enforce the no-fly zone over northern Iraq. Erbakan removed Islamist officers from the military because they violated Turkish military law. He even let the military improve relations with Israel in a series of military cooperation and training agreements.

G ⋮ *Geography*

TURKEY AND THE EUROPEAN UNION

Is Turkey in the Middle East or in Europe? Most Turks are adamant that Turkey belongs in Europe, but many Europeans think not. The **European Union** (EU) doubts Turkey's commitment to human rights and its economic and democratic credentials, and, although it rarely says so in public, it doubts that a Muslim country belongs in the EU. Many Turks want to preserve Turkey's traditional Muslim character, and, spurned by Europe, more Turks are turning to Islamism. We cannot count on Turkey facing forever westward.

Only two countries with Muslim populations have ever applied for EU membership, Morocco and Turkey. Brussels said that Morocco was not a European country. Brussels did not reject Turkey's application but delayed it forever with a variety of reasons: Turkey must liberalize its politics, improve its economy, and clean up its (at times brutal) human-rights record. Many Turks believe former German Chancellor Helmut Kohl gave the real reason when he said Europe was a Christian club that would never accept a Muslim country.

Turkey first applied for EU membership in 1959 and signed an "association" agreement in 1963 that cut tariffs between Turkey and the EU. In 1970 the EU set up a **customs union** with Turkey, to be implemented over twenty-five years. In 1987, Prime Minister Turgut Özal applied for full EU membership. The EU Commission took thirty months to respond and said the fuller unification of present members took precedence.

In 1996, the EU tried to give Turkey a "special status" by implementing the long-promised customs union, but withholding membership in the organization itself. Disappointed Turks waited until December 1997 to learn they were not a "candidate" country. Under incredible pressure from the United States, which was seeking to support a vital ally, however, the EU reversed itself two years later and accepted Turkey's application for membership. Brussels placed heavy conditions on Turkey, requiring it to make numerous, substantive changes in government. These changes, codified at the 2002 Copenhagen summit and since known as the Copenhagen criteria, obliged the military to remove itself from politics, and the government to abolish the death penalty, cease torturing prisoners, and implement numerous human rights reforms. Prominent in the European demands were requirements for Turkey to recognize the rights of its Kurdish citizens.

In 2000 the EU announced accession dates for twelve of thirteen applying states. The odd man out, as usual, was Turkey. The Christian former-Communist countries of East Europe were good Europeans; Muslim Turkey was not. Many Turks began to suspect they never would be. Turks have nevertheless united in their efforts to join the EU; even the moderately Islamist ruling Justice and Development (AK) party has accepted Atatürk's dream that a modern Turkey will be recognized as being a part of Europe. As a result, Parliament has passed numerous changes in the Turkish constitution, laws, and penal codes to bring them into compliance with European demands.

In 2004, the EU noted with favor Turkish progress but cautioned it could take another decade before the EU voted on Turkey's application, and that, even if Turkey implements all the reforms Europe was demanding, they were giving no guarantees that Turkey's application would ever be accepted.

European Union   Federation of most European states with main institutions in Brussels; began as Common Market in 1957.

customs union   Pact providing same external tariffs for members.

On the other hand, Erbakan tried to reinforce his Islamist credentials in foreign policy. He ostentatiously first visited his Muslim neighbors of Iran, Libya, and Egypt. In Iran, he thumbed his nose at the United States by signing a $23 billion deal for Iranian gas, less than a week after a new U.S. law ordered sanctions (unenforceable) for those who did business with Iran. In Libya, Erbakan urged Libya to pay the debt it owed Turkish construction companies, but Qaddafi lectured Erbakan publicly on Kurdish rights and the need for a Kurdish homeland. In Egypt, there were no Turkish flags at the airport for the welcoming ceremony, an insult the Turkish military noted.

At home, Refah sought to change the national education system, giving greater rights to Muslim seminarians. They also attempted to place the General Staff under the defense ministry, and thus under the Islamist government's control. Refah parliamentarians sought to cut the military budget by a half billion dollars to protest the continuing expulsions of Islamists from the military.

MILITARY MOVES AGAINST REFAH

The army wanted the Islamist government out but was divided on a coup. They were especially incensed at the Iranian ambassador urging a Turkish audience to support an Islamic revolution. In 1997 the General Staff told the government to repudiate Refah's ideology, asserting the internal threat to the Turkish state from Islamists was greater than any external threat. In return, some Refah members urged withdrawing from the government.

As Refah and True Path had earlier agreed when forming their coalition government, Tansu Ciller was supposed to become prime minister in 1997, but Turkey's president rejected the promised swap in leaders and instead named the chief of the Motherland party. Now out of power, Refah's supporters protested violently in the streets. Accused of fomenting Islamism, Refah was banned in early 1998 by the Constitutional Court, which then barred seven leaders, including Erbakan, from all political activity for five years. Refah parliamentarians and other officials kept their positions, but as independents. Some Refah members had already organized another party, the Fazilet (Virtue) party.

The state continued to pressure Islamists. Istanbul mayor Recep Tayyip Erdogan (pronounced "Erdowan") went on trial for reading an Islamist poem that called for the liberation of the oppressed from the rule of "Pharaoh." The State Security Court ruled the speech was an incitement to hatred based on religious and racial differences, and Erdogan was jailed and banned from public office. The centrist government fell in late 1998, accused of awarding bank privatization to friends, the latest in a long line of scandals touching centrist prime ministers. Corruption is one big reason Turks often vote for Islamist parties, which are relatively clean and deliver welfare.

In 1999, Turkish security forces captured the leader of the Kurdistan Peoples party (PKK), Abdullah Ocalan (pronounced "Ojalan"), who had been hiding in

G : *Geography*

TURKEY, IRAQ, AND THE UNITED STATES

Turkey has had problems with its border with Iraq going back to the founding of the Turkish Republic. Under the Ottomans, Iraq had simply been three Ottoman provinces. The Treaty of Lausanne awarded the oil-producing cities of Mosul and Kirkuk to Iraq, then under British supervision. Turkey objected strongly, and some Turks have kept Turkish claims to these oil fields alive. In addition, Turkey asserts a right to protect the Turkic minority of Iraq, the Turkomans, 2 percent of Iraqis.

Turkey also has national security reasons to watch northern Iraq. Having fought a murderous Kurdish insurgency for fifteen years, Turkey opposes any independence or autonomy for Kurds in Iraq for fear of creating a safe haven for Turkish Kurdish insurgents and an example for Turkish Kurds to resume their struggle.

When Iraq invaded Kuwait in August 1990, Turkey joined most of the world in condemning it. Turkey allowed coalition aircraft to fly from the NATO airbase at Incirlik. Turkey also agreed to the U.S.-led economic embargo of Iraq, cutting the crucial oil pipeline into Turkey and costing Turkey billions of dollars in trade and transit revenues. President Turgut Özal relied on promises from President Bush 41 of massive economic aid, but the U.S. Congress only passed a fraction of it. Turkey felt it had given America much and gotten little in return.

Following the Gulf War, Iraq's Kurds rebelled against Saddam Hussein at American instigation. The U.S. military stood by and did nothing while Saddam destroyed the rebels, and half a million Kurds fled into Turkey. Alarmed both at the costs of caring for these refugees and at the security situation created by an influx of Kurds (who possibly sympathized with Turkish Kurdish rebels), the Turks agreed to a no-fly zone in the north of Iraq. That way, Iraqi Kurds would stay in Iraq.

Every six months for a decade, the Turkish parliament reluctantly renewed permission for U.S. warplanes to patrol northern Iraqi skies from Incirlik. Ankara did not like the way Iraqi Kurds took advantage of the relative peace to establish a northern Kurdish zone independent of any central authority in Baghdad or Ankara. Again, it might give Turkish Kurds ideas. In 1991, however, Turkey did not participate in the invasion of Iraq. They massed troops along the border, giving Iraq a potential threat to defend against, but Turkey did not actually fight.

In early 2003, President Bush 43 asked Ankara to let the United States stage the U.S. Fourth Infantry Division's invasion of Iraq from Turkey. Washington promised $6 billion in outright grants and $24 billion in concessional loans. The Turkish General Staff wanted to accept and even send Turkish troops into Iraq to keep the Kurds under control, a deployment of Turkish troops that required parliamentary approval. The new government would go along with this if the UN authorized it, but when the UN deadlocked the Turkish parliament refused to authorize either the U.S. transit or use of Turkish troops.

At first, the Turkish public applauded parliament for preserving Turkish honor: "We cannot be bought for a bribe, no matter how large." When the public began to realize it had lost major financial aid, a voice in the future of Iraq, and the goodwill of its primary Western ally, Turkey later granted U.S. forces overflight rights. With the Iraq War underway, the Fourth Infantry Division pulled its equipment out of Turkish ports and sailed through the Suez Canal to enter Iraq from the south. Parliament granted the United States permission to use Incirlik to bomb Northern Iraq, earning about $1 billion in grants and $5 billion in loans. But Turkey had lost U.S. aid and goodwill. U.S.-Turkish relations are still good but not what they used to be.

the Greek ambassador's residence in Kenya. The Turkish public held Ocalan personally responsible for over 30,000 deaths from the long PKK insurrection. The arrest gave Bülent Ecevit's caretaker government a tremendous boost in public support, and his Democratic Socialist party won the most votes in the 1999 elections. Second place went to the Nationalist Action party. Fazilet drew only 15 percent of the vote. The electorate had heeded the military's warnings to not return Islamists to power. The electorate's message, however, was neither pro- nor anti-Islamist; it was for clean government.

Ecevit formed an alliance with the right-wing Nationalist Action party but faced Turkey's second economic crisis in ten years (the first was under Ciller in 1994), a crisis that did not abate for almost five years. They brought Kemal Dervis, a technocrat economist who worked for the World Bank, back from Washington to lead an economic recovery team. Dervis and his team failed but did win a law bringing Turkey into alignment with EU laws. In August 2002, parliament abolished the death penalty and legalized teaching and broadcasting in a language other than Turkish (meaning Kurdish). This did not help the Ecevit government, which collapsed the same year.

Now in opposition, Fazilet began to show internal divisions over getting Erbakan out of jail or keeping distant from him in order to avoid being shut down as a continuation of the Refah party. In 2001, the Supreme Court banned Fazilet as a focus for illegal Islamist activities.

THE JUSTICE AND DEVELOPMENT PARTY

As usual, a new Islamist party took the place of Fazilet. The Justice and Development party (AK), led by the reformers Abdullah Gül and Tayyip Erdogan, took a conciliatory tone with the secular establishment, saying it was culturally conservative but committed to a secular state. The 2002 elections swept AK into power. The previous coalition parties, as well as all opposition parties except the Republican Peoples' party, each failed to reach the 10 percent national threshold and therefore did not receive a single seat in Parliament. For the first time since 1987, one party had a parliamentary majority, and for the first time since 1954 parliament had a two-party system.

Although Erdogan was leader of the AK, he was ineligible to sit in parliament because of his conviction for inciting religious hatred as a Refah party leader. Abdullah Gül became prime minister with the understanding that he would soon turn the office over to Erdogan. In late 2002, parliament amended the constitution to restore the rights of those banned for ideological crimes, such as Erdogan. In 2003, Erdogan won a seat in a by-election in a conservative town and a week later was named prime minister. Gül became foreign minister. The new government declared their three main priorities were joining the EU, improving relations with the West, and increased regional cooperation. Turkey's strategic relationship with Israel was unchanged despite the Islamist character of the new government.

G : *Geography*

PIPELINE POLITICS

With the demise of the Cold War and Turkey's refusal to be a Western proxy in battles with Middle Eastern countries, why is Europe or the United States still interested in this country? It is an example of a democratic, Muslim-majority country, and its geographic location is still strategic. But one of the main reasons that Turkey has become important today is oil. Turkey has negligible petroleum of its own, but without the pipelines that criss-cross its length and breadth, Caspian energy reserves would be unable to reach world markets.

The Caspian region holds an estimated 16 billion barrels of oil, but the fields are completely landlocked. The only way Caspian oil could move was via the antiquated Russian pipeline system, built in the Soviet era and already straining under the weight of Russian oil. In 1997, Western oil companies began to discuss a new pipeline that would make it commercially feasible to invest in the Caspian fields. One proposal was to improve the Russian pipelines; another was to run a pipeline straight south through Iran. Either of these options would have been economically more feasible than the route that was eventually chosen. Under pressure from the United States, which did not want to reward its Russian strategic rival or the mullahs of Iran, the pipeline consortium decided on a 1,094-mile line from the Azerbaijani capital of Baku, through the Georgian capital of Tblisi, to the Turkish Mediterranean port of Ceyhan (pronounced Jayhan). If the pipeline carries its estimated million barrels of oil per day, Turkey will collect some $1.5 billion annually in transit fees. This pipeline, known as either the BTC or the main export pipeline, may eventually also open up the Khazakh oil fields to world markets as there are plans for a pipeline under the Caspian to link up with the BTC.

Because of environmental concerns, in the early 1990s Turkey banned the burning of its most popular fossil fuel, soft coal. It was replaced by natural gas. Frightened at the prospect that economic growth would exceed Turkey's ability to import the precious commodity, Turkey signed several pipeline agreements in the late 1990s to build natural gas pipelines: from Turkmenistan along the BTC route, from Russia under the Black Sea, and from Iran. As of 2002, both the Russian "Blue Stream" pipeline and the Iranian pipeline had been completed. Turkey briefly halted the importation of natural gas from both pipelines, citing variously either lack of demand because of the Turkish economic turndown or price disputes with the Russians and Iranians. Should Turkey begin to export the quantities it has committed to in the initial contracts from these two sources, and the Turkmenistan gas come on line, the amount of imports will far exceed Turkey's needs. This means that Turkey has the capability of developing into an exporter of natural gas to Europe. There are already plans to build a pipeline between Ankara and the Greek city of Alexandropoulus.

TERRORISM RETURNS

After the 1999 capture of PKK leader Ocalan, Turkey enjoyed a respite in terrorist violence. In November 2003, however, a group that claimed association with al Qaeda killed twenty-five when two car bombs exploded outside of Istanbul's main synagogue. The entire country was moved in solidarity when the Jewish community's leaders insisted that the coffins be draped with Turkish flags rather than any religious insignia. The same group then used suicide bombers to kill twenty-eight at a British bank and at the British consulate.

The PKK announced in May 2004 they were abandoning their cease-fire, claiming the Turkish government had not honored the conditions of the peace and were engaging in "annihilation operations." The Kurdish charges were not without foundation: At one point during the ceasefire, local security forces stopped an individual whose car was full of bomb making materials and who had the names and addresses of prominent Kurds in the area. He turned out to be a military intelligence operative.

There were occasional bombings over the next two years, but the PKK usually denied having any involvement. Then, in April 2006, PKK-sponsored bombings resumed in Southeastern Turkey. Turkish security forces killed a number of individuals they identified as PKK militants, an echo of the previous anti-PKK campaign. An increase in Kurdish violence could lead to the military's reassertion of its former rights and role, with unknown consequences for Turkey's EU candidacy.

Turkey remains tense. Writers bold enough to discuss the 1915 Armenian massacres face prosecution for "insulting Turkishness." Even Nobel Prize winner Orhan Pamuk was charged and fled to New York. A nationalist youth shot to death Armenian editor Hrant Dink; thousands of secular Turkish intellectuals turned out for his funeral. Turkish security forces have formed a sinister "deep state" conspiracy to return Turkey to authoritarian nationalism. One cannot predict a smooth path for Turkish democracy.

CONCLUSIONS

Turkey is a case study in the difficulty of modernizing a Muslim country. Turkey is the first Muslim country to attempt modernization and has not yet fully succeeded. Significant elements resist. Generals who had earlier tried to modernize the Ottoman Empire founded the Republic of Turkey with Atatürk, one of their own, as first president. Atatürk, an authoritarian reformer, led the country on a secular, Western course. His successor, Ismet Inönü of the Republican Peoples party, democratized Turkey by legalizing opposition parties, some of which tried to roll back Atatürk's reforms, leaving Turkey "torn" between a Westernizing elite and Islamic mass parties. Turkey seemed to be permanently praetorian.

In 1950, the Democratic Party came to power and tried to disenfranchise the Republicans and their military supporters. This triggered the 1961 coup. Having tasted power, military officers tried twice more in the 1960s to overthrow the government. In 1971, they threatened a coup if the government did not improve security, and the government resigned. In 1980, the military intervened again, to restore security to the streets.

In the 1990s, a series of Islamist parties took power, either in coalitions or on their own. The current AK party is run by Islamist reformists. While an Islamist government cooperated with the United States in the First Gulf War, the current party did not. As the country struggled to come out of the worst depression in sixty years, it turned down a major U.S. aid package rather than assist the second Bush administration to invade Iraq.

The Islamist Justice and Development party has united the country behind a long-held secularist goal: integration of Turkey into Europe. Turkey's reaction to an upsurge in terrorism has the potential of derailing efforts to meet European modernization standards, but Turkey will remain important to Europe because of the oil and natural gas in Turkish pipelines.

KEY TERMS

customs union (p. 139)

disestablish (p. 130)

Entente (p. 127)

European Union (p. 139)

Islamism (p. 131)

junta (p. 134)

Lausanne (p. 127)

nationalist (p. 126)

reactionary (p. 129)

republic (p. 128)

Sèvres (p. 127)

statism (p. 131)

technocrat (p. 137)

FURTHER REFERENCE

Ahmad, Feroz. *The Making of Modern Turkey.* New York: Routledge, 1993.

Henze, Paul B. *Turkey and Atatürk's Legacy.* Haarlem, Netherlands: SOTA, 1998.

Heper, Metin, and Jacob M. Landau, eds. *Political Parties and Democracy in Turkey.* New York: I. B. Tauris, 1991.

Larrabee, F. Stephen, and Ian O. Lesser. *Turkish Foreign Policy in an Age of Uncertainty.* Santa Monica, CA: RAND, 2003.

Lewis, Bernard. *The Emergence of Modern Turkey,* 2nd ed. New York: Oxford University Press, 1968.

Macalester International. *Hybrid Geographies in the Eastern Mediterranean: A View from the Bosporus,* vol. 15, winter 2005.

Mango, Andrew. *The Turks Today.* New York: Overlook, 2006.

———. *Turkey and the War on Terror.* New York: Routledge, 2005.

Pamuk, Orhan. *Istanbul: Memories and the City.* New York: Vintage, 2007.

Pope, Nicole, and Hugh Pope. *Turkey Unveiled: A History of Modern Turkey.* New York: Overlook Press, 1998.

Zurcher, Erik J. *Turkey: A Modern History.* New York: I. B. Tauris, 1993.

8   The Kurds

Points to Ponder

- Are the Kurds a separate nationality?
- Can one nationality have several languages?
- Should all nations have their own state?
- What has prevented the Kurds from establishing a state?
- If Kurds establish a state in one country, what will be the effect on Kurds in other countries?
- Is it right for nationalist movements to constantly switch allies in order to get powerful supporters?
- Is this region especially full of violence and betrayal, or no worse than many others?

Largely forgotten, the Kurds have been a long-smoldering problem that took on new urgency with the two wars against Iraq. Should these strange, divided people have their own country, or should they be content to be citizens of other countries? To answer these questions, we have to understand the concept of nationalism.

WHO ARE THE KURDS?

The Kurds are at least 25 million people who live in Turkey (14 million), Syria (2 million), Iraq (5 million), Iran (4 million). They have no country of their own and never did. They have usually been divided and do not form one single ethnic group. The biggest concentration of Kurds is probably Istanbul, home to some 3 million Kurds.

The ancestral home of the **Kurds** is in the mountainous region where these countries come together, a land of plateaus and mountains, many with peaks over 10,000 feet. Even the cities are at altitudes of over 4,000 feet. Winters are extremely

---

Kurds   Nationality, neither Turkish nor Arab, inhabiting mountains where Iran, Iraq, and Turkey meet.

The Scattered Kurds

cold; snow isolates many mountain villages. The harsh climate and terrain breed self-reliant people used to hardship. The same conditions produce social isolation and difficulties in communication.

The Kurds speak a variety of dialects. The two most common are Kurmanji and Sorani—Indo-European languages related to Persian. The third dialect (known as Macho-Macho by the Kurds, Zaza by the Turks, and Gurani by the Persians) is not linguistically related to the other two. Kurmanji and Sorani reflect a common origin, but there are numerous differences between them. Kurmanji has gender and case endings; Sorani does not. Differences in pronunciation often make the languages mutually unintelligible. The Kurmanji-Sorani divide reflects an underlying cultural chasm. Kurmanji speakers are organized along tribal lines, whereas the Sorani are more urbanized. Written Kurdish also varies with the countries Kurds live in. In Iraq and Iran, Kurdish uses a modified Arabic script, in Armenia a Cyrillic one, and in Syria and Turkey a Latin script.

While most Kurds are Sunni Muslims, some are Shi'a or Christians. Most Kurds are tolerant of religious minorities. Some Kurds believe in sects that most orthodox Muslims reject, such as the Yazidi and the Ahl al Haq or Ali Allahi. Even among the traditional Sunni Kurds, many are members of Sufi religious orders, primarily the Qadiri or the Naqashbandi.

Kurds are divided among nomadic tribesmen, sedentary tribesmen, and city dwellers. Traditionally Kurds have looked to the nomads as their real fighters. Feuds between tribes often interfere with nationalist aspirations. Even when tribal chiefs

K Key Concepts

NATIONALISM

As we discussed in Chapter 4, nationalism is the belief that a people ought to govern themselves with their own state. The basis for this feeling can be language, ethnicity, religion, or ideology. Nationalism often emphasizes the greatness and unity of one's people and a dastardly Other, those who are not like us but occupy us, misrule us, oppress us. Nationalism can be very negative and nasty.

Ethnic nationalists look at physical appearance, common ancestry, common language, and common religion. Few nations are ethnically pure, as you always find mixed marriages, immigrants, emigrants, contrived histories and ancestries, and converts into or out of the religion. Nationalism based on ideology accepts a variety of people who believe they are part of the nation. **Self-identification** is what matters here. We are Americans because we wish to be, not because of a common ethnic origin. Few countries are like that. The Kurds, divided by dialects, have trouble defining themselves as a nation based on purely ethnic criteria. Do they have sufficient self-identification to form a nation on ideological grounds?

support a nationalist movement, other tribes oppose it out of tribal rivalry. Kurds do not have a long written history; instead they have a rich body of folklore. The bulk of Kurdish literature is poetry, transmitted orally.

A HISTORY OF SEEKING A NATION

Ancient Sumerian records describe a people called Gutu, or Kuti, who held the middle Tigris region between 2400–2300 B.C. These could have been early ancestors of the Kurds, as could the Kardukhia who lived on the Armenian plateau between the ninth and sixth centuries B.C. Other possible ancestors are the Cyrtii, first mentioned by Polybius in 22 B.C. as rioters among the troops of the governor of Media.

By the fourth century A.D., Armenians gave the name Kerchkh to the region northwest of Lake Urumiyeh, and they referred to the residents by the same name. When the Arabs conquered the area in 644–656, they called the inhabitants Kurds. Between 951 and 1096, numerous Kurdish dynasties ruled in Eastern Turkey, Western Iran, and Azerbaijan. The Kurdish general Salah-ad-Din, better known as Saladin, defeated the Crusaders, recaptured Jerusalem, ruled over central Arabia, and reconquered Fatimid Egypt for the caliphate.

In 1501 Shah Ismail founded the Safavid dynasty in Iran and tried to convert his subjects to Shi'a Islam. Many of the Sunni Kurds migrated out of Iran and into

---

self-identification   Group formation based on subjective feeling of solidarity.

Cultures

CREATION MYTHOLOGY

Persian creation mythology is found in the Shahname; Kurdish creation mythology is in the Sharafname. Much of the creation is the same in both accounts, suggesting a common ancestry. The differences emphasize group attributes in which Kurds take great pride.

The fifth king in the Pishdadides dynasty of Iran was Zohhak, son of Jamshid. Zohhak had a peculiar illness in which serpents grew from his shoulders. To assuage this malady, Satan advised Zohhak to apply the brains of young men to each of the shoulders. Zohhak accordingly ordered the execution of two youths daily. In the Persian version, this practice continued until a hero killed Zohhak.

In the Kurdish version, the executioner took pity on the intended victims and only sacrificed one youth. The executioner then mixed the brains of the one victim with the brains of a sheep. As for the youths who were saved, they were forced to escape and hide in the most inhospitable mountains in the country, where they multiplied and became the original Kurdish people. Thus, this creation story emphasizes the oppressed nature of the Kurds, and their ability through cunning and perseverance to survive.

---

the Ottoman Empire, especially after the battle of Chaldiran (1514) when the Turkish Sultan Selim the Grim defeated the Persian shah. The Sultan established a series of five independent Kurdish principalities on the border to act as a buffer. Iran followed suit. The last of these semi-independent emirates lasted until 1865. During the reign of Shah Abbas the Great (1585–1628), many Kurds left their traditional heartland forever. To protect his borders against invading Uzbeks and Turkomans, the shah transferred several Kurdish tribes from the western borders of his kingdom to the far northeastern corner of Khorasan. These tribes were Shi'a Kurds and gave their loyalty to the shah of Iran rather than the Sunni caliph in Istanbul.

In the nineteenth century, nationalism began to stir among the Kurds. Emir Badr Khan of Botan began to unite Kurds in a single state. He struck his own coins and the Friday prayer was said in his name—both signs of sovereignty. In 1843 and 1846, Badr Khan sent expeditions against his **Nestorian** Christian neighbors, but the Ottomans, under European pressure, forced his surrender. Badr Khan was exiled to Canada and later to Damascus, where he died. Some Kurdish historians consider him the father of Kurdish nationalism.

In 1872, the Persian government demanded that the Kurds pay taxes to the central government. They refused, claiming that in 1836 the shah had let them pay whatever taxes were owed to their own leader, Shaykh Taher. The Persian government sent an army to collect the revenues. Shaykh Taher, head of the Naqashbandi order in the region, had died, but his son, Shaykh Ubaydallah, saw

---

Nestorian   Branch of Christianity that spread from Byzantium into Caucasus, Central Asia, and China.

his authority was being challenged and appealed to the Ottoman Sultan for protection. The shaykh also sent a small force to the Russo-Turkish war of 1877–1878; in recognition, the Ottomans appointed him commander of Kurdish tribal forces, bolstering his claim of leader of the Kurdish lands. With little Ottoman help, the shaykh decided Kurds could rely only on themselves.

The Treaty of Berlin ended the war and obligated the Ottoman government to protect Christian Armenians from Kurds. Ubaydallah interpreted this as a European guarantee of Christian ascendancy in Kurdistan. Hearing the Armenians were to get an independent state around Van, Ubaydallah stated he would never permit it, even if he had to arm *women* to stop it!

In 1879, Kurds from the Haraki tribe plundered a village, and the Ottomans retaliated against them. In response, Ubaydallah launched an armed uprising against the Turkish government. The insurrection, under command of his son Abdul Qadir, was easily put down, and the shaykh bowed to the central government. In 1880, Persian troops crossed the border and killed or kidnapped some young Kurds. In retaliation, the shaykh attacked Iran and threatened to set up an independent Kurdish kingdom. He attacked with 80,000 soldiers and, joined by Iranian tribesmen, reached Tabriz before being repulsed. The Ottoman government tired of Ubaydallah's attempts at a Kurdish kingdom. In 1882 Ubaydallah sought Russian support for yet another Kurdish movement. Weak political movements seek help everywhere and anywhere. Istanbul soon heard of it and deported the shaykh and his tribal chiefs to Mecca.

To guard against another Ubaydallah, in 1890 Sultan Abdul Hamid II established the Hamidiye, cavalry regiments of native tribesmen. They had to provide their own weapons and horses, and the tribal chieftains were made unit commanders. The Hamidiye continued in one form or another until the establishment of the Turkish Republic. Local residents remember these units with revulsion, because the tribal leaders used them to oppress all in the area not allied with them.

WORLD WAR I AND ITS AFTERMATH

Allied pronouncements after World War I fueled nationalist aspirations among Kurdish leaders, as they did worldwide. Woodrow Wilson in his 1918 **Fourteen Points** speech said territorial settlements at the upcoming peace conference should be based on national self-determination. Point twelve specifically said that in the Turkish portions of the Ottoman Empire, other nationalities should be assured an opportunity for autonomous development. Britain, less enamored with nationalist rights than Wilson, suggested a Kurdish buffer state between Turkey and Mesopotamia.

The allies met at Versailles to negotiate a peace. The Kurds sent a delegation but, as usual, the Kurds could not maintain a united front. In November 1919, several Kurdish chieftains under Turkish influence telegraphed the conference

---

Fourteen Points   President Wilson's plan for ending World War I, based on national self-determination.

P : *Peace*

TREATY OF SÈVRES

As we considered in Chapter 7, Turkey actually had two treaties marking the end of World War I. The first, the Treaty of Sèvres was signed on August 10, 1920, by the Ottoman, British, French, Italian, and U.S. governments. Article 62 provided for the establishment of a Kurdish autonomous area within Turkey, and pointed out that the Turkish border could be redrawn if necessary to fulfill this commitment. Article 64 said that if the Kurds then petitioned the League of Nations for independence and the League accepted the petition, Turkey would recognize the independent country and renounce all claims to its territory.

It looked like the Kurds had international recognition for a country of their own, but that recognition had been granted by the Ottoman representatives. When Atatürk's Nationalist forces took over Turkey, they refused to recognize the treaty, claiming that the Sultan was under the thumb of foreign occupation. Atatürk demanded the treaty be renegotiated, and the new treaty, the 1923 Treaty of Lausanne, avoided all mention of an independent Kurdistan. What the Kurds thought they had won was snatched away from them. Kurds still refer to the Treaty of Sèvres as granting them independence.

protesting plans to separate them from Turkey, especially if the new entity would be under a foreign mandate, namely Britain as the mandatory power of Iraq. Britain had no intention of turning oil-rich Mosul province over to an independent Kurdistan. It kept Mosul as part of the new country of Iraq it was setting up.

THE SIMKO REBELLION

The leader of the Shakak tribal confederation was Ismail Agha Simko, husband of Shaykh Ubaydallah's granddaughter. Simko, an opportunist, first achieved prominence during the Iranian Constitutional Revolution of 1906. Originally aligned with the constitutionalists, he switched to the monarchists. As a reward, the Iranian government appointed him subgovernor of the district of Qotur. During World War I he fought as a Russian ally against Turkey and later against the Russians to defend Iranian territory from their occupation. In 1918, he personally shot Assyrian Christian pope Mar Shimun XIX in the back to eliminate the Assyrians as a political or military threat. By the end of the war, Simko was the only power in the Turkish-Iranian border area. By July 1922 he appointed both tribal leaders and governors for the area.

Simko's rebellion was less a nationalist uprising than a bid for personal control. In July 1922, in British-ruled Iraq, another Kurdish ruler decided to join in Simko's revolt. In an attempt to obtain British support for his own movement, Simko opposed the Iraqi revolt and convinced the other Kurdish tribes to deny the Iraqi movement any support. In August 1922, the Iranian government sent its Cossacks against Simko, defeating him decisively and forcing him into exile.

Reza Khan Pahlavi pardoned Simko in 1924, paving the way for Simko's return to Iran. In 1926, Simko again tried to regain leadership of the Kurdish tribes. This time, the Turks and Iranians combined forces and worked jointly against him. When the Kurds retreated across the Turkish border, the two armies encircled, disarmed, and interned Simko. In 1929, the Iranian government again invited Simko to return. Immediately, tribal chieftains gave him obeisance. Before he could reorganize, however, the tribes betrayed Simko to the Iranian government, which killed him in an ambush. The tricky Simko is a dubious Kurdish national symbol.

THE MAHABAD REPUBLIC

World War I gave Kurds their first chance at nationhood; World War II gave them a second. After Hitler invaded the Soviet Union in 1941, the allies supplied the Soviets heavily through Iran. In August 1941, the British took control of southern Iran and the Soviet Union took over the northern part of the country. Both agreed to evacuate six months after the end of the war. The central part of the country, including some Kurdish territory, fell between the two zones, an area that achieved de facto autonomy. Barely a third of Iranian Kurds fell inside the borders of this area.

In the absence of government authority, the Kurdish tribes began to reassert themselves and establish independent principalities. In the town of Mahabad, middle-class Kurds replaced Iranian government employees. With Soviet permission, Tehran appointed the chief of the Dehbokri tribe governor of the region, but the leaders of other tribes did not accept him. In August 1942, the Iranians appointed Seif Qazi to the position, the son of a Sunni religious leader and ally of Ismail Simko. Iran was attempting to hold itself together.

Stalin played his own game, namely, expanding Soviet power in the **Caucasus** by detaching Iran's Kurdish and Azeri areas and amalgamating them into his own Soviet Kurdish and Azerbaijan republics under the name of ethnic unification. Some say Stalin's attempt at this was the opening shot of the Cold War. In November 1941, the Soviets took several important Kurdish leaders to Baku in Soviet Azerbaijan to convince them that the USSR would support a Kurdish republic. Later Kurdish chiefs in Western Iran submitted a petition to the Soviets, requesting freedom for the Kurds in their national affairs. Meanwhile, a secret Kurdish nationalist society, Komala, formed and called for political and cultural autonomy within Iran but ultimate unification of all Kurdish lands into an independent state.

The Tehran government lost control of the area in May 1943, when Kurdish townspeople stormed a police station to obtain arms. An Iranian army detachment set out to restore order, but the Soviets stopped it on the pretext that the troop movement would upset the balance of military forces in the region. By 1944, Soviet political agents were situated throughout Northwest Iran, centered on the Soviet Consulate in Rezaiyeh. In 1944, Komala affirmed its unity with groups seeking

---

Caucasus   Mountains between Black and Caspian Seas, home to a bewildering variety of peoples.

Kurdish independence in other countries and asked the pro-Soviet Qazi Muhammad to join them, although some feared he would quickly draw the group's power into his hands—which is exactly what he did.

In 1945, the Soviets convinced the Qazi to accept leadership of the Komala and also invited the group to use the Soviet cultural center in Mahabad as headquarters. Komala changed its name to the Kurdish Democratic party, and went from a clandestine party to an open party that many Kurdish leaders joined, convinced that the party's goal was democracy. But the Soviets had other plans—namely, to use it as a front to grab another country. Qazi Muhammad and 105 Kurdish notables signed a democratic-sounding party program that may have been drawn up under the direction of the Soviet consul in Rezaiyeh. Qazi Muhammad denied the party was Communist but recognized the USSR as a true democracy and worthy of emulation. Setting up such "democratic fronts" was the standard Soviet technique for slowly taking over parties and governments in other countries.

In September 1945, a Kurdish group returned to Soviet Azerbaijan where they were promised everything: military and financial support for independence and positions at the Baku Military College for Kurdish military cadets. Except for some light arms, none of the promised aid arrived. The Soviets also purchased the Kurdish tobacco crop as an indirect form of financial support. The Tehran government, of course, was furious at the dismemberment of Iran. The United States, which had replaced the British in southern Iran, complained that the Soviets had not evacuated six months after victory in Europe as they had promised. Some historians once said that the continued Soviet presence in northern Iran caused President Truman to turn against Stalin and thus started the Cold War, a view now discarded.

On December 17, 1945, the Kurdish Republicans raised their flag in the Kurdish area of Iran. Men who had served in the Iranian army were recalled into a new Kurdish army. In January 1946, Qazi Muhammad formally declared the establishment of the **Mahabad Republic**, named after the local town. For protection against Tehran, the Republic turned to the tribes. Some, but not all, at first agreed to support the experiment but soon abandoned it in favor of Tehran. Many tribes did not support the nationalists because they had a historical hatred of Russians and regarded the Kurdish republic as a Russian creation. The communist orientation of some of the nationalists such as Qazi Muhammad disturbed traditional leaders. In addition, many tribal leaders had had good relations with Tehran for decades.

With Iranian Kurdish tribal support insufficient, the republic accepted the help of an Iraqi Kurdish leader, Mullah Mustafa Barzani. The Barzani tribe was the most loyal defender of the republic, but in the end they also negotiated with Tehran through the Americans. The Barzanis had entered Iran in late 1945, before the Republic had been announced, en route to the Soviet Union to seek Soviet help for Iraq's Kurds.

Soviet and Kurdish aims frequently clashed. Stalin wanted to speed up the secession of neighboring Iranian Azerbaijan and its union with his Azerbaijan SSR.

Mahabad Republic   Brief 1945–1946 Soviet-sponsored Kurdish state in northwest Iran.

The Soviets were worried, however, that the Mahabad Republic, led by members of the middle class and tribes, could become a nucleus for a Western-style democracy instead of a Communist state. By February 1946, Soviet unhappiness with the Kurdish Republic was clear. Stalin hated what he did not control.

The Mahabad Republic introduced measures to attract support of the Kurds. It allowed the use of Kurdish national dress, previously banned by the shah. It established universal elementary education, with textbooks in Kurdish. Using a printing press probably supplied by the Soviets, they issued a Kurdish-language newspaper, a periodical, and two literary magazines. Barzani was named "marshal" of its armed forces.

The Kurdish republic never formally declared independence from Iran because its backers, the Soviets, were not willing to burn their bridges with Tehran by supporting such a move. The Kurds themselves recognized that Tehran would oppose with force the creation of an independent Kurdistan but hoped Tehran would accept an autonomous Kurdish region within Iran. The republic also had problems with its neighbor, the other Soviet creation, the Azerbaijan Republic, as both claimed the same territories.

On May 9, 1946, a year after the war's end, the Soviets withdrew the last of their troops from northern Iran and the Iranian central government moved troops against the breakaway republics. Qazi Muhammad realized he had to negotiate with Tehran if he wanted to preserve any Kurdish gains. Iranian Prime Minister Qavam proposed that Iranian Kurdish lands be combined into a single province to be directed by a governor general, probably the Qazi himself. Qazi sought the advice of the Soviet Embassy, which told him not to accept, so Qazi never agreed to Qavam's proposals.

The Azerbaijan Republic fell to Iranian forces first, and the Kurdish tribes turned against the Kurdish government. Qazi Muhammad surrendered Mahabad on December 14, 1946—eleven months after having announced the creation of the republic there. Mullah Mustafa Barzani tried to convince Qazi Muhammad and the rest of the government to flee, but they refused. Iran hanged the Qazi, his brother, and his cousin for treason.

Within a few days, all traces of the Mahabad Republic had been erased. The government forbade the teaching of Kurdish. Iranian soldiers destroyed Kurdish books in the Mahabad public squares. Kurds who had been active in the movement hid any compromising documents. The Kurdish Democratic party was banned, but continued as a clandestine organization. Barzani escaped to Iraq and then passed into the Soviet Union where he would remain in exile until 1958. His stay in the USSR earned him the title, "the Red Mullah" and the rank of Soviet general.

THE RISE OF BARZANI

Amidst the confusion of the 1958 Iraqi revolution, Mullah Barzani went back to his tribal homelands. Based on his military reputation, his role as defender of Mahabad, his Soviet backing, and his lack of competition, Barzani was immediately recognized by Kurds in Iran and Iraq as their leader. Barzani treated Iran as his guerrilla army's hinterland. The Iraqi army blockaded Iraqi Kurdish territory, but neither Iran nor Iraq had the power to close their border. This let Iraqi Kurds escape the blockade and import the materials they needed. Iranian Kurds sent provisions, clothing, tents, arms, and munitions. To ensure that aid continued, Barzani established a network of contacts throughout Iran and appointed a close aide as leader of the Iranian Kurdish Democratic party. Many Iranian Kurds were so convinced of Barzani's role as nationalist leader that they moved to Iraq, some to fight alongside the Barzani forces.

As usual, the Kurds were split. Mullah Barzani clashed with Ibrahim Ahmad Jalal Talabani for the leadership of Iraqi Kurds in the summer of 1964. Barzani sought support from Iraq's historical enemy, Iran. The shah provided Barzani with money, weaponry, and intelligence. The shah believed he could use the Iraqi Kurds as leverage in his boundary dispute with Iraq over the **Shatt al-Arab**.

In return, Barzani promised to maintain peace in Iranian Kurdistan. He told Iranian Kurds that with the shah's help they could get Kurdish **autonomy** in Iraq first, so in the interest of Kurdish nationalism the Iranian Kurds should "freeze" their anti-Tehran activities. Many Iranian Kurds were outraged at this backdown, and some broke with Barzani. About a hundred Iranian Kurdish fighters in Iraq returned to Iranian territory, where the central government arrested and shot them. Barzani's fighters even assisted the shah's police in their efforts. This is a sharply divided nationalist movement.

Barzani saw the shah as his only support and in 1968 even killed Iranian revolutionaries who were trying to transit Iraq into Iran. Their bodies were turned over to Iranian authorities as proof of Barzani's fealty. The shah in return sent Iranian troops across the border to support Iraqi Kurds in 1969. Worried, Baghdad sent a secret delegation to Tehran to negotiate. The Iranian prime minister toyed with the Iraqis, refusing to admit Iran's complicity with the Iraqi Kurds, but claiming inability to control the border.

In 1970 Baghdad and Mullah Barzani signed a peace accord and autonomy agreement committing the ruling Baath party to recognize that Iraq had two peoples, Arabs and Kurds, and to give Kurds a role in government. The shah was furious at this switch, but he was a realist. In 1972 he renewed contact with Barzani because the Soviet-Iraqi Friendship Treaty alarmed him and he saw Barzani as a possible foil to the Baghdad government. The shah feared encirclement.

By July 1972, Barzani was receiving heavy weapons from Iran and had begun broadcasting from Iran. Washington approved of this renewal of Iranian-Barzani contacts. President Nixon, like most U.S. presidents, saw Iran as an anti-Soviet ally and Iraq as a Soviet client. The 1970 accord fizzled, and by 1974 Iraqi forces had several military successes against the Kurds. In reaction, Iran aimed artillery fire into Iraq from Iranian territory. In February 1975 Iran sent 400 men and twelve 155mm howitzers into Iraq to protect Barzani's forces with two other artillery batteries in

---

Shatt al-Arab   "River of the Arabs," confluence of Tigris and Euphrates that flows fifty miles to Persian Gulf.

autonomy   Partial independence.

G Geography

THE SHATT AL-ARAB BORDER DISPUTE

The border between Iraq and Iran was first settled in a 1555 treaty between the Ottomans and the Persians. With the British in charge of Iraq, the 1937 Iran-Iraq treaty set the border along the river's eastern edge, placing the entire Shatt solely under the control of Iraq. Iranian navigation was only with Iraqi permission. Iran wanted the border redrawn, to run along the **thalweg**, the midpoint of the deepest channel in the river.

reserve. Fire was not very precise, and the Iranian soldiers quickly learned to fear Iraqi airpower. To protect their military assets, the Iranians sent the Iraqi Kurds surface-to-air missiles. Quietly, in the Kurdish region, Iraq and Iran fought years before Iraq's 1980 invasion.

While Iran provided enough support to allow Barzani to continue his battle against overwhelming Iraqi military force, he did not provide enough to let the Kurds win. The shah opposed Iraqi Kurdish autonomy for fear of the precedent spreading to Iranian Kurds, precisely the same fear that Turkey has. As the shah was providing Iraqi Kurds with military support, he was violently suppressing his own Kurds. As early as October 1972, the shah sent word to Iraq that he would assure peace among the Kurds if Iraq gave Iran part of the Shatt al-Arab.

Iraq gave in and signed the Algiers accords on the Shatt boundary on March 6, 1975. Both sides agreed to discontinue support to the others' Kurdish populations, and the river frontier was to run along the thalweg. That evening, Iran withdrew its artillery back to its border. The following morning, Iraq systematically bombed Kurdish forces. After a week of aerial massacre, Baghdad let Kurds either submit or flee to Iran. Mullah Barzani and his tribe crossed into Iranian territory to await a chance to fight another day. The shah, having gotten the border he wanted, cynically sold out the Kurds who had counted on him. In this region, betrayal is a way of life. An old Kurdish saying: "The Kurds have no friends."

THE ROLE OF THE UNITED STATES

The United States had no national-security interests in the Kurdish question. Because the United States wanted to build up Iran as its major ally in the region, to protect the Persian Gulf from Soviet encroachment, Nixon agreed to aid Barzani, but it had to be covert. If it became public, our NATO ally Turkey—itself facing a

---

thalweg   German "valley path"; line drawn along the deepest part of a valley or river, often used as a ship channel and boundary.

Kurdish separatist movement—would be furious. The United States followed the Iranian lead in providing aid but not enough for the Kurds to actually gain independence. The U.S. House's Pike Commission later remarked that even in the context of covert action it was a cynical enterprise. News reports said the commission quoted a "high government official" (supposedly Henry Kissinger) who defended himself and his policies: "Covert action should not be confused with missionary work."

According to press accounts, the United States subsidized the shah's efforts to the tune of approximately $12–16 million. U.S. aid probably began in the 1960s. In 1971–1972, National Security Advisor Henry Kissinger (for more on this office, see Chapter 14) rejected Kurdish requests for funds, but the administration reversed itself after Iraq signed its friendship treaty with the USSR. The United States halted the aid again when Iraq signed the 1975 Algiers accords.

THE KURDS IN IRAN'S ISLAMIC REVOLUTION

The Soviets and Iranians, cutting deals of their own, abandoned the Kurds. The Soviets wanted Iraq as a client state, and the Iranians wanted a better border in the Shatt. So Barzani switched sides again, this time to the United States. Actually, every step in gaining and shifting allies that Barzani made was rational. Americans tend to get sentimental and want to keep allies.

Mullah Mustafa Barzani died in 1979 in a Washington hospital, where he befriended columnist William Safire, who continued to support the Kurdish cause in the *New York Times.* Barzani's sons, Idris and Masoud, took over leadership of the movement. The Barzanis called their group the Kurdish Democratic party of Iraq (KDP) and got Iranian support.

In Iran, the Kurds sympathized in general with the growing opposition to the shah. The Kurds felt the monarchy had crushed and betrayed them. Iran's Kurds, however, were not active during 1978, as the Iranian Revolution was an urban phenomenon. As it grew, though, Kurdish tribes seized the lands the shah had appropriated from their chiefs in the 1963 White Revolution (see Chapter 9). The Kurds established local committees to manage their own affairs, the only way to maintain law and order with no central government. When the Islamic Republic was declared, many Kurds joined it. In the Bazargan government, the ministers of foreign affairs and labor were Kurds, as was the assistant army chief of staff. The leader of the Iranian Kurds, Ahmad Kazem Qassemlu—newly returned from exile in Europe—appealed for Kurdish autonomy but to no avail. By September 1979, the Kurds were in armed opposition to the new Islamic government.

The Supreme Leader of the Islamic Revolution, Grand Ayatollah Ruhallah Khomeini, refused to recognize the existence of a separate Kurdish minority and labeled the Iranian Kurdish Democratic party as agents of America. The government annulled the election of Kurdish delegates to the new parliament, despite the fact they received 80 to 85 percent of the votes in their area. Their leader, Qassemlu, was elected to the Assembly of Experts that wrote a constitution for the Islamic Republic, but Khomeini banned his participation. At first, Kurds tried to fight the central government, but the Iranian military easily overcame them. By late 1979, the Kurds turned to guerrilla warfare. The Islamic revolutionaries in Tehran rejected Kurdish cease-fire proposals.

The Barzani brothers, driven by their hatred of the Baathist regime of Saddam Hussein, allied with the Iranians. Tehran did not use the Barzanis to fight Iraq but to pacify their fellow Kurds in Iran. The Barzanis played upon tribal and linguistic ties to split the Kurds and to deprive the Iranian Kurdish Democratic party of many of its followers. Iranian Kurdish leader Qassemlu tried to negotiate another cease-fire, and Iranian President Hassan Bani Sadr appeared ready to accept. The head of the Islamic Republican party, Ayatollah Muhammad Beheshti, overlooked the fact that the Iranian army was collapsing in the provinces and insisted on continuing the war against the Kurds.

By May 1980, Tehran sent Rashid Jahruquiri, an Iranian Kurd who was cooperating with them, to close the road along the Soviet border to insure the rebellious Kurds would receive no support from that direction. Rashid was unsuccessful, and the Iranians sent the 64th Division to do the job. By the end of June 1980, the cities of Kordestan Province had returned to normal, and Kurdish rebels either surrendered or returned to the hills. The war degenerated into night raids.

THE IRAN-IRAQ WAR

The Iraqi army invaded Iran on September 22, 1980 (see Chapter 12). With active Iraqi military assistance, Kurds opened a northern front against the Iranians while the Iraqi regular army fought in the south. At a time when Iran needed every soldier in the southwest province of Khuzistan, the Kurds tied down at least a quarter of Iran's army. In 1981 Tehran offered to recognize oppositionist ethnic groups if they would lay down their weapons. The Kurds doubted the offer and continued fighting.

Iran's Kurds aligned themselves with the Mujahidin-e Khalq (People's Warriors), a cultist Islamic-Marxist organization that had originally supported but then broke with the Islamic Republic. The alliance did not have sufficient military power to challenge the central government. In May 1982 Iranian forces militarily destroyed the Iranian Kurdish Democratic party. Qassemlu went into exile and was negotiating for Kurdish autonomy with an Iranian delegation in Vienna in July 1989 when he was assassinated, probably by the Iranian negotiators. Dr. Sadeq Sharafkandi then took over but was assassinated in Berlin in 1992. Tehran conducted a bloody "war in the shadows" with its opponents for several years.

Despite the Iranian Kurds' military defeat, low-level violence has continued. Kurds remained dissatisfied with the Tehran government, as evidenced by low levels of participation in the 2005 presidential elections. While the average turnout nationwide was almost 60 percent, Kordestan province turnout was only 25 percent In Mahabad and Piranshahr in West Azerbaijan, turnout dropped to as low as 15 percent.

⎇ *The United States in the Middle East*

CHEMICAL WEAPONS AND MORAL CLARITY

The United States in the 1980s supported Iraq out of anger with Iran, which had held American diplomats hostage for over a year. Washington knew Iraq was using massive quantities of chemical weapons against both Iran and against its own Kurds but said little and did nothing. Actually, no outside power did. U.S. intelligence even forwarded satellite data to Baghdad so it could more accurately use poison gas against Iran.

In 1990, however, we "discovered" that Iraq had chemical weapons after it invaded Kuwait. In 2003 we went to war with Iraq over these same chemical weapons, which it turned out they did not have. Consistent U.S. leadership in opposing any chemical weapons by any country at any time would have set a standard for moral clarity in the 1980s that we could have used in later decades.

THE KURDISH BREAK WITH IRAQ

Kurds on both sides of the border took advantage of the Iran-Iraq war to further their cause. In Iraq, the head of the Patriotic Union of Kurdistan (PUK) attempted to negotiate with Baghdad. Saddam Hussein, desperate for peace in the north while he battled Iran, agreed to a Kurdish autonomous region that included the oil city of Kirkuk. The deal collapsed, however, when Turkey brought pressure on Baghdad so that Turkey's own restive Kurdish population would not demand similar treatment.

With the collapse of the negotiations, Iraqi Kurds resorted to armed resistance to Saddam. But Saddam was not governed by any rules of civilized warfare and launched the al-Anfal campaign that used poison gas against his Kurdish citizens, supervised by Saddam's cousin, Ali Hasan al-Majid ("Chemical Ali"). The most horrible case was in the village of Halabja, where up to 5,000 Kurds died and 10,000 suffered injuries from air-dropped gas. In a three-day period, the Iraqi military dropped conventional bombs, mustard gas, Sarin, Tabun, and VX on Iraqi Kurds. Halabja was only the latest in a long line of Baathi efforts to eliminate Kurdish opposition to their rule, going back to 1963 when the Baath first took power in Iraq.

THE FIRST GULF WAR

In August 1990 Iraq invaded Kuwait. After a U.S.-led coalition drove the Iraqi army out of Kuwait, President Bush 41 urged Iraqis to rise up and overthrow Saddam. The Shi'a in the south and Kurds in the north responded and began seizing control. Bush did not back the rebellion, however, and Iraqi forces easily and bloodily put down the Shi'a rebellion. Then the Iraqi army turned north, and half a million Kurds fled into Turkey.

Conflicts

UN RESOLUTION 688

The Security Council approved Resolution 688 in the middle of the 1991 crisis precipitated by the Kurdish flight from northern Iraq into Turkey. The resolution was passed without citing Chapter 7, a necessary prerequisite for UN sanctioned resort to violence. Instead, it called for Iraq to cease oppressing its Kurdish population and requested that the Secretary General pursue humanitarian efforts in the region.

The United States and Great Britain frequently used 688 as justification for its establishment and military enforcement of no-fly zones in the northern and southern thirds of Iraq. This was invalid on two counts: There was no Chapter 7 authorization, and 688 did not include any enforcement measures in the event Iraq continued to repress Kurds. This was in accord with traditional UN philosophy of limiting intervention in the internal affairs of a member state.

The Turkish General Staff was appalled. Not only did they worry about the cost of the refugees to their weak economy, they were concerned that the new Kurds would strengthen their own, indigenous Kurdish rebellion. Ankara demanded that the coalition put the Iraqi Kurds back into their own land. The United States established a northern, no-fly zone above the 36th parallel claiming the move was justified by UN Security Council Resolution 688.

Deprived of their airpower, Baghdad could not defeat the Kurdish militias, known as *peshmerga* ("those who stand before death"). The Iraqi Kurds left Turkey to live in their own homes and receive humanitarian aid. From the March 1991 implementation of the no-fly zone until the 2003 invasion of Iraq, the Kurds living above the 36th parallel were happily free of Baghdad's control. They established an autonomous region with its own government and parliament, supposedly democratically elected. Their finances came from customs tolls, collected at the crossings with Turkey and Iran.

In reality, the region is governed by an uneasy alliance between two factions: Talabani's PUK and Barzani's KDP (which crossed back into Iraqi Kurdistan during the first Gulf War). Idris Barzani died in 1987, and Masoud Barzani ruled the KDP as Mullah Barzani's sole surviving son. The KDP controlled the northern, tribal regions of the autonomous zone while the PUK derived its strength from the zone's southern cities.

The parliament, the Kurdistan National Assembly, was chosen in 1992 elections under international observers, and most believe the election itself was free and fair. The results, however, were never announced because it could have destabilized the new Kurdish regional government if one faction held sway over the other. KDP and PUK leaders decided to divide the parliamentary seats 50–50, with five of the 105 seats going to Christians.

The new government organized itself around the March 1970 Autonomy Agreement the Kurds had negotiated with Saddam Hussein. The prime ministry and cabinet were divided between the two factions. In 1994 fighting broke out between the KDP and PUK over customs revenues. The main collection point was the Habur Gate between Iraq and Turkey, located in KDP-controlled territory. Barzani was taking a share for his followers before turning the revenues over to the Kurdish government. Talabani wanted a more equal division, and armed conflict erupted. In 1996, during a cease-fire, they established two administrations: a KDP administration in Irbil, and a PUK one in Sulaymaniyeh. The area remained divided until October 2002, when the two factions again united in anticipation of a U.S. invasion of Iraq. These two groups have been intense rivals for over thirty-five years. Kurds do not easily unite into one movement.

Combined with the U.S. Fourth Infantry Division invading from Turkey, the Kurds were supposed to open a northern front against Saddam in the 2003 invasion. But Turkey refused to allow U.S. troops to launch from its territory (see Chapter 7), so the Kurds missed most of the fighting. The new, American-tutored Iraqi government established a post-Saddam governmental structure that awarded much autonomy—some call it de facto independence—to the Kurds. This was the result of influence from Iraq's new president, longtime KUP leader Jalal Talabani.

Because of its decade of relative prosperity under the American no-fly zone, where the Kurds received their share of international aid for the first time under the UN-administered oil-for-food program, northern Iraq is one of the most pro-American areas in the Middle East. While it shares in the unrest plaguing the rest of Iraq, there has been relatively little violence. To attract tourism, the Kurdish autonomous government hired an American public relations firm, which used the slogan: "Kurdistan, the other Iraq."

THE RISE OF THE PKK

The Kurds of Turkey, the biggest group of Kurds, were not affected by rivalries between the great powers or between Iran and Iraq. Compared to their cousins across the borders, Turkish Kurds had it pretty good: They were full citizens of the Turkish Republic, and many of their notables advanced to the highest levels of Turkish government. There were scores of Kurdish members of parliament and of the cabinet and prominent party officials. Even the former president of Turkey, Turgut Özal, was rumored to have a Kurdish mother. To achieve these positions in Turkish society, however, a Kurd had to fully identify with Turkey—at the expense of a Kurdish identity. As a Turkish citizen, one could achieve much. Those who emphasized Kurdishness, however, by demanding Kurdish cultural or political autonomy, would be jailed as separatists.

Abdullah Ocalan (sounds like "Ojalan") founded the group that eventually became the Kurdistan Workers' Party (PKK) in Ankara in 1974. Ocalan had been one of many students caught up in the left-right violence that tore Turkey apart in the 1970s (see Chapter 7), and served prison time for leftist activities. The group was Marxist and Kurdish-nationalist, not Islamic. In 1978, Ocalan established a PKK central committee to direct the struggle. As did many liberation movements inspired by Vietnam in the Third World, Ocalan declared guerrilla warfare the method for achieving Kurdish rights.

Conflicts

TURKEY'S KURDISH WAR

In the 1980s, armed PKK insurgents established camps in Iraq south of the Turkish border, from which they attacked southeastern Turkey. (Some PKK fighters are still in Iraqi Kurdistan.) To counter them, Ankara organized a "village guard" system that paid and armed loyal villagers to keep out the PKK. These village guards soon became the primary target for the PKK. Schools, a symbol of central government authority, were also a major target.

At its height, the PKK claimed 10,000 to 15,000 armed fighters. Ankara evacuated some villages, either because they were too distant to protect or because they were suspected of giving aid to the guerrillas. Commandos trained in counterterrorist operations operated in Kurdish areas, and locals accused them of brutal tactics against noncombatants. It was a long, nasty war that took some 37,000 lives and could break out again.

In 1980, the Turkish military seized power to stop left-right violence and arrested thousands of activists, most of them from the left. They hit the PKK heavily, and imprisoned several members of the Central Committee. Ocalan, known as Apo, escaped to Syria, whose government provided him with a safe villa in Damascus, a Mercedes, and security protection. The Syrian government considered the PKK a strategic resource to force Ankara to abandon plans to dam the Tigris and Euphrates Rivers and to prevent Turkish cooperation with Israel. Ocalan also sought relations with Iraqi Kurds, but ultimately they were at cross-purposes and opposed each other.

The Turkish government tried to win Kurdish hearts and minds. Recognizing that the southeast was underdeveloped and that poverty fueled the terrorists, Ankara instituted a major project to build dams on the headwaters of the Tigris and Euphrates Rivers that would irrigate fields and generate electricity for industrial development. The theory was that gainfully employed Kurdish men would not "go to the mountains" and join the rebels. In 1991, the government lifted its ban on the use of the Kurdish language in homes and unofficial settings. Kurdish remained illegal in schools, government offices, or political campaigns.

The PKK did not limit its activities to the military field. In October 1991, its allies in the Social Democratic party broke with the party, and organized an ethnically Kurdish political party, the People's Labor party (HEP). Eighteen Kurdish nationalists were elected to the Turkish parliament. They arrived on the floor dressed in Kurdish national colors and insisted on taking their oath of office in Kurdish instead of in Turkish. The parliament voted to strip seven of the newly elected members of their parliamentary immunity, and they were eventually jailed for advocating separatist activities.

Key Concepts

Opportunism and Rationality

We have seen numerous cases of Kurdish opportunism, of switching sides to aid their cause. Ubaydallah, Simko, Mullah Mustafa Barzani, and others changed allegiances frequently among the Ottomans, the Persian shahs, the Soviets, or the Americans. Barzani went from a religious leader to Soviet marshal to friend of the United States. Is this dastardly or rational? What other choice does a small nationality, surrounded by more powerful forces, have? Consistency and purity could cost you your goals and your life.

Since the 1960s political scientists have developed **rational-choice theory** to explain the positions politicians take at any given time. They constantly scan the horizon and ask, "How can I get and keep power?" In U.S. elections they ask, "What do the voters back home like? I'll give it to them." They look at the very real differences of "red states" and "blue states." In international relations, leaders ask "How can my country survive and thrive?" They let little else stand in the way. Change the situation, and they change their policies. This is not slippery; it's rational.

For example, Israel had informal but good relations with Tehran (the shah did not publicly recognize Israel) and sent arms captured in the 1967 Six Day War to the Kurds in Iraq via Iran. Israel was undermining its blood enemy Iraq and the Kurds were carving out their Kurdish homeland. Perfectly rational. Israelis and Kurds could not care less about religion. Countries and political movements are highly opportunistic: They ally with whomever they think will further their cause. The United States does it, too.

The PKK established foreign chapters in Europe to raise money from Kurds living abroad (often using extortion, threats, and robbery), from drug smuggling, and to spread PKK propaganda that was accepted uncritically by European leftists. The PKK even had its own television station, MED-TV, broadcast from Britain.

The Capture of Ocalan

By the late 1990s the Turkish General Staff decided to end the Kurdish rebellion once and for all. It massed units of its 600,000-man army on the Syrian border and told Damascus that if they did not expel Ocalan, Turkey would invade. Turks and Arabs do not like each other. Syria expelled Ocalan, who traveled through many European countries that kept quiet about it. In November 1998, Ocalan requested political asylum in Italy. Turkey, Italy's NATO ally, pointed to the outstanding Interpol arrest warrant for Ocalan, charging him with the responsibility for 37,000 deaths. Washington supported Turkey's demands. Rome did not want to oppose allies, but many Italians wanted to protect a "freedom fighter." In January 1999, the Italians put Ocalan on an airplane and informed the allies they had no knowledge where he had gone.

---

rational-choice theory   Argues that political positions reflect intelligible needs and wishes.

Finally, in February 1999, Turkish intelligence located Ocalan in the Greek Embassy in Nairobi, Kenya. Ocalan was traveling on a Greek Cypriot passport. In a daring raid, Turkish commandos captured Ocalan and smuggled him out of Kenya. When Apo realized he was in the hands of Turkish authorities, he denounced his comrades and offered to be a Turkish government penetration agent against the PKK. Unhappily for Apo, the Turks filmed the entire event and broadcast it to the world.

Apo's supporters were not discouraged and demonstrated in sixteen European cities. Turkish courts found Apo guilty of murder and incitement to murder. His sentencing was postponed while Apo made public calls renouncing violence. He asked his followers to lay down their arms. The PKK at first said they would hold off any armed attacks as long as their leader remained alive; if Turkey executed Apo, the PKK would renew its terrorism strategy. As an armed force, the PKK was weakened but not finished.

In February 2000, the mayor of Diyarbakir and twelve other Kurdish leaders were arrested for aiding the PKK. Evidence of their crimes included their organizing a protest against Turkey's attempts to extradite Ocalan from Italy in 1999, something that would have been in the common interest with the PKK. They were sentenced to four years in prison.

As for Apo himself, he eventually got a death sentence, but it was never carried out. In 2002 Turkey ended its death penalty to meet criteria to enter the European Union. Ocalan now faces a life in prison. The PKK renounced violence as a tactic and changed its name to KADEK. Some PKK fighters, however, now calling themselves the Kurdistan Freedom Falcons, have bombed targets in Turkish cities. Others have shot Turkish policemen. Perhaps 5,000 PKK guerrillas took refuge in Iraqi Kurdistan; Turkey itches to invade to wipe them out. The Kurdish war in Turkey is not over.

CONCLUSIONS

The Kurds have always suffered two insurmountable obstacles. First, they never had a unified kingdom and are divided along lines of dialect, tribe, and nation of residence. Their factions often fight each other. Second, in the game of international politics, regional powers have always used the Kurds as a pawn. They used the Kurds to fight battles and then ditched them when their interests shifted. No one ever took Kurdish wishes and aspirations seriously. This has left the Kurds an angry and unpredictable force in the region.

Kurds have occasionally risen up for autonomy or independence when the great powers stalemated one another, leaving some room in which the Kurds could maneuver. Ubaydallah and Simko managed to gain power when the Turks and Persians balanced each other; Qazi Muhammad had limited success when the Russians and Persians were at loggerheads. The Iraqi Kurds recently achieved some autonomy when allied airpower kept Baghdad at bay, but Ocalan's rebellion never had a chance since there were no powers to oppose Ankara in southwest Turkey.

The Kurds have made it clear that they want to rule themselves. What is less certain is what form this self-government should take, how large an area it should encompass, and how a Kurdish government could support itself economically. Iraqi Kurdistan is de facto independent. Some Kurds think the oil fields of Kirkuk could give them an economic basis, but the United States has not been any more willing to let that happen than were the British between the two World Wars. Until someone can unite the various Kurdish factions, they will continue to fight among themselves. Similarly, until the countries of the area are comfortable with a Kurdish entity, history has shown the Kurds have little chance of success.

Key Terms

autonomy (p. 155)

Caucasus (p. 152)

Fourteen Points (p. 150)

Kurds (p. 146)

Mahabad Republic (p. 153)

Nestorian (p. 149)

rational-choice theory (p. 163)

self-identification (p. 148)

Shatt al-Arab (p. 155)

thalweg (p. 156)

Further Reference

Arfa, Hassan. *The Kurds: An Historical and Political Study.* New York: Oxford University Press, 1966.

Bidlisi, Sharaf Khan. *C'heref-nameh, ou, Fastes de la Nation Kourde,* translated from Persian and commentary by François Bernard Charmoy. Westmead, Eng.: Gregg International Publishers, 1969.

Bruinesen, Martin van. *Agha, Shaikh, and State.* Utrecht: Ph.D. dissertation, 1978.

Eagleton, William, Jr. *The Kurdish Republic of 1946.* New York: Oxford University Press, 1963.

Entessar, Nader. *Kurdish Ethnonationalism: Politics and Identity in the Middle East,* 2nd ed. Boulder, CO: Lynne Rienner, 2007.

Ghareeb, Edmund. *The Kurdish Question in Iraq.* New York: Syracuse University Press, 1981.

Imset, Ismet G. *The PKK: A Report on Separatist Violence in Turkey.* Ankara: Turkish Daily News Publications, October 1992.

Izady, Mehrdad R. *The Kurds: A Concise Handbook.* Washington, D.C.: Taylor and Francis, 1992.

Kutschera, Chris. *Le Mouvement National Kurde.* Paris: Flammarion, 1979.

Latham, Aaron. "Introduction to the Pike Papers," *Village Voice,* February 16, 1976, 70–92.

McKiernan, Kevin. *The Kurds: A People in Search of Their Homeland.* New York: St. Martin's, 2006.

More, Christiane. *Les Kurdes Aujourd'hui: Mouvement National et Partis Politiques.* Paris: Editions L'Harmattan, 1984.

Nikitine, Basile. *Les Kurdes: Etude Sociologique et Historique.* Paris: Imprimerie Nationale Librairie C. Klincksieck, 1956.

Olson, Robert. *The Emergence of Kurdish Nationalism and the Sheikh Said Rebellion, 1880–1925.* Austin, TX: University of Texas Press, 1989.

Romano, David. *The Kurdish Nationalist Movement: Opportunity, Mobilization and Identity.* New York: Cambridge University Press, 2006.

Yildiz, Kerim. *The Kurds in Turkey: EU Accession and Human Rights.* London: Pluto Press, 2005.

9 Iran

Points to Ponder

- What is the difference between "high" and "low" Islam?
- What is the origin of the Baha'i faith?
- When did Europeans first arrive in the Persian Gulf?
- Describe the Shi'a hierarchy. What does it resemble?
- How were the Pahlavis "modernizing tyrants"?
- Who took over Iran in World War II? Why?
- What did Stalin try to do in northern Iran?
- Who was Mossadeq and what did he try to do?
- What is OPEC and what does it attempt?
- Who was Khomeini and what was his political theory?

The Arabian peninsula has a number of independent Arab countries, most of which were invented by the British as they were protecting their sea lane to India. These include Bahrain, Qatar and what used to be called the Trucial States—now the United Arab Emirates. Each of these countries has a fascinating history, and many play important roles in the area. The UAE is an international transit point and major trading center. Bahrain was one of the first places in the region to produce oil. Qatar is the current headquarters for U.S. CENTCOM forces in the area. In discussing the Persian Gulf since World War II, however, the major players are the oil states of Iran, Saudi Arabia, Iraq, and Kuwait.

THE SAFAVIDS

At the end of the thirteenth century, a Sufi order sprang up in north-central Iran known as the Safavids. Within two centuries it had spread throughout the Turkic world. Its leaders sought political power as well as spiritual influence. The Safavids were originally a Sunni order, but the majority of its followers were Turkic tribesmen who looked for salvation through the Prophet's son-in-law, the Imam Ali.

167

R Religions

HIGH VERSUS LOW ISLAM

The Islam of textbooks is sometimes referred to as "High Islam." It is the religion of the learned, with a thousand years of rules and regulations, historical interpretations, and judicial rulings. Many Muslims find High Islam a rather dry faith that does not fill needs for an inner spirituality. Enter "Low Islam," namely Sufism, which we mentioned in Chapter 2 in connection with the Abbasid Empire. Rather than concentrate on the God of 99 names (such as "The All Powerful," "The Great," "The Merciful"), Sufism concentrates on manifestations of God in the hearts of individuals. It is a creed of love and a desire for oneness with God through extinction of one's self.

Sufism is a powerful, mystical movement within Islam. High clerics condemn it because it incorporates pre-Islamic themes and rituals into Islamic ceremonies. Most Sufis belong to religious orders that trace their origins back to the original companions of the Prophet. Sunni orders often cite Abu Bakr while Shi'a orders often cite Ali as the ultimate source of the "hidden knowledge," which they pass on to their followers. The largest Sufi orders are the Naqshbandi, the Qaderi, the Bektasi, and the Sanussiya.

In 1501, the Safavid Shaykh Ismail captured Tabriz in Persia and declared himself **shah**. He also declared that his kingdom would embrace Shi'ism as the official religion. It has often been debated whether Ismail took this move because he truly embraced Shi'a doctrine or if he wanted to differentiate himself and his movement from the Ottomans ruling the Anatolian plateau immediately to the west. Whatever the reason, Ismail believed his own propaganda and declared himself the "Shadow of God on Earth."

By 1509, the Safavid Empire ruled all Iran. The Ottomans invaded Iran and defeated the Safavids in 1514 at the battle of Chalderan. The borders established in the peace treaty have held, with only minor (sometimes nasty) variations, as the dividing line between Turkey and Iran for almost six hundred years.

The greatest Safavid ruler was Shah Abbas. Prior to his coronation in 1588, the kingdom had begun to disintegrate because most Iranians were Sunni Muslims who did not accept the Shi'ism of the Safavids. Iran is an empire in the true sense of the word because it is composed of many ethnic groups under the rule of one executive. Within Iran are Persians, Azeri Turks, Kurds, Baluch, Uzbeks and other nationalities. As we saw with the Kurds, when central authority is weak these ethnic groups tend to drift away and rule themselves. Through force of arms, Abbas reunited his empire and established strong central government.

---

shah   Persian for "king."

G : *Geography*

THE NAME OF THE GULF

Even the name of the Persian Gulf is disputed. It was known for centuries as the Persian Gulf, which Iranians like—Arabs say it should be called the Arabian Gulf. (There is already an Arabian Sea east of the Gulf of Oman that blends into the Indian Ocean.) One of the authors, working on AP's World Desk long ago, sent out a story from an Arab Gulf emirate that called it the "Arabian Gulf"—and quickly got an angry response from AP's Tehran bureau. The shah of Iran ordered his diplomats to walk out of any meeting that did not call it the Persian Gulf. At stake was not just a name but an understanding as to who was the dominant power in the region.

When the Americans entered the region in the late 1980s, Pentagon briefers began to refer to the Arabian Gulf in an effort to win Arab support, despite the fact that the official name recognized by the U.S. government was the Persian Gulf. To sidestep the issue, the Department of State began to refer to the water as just "the Gulf," an unsatisfactory solution because you cannot be sure to which gulf spokesmen are referring. Washington has yet to come up with a solution, and each department calls the Persian Gulf whatever works.

Shah Abbas was the first Iranian ruler to invite British troops onto Iranian soil. Portuguese merchants had established an outpost on one of the islands near the Strait of Hormuz, and Abbas did not have the naval power to oust them. He invited the British, rivals with the Portuguese in India, to do it. This opened the door over time to British influence on both sides of the Persian Gulf, as the British recognized the importance of the Gulf to their control of India.

Abbas's successors could not hold the kingdom together. Raised in the harem with little training for governance, they soon faced fissiparous tendencies, halted briefly by Nader Shah, who reunited the empire at the beginning of the eighteenth century. Nader is most famous for raiding India in 1738 and seizing the Peacock Throne that he brought to Iran. It has been there ever since. With Nader's death in 1747, however, the kingdom resumed breaking into smaller units ruled by military commanders.

THE QAJARS

At the end of that century, one of the military commanders managed to reunite the country. He was Mohammad the Eunuch, better known as Shah Mohammad Agha, a member of the Qajar tribe. He started the Qajar dynasty that ruled Iran through the nineteenth century. Shah Fath Ali succeeded Muhammad Agha and presided over two disastrous wars with the growing Russian power in the north. In 1813, Iran signed the treaty of Golestan and in 1828 the treaty of Turkmanchai, both ceding to the Russians Iran's claims in the Caucasus.

R⋮ *Religions*

THE BAHA'I

Every hundred years or so, a messianic movement rises in Islamic territories. In the 1840s, it was Mirza Ali Muhammad of Isfahan. He accepted Shi'a teachings that there would be no more prophets after Muhammad and that the twelfth Imam was hidden. Mirza Ali Muhammad claimed that he was the gateway (*bab* in Arabic) to the twelfth Imam.

The Shi'a religious hierarchy suppressed his teachings and persecuted his followers. The leading clerics in Iran were supreme leaders to their followers and disliked a new figure whose claims would place him above them. The government did not want anyone claiming to rule as spokesman for the Imam. The Bab's followers revolted; he was arrested and condemned to death.

After Mirza Ali Muhammad's execution, Mirza Husayn Ali Nuri took over the movement and called himself the Glory of God, *Baha' Allah*. His followers named themselves after this title, the Baha'i ("those who are part of the Glory"). Mirza Husayn claimed to be the Mahdi, the individual who would come at the end of the world to prepare mankind for the Second Coming. Traditional Muslims, Sunni and Shi'a alike, condemned Mirza Husayn and his followers as heretics. Under official sanction, Mirza lived in exile in Acre, Palestine, from where his religion spread worldwide.

ENTER THE WEST

The Qajars are not remembered fondly in Iran. They were corrupt and let Western influences penetrate the land. The Qajars received official subsidies from the British to keep the sea lanes to India open and keep the Afghans off balance so they could not attack the **Raj**. When they ran short of money, the Qajars sold "concessions," monopoly rights to a particular Iranian commodity. It began in 1872 when Naser al din Shah sold Iran's mineral rights (not including gold, silver, and some precious stones) to Baron Paul Julius von Reuter for 60,000 pounds and a percentage of the revenues. Other concessions to the British included the right to print banknotes and run shipping and roads. The Russians got the telegraph concession, road-building contracts, and a monopoly on Caspian fishing. The imperial competition between Britain and Russia often led to concessions granted to one and then cancelled when the other protested, to be settled by whichever government offered more money or bigger threats. The wishes of the Iranian people were never considered. To many, the Qajars were no more than puppets of the infidels.

The biggest flareup was the Tobacco Rebellion of 1891–1892. Naser sold the rights to sell Iran's tobacco crop to a British major in return for a bribe, a payment to the state, and a percentage of future revenues. The Iranian clergy spread the rumor that the Christian British handling of the crop made it religiously impure.

Raj   British India.

R ⋮ *Religions*

SHI'A HIERARCHY

Traditional Shi'a Islam has no single religious authority that rules supreme in matters of faith and morals, like the pope does in Catholicism. Rather, there are a number of senior clerics, each free to agree or disagree with the other clerics. Their rulings are binding on all Shi'a who follow that particular cleric. These clerics, in descending order of importance, are as follows:

Grand Ayatollah—literally, the "Word of God." Grand ayatollahs are teachers with religious students following them, but they also have the rank of *Marja'ye Taqlid,* "source of emulation." These learned men make religious rulings based on the primary sources in Islam, using their own judgment. All Shi'a are supposed to follow the teachings of a living Marja'. Times and circumstances change, and so the Marja' needs to constantly reinterpret Islamic law. Since a dead man cannot reinterpret the law, when a Marja' dies his followers are supposed to change their allegiance to another Marja'. A Marja's rulings are no longer binding after his death and need to be reaffirmed by a living Marja'. There can be anywhere from one to ten grand ayatollahs at any one time. One achieves the rank of grand ayatollah by acclamation of one's followers.

Ayatollah—Slightly lower in importance than a grand ayatollah, they number in the hundreds. Ayatollahs have the equivalent of a Ph.D. in Islam and, after long study in seminaries, have to write a dissertation accepted by their professors. Grand ayatollahs are always ayatollahs first.

Hojatollah—literally, "Sign of God." These men, numbering in the thousands, hold the equivalent of a master's degree in Islam.

Alem or *Mullah*—one who is educated in Islam, the equivalent of the parish priest or minister in Christianity.

This hierarchical structure, familiar to Catholics (think cardinal, bishop, priest), has no equivalent in Sunni Islam. While the Sunni tradition has a special place for those who study their religion, any man can legally lead prayer in a mosque. This is based on the opening verses of the Qur'an, the *Fatiha,* that Muslims repeat several times a day at prayer. In these verses, Muslims acknowledge that they are creatures of God, and no one stands between a Muslim and God. In Shi'ism, however, sacerdotal roles are reserved for the mullahs alone.

Smoking tobacco, beloved in Iran, was thus damned because a Muslim would be ingesting impure materials. When British agents arrived in Iran to handle the new concession, **bazaars** across the country closed in a general strike, and the mullahs issued a **fatwa** forbidding the use of all tobacco. The boycott brought the shah to his knees, and he cancelled the concession. Once the shah had been proven vulnerable, a wave of street protests began, culminating in the shah's assassination in 1896.

---

bazaar Persian for "market."

fatwa Muslim religious ruling.

Despite his personal corruption, Naser had been committed to modernizing Iran. He copied his neighbors to the west, the Ottomans, who were trying their own reforms in the *Tanzimat*. Naser did the same, reintroducing sciences to the school curriculum, creating a civil service, and modernizing the army. One of his reforms was the creation of a Russian-style Cossack brigade in 1879. This light cavalry drew many of its members from Central Asia. Naser's successor was Muzaffar Shah, who had learned from his predecessor the easy way to raise money. In 1901 he sold the concession to explore for and exploit petroleum in the southern half of the country to a British financier, William Knox D'Arcy. He drilled for and found oil, the oil that allowed the British navy to convert from coal to oil.

THE CONSTITUTIONAL REVOLUTION OF 1906

While the Tobacco Rebellion showed the people of Iran that they could force their ruler to change an economic policy, the first mass challenge to Qajar rule was the 1906 Constitutional Revolution. Pressure had been growing in the bazaar for a year, marked by strikes and violence, as the *bazaaris* sought a voice in national politics and the cancellation of foreign concessions.

Almost like the 1978–1979 upheaval, events were precipitated by a funeral and overreaction by the government. The police arrested a local cleric who had delivered a sermon critical of the government; his students launched a demonstration at the police station. The police shot one of the protesters; the next day after the funeral, the Cossack brigade beat all who attended as they exited the mosque. Outraged at this breach of religious etiquette, all the clerics in the capital exited en masse for Qom, Iran's Shi'a holy city, vowing not to return until the shah instituted political reform. In sympathy, the bazaar closed and the country as a whole went on strike.

The protesters then took refuge in the garden of the British Embassy. In the end, over 10,000 Iranians crowded into the diplomatic compound. After some weeks, the shah agreed to the creation of a parliament. Political groups organized throughout the country, elections were held, and in October, 1906, Iran's first National Assembly met. It immediately wrote a constitution, which the shah signed, making the National Assembly answerable only to the people of Iran. The shah dropped dead five days later and was succeeded by his son, Muhammad Ali Shah, who wanted to rule in the old, imperial manner. With Russian encouragement, the shah and his government ignored the parliament.

In 1907, the parliament passed the Supplementary Fundamental Laws, based on the Belgian constitution and limiting royal authority. The shah refused to sign. Vast crowds of protesters took to the streets, and the prime minister was assassinated. Over 100,000 people attended the funeral. Appalled at the assassination and frightened by the size of the protests, the shah retreated and signed the laws.

The shah struck back the following year. Backed by tribal elements and a senior cleric, he declared he could not support constitutionalism because it was alien to Islam. He directed the Cossack Brigade to open fire on parliament. Many of the parliamentarians fled to the Ottoman Embassy; those who did not were arrested. The shah had completed a coup against his own government.

R : *Religions*

CLERICS AND POLITICS

Traditional Shi'a political theory encourages clerics to avoid politics, but their political involvement began long before the 1979 Iranian Revolution. The Tobacco Rebellion would never have succeeded without Ayatollah Behbahani issuing a *fatwa* forbidding tobacco. Similarly, the leaders of the Constitutional Movement included Ayatollahs Behbahani, Tabatabai, and Nuri. The shah felt strong enough to move against the reformers only when Ayatollah Nuri defected from the Constitutionalists and threw his support behind the monarchy. Shi'a clerics have not been perfectly apolitical.

While the shah controlled Tehran, the rest of the country revolted against his arbitrary attack on the people's representatives. Fighting ended only when the shah's foreign bankers ceased providing him funds to pay his tribal supporters and the Cossacks. Many of the senior clerics in Qom supported the constitutionalists against the shah. The shah's supporters left him when their checks bounced, and he abdicated, taking refuge in the Russian Embassy. His son, a child of twelve, assumed the throne.

The second National Assembly opened in November 1909, but it was too late. Without strong guidance from the palace, the country slid into anarchy. As always in Iran, when the central government is weak, the outer provinces and the tribes pulled away and started to rule themselves. Ottoman, British, and Russian troops seized various parts of the country as the Great Powers sought positions in advance of World War I. In the south, the British were particularly active in arming tribes who opposed the central government. The British were motivated by a desire to protect "their" oil fields and route to India.

In the north, the Russians also supported tribes fighting the central government. While this policy began under the tsars, the Bolsheviks continued it after the Russian Revolution of 1917. Very early, the Soviets supported the "Jangal Movement," a group that established a Soviet Republic of Gilan on the southern shore of the Caspian Sea. They even sent Red Army troops to prop up their puppet government.

In 1919, the government signed the Anglo-Iranian agreement, which guaranteed the British a monopoly to sell the government weapons and provide Iran with all its military and civilian advisors. The opposition enlisted the new Soviet government to help fight the ever-increasing British control of the government, and they allied with the Gilan republic.

In the middle of all this, the Cossack Brigade flexed its muscle. Its leader, the illiterate Colonel Reza Khan, marched on Tehran. Reza got the support of the British, the police, and gendarmerie and in 1921 overthrew the government (but not the shah). The new government signed a friendship treaty with Moscow, which gave the Soviets the right to intervene in Iranian affairs if something threatened

Soviet security. The treaty also cancelled the 1919 Anglo-Iranian treaty and pledged that Iran would never be used to launch an attack against the Soviet Union. The Soviets, in turn, withdrew their forces from Iranian soil. Without their support, the Gilan Republic collapsed.

In 1923, Reza assumed the position of prime minister. Despite the fact that he had achieved his position with British backing, Reza established himself as a nationalist. He negotiated the withdrawal of the British army from Iran in 1924 (still there from World War I), and he removed British military advisors from the Iranian army. In 1925, he convened a parliament that deposed the last of the Qajars, Ahmad Shah, while Ahmad was on one of his frequent trips to Europe. The parliament then crowned Reza the new shah of Iran. The leading opponent to this move was a parliamentarian with royal blood from the old regime: Dr. Muhammad Mossadeq, educated at Paris's prestigious Political Science School.

Wishing to give his newly founded dynasty a link with Iran's imperial past, Reza Khan took the name of the ancient language of Iran, Pahlavi, as his family name. Reza's blood was quite ordinary, but he liked to pretend to continue two and a half millennium of Persian monarchy.

Shah Reza Pahlavi embarked on a massive modernization campaign. He decided that the path to modernization was not to follow the liberal democracies of the West but rather to emulate the totalitarian regimes that had begun to sweep Europe. He abolished political parties, closed presses, outlawed trade unions, and broke the power of the tribes to oppose the central government. He also built thousands of miles of railroads and paved highways, enlarged the military, and streamlined the bureaucracy by eliminating the thousands of hereditary positions in the provinces. He replaced them with a centralized hierarchy, staffed by graduates of the new schools and universities he created. He ordered the country to be called by its original name, Iran. Like Atatürk, he was a modernizing tyrant.

Pahlavi shared Atatürk's views that Islam held his country back. He did what he could to limit the role of the mullahs in the public sphere. He abolished Shari'a courts, seized traditional lands controlled by religious institutions, and established a secular court system based on European legal codes. He also eliminated clerics from government positions and the parliament.

Pahlavi wanted to change not just the economy but the whole society. He ordered men to wear European-style hats in place of more traditional or ethnic headpieces, and he ordered women out of the veil. (Atatürk did the same, but by leading parliament to pass laws.) In Mashad, this led to massive protests and the takeover of the Shrine of the Eighth Imam by the opposition. Traditionally, Iranians recognized the concept of sanctuary, which is why the opposition had taken over the gardens of the British legation in 1906. Mosques and religious shrines were places of sanctuary, just as cathedrals were in medieval Europe. Shah Reza, however, ordered troops from Azerbaijan to invade the Shrine and attack the protesters.

Pahlavi's opposition to the religious and his support of women's rights are exemplified by a supposedly true story. The shah's mother visited the main mosque in Tehran where the Imam berated her for entering the building uncovered. Returning to the palace, the mother reported to her son what had happened. Enraged, the shah personally went to the mosque and beat the Imam severely with

Cultures

THE SHAH'S PUSH FOR EQUALITY

With the Constitutional Revolution of 1906, Iran was on its way to establishing a liberal democracy. The Pahlavis reversed this course in favor of rapid modernization. In one respect, however, the Pahlavis were ahead of most of the Middle East: advancing the role of women.

Reza Shah moved slowly and did not try to change the superior role of men in Shari'a family law. He did, however, allow women to advance socially. He opened the universities to them, forbade gender discrimination, and outlawed the **chador**. To set an example, in 1935 he ordered government officials fired if their wives wore the chador. It was a major step that the ayatollahs tried to reverse after 1979. Women traditionally wore the chador, usually black, anytime outside the house. It is still used in Afghanistan and on the Arabian peninsula.

Muslim jurists in the tenth century declared that the Qur'an prescribed the chador so that women would conceal their "adornments." In fact, use of the chador probably began in Damascus before Islam to protect the expensive clothing of rich women when moving through the dust and grime of fifth-century streets.

a walking stick. The majority of Iranians were conservative, and the shah's efforts to modernize the country usually met public opposition. The shah relied more on his army and security forces to rule than on the support of the populace.

WORLD WAR II

In the late 1930s the clouds of war gathered over Europe and Asia. Almost too late, Britain, France, and some small countries allied against the growing Axis powers of Germany, Italy, and Japan. In August 1939, Germany signed a Non-Aggression Pact with the **Soviet Union**; a secret protocol divided East Europe between the Germans and the Soviets. A week later, Germany invaded Poland and started World War II with no Soviet protest. Indeed, Stalin was in on the deal and took the eastern third of Poland.

Joseph Stalin, leader of the Soviet Union, played down Adolph Hitler's hatred of Communists—a hatred Hitler explained in his autobiography *Mein Kampf* ("My Struggle"). Hitler's 1939 pact with Stalin was intended to be very temporary, although Stalin had trouble understanding that. Once Hitler conquered most of Europe, he ordered the *Wehrmacht* to invade Russia in Operation Barbarossa in June 1941, the largest invasion in history.

---

chador   Persian for "tent"; women's head-to-foot garment.
Soviet Union   Communist Russia and some adjoining republics, 1922–1991.

G ⋮ *Geography*

BOUND IRAN

Iran is bounded on the north by Armenia, Azerbaijan, the Caspian Sea, and Turkmenistan;
on the east by Afghanistan and Pakistan;
on the south by the Gulf of Oman and Persian Gulf;
and on the west by Iraq and Turkey.

In Britain, Prime Minister Winston Churchill was both thrilled and frightened by events. Germany now had a two-front war, something the German General Staff had long predicted would lead to their ultimate defeat. Churchill looked at the Soviet Union's size and the millions that could be mobilized into its Red Army and proposed that Britain seek an alliance with the formerly hostile giant. Justifying this stand, he told critics that if Hitler invaded hell, he would give favorable mention to Satan in the House of Commons.

These developments made Iran important. Britain had long been unhappy with Shah Reza's preference for Nazi Germany. (Actually, German agents in Iran had also been active during World War I.) As the British fleet was powered by Iranian oil, the British landed troops in Southern Iran to protect their energy source. In addition, now the Soviet Union was an ally and had to be supplied. Nazi armies blocked all routes through Europe, so the British set up a supply corridor through Iran.

British and Soviet troops invaded Iran in August 1941. The British seized the south, the Russians the north, leaving a narrow band that included the capital in the hands of the Iranian government. The Iranian army tried to halt the invasion, but fled the battlefield and deserted in a matter of days. The government fell, and the new prime minister negotiated in secret to remove the shah. The British, on their part, began a propaganda campaign against the shah to encourage members of parliament and others to jump on the victors' bandwagon and condemn the shah.

SHAH MUHAMMAD REZA

As the Soviet army moved on Tehran, Reza Shah knew there was nothing he could do to avoid capture. He abdicated in favor of Crown Prince Muhammad Reza Pahlavi, a Western-educated youth (Swiss boarding schools) without any government experience. Reza Shah sailed into exile like many maharajahs of India, aboard a British battleship. He died in South Africa in 1944.

The new shah was aware that he had neither domestic nor international allies. His best path to survival was to win over as many supporters as possible. He turned much of his administration over to American advisors, who by early 1942 had generally replaced the British in southern Iran. He then concentrated his attention on the Iranian army, which had deserted during the allied invasion but was still the most powerful element in Iran. He also pledged full cooperation with the Allies and even hosted the 1943 Tehran Conference, where Roosevelt, Stalin, and Churchill outlined measures for ending the war and carving up Europe afterward. Significantly, the Allies decided to hold the conference in the shah's capital city before they asked him, and they did not allow him to participate. The Allies allowed him only to pose for pictures with the world leaders at the end of the summit.

With the heavy hand of Reza Shah removed, groups that had been held down by the central government revived. New newspapers gave intellectuals a voice. In politics, Muhammad Mossadeq, who was briefly jailed for opposing the Pahlavis and who spent the fifteen years in seclusion on his estates, returned to parliament in November 1941. The parliament, or **Majles**, began to reassert itself after fifteen years as a rubber stamp. Political parties, including the Communist Tudeh party, organized and/or surfaced from the underground.

In parliament, Mossadeq picked up where he had left off years before: opposing the unlimited power of the Pahlavi monarchy. The opposition recognized that Muhammad Reza's power depended on the military, so they unsuccessfully attacked the military's privileges. When workers in Isfahan revolted, several of the oppositionists returned to the royalist fold out of fear of the masses.

THE SOVIET THREAT

The conventional story of the Cold War is that it began in Europe in 1946 or 1947 as Stalin turned East European countries into obedient satellites. Some argue that it began months earlier, in Iran. In August 1944, Iranian Prime Minister Muhammad Sa'id gave oil concessions in the southern sector to a consortium of American and British oil companies. The Soviets in October in turn demanded oil concessions in the zone they occupied. When the prime minister played for time, the Soviets offered to drop their demands if the shah replaced Sa'id with someone who was not anti-Soviet. After Sa'id's downfall, Iran stumbled through a series of political crises and prime ministers, none of whom could unite the country.

Moscow and London (later Washington) had agreed to evacuate Iran within six months of the end of the war in Europe. We did and they did not. Some see this as the opening round of the Cold War. The Soviets had not abandoned their desire for a piece of northern Iran and its oil. In September 1945, Ja'afar Pishevari established the Democratic party of Azerbaijan and called for the province's autonomy from Tehran. Pishevari, an old Iranian leftist ideologically attuned to the Soviet Union, coordinated his actions with Soviet representatives, such as the Soviet consul and military advisor in Tabriz and Rezaiyeh and shadowy figures of the Soviet intelligence apparatus. In addition to Pishevari, the Soviets encouraged the Kurds to establish the Mahabad Republic (see Chapter 8).

To protect their ally and further their aims in northern Iran, the Soviets interposed military forces between Tabriz and Tehran. The only way the central government could reassert its authority in the area would have been to fight through the Red Army. U.S. President Harry Truman issued an angry ultimatum to Moscow to withdraw or face a hostile America. Scholars now doubt that this was the start of the Cold War and the effectiveness of Truman's threat.

Majles   (Also *majlis*.) Arabic for "meeting, convocation, or audience." In Saudi Arabia, princes' local meetings; in Iran, national parliament.

The latest prime minister, the wily Ahmad Qavam, in March 1946 negotiated a Soviet withdrawal by seeming to grant the Soviets' demand for the northern oil concession. Qavam noted that the Iranian constitution required parliamentary approval to grant such a concession, and the Majles was in recess. He promised to get parliament to pass the concession. In fact, the oil concessions were worthless. No one ever had or has found oil in northwest Iran. Once the Soviet troops were out, the shah's army moved in and crushed the Azerbaijani and Kurdish Republics. The Majles refused to grant the oil concession. Some historians say it was Qavam's craftiness that got the Soviets out of Iran, not Truman's warning.

Iran's parliament continued frozen among squabbling factions, leaving the shah as the only power on the national scene. In February 1949 the shah was shot and wounded at Tehran University. Taking political advantage of the incident, the shah declared martial law and cracked down on opponents. After eight years in the shadows of others, the shah followed his father's footsteps and reclaimed the country with his military and security forces.

MUHAMMAD MOSSADEQ AND OIL

In June 1950 the government submitted its proposals to parliament for the revision of the 1933 Anglo-Iranian oil agreement. Oppositionists claimed that the Anglo-Iranian Oil Company (AIOC) was a state within a state, paid too small a percentage of the profits (somewhat over 20 percent) to the government, and did not pay enough taxes. Some radicals demanded nationalization of the AIOC, arguing the Iranian oil belonged to the nation and not to a British corporation. The hot question brought yet another prime minister through the revolving door. Prime Minister Razmara tried to lead the bill through the Majles but was assassinated in 1951 in Tehran's Friday mosque. Parliament passed a law nationalizing the oil company as Muhammad Mossadeq, the fiery nationalist and crowd manipulator, emerged as prime minister in May 1951. A hypochondriac, when in trouble Mossadeq retreated to his sickbed and was often interviewed in pajamas.

Mossadeq led a patchwork alliance of nationalists, leftists, and some religious leaders, united in their opposition to royal power. One of his major allies against British power was Ayatollah Abdul Qassem Kashani, who appealed to the conservative masses in his efforts to restore Shari'a law to Iran. The Mossadeq-Kashani marriage was one of convenience, but an effective one. The group was known as the National Front.

The British refused to recognize the legality of the nationalization. Oilmen from around the world pressured their governments to refuse to accept Iranian oil. They were afraid of the precedent: If the Iranians could nationalize oil, what would the Arabs and Venezuelans do? The AIOC said they would sue any company that accepted Iranian oil for receiving stolen goods. The British navy steamed into the Persian Gulf to threaten Iran with possible invasion, and British diplomats condemned Iranian actions in the UN. Mossadeq accused the British of interfering in the domestic affairs of Iran and ordered British diplomatic posts closed. The royalists secretly sided with the British but did not have the strength to oppose Mossadeq openly.

Mossadeq upped the ante by appointing a new war minister the shah would not accept. Mossadeq resigned, releasing a letter to the public protesting the shah's interference in the workings of government. The National Front called for strikes that the shah tried to put down with military force. When he failed to halt the protests, he turned back to Mossadeq and asked him to form a new government.

Mossadeq sought revenge. He seized royal lands, confiscated royal charities, reduced the palace's budget, demanded that the military report to him as head of government instead of the shah, and isolated the shah in his palace. He ruled the country with a series of emergency powers he obtained from parliament. Mossadeq brooked no opposition, disbanding the upper house and forcing the lower house to resign. In establishing his rule, Mossadeq lost the support of many in the National Front, including the religious wing.

OPERATION AJAX

Mossadeq had risen to power claiming the shah had usurped the constitution. Now the shah tried to use the constitution against Mossadeq. In August 1953, a colonel of the Imperial Guard tried to deliver a royal decree firing Mossadeq, but Mossadeq's home was surrounded by military loyal to him. Faced with his total lack of control in the country, on August 17 the shah fled to exile in Baghdad and then to Rome, never expecting to return.

London was alarmed with the loss of the AIOC and took its concerns to Washington, which viewed Iran in Cold War terms as a Soviet takeover target. The Communist Tudeh party, after all, was among Mossadeq's supporters. Eisenhower's militant anti-Communist Secretary of State John Foster Dulles had no trouble seeing a Communist threat in Iran, and neither did his brother, Director of Central Intelligence Allen Dulles. Ousting Mossadeq became a top Washington priority in 1953. Some now wonder if the Communist threat was that great or if Mossadeq was merely an Iranian nationalist.

Two days after the shah fled, British and American agents implemented "Operation Ajax," a secret plan to restore the monarchy. CIA Near East Director Kermit Roosevelt (Teddy's grandson) arrived with a suitcase containing $1 million and spread dollar bills throughout the slums of South Tehran, buying a demonstration that chanted, "Long live the shah!" Meanwhile, military coup plotters loyal to the throne attacked Mossadeq with tanks. They captured the prime minister, and the shah returned to Iran. Backed by his military, the shah arrested his political foes and crushed those who opposed him in the streets. Muhammad Reza Pahlavi had regained his throne with the military he had so assiduously cultivated.

Back in power, the shah cancelled the nationalization of the oil companies that had started the whole crisis. He did negotiate a new deal that split the oil revenues equally between the government and the oil companies. (At the beginning of the crisis, the British had rejected a Mossadeq offer of an equal split of the proceeds.) This represented a giant boost in Iran's share of the take over previous arrangements. In the end, the shah was as big a hawk on Iran's oil as Mossadeq. The shah did not forget, however, the help the Americans gave him in returning

G Geography

OPEC

With plenty of oil coming on line in the 1950s and 1960s, world oil prices were low. To boost their revenues, several oil countries founded **OPEC** in 1960 to keep oil prices up by limiting production. At its headquarters in Vienna, OPEC negotiates members' production quotas to try to keep production low enough so that prices stay up. OPEC is not just an Arab organization; it has several Latin American and African members. Some major producers—Russia, the United States, Mexico, Canada, and Norway—are not OPEC members.

OPEC got noticed when the 1973 Arab-Israeli war (see Chapter 5) prompted Arab producers to cut the flow of oil, creating a worldwide economic slowdown but increasing fivefold the price they got for oil, from about $2.25 a barrel to $11. Furthermore, Gulf producers rewrote their deals with the oil companies to give themselves some 90 percent of the revenues. Now the oil companies worked for their host countries as their technical and marketing agents. Staggering sums of oil revenue flowed into the Gulf countries. In 1979, with the turmoil created by the fall of the shah, prices again climbed, to over $30 a barrel.

In the long run, OPEC cannot permanently set world quotas or prices. All producers' cartels eventually leak. Nonmembers do not obey and even some members, strapped for cash, cheat by quietly producing more than their quotas. In times of crisis OPEC may tighten quotas and boost prices, but the quotas soften after the crisis passes. In the short term, however, OPEC can cause disruption, contributing, for instance, to the U.S. **stagflation** of the 1970s.

to the throne: After the Mossadeq coup, the vast majority of Iranian oil concessions went to American rather than British oil companies. The shah's opponents also remembered—with great bitterness—the American hand.

The shah ruled through the 1950s without any real opposition. He tamed parliament by dividing it into two parties—both loyal to him. He increased the size of the military and created SAVAK, his brutal intelligence and security service. He had the support of traditional clergy and recaptured Ayatollah Kashani's support when the shah released him early from prison.

KHOMEINI'S OPPOSITION TO THE WHITE REVOLUTION

Like his father, the shah believed in modernization. He launched a **White Revolution** (as opposed to a Bolshevik-type Red Revolution), which included land reform. This limited reform alienated large landowners and the clergy

OPEC Organization of Petroleum Exporting Countries, a producers' cartel aimed at keeping up oil revenues.

stagflation Slow economic growth plus inflation; came in 1970s from high oil prices and faulty fiscal policies.

White Revolution Major reform program controlled by the monarchy from the top down.

R Religions

KHOMEINI'S POLITICAL THEORY

Recall that the Shi'a in Iran believe that the world's rightful rulers were the Twelve Imams, direct descendants of the Prophet through his daughter, Fatima, and his son-in-law, Ali. The twelfth Imam did not die but is hidden, still in the world but not in time. Since the true ruler of the world is still alive, any temporal government is usurping the rightful position of the Imam. Some clerics theorized that it was acceptable to support these temporal governments if the government protected the Islamic lands and tried to shepherd the citizenry toward salvation. This support did not imply, however, that the usurping regimes were legitimate.

   Enter the Ayatollah Khomeini, who turned twelve hundred years of Shi'a theory on its head. Khomeini noted that no one had seen or heard from the Imam in a thousand years, and it could easily be another thousand before he was seen again. He also reasoned that neither God nor the Imam would want Muslims to be without guidance. He concluded that the only people who were qualified to guide were those who understood the faith fully: the clergy who spent their lifetimes studying the Qur'an and other religious texts. If one cleric could be found who epitomized Muslim learning and virtue, he should rule an Islamic Republic. If that cleric could not be found, then a committee of clerics could rule. The theory for the committee was that even though no cleric alone might possess all the qualities, each would have some of the necessary qualities. The clerics could band together, making sure that all the qualities were represented in the group. This concept, rule by those who knew Islamic law, became known as the "Guardianship of the Islamic Jurist." After 1979, Khomeini used his new doctrine to make himself ruler of Iran.

---

by nationalizing their holdings for redistribution to peasants. Traditionalists in 1963 mobilized the population into a series of demonstrations in Iran's major cities, which the shah crushed with the army, as usual. Paratroopers dropped on the holy city of Qom.

   Handing over land deeds personally to some peasants provided great photo opportunities for the shah, but the land reforms did little good. The peasants' small new holdings, unsupported with loans, training, or marketing infrastructure, netted them little. Many felt the loss, however, of traditional protections they enjoyed from their feudal masters. Much of the land for redistribution was taken from traditional Islamic foundations, earning the shah the hatred of the mullahs.

   In the meantime, Iran did modernize, but in a way that undermined the shah's regime. The shah had always favored higher prices for oil, and Iran had been a big supporter of OPEC. In effect, the shah nationalized Iran's oil much like Mossadeq tried to do. Awash with petroleum revenues, the shah hatched grandiose plans for a rich, modern Iran that would not get distracted by democracy. Ties with the United States were strong. Tens of thousands of Iranian students attended U.S. universities, and thousands of U.S. contractors and advisors worked in Iran. The shah bought much U.S. military equipment, a point that rankled opponents, who thought he was spending too much on the military. A journalist once asked the

G : *Geography*

Twin Pillars in the Gulf

When the world's leaders met in Tehran in 1943, they assigned responsibility for maintaining peace in the Middle East to Britain, long the regional power. But postwar Britain was too weak for its traditional burdens and in 1968 announced it could no longer supervise the Persian Gulf. As the British retrenched, the shah of Iran sought to fill the void in the Persian Gulf. Days before the British were to grant independence to the oil sheikdoms on the Arabian side of the Gulf, the shah ordered his troops to seize the islands of Abu Musa and the Tunbs near the strategic Strait of Hormuz.

President Richard Nixon recognized the important role the shah could play in keeping the Soviets out of the region. He announced that Iran, along with Saudi Arabia, would be the "twin pillars" of U.S. security policy in the Middle East. The Nixon administration approved the sale to Iran of the most advanced weaponry in America's arsenal. The shah, loaded with oil dollars, could afford it.

To protect their new protégé, the United States supported Iran in its dispute with Iraq. The United States provided covert assistance to the shah's allies in Iraq, the Kurds, and discontinued the aid when the shah and (then) Iraqi Vice-Premier Saddam Hussein signed the Algiers Accords, in which the two promised to settle all outstanding differences, split the Shatt al-Arab between the two countries, and not interfere in the internal affairs of the other.

Nixon's closeness to Iran and Saudi Arabia were part of a larger strategic effort to rely on regional powers to contain Soviet expansion. In Asia, the United States turned more toward Japan; in Europe, it called on NATO to accept more "burden sharing." U.S. resources had been stretched thin by the Vietnam war, and an American proxy like Iran in the Persian Gulf seemed the perfect answer to Washington's need to project power. The United States and the shah became very close, perhaps too close.

shah if he could become a figurehead monarch, like the king of Sweden. "I'll become like the king of Sweden," replied the shah, "when Iranians become like Swedes."

The 1960s brought a new voice to the opposition, one previously unnoticed. Ayatollah Ruhallah Khomeini had criticized the shah for a number of reasons and had tried to mobilize his students against the crown. His arrest in 1963 sparked demonstrations in Qom. In 1964 he denounced the Status of Forces Agreement, whereby U.S. soldiers in Iran would be tried in an American military court rather than an Iranian court. To Khomeini, this was much like the hated capitulations that the Qajars had agreed to as they sold the country to Europeans.

The shah sent Khomeini into exile. In 1965 Khomeini started teaching at a seminary in the holy Shi'a city of Najaf, Iraq (historically far more important than Qom). Khomeini attracted a large following both for his political views and his learning in Islamic mysticism. During his years of exile, he developed a new political theory, that of **Velayat-e Faqih**.

Velayat-e Faqih   Guardianship of the Islamic Jurist.

Khomeini and his followers in exile recorded audiocassettes condemning the shah and his government. These cassettes were smuggled into Iran and passed hand-to-hand in the mosques and bazaars. SAVAK monitored this flow, arresting those who were most active. This underground communication, popular among Iran's lower classes, escaped the notice of foreign diplomats, including the U.S. Embassy. The stage was thus set for the Islamic Revolution of 1979.

CONCLUSIONS

Iran differs from Arab lands not only in language and culture, but also in religion. The Safavid takeover of Iran in 1501 made Shi'a the official faith, and its mullahs, more hierarchically organized than their Sunni counterparts, gained a certain political role. In the early seventeenth century, the British presence began in Iran and grew as the corrupt Qajar dynasty sold numerous monopolistic "concessions" to British business, all of them resented by the Iranian people.

In the early twentieth century, with Tehran's rule in decay and a Russian sphere of influence in the north and a British one in the south, an illiterate cavalry officer, Reza Khan, seized power and crowned himself shah. Both Pahlavi shahs were modernizing tyrants, but more dictatorial than Atatürk. World War II made Iran an important transportation corridor into the Soviet Union and brought Soviet domination in the north and British (later U.S.) domination in the south. This began the massive U.S. involvement in Iran and support for the shah as one of the "twin pillars" to block Soviet power in the Gulf region.

When populist premier Mossadeq tried to oust the shah and the British oil company, the United States helped oust Mossadeq in 1953. Oil prices, bolstered by OPEC, brought Iran new wealth. As the shah modernized, however, he also alienated much of the population, especially the Shi'a clergy and Ayatollah Khomeini, who eventually brought down the regime in 1979.

KEY TERMS

bazaar (p. 171)

chador (p. 175)

fatwa (p. 171)

Majles (p. 178)

OPEC (p. 181)

Raj (p. 170)

shah (p. 168)

Soviet Union (p. 175)

stagflation (p. 181)

Velayat-e Faqih (p. 183)

White Revolution (p. 181)

FURTHER REFERENCE

Bakhash, Shaul. *Iran: Monarchy, Bureaucracy, and Reform under the Qajars, 1858–1896.* London: Ithaca, 1978.

Banani, Amin. *The Modernization of Iran, 1921–1941.* Stanford, CA: Stanford University Press, 1961.

Bill, James A. *Iran: The Politics of Groups, Classes, and Modernization.* Columbus, OH: Merril, 1972.

Binder, Leonard. *Iran: Political Development in a Changing Society.* Berkeley, CA: University of California Press, 1962.

Cottam, Richard W. *Iran and the United States: A Cold War Case Study.* Pittsburgh, PA: University of Pittsburgh Press, 1988.

———. *Nationalism in Iran.* Pittsburgh, PA: University of Pittsburgh Press, 1979.

Farmanfarmaian, Manucher, and Roxane Farmanfarmaian. *Blood & Oil: A Prince's Memoir of Iran, from the Shah to the Ayatollah.* New York: Random House, 2005.

Kinzer, Stephen. *All the Shah's Men: An American Coup and the Roots of Middle East Terror.* New York: Wiley, 2003.

Lenczowksi, George. *Russia and the West in Iran, 1918–1948.* Ithaca, NY: Cornell University Press, 1949.

Mackey, Sandra. *The Iranians: Persia, Islam, and the Soul of a Nation.* New York: Dutton, 1996.

Pollack, Kenneth. *The Persian Puzzle: The Conflict between Iran and America.* New York: Random House, 2005.

Yergin, Daniel. *The Prize: The Epic Quest for Oil, Money, and Power.* New York: Simon & Schuster, 1992.

Yu, Dal Seung. *The Role of Political Culture in Iranian Political Development.* Brookfield, VT: Ashgate, 2002.

Zahedi, Dariush. *The Iranian Revolution Then and Now: Indicators of Regime Instability.* Boulder, CO: Westview, 2001.

10 Saudi Arabia

Points to Ponder

- How did a religious alliance bring al-Saud to power?
- What are the strategic waterways of the Middle East?
- Since when has Arabia been "Saudi"?
- Why did the Saudis and Hashemites mistrust each other?
- How old and deep is the U.S.-Saudi relationship?
- How did Nasser jolt the Arab world?
- What are the weaknesses of the Saudi monarchy?
- How could Saudi Arabia tolerate U.S. support for Israel?

There are great and deep rivalries among Arabs. The rise of the House of Saud illustrates some of this complexity. The al-Saud had been trying to rule the peninsula for two centuries; the present kingdom is their third effort. Back in the 1740s, the Arabian peninsula was a desolate place. The east and west coasts were ruled by the Ottoman Empire, and the protector of Mecca and Medina was the Sultan in Istanbul. The south coast and the desert interior were tribal and independent, probably because the blowing sands had no apparent economic value.

MUHAMMAD IBN SAUD

In a small **Najd** hamlet near what is today Riyadh, in 1744, a tribal chieftain cast his lot with a local preacher. Their alliance ultimately founded today's kingdom. The chieftain, Muhammad ibn Saud, ruler of a small clan in the town of Dar'iyya, in 1744 signed a pact with Muhammad ibn Abd al-Wahhab to support one another.

Najd   Large north-central interior of Arabian peninsula.

R : *Religions*

"Wahhabism"

Wahhabism is a term for a religious interpretation whose adherents do not accept the label. Believing in the unity of God alone, the believers do not think they should be named after a man, because that raises the man to a level close to God. Eighteenth-century Najd preacher Muhammad ibn Abd al-Wahhab was obsessed with the unity of God, the basic tenet of the Islamic faith: "There is no God but God." Ibn Abd al-Wahhab took this message to an extreme not practiced in other lands. He said that a sinner places himself as either the equal to God or superior to God's will, implying that a sinner was declaring himself a god. Ibn Abd al-Wahhab therefore argued that anyone who did not practice Islam as he described it was a heretic to be thrown out of the community and/or killed.

This radical interpretation of Islam—a form of the older salafiyya doctrine (see Chapter 16)—might never have caught on in the luxury of the ancient capitals, but it found an audience in the unremitting heat of the Arabian desert, where nomads and farmers found the harshness of this interpretation a reflection of the harshness of the world in which they lived. Saudis do not call their Islam Wahhabism—which has a pejorative connotation—but Hanbali Islam, the smallest and most conservative of the four main Sunni schools. Nonetheless, Saudi money spreads Wahhabism through the schools it supports in Pakistan and Central Asia.

It is not quite certain why Saud agreed to sponsor the preacher and his rigid creed; one must assume that Saud believed in the preacher's message. Saud backed the preacher with the arms of his tribe; ibn Abd al-Wahhab provided the motivating ideology. Within a generation, this band of holy warriors had conquered half the peninsula. In 1801, a Saudi raiding party reached Karbala in Iraq and ransacked the tomb of Husayn, the Shi'a Third Imam and grandson of the Prophet. This was fair game for the warriors, since the Shi'a, in their eyes, were worshipping Husayn and the Imams instead of God alone.

The Saudi forces even captured the cities of Mecca and Medina briefly but were unable to hold them. The Ottoman Sultan ordered his Albanian viceroy in Egypt, Muhammad Ali, to retake the towns in the name of the caliph. This was the beginning of the end for the first Saudi kingdom. Members of the al-Saud clan began to squabble among themselves over position and were unable to unite against Muhammad Ali's forces. Eventually, the viceroy attacked Dar'iyya itself in 1818, and the leading member of the al-Saud was taken to Istanbul and beheaded. The family's first bid for supremacy had failed.

Round Two

The fate of the al-Saud now became intertwined with the fate of the Ottoman Empire and Muhammad Ali. Once the viceroy had declared victory over the al-Saud, Muhammad Ali left the peninsula. Almost immediately, the Saudis

G ⦙ *Geography*

MIDDLE EASTERN STRATEGIC WATERWAYS

The Middle East contains at least four maritime choke points, narrow waterways of great strategic value. Two of them are at corners of the Arabian peninsula but not under Saudi control. Closing any of them would damage the world economy. They are as follows:

Strait of Hormuz—The narrow entrance to the Persian Gulf is at one point only twenty-one miles wide; the channels for supertankers less than half that. Most of Japan's oil passes through Hormuz. Iran is on the north; U.S.-friendly Oman is on the south.

Bab al Mandab—Arabic for "Gate of Tears," it is the narrow southern entrance to the Red Sea. Yemen is to its east.

Suez Canal—Completed in 1869, it is not quite as important as it once was, as supertankers are too big for it.

Turkish Straits—Connecting the Mediterranean and Black Seas, the Straits, now crowded with merchant shipping, were long a Russian goal but are now internationalized.

How strategic are they? When Turkey did not allow the U.S. Fourth Division to invade Iraq from Turkey in 2003, it had to move its equipment quickly through Suez, the Bab, and Hormuz. In addition, the Tiran Strait, entrance to the Gulf of Aqaba, is strategic for Israel and Jordan.

---

reclaimed much of the territory they had previously held. Fighting for supremacy within the tribe continued, however, and ultimately brought the tribe down a second time.

Meanwhile, Muhammad Ali realized that the reason Istanbul had asked for his help was because he controlled the strongest army in the Ottoman Empire. With a small jump in logic, Muhammad Ali realized the Sultan needed him, but he didn't need the Sultan. So in 1834 Muhammad Ali renounced his allegiance to the Ottomans and set out to conquer his own kingdom. On the peninsula, this meant again subduing the al-Saud. This time, however, Muhammad Ali did it with diplomacy. He brought a rival claimant to the al-Saud leadership with his army and forcibly placed him on the throne. Muhammad Ali then became the military arm of the al-Saud family's ambitions.

The European powers knew the Ottoman Empire was decaying, but they were not ready to dismember it; they favored the status quo. They forced Muhammad Ali to return to Egypt but guaranteed him that his family would be the hereditary rulers of Egypt (but as vassals of the Ottoman Sultan). In 1841, the last of the Egyptian troops left the peninsula and the rival claimants to al-Saud leadership resumed fighting among themselves. For a brief period, the family was able to maintain control, but as Ottoman subjects. In the end, weakened by internal dissension, the al-Saud were defeated by the al-Rashidi clan in 1886. These Arab rivals were loosely allied with the British on the Persian Gulf coast.

G : *Geography*

THE TRUCIAL STATES

As early as 1820 the British (through their Indian colony) signed treaties with the various **shaykhs** who ruled along the southern shores of the Persian Gulf. Collectively they were known as the Trucial States, named after the 1853 Perpetual Maritime Truce they signed with Britain and one another. The British wanted suppression of the piracy that threatened shipping to India; the shaykhs wanted British support against local rivals. Depending on the era, these rivals included the Saudis, the Hashemites, the Ottomans, and/or smaller neighbors. In 1869, treaties formalized this arrangement. The British guaranteed the shaykhs protection in return for the shaykhs giving Britain control over their foreign relations. Britain assigned Political Officers to Kuwait, Qatar, Bahrain, and the seven emirates that eventually united into the United Arab Emirates (Abu Dhabi, Dubai, Sharjah, Ajman, Umm al Qaiwan, Fujaira, Ras al-Khayma).

In Muscat, the British had a consul, indicating British acceptance of an independent status for the Sultanate of Oman. The British also granted formal protectorate status to Aden, an essential port for fuel and supplies on the long voyage to India. The British were concerned only with the foreign policies of the rulers and played little or no role in the internal government of the sheikdoms, which gave the British a good reputation in the region. Goods sold in the Trucial States today, from refrigerators to underwear, are still more likely to be imported from Great Britain than from any other country.

The Saudis tried to reclaim their land in 1891, but the military defeat was so decisive that the family had to flee to Kuwait to avoid capture and possible death. The Rashidis could not capture Kuwait (although they tried) because the ruler of Kuwait had a treaty with the British. The British navy defended Kuwait City against a Rashidi attack with an artillery barrage.

ROUND THREE

Much has been made of the events of January 1902, when Abd al-Aziz ibn Saud began the third and successful conquest of the peninsula. As an ally of Emir Mubarak of Kuwait, Abd al-Aziz continued his family's quarrel with the Rashidis. In one popular account, Abd al-Aziz slipped into Riyadh with sixty men. Under a full moon, he personally led them up the walls of Riyadh castle, holding his scimitar between his teeth, and battled the governor of Riyadh in a sword duel to the death. This Hollywood story may not be totally accurate. More probably, Abd al-Aziz and his men ambushed the governor. The Saudis were victorious in the skirmish, and the people of Riyadh rallied to the cause of the al-Saud, whom they regarded as their religious and legitimate rulers.

---

shaykh   Literally, "old man"; Arab chief. More commonly spelled *sheik,* but pronunciation is closer to "shake" than "chic."

The peninsula saw fierce fighting over the next few years. The Ottoman Empire aided the Rashidis, believing the Saudi attacks were British-supported efforts to seize control of the new German-built Hijaz railroad, which carried pilgrims from the Levant to Mecca. (Lawrence of Arabia helped blow it up in World War I, and it has never been repaired.) Abd al-Aziz defeated the Rashidi but swore allegiance to the Sultan and was appointed governor of the Arabs.

The Saudis still did not control the peninsula. In the western **Hijaz** the Sultan appointed a member of the Hashemite dynasty, who could trace its lineage directly to the Prophet, to be the **sharif** of Mecca. Sharif Husayn had pure blood, Ottoman backing, and possession of the holy places. The Hashemites and the Saudis were headed for conflict; the peninsula was not big enough for two leaders with ambitions of conquest.

The Ottomans did not oppose Saudi rule in the eastern part of the peninsula and Hashemites in the west, because both were nominal subjects and paid taxes. The Saudis, however, wanted the other Ottoman-backed power, the Hashemites, out. To obtain leverage against the empire, Abd al-Aziz approached the British on numerous occasions and proposed an alliance similar to British treaties with the coastal tribes. For a decade before World War I, however, the British refused to deal with Abd al-Aziz ibn Saud.

WORLD WAR I

Once the war broke out in 1914, the British rushed to obtain an alliance with ibn Saud against the Ottomans and their allies on the peninsula, the Rashidis. This treaty gave him British recognition as ruler of the provinces he held in return for Saudi guarantees not to attack the Trucial States and not to sign any treaties without British permission. This latter clause was standard in British treaties with all Arab countries.

Of note, Ibn Saud did not agree to join the war as a British ally. To weaken Germany's ally, the Ottomans, the British relied on another Arab leader, Sharif Husayn of Mecca. The sharif and his sons, encouraged by British military officer T. E. Lawrence, led the Arab revolt that brought the Hashemites into modern Jordan, Syria and Iraq. Abd-al-Aziz considered British agreements with his enemies, the Hashemites, a betrayal of the relationship he thought he had with the British.

THE IKHWAN

It took almost twenty years for the Saudis to win British backing; even then, the Saudis would never be Britain's closest allies. Ibn Saud felt that the British had been responsible for too many betrayals. In the meantime, Abd-al-Aziz used the same ideology as his forefathers to unite the tribes under his banner: Islam

---

Hijaz   Western area of Arabian peninsula, holds Mecca and Medina; sometimes spelled *Hejaz*.

sharif   Prince or chief, a descendant of Muhammad (not the origin of our sheriff).

G : *Geography*

BOUND SAUDI ARABIA

Saudi Arabia is bounded on the north by Jordan, Iraq, and Kuwait;
on the east by the Persian Gulf, Qatar, and the United Arab Emirates;
on the south by Oman and Yemen;
and on the west by the Red Sea and Gulf of Aqaba.

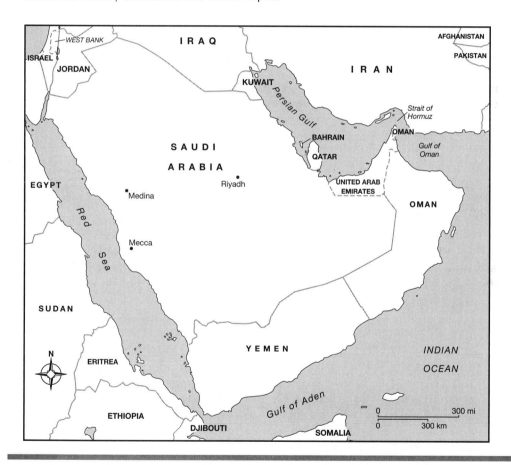

as interpreted through the teachings of ibn Abd al-Wahhab. Rival tribal forces could never defeat his troops, known as the **Ikhwan**, but they were no match for the British army.

ikhwan   Arabic for "brothers" or "brotherhood." In Saudi context, tribesmen who spread Wahhabi Islam by the sword. In Egypt, used for extremist Muslim Brotherhood.

R : *Religions*

THE ULAMA

Islam has no clergy with sacerdotal duties as has Christianity. Any man can be a prayer leader. Islam does have an important group of scholars responsible for interpreting religious law. These are the **ulama,** Arabic plural for *mu'alim,* meaning "one who is knowledgeable in the science of religion." In Saudi Arabia, the king's legitimacy is based heavily on his role of defender of Islam's two holy places (Mecca and Medina). Because of this, the ulama have a lot of influence. If they declare an action of the royal family to be un Islamic, support for the monarchy decreases.

Since 1990–1991 (the First Gulf War), establishment ulama, whose salaries are paid by the state, have continued to support the house of al-Saud, even after King Fahd invited U.S. troops onto the peninsula to protect the kingdom from feared Iraqi aggression. A minority of ulama, however, circulated petitions denouncing the king. This group of ulama argue that "crusader" armies are forbidden on the peninsula because the Prophet had said there could not be two religions there. Followers of this minority believe the king lost his legitimacy by ignoring the Prophet's prohibitions. The strength of this minority group is unknown.

The last of the Rashidis surrendered to ibn Saud in 1921, and the Ikhwan captured the peninsula between the mandate territories in the north and the Trucial States in the east and south. The British-backed Hashemites remained the only other rival for power on the peninsula. Sharif Husayn, with an overdeveloped opinion of his own importance and unwillingness to compromise, soon alienated his British overlords. By late 1925, the Saudis had evicted the Hashemites from the peninsula. When Abd-al-Aziz attacked the Hashemite stronghold of the Hijaz, Sharif Husayn's sons—whom the British had made kings of Jordan and Iraq—were prevented from coming to his aid by British instructions to maintain neutrality in the conflict.

Abd-al-Aziz had to face internal challenges to his power. The problem with using an ideology to motivate troops is that ideologies often have no limits. Ibn Saud had unleashed the Ikhwan as holy warriors to battle unbelievers, meaning those who practiced Islam in a slightly different manner. But there were still "unbelievers" in Iraq, Jordan, and among the Hijazis who had been ruled by the Hashemites. Ibn Saud tried to make the Ikhwan stop raiding British-controlled territory and in his newly conquered territory of the Hijaz, so the Ikhwan declared him an apostate. As the Ikhwan continued their forays, including attacks against British-controlled Iraq, Abd-al-Aziz realized the magnitude of the problem and recruited new and different military forces. This use of multiple armed forces to control each other has been a feature of the Saudi military to the present day.

---

ulama   Literally, "learned men"; Muslim scholars as a whole; sometimes spelled *ulema.*

⑆ *The United States in the Middle East*

SAUDI-AMERICAN RELATIONS

With the British government supporting the Hashemite kingdoms of **Transjordan** and Iraq, ibn Saud sought to balance the British. He found the counterweight when American oilmen approached him in the early 1930s. Not only did they promise money for his depleted treasury, they held out the possibility of U.S. backing. America was especially good because it was far away. Seeing all the problems he had over the years with Britain on his doorstep, ibn Saud calculated that if he let any power into his country, it would be one that could not intervene easily. Washington was in no hurry to deepen a relationship with ibn Saud; President Franklin D. Roosevelt had an understanding with London that the Middle East was in Britain's sphere of influence.

Ibn Saud signed a deal with Standard Oil of California (SOCAL, later Exxon) in 1933, which found oil in commercial quantities in 1938. The revenues did not really flow until after World War II. SOCAL had promised royalties of roughly $1 per barrel of oil. Abd-al-Aziz existed on revenues from the hajj, on British subsidies, and on the limited oil payments. During World War II, all his sources of revenue were strained. Ibn Saud looked everywhere for income, recognition, arms, and a counterweight to Britain. He concluded arms deals with Mussolini's Italy and Nazi Germany, and signed a treaty of friendship and trade with Japan. Washington saw that an assured source of foreign oil was a national-security interest and agreed to provide the Saudis with money under the Lend-Lease Act, even though the Saudis were not in the war.

With World War II, Saudi Arabia became really important. By 1945, the United States saw that the West's future economic health would rely in large part on access to Saudi oil. FDR understood that Saudi oil was important enough for a personal meeting with ibn Saud. In February 1945, following the Yalta Conference to divide up postwar Eastern Europe, FDR met the king aboard the USS *Quincy* in the Great Bitter Lake in the Suez Canal. It was a triumph of American diplomacy and cemented the "special relationship" that bound the United States and Saudi Arabia for the rest of the twentieth century. The bedrock of the relationship: The United States wanted access to the oil, and Saudi Arabia wanted to sell it to us. FDR also assured the king that the United States had no territorial desires in the area.

The only discordant note was when FDR tried to sell Abd-al-Aziz on the establishment of Israel. FDR eloquently described the plight of the Jewish people and the Nazi genocide. Ibn Saud was sympathetic and recommended that the allies award the Jews the best German lands but would not agree to a Jewish state in an Arab and Muslim area. After all, he pointed out, why should Arabs have to pay for crimes committed by Germans? FDR promised to consult the king before taking any actions that would impact negatively on the Arabs, a promise that died with FDR less than a month later.

The British, not wishing to be cut out, insisted that Prime Minister Winston Churchill also meet with the king, a meeting that turned into a disaster. The Americans had been scrupulous in observing Muslims' rules and regulations so as not to offend their royal guest. (FDR even hid in his private elevator when he needed a cigarette.) Churchill insisted on his usual after-dinner cigar and brandy in front of Abd-al-Aziz. Instead of promising consultations as the Americans had, Churchill demanded ibn Saud's cooperation on Palestine as a price for the subsidies Britain had paid him for the previous twenty years. When the king did not acquiesce, Churchill showed how little he understood of the Arab world by mentioning to an aide that the al-Saud family should be grateful for the aid the British had provided the Hashemites, the Saudis' old enemies.

Transjordan   Original name of British-created Hashemite kingdom in the Palestine mandate territory east of the Jordan River.

Ibn Saud's forces in 1929 defeated the Ikhwan revolt. Those members of the tribal levies who surrendered were resettled; others escaped to Iraq and submitted to Hashemite authority. Abd-al-Aziz proclaimed that tribal chieftains were not trained to interpret Islam, a function reserved to the ulama. This edict led to the religious authorities eventually controlling not only religious activities in the kingdom, but also the judiciary, education, and much of the police powers of the state.

SAUDI ARABIA ENTERS THE WORLD STAGE

In 1945, Britain established the Arab League in Cairo to give the Arabs a united voice in world politics. Ibn Saud was wary of it because it might give too much voice to the Hashemites. His foreign policy was always to check the Hashemites. In 1947 he sent his son, Crown Prince Saud ibn Abd-al-Aziz ibn Saud, to Washington. Shortly afterward, the United States voted for the partition of Palestine, opposed by all Arab countries. The Hashemite kingdoms demanded that the Arabs stop selling oil to any country that supported the "Zionist" resolution.

King Saud sent a message to President Truman affirming his opposition to the UN resolution and advising that he would not allow his Hashemite rivals to embroil him in a conflict with his good friend, the United States. To strengthen his hand against the Hashemites, he opened relations with Syria and Egypt. Embarrassingly, the only victorious Arab army against Israel was that of Hashemite Jordan. The Saudi king asked the United States for a treaty, but Washington gave him only a military assistance agreement, which effectively brought Saudi Arabia into the U.S. strategic orbit.

SAUDI-EGYPTIAN RIVALRY

Abd-al-Aziz died in 1953 at the age of seventy-seven. He had founded the third Saudi realm over most of the Arabian peninsula, defeated his enemies the Rashidis and the Hashemites, and made deals that brought great financial wealth. Now it was the turn of his son, Saud, who was as devoted to Islam as his father was. He paid to renovate the mosques in Mecca and Medina and abolished the taxes that pilgrims had to pay on the hajj. He reasoned that God had given him oil and that was all the money he needed.

Saud, however, like many Arabs, was captivated by Egypt's new President, Gamal Abdul Nasser. Nasser's heady rhetoric called for Arab unity and social justice. Saud even followed Nasser's lead in establishing contact with the Soviet bloc for an arms deal.

Saud's alignment with Nasser was based on the family's old rivalry with the Hashemites. Britain, with the support but not the participation of the United States, organized the Baghdad Pact. King Saud opposed it because he believed the British

C | *Cultures*

GAP ON PENNSYLVANIA AVENUE

The Saudi crown prince's 1947 Washington visit illustrates the cultural gap. In keeping with the usual honor for foreign dignitaries, he stayed at the official guesthouse, Blair House, across Pennsylvania Avenue from the White House. (Truman resided there while repairs were made to the White House a year later.) It is a charming federalist brick building, furnished with early American antiques. Americans think Blair House is beautiful and historic, but the crown prince was furious at what he thought were shabby lodgings. He demanded to know what he or his father had done to be insulted with rooms full of old furniture. Wasn't his country important enough to warrant new furnishings?

were creating an alliance that gave his Hashemite rivals supremacy in the Middle East. Instead, he aligned with Egypt in an effort to stop the growth of Hashemite influence.

Saudi-Egyptian amity could not last; the two are culturally and politically vastly different. Saud realized that Nasser was costing Saudi Arabia money, influence, and power. In 1955, military officers in Ta'if plotted to kill the king, just as the Free Officers in Egypt had overthrown their monarchy. Saud responded by recruiting a Royal Guard from among the Ikhwan his father had resettled a quarter century ago. This tribal force persists to this day as the National Guard, headed by Crown Prince Abdallah.

The big break came in 1956, when Nasser nationalized the Suez Canal without consulting his Saudi allies. This triggered the 1956 Arab-Israeli war, which closed the Suez Canal and deprived Saud of revenues from oil that ordinarily passed through it (then 40 percent of the country's output). Because Saud had signed a military alliance with Egypt (he thought it was against the Hashemites), he was forced to support Nasser and grant him basing rights. Saud even broke diplomatic relations with its longtime ally Britain.

Despite his public support of Egypt, Saud seethed. He believed Nasser had deceived him into joining an alliance that put him on a collision course with the European powers. He also was upset at the loss of oil revenues. Most alarming, when Nasser visited the Kingdom, Saudi subjects turned out by the thousand in spontaneous demonstrations. Saud saw a threat to his throne and vowed to oppose any additional incursions by Nasser.

Saud's opportunity came in 1957, when King Hussein of Jordan dismissed his pro-Nasser government. Saud sent reinforcements to help the Jordanian king against pro-Egyptian elements. The two monarchs established a "Royals Alliance" against Nasser that finally buried the enmity between the Hashemites and the Saudis. Washington, which had been alarmed at the king's flirtations with Nasser's anti-U.S. Arab nationalism, again regarded the Kingdom as an ally. The king visited Washington and renewed military cooperation.

G : *Geography*

THE BAGHDAD PACT (CENTO)

The 1950s were the height of the Cold War in which the United States and the Soviet Union regarded international relations as a zero-sum game where countries were traded like playing cards. Every card held by one side was one less for the other. The superpowers looked at the Middle East, like other parts of the world, as a playing field for their rivalry.

Eisenhower's Secretary of State John Foster Dulles wanted to unite the world in a series of anti-Communist alliances. This world-wide strategy to stop Soviet expansion was known as containment. Copying the North Atlantic Treaty Organization (NATO) in Asia, Dulles created the Southeast Asia Treaty Organization (SEATO). To stop feared Soviet expansion into the Middle East, he encouraged the organization of the Central Treaty Organization (CENTO)—an anti-Soviet, Middle Eastern coalition designed to keep the Soviets from fulfilling their age-old ambition of obtaining a warm-water port to their south. CENTO was never worth much.

Egypt's Nasser, through his position in the Arab League, lined up opposition to CENTO. When the League rejected CENTO, the only Arab country to join it was Iraq, still under British influence. The United States did not participate in CENTO because Ike believed it would overextend U.S. commitments in an area that was not America's traditional responsibility. Instead, Britain fulfilled its usual role as guarantor of security in the Middle East.

CENTO's five member countries were Britain, Turkey, Iraq, Iran, and Pakistan, the so-called "Northern Tier" of countries blocking Soviet penetration into the Middle East. They signed the mutual defense treaty in the Iraqi capital of Baghdad, earning them the name "Baghdad Pact." After the Iraqi revolution of 1958, Baghdad withdrew from the Baghdad Pact, leaving Britain and only non-Arab countries in CENTO.

FAISAL'S TWO TURNS

King Saud tried to buy a revolution in Syria, which in 1958 had joined Egypt in an experiment of Arab nationalism, the United Arab Republic. The Saudi covert action ended badly, embarrassing the Saudis and the king, who may have suffered a nervous breakdown. The sons of Abd-al-Aziz, Saud's brothers, met in council and transferred governmental authority from the king to a regent, Crown Prince Faisal. The regent ruled two years and concentrated on reform of the state bureaucracy.

Faisal decided he could not defeat Nasser but could appease him by distancing himself from his British and American allies and withdrawing his troops from Jordan. In 1958 Arab nationalists inspired by Nasser overthrew the Iraqi monarchy, the United States stood by, and Britain was unable to protect the monarchy it had created and nurtured. The safe bet was on Egypt.

The United States invoked the new Eisenhower doctrine to justify landing Marines in Lebanon to prop up the government there. The real goal of the 1958 action was to show the countries of the region that America was prepared to oppose expansion by Nasser. King Saud supported Egypt in its opposition to the Beirut landing, but Nasser's propaganda offensive against monarchies continued. Ultimately, traditionalists cannot work with radicals.

The United States in the Middle East

THE EISENHOWER DOCTRINE

President Dwight Eisenhower obtained a joint congressional resolution in 1957 allowing the president to use "such assistance and cooperation to include the employment of the armed forces of the United States to secure and protect the territorial integrity and political independence of such nations, requesting such aid, against overt armed aggression from any nation controlled by International Communism."

Eisenhower invoked the doctrine only once, to send troops into Lebanon in 1958 (for more, see Chapter 17). In reality, there was no Communist threat, but a spat between an outgoing Lebanese president and an incoming candidate who was supported by Nasser. Eisenhower felt that, after the Iraqi revolution, he had to intervene to demonstrate Western commitment to the area.

Saud returned to power in 1961 and continued Faisal's policies of appeasing Nasser. He did not renew the U.S. lease on the important Dhahran airfield. He joined Egypt in providing troops to oppose Iraq's efforts to annex Kuwait. Even then, Baghdad claimed that Kuwait never should have been broken away from Iraq.

A military coup in Damascus in 1961 brought to power officers who withdrew Syria from the United Arab Republic. Feeling betrayed, Nasser called on the Arab world to rebel against their governments so that Arab unity could proceed. Saud could not countenance this and again aligned the Kingdom with the Western powers and built up Saudi armed forces.

In 1962, a military coup overthrew the traditional ruler of Yemen, the Imam Muhammad al-Badr. When a civil war broke out in Yemen, Egypt sent a military force to support the new, socialist government. Egyptian troops—who reportedly used poison gas in Yemen—thus gained a toehold on the Arabian peninsula, and they may have had designs on Saudi territory. Dissident Saudi princes flocked to Cairo, and some military aircraft defected to the Egyptians in Yemen. King Saud suffered a nervous breakdown, and the Council of Ministers again bestowed authority on his brother Faisal.

Faisal now acted as king, not as regent, and supported the Imam in Yemen by providing military aid, but, not wanting to tangle with Egypt directly, sent no troops. He also turned to the United States and Britain for assistance. Washington promised to protect the kingdom against direct Egyptian attack but would not intervene in Yemen. Even when Egyptian jets attacked Saudi border towns, the United States did not react because the Kennedy administration was trying to woo Egypt. Britain, by contrast, began to provide aid immediately.

Faisal built up his National Guard, and the British increased their presence in the area. Nasser concluded he could not win in Yemen and agreed to UN arbitration and to a summit meeting with Faisal. In 1964 this caused one of the greatest crises in modern Saudi Arabia.

A rested King Saud returned from abroad and demanded to lead the Saudi delegation. Faisal and his other brothers did not recognize Saud's authority. The Royal Guard loyal to Saud surrounded Faisal's palace while the National Guard loyal to Faisal surrounded Saud's. The brothers turned to the ulama, which decided that Saud should lead the delegation as he was still the country's king, but Faisal should continue to run the country because of Saud's ill health. Saud, claiming his health had been restored, tried to dismiss Faisal.

The dispute continued for eight months with military standoffs and arrests of royal brothers. Finally, in November 1964, the ulama issued a *fatwa* that stated Saud had been deposed as king, and that King Faisal reigned in the Kingdom of Saudi Arabia. Saud then moved to Cairo to oppose his brother, under the sponsorship of Nasser.

THE 1967 ARAB-ISRAELI WAR

Faisal immediately moved to consolidate power. He abolished the post of prime minister and made the Council of Ministers purely advisory. To balance the Nasser-controlled Arab League, in 1964 Faisal formed the Organization of the Islamic Conference. Just as the al-Saud had used religion domestically to prop up its legitimacy, now al-Saud used it internationally.

Saudi Arabia played no role in the 1967 war. Israel's defeat of Egypt forced it to withdraw its broken army from Yemen, where tribal loyalists again tried to dislodge the republicans and failed. In nearby Aden, leftists founded the People's Democratic Republic of Yemen (PDRY), whose goal was to unite with the Yemen Arab Republic against the Saudis. The new rulers turned to the Soviet bloc for military help. Egypt had been replaced by the Soviets on the toe of the Arabian peninsula. Yemen unified in 1990 and became, by some accounts, the only Arab Communist country.

In Oman, the Saudis had supported a long-smoldering rebellion in Dhofar province that now burst into flames, supported by leftist elements from the Yemens. By 1970, rebel troops were at the palace doors in Muscat, capital of Oman. The British convinced Qabus ibn Said, the British-educated son of the sultan, to depose his father so the military could respond effectively to the rebel offensive. Faisal did nothing to help the young sultan, who eventually asked Iran to intervene.

This could have led to increased rivalries with the shah but did not. The king of Saudi Arabia and the shah of Iran reached an informal understanding whereby the king's sphere of influence extended to water's edge, while the shah could guarantee the safety of shipping in the Persian Gulf. This became important after Britain withdrew from the Gulf in 1971, and America began to look for someone to police the area. They found the Saudi-Iranian partnership workable, and President Richard Nixon declared his support for the "twin pillars" of stability in the Gulf.

The Soviets moved to counter the U.S. foray into Gulf politics by signing a treaty of friendship in 1972 with Iraq, turning Iraq into a dangerous and well-armed client state. With the backing of a superpower, Iraq invaded Kuwait in 1973, the second time in twelve years that it tried to lay claim to the country.

Saudi Arabia immediately responded by sending troops to support Kuwait in its battle, and the Iraqis quickly withdrew. Iraq's 1990 invasion was its third attempt to grab Kuwait (see Chapter 13).

THE 1973 ARAB-ISRAELI WAR

Ever since Abd-al-Aziz met FDR in 1945, American support for Israel has irritated U.S.-Saudi relations. King Faisal opposed Israel, and it was only his antipathy to Nasser that prevented the Saudis from doing more in 1967. By 1973, however, things had changed in the Middle East. Nasser died of a heart attack in 1970, and Anwar Sadat took over. Sadat traveled to Riyadh to consult with the Saudi king and told Faisal of his plan to renew the war with Israel. He got both Saudi financial pledges and a Saudi agreement to use the oil weapon.

Egypt and Syria launched their attacks on October 6, 1973 (see Chapter 5). As Israel quickly used up its munitions, the United States airlifted supplies directly to the front lines. The Saudis interpreted this as direct American intervention on behalf of the Israelis—this after President Nixon had given his assurance that he wanted to see a peace based on Resolution 242 (see Chapter 6). Faced with what Faisal doubtless saw as a personal betrayal, he and the Arab nations of OPEC declared an embargo on oil sales to any country that supported Israel. In December 1973, OPEC (see page 181) quadrupled the price of oil. For the first time OPEC worked as a unit and actually set the price of oil. OPEC, founded as a defensive cartel to keep oil prices from dropping, went on the offensive.

The embargo hit the world oil market at precisely the wrong time. Europe and Japan depended heavily on Arab oil, and the United States could not make up the shortfall as it, too, relied on imports. In economic terms, there was no "elasticity" in the market. Even a few-percent shortfall kicked prices to the sky. As Americans tasted rationing, gas lines, and odd-even fill-up days, the Europeans abandoned Israel and the United States. Many date the U.S.-European split over the Middle East to 1973.

The Saudis ended the boycott against the United States in March 1974. After both sides adjusted to the new relationship between the powers, they signed a Saudi-U.S. military cooperation agreement in June. The Americans agreed to provide security assistance in return for Saudi pledges to work to guarantee American energy supplies. The Saudis could have sold large quantities of oil on the open market and driven the price back down. Many in the Kingdom were concerned that the high cost of crude would drive consumer countries to develop alternative fuels. In the end, the king allowed the new prices to stand, and Saudi oil revenues jumped 330 percent. America tried to regain the money it was sending to the Kingdom for oil by selling the Saudis modern armaments, part of the practice known as "recycling petrodollars."

In 1975 King Faisal was assassinated by his nephew for unknown reasons. Crown Prince Khalid was crowned king. The elder in the family, Muhammad ibn Abd-al-Aziz, decided that Fahd should be the crown prince, and two princes in the middle were passed over. Succession was thus determined by the family elder and not by the king of the country.

When Egypt signed its peace treaty with Israel in 1979, it immediately became a pariah state to the rest of the Arab world. Washington asked the Saudis to support the peace treaty, something the king rejected. This forced the Saudis to side unwillingly with the rejectionist front: Palestinians, Iraq, and Syria. The United States sought to maintain its special relationship by agreeing to separate the Arab-Israeli conflict from the rest of its dealings with the Kingdom. This awkward compartmentalization could only work as long as there was a common enemy to unite the two countries. The Iraqi invasion of Kuwait in 1990 brought the two together for a while, but the demise of the Soviet Union at the end of 1991 brought a very different Saudi-U.S. relationship.

KINGDOM OF DENIAL

Iraq and Iran are important, but Saudi Arabia is far more important to us in the Middle East. Saudi Arabia sits atop the world's biggest pool of oil, one quarter of all proven reserves, and supplies one-sixth of U.S. oil imports. (Our biggest supplier, however, is Canada.) Saudi oil is also cheap to produce, about $2 a barrel, a fraction of the cost of most other oilfields. The United States and Saudi Arabia are strongly interdependent, and in recent years both turned scared. The traditional Saudi regime could collapse like the shah's in 1979.

For decades apologists (some paid by the Saudi embassy) assured us that the Kingdom was firmly built on traditional legitimacy and a contented population. With essentially no news coverage, this was hard to confirm or refute. One got only hints of trouble, all of it denied by Saudi officials. Some observers say the beheading of a Saudi princess in the late 1970s for premarital sex was a cover-up for widespread un-Qur'anic behavior among the royal family. (Her commoner lover was simply shot.) French special forces dislodged the Saudi extremists who took over Islam's holiest site in Mecca in 1979. Saudi troops could not do the job, so the regime requested French or Pakistani (sources disagree on which) special forces but kept their presence quiet. In 1990, the Saudi government waited three days before allowing its mass media to report on Iraq's invasion of Kuwait. This is a frightened regime.

The events of 9/11 made clear that America and Saudi Arabia are no longer close. In Internet chat rooms Saudis show deep hatred for the West and praise for 9/11 and al Qaeda. In a survey done by Saudi intelligence, 95 percent of educated Saudis supported Osama bin Laden. Some American observers now see the Saudis as false friends. The Bush 43 administration, like all previous U.S. administrations, was restrained in its comments on the Saudis, but Congress and the media grew increasingly critical. The Saudis lied and denied that fifteen of the nineteen skyjackers were Saudis. Some Saudis still say it has not been proved. If they admitted that most of the 9/11 murderers were Saudi, they would be admitting that there is revolutionary rage in the Kingdom, a fact they do not want to face. Riyadh was slow and lazy in investigating the Saudi friends of Osama bin Laden and Saudi "charity" funds for al Qaeda. They likely do not want prominent Saudis named. Best to keep some things quiet, was the Saudi response; we'll solve this in our own way. But the old way of denying unrest while quietly buying it off is no longer feasible and merely telegraphs fear and weakness.

U.S.-Saudi relations became strained over the issue of terrorism in the mid-1990s. Saudi police caught and quickly executed the 1996 bombers of the Khobar Towers but did not allow U.S. officials to interrogate the suspects out of fear they might name highly placed Saudis. American officials were outraged but said nothing. The U.S. embassy and State Department blandly reassured us of Saudi cooperation and friendship, and no U.S. official said a critical word in public about the Saudis, for that might undermine the regime.

Terrorism in Saudi Arabia has killed over 280 since 2003, mostly by bombs, indicating that al Qaeda is trying to overthrow the House of Saud. A related aim is to get foreigners out; the U.S. embassy urges Americans to leave. The Saudis long claimed their **mukhabarat** is thorough and well-informed, but some feared it had been infiltrated and compromised by al Qaeda sympathizers. Finally, with the 2003 bombings came the realization that al Qaeda cannot be bought off or sent to other countries. The House of Saud ordered the mukhabarat to get serious; it cracked down on "charitable foundations" and killed or arrested some 500 al Qaeda suspects.

Osama bin Laden was born and raised in Saudi Arabia, and most of his funds and many of his recruits come from there. Much of Saudi education is in the hands of Wahhabi clerics, who teach Qur'an and hatred of all non-Muslims. "Well, of course I hate you because you are Christian," a Saudi professor of Islamic law explained to an American, "but that doesn't mean I want to kill you." Some failed to grasp the distinction.

Saudi-funded Wahhabi **madresas** in Pakistan were the religious basis of the Afghan Taliban movement, which we overthrew in 2001. John Walker Lindh, the California youth now in a U.S. prison for aiding the enemy, got his fundamentalist education in one such madresa. Although the Saudi regime sponsors salafiyya, it is itself a target of salafis, another example of blowback.

Washington presses Riyadh to democratize, but it proceeds with glacial slowness. Pushing too hard on Riyadh, however, could destabilize the Kingdom. Saudi Arabia denounced the Iraq War out of fear of further regional and domestic destabilization. Arabs do not like the United States attacking brother Arabs, even if they disliked Saddam Hussein. In 2007 King Abdullah called the U.S. presence in Iraq "an illegal foreign occupation." In 1990 and 1991 Riyadh let U.S. forces use Saudi territory to attack Iraq; in 2003 it did not. The U.S.-British attack had to mass in little Kuwait. Quietly, the Saudis did let Americans use the Prince Sultan airbase (built and run by Americans) to direct the air war in 2003, but not to launch strikes from there. The Saudi government quietly requested that all 5,000 U.S. military personnel be withdrawn in 2003, and Secretary Rumsfeld honored this request. The feeling of estrangement was mutual.

Saudi Arabia (and Egypt) condemned Lebanese Hizballah, a Shi'a force sponsored by Iran, in 2006 for excessive provocation when Hizballah kidnapped two

---

mukhabarat   Arabic for security police.

madresa   Muslin school, chiefly for memorizing the Qur'an.

D : *Domestic Structures*

Saudi Arabia

The Kingdom, as Saudis call it, is a family-owned business run by tradition rather than a constitution, claiming that God's holy Qur'an is their constitution. Only in 1992 did King Fahd decree a "basic law" specifying state structures. All power is in the hands of roughly 200 al-Saud princes, government by half-brothers. The king both reigns and rules but usually in consultation with these high-ranking princes.

In August 2005 Abdullah ibn Abd-al-aziz al-Saud (born in 1923, the fifth son of founder Ibn Saud) became the sixth king of Saudi Arabia and its prime minister. Abdullah had been crown prince for twenty-three years and de facto ruler for ten years until his ailing half-brother, King Fahd, passed away. Saudi flags could not fly at half-staff because they contain the words "God is One and Muhammad is His Prophet" and so must not be lowered. Abdullah's age predicts another successor soon. By tradition, succession goes to a brother, not a son.

The king appoints a cabinet, the Council of Ministers, composed largely of hereditary princes. The Council is not responsible to parliament, the 150-member Majlis al-Shura (Consultative Assembly), which is appointed for four-year terms and has little influence. In steps over a few years, one-third of Majlis members are to be elected by adult male Saudis, but political parties are prohibited. The state budget is secret; not even the Majlis debates it.

Israeli soldiers and precipitated the Israeli invasion of southern Lebanon. Saudi antipathy toward Shi'ism and fear of growing Iranian power has led to Iranian-Saudi confrontation.

Conclusions

Arabia became Saudi starting with the 1744 alliance of a tribal chief, Saud, and a fundamentalist preacher, ibn Abdul Wahhab. It took three attempts, but finally in 1925 the al-Saud evicted their last rivals, the Hashemites. Saudi-U.S. relations have been long and deep, starting with U.S. oil developers in the 1930s. FDR met with the king in early 1945. Although Israel was an irritant, the two countries needed each other: their oil for our security protection.

Initially impressed by Nasser of Egypt, the Saudis soon learned that conservative regimes must fear revolutionary ones. With the 1973 Arab-Israeli war, OPEC quadrupled oil prices, making the Kingdom very rich and possibly beginning its destabilization. Saudi Arabia is the great prize of the region, but it is showing signs of unrest, although it denies any problems. Much Islamic terrorism originated in the Wahhabi faith of the Kingdom, including Osama and fifteen of the nineteen 9/11 skyjackers. Constantly afraid of mass anger, Saudi Arabia did not let U.S. forces use Saudi soil for the 2003 war and asked U.S. forces to leave after the war. The House of Saud, however, was smart enough to begin a cautious democratization to head off smoldering extremism. There is no guarantee it will work.

Key Terms

Hijaz (p. 190)   sharif (p. 190)
ikhwan (p. 191)   shaykh (p. 189)
madresa (p. 201)   Transjordan (p. 193)
mukhabarat (p. 201)   ulama (p. 192)
Najd (p. 186)

Further Reference

Aburish, Said K. *The Rise, Corruption, and Coming Fall of the House of Saud*. New York: St. Martin's Press, 1995.

Al-Rashid, Madawi. *A History of Saudi Arabia*. New York: Cambridge University Press, 2002.

————. *Contesting the Saudi State: Islamic Voices from a New Generation*. New York: Cambridge University Press, 2006.

Bronson, Rachel. *Thicker Than Oil: America's Uneasy Partnership with Saudi Arabia*. New York: Oxford University Press, 2006.

Caudill, Mark A. *Twilight in the Kingdom: Understanding the Saudis*. Westport, CT: Praeger, 2006.

Champion, Daryl. *The Paradoxical Kingdom: Saudi Arabia and the Momentum of Reform*. New York: Columbia University Press, 2005.

Cordesman, Anthony H., and Nawaf Obaid. *National Security in Saudi Arabia: Threats, Responses, and Challenges*. Westport, CT: Praeger, 2005.

————. *Saudi Arabia Enters the Twenty-First Century: The Political, Foreign Policy, Economic, and Energy Dimensions*. Westport, CT: Praeger, 2003.

Esposito, John L. *Islam: The Straight Path*. New York: Oxford, 1991.

Helms, Christine Moss. *The Cohesion of Saudi Arabia: Evolution of Political Identity*. Baltimore, MD: Johns Hopkins University Press, 1981.

Holden, David, and Richard Johns. *The House of Saud: The Rise and Rule of the Most Powerful Dynasty in the Arab World*. New York: Holt, Rinehart & Winston, 1981.

Howarth, David. *A Desert King: Ibn Saud and His Arabia*. New York: McGraw-Hill, 1964.

Lacy, Robert. *The Kingdom: Arabia and the House of Saud*. New York: Harcourt Brace and Jovanovich, 1981.

Lippman, Thomas A. *Inside the Mirage: America's Fragile Partnership with Saudi Arabia*. Boulder, CO: Westview, 2005.

Long, David E. *Culture and Customs of Saudi Arabia*. Westport, CT: Greenwood, 2005.

Miller, Aaron David. *Search for Security: Saudi Arabian Oil and American Foreign Policy, 1939–1949*. Chapel Hill, NC: University of North Carolina Press, 1980.

Simpson, William. *The Prince: The Secret Story of the World's Most Intriguing Royal, Prince Bandar bin Sultan*. New York: Harpercollins, 2007.

11 *Iraq and Kuwait*

Points to Ponder

- When and why did Britain conquer Iraq?
- Is the British experience in Iraq a good analogy for the present situation?
- How did Iraq get its king? What royal house was he from?
- What was the Baath party? What was its ideology?
- What are the population groups of Iraq?
- Why do "Saladin figures" arise in the Arab world?
- Was Kuwait always independent or part of Iraq?
- Did Britain invent both Iraq and Kuwait?

IRAQ

World War I brought Britain into what it then called Mesopotamia for two reasons. First, the Ottoman Empire sided with Germany in 1914, and, second, London knew of Mesopotamia's oil potential. Forces from Britain's Indian Army landed on the Faw peninsula at the head of the Persian Gulf in 1914 and soon took Basra (which British troops took again in 2003). They moved rapidly up the Euphrates Valley (as U.S. forces did in 2003) and by the fall of 1915 tried to take Baghdad, but a Turkish counteroffensive pushed them back to Al Kut on the Tigris, where, after a 140-day siege, the British surrendered in April 1916. In March 1917, however, British forces took Baghdad and in November took Mosul, so that by the end of World War I they held all but the north of what was now called Iraq, after the old Arabic name.

In a parallel to the 2003 Iraq War, victorious British General Stanley Maude in 1918 proclaimed that Britain, having liberated Iraq from foreign (Turkish) rule, intended to return control to Iraqis. Iraqi nationalists for some time had opposed Ottoman rule. Indeed, the British-sponsored Arab Revolt of 1916 had encouraged Arab nationalism against the Turks. These Iraqis therefore bitterly resented

G Geography

Collapsed Empires

The collapse of an empire always leaves a terrible political mess behind, like a vacuum that many rush in to fill. World War I collapsed four empires—the German, Austro-Hungarian, Russian, and Ottoman—leaving a wide swath of chaos and instability from Central Europe, through the Balkans and Middle East, and into Asia. When you collapse a political entity in war you must always ask what will come after it. In Europe, the collapse of the German, Austro-Hungarian, and Russian empires led straight to communism, Nazism, and World War II. It was, in the words of E. H. Carr, "the twenty years crisis."

What it left behind in the Middle East might be termed "the hundred years crisis." Ottoman power was out, but British and French power could not bring stability. Local nationalists opposed them and strove constantly to oust them. The new states set up by the imperialists had ancient roots but only a weak sense of themselves as modern states. Britain invented a modern state called Iraq out of three Ottoman provinces. Boundaries were open to question and drawn mostly by the British and French. The British, over Iraqi objections, allowed a separate Kuwait to continue. The French took Syria's Bekaa Valley and made it part of Lebanon. Empires may be bad, but what comes after them can be worse.

the "mandate" over Iraq that Britain had given itself through the League of Nations. Britain ran Iraq like a colony, staffed with experienced British and Indian administrators from India. Initially, no Iraqi administrators were appointed.

Compounding the problem was the fact that, at the end of World War I, the triumphant Arab armies of Hashemite Prince Faisal were in Damascus. With British promises and encouragement, they had pushed the Turks out of much of northern Arabia and Syria. Now they turned to the British and demanded what they believed they had been promised in the 1915–1916 Husayn-McMahon correspondence: self-determination for the Arabs in the lands that they conquered. In March of 1920 the Syrian National Congress proclaimed Faisal their king. The only problem was that Britain had also promised Syria to the French in the Sykes-Picot agreement, a deal that was confirmed at the San Remo Conference in April.

French forces in Lebanon hesitated to press their colonial claims until Faisal accepted the Syrian kingship. The French considered this move a direct threat to their interests, especially since Faisal was a British ally. The French commander marched on Damascus and deposed the king in August 1920. The French then escorted Faisal to Palestine and to the protection of his British masters.

In the lands of the Tigris and Euphrates, a British army of 130,000 men kept order as they waited for a new British mandate to be established. When the Syrians proclaimed Faisal king, however, it inspired officers of the Arab army to proclaim Faisal's older brother, Abdallah, king of Iraq. The British did not recognize this Arab move for self-government. Probably triggered by the April 1920 announcement of a British mandate over Iraq, Arab nationalists rebelled in Mosul in July, and the rebellion spread down the Euphrates Valley. The British response

G ⋮ *Geography*

BOUND IRAQ

Iraq is bounded on the north by Turkey;
on the east by Iran;
on the south by the Persian Gulf, Kuwait, and Saudi Arabia;
and on the west by Jordan and Syria.

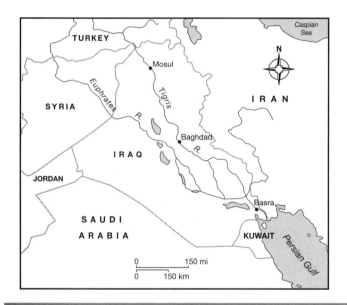

was fierce and, after a few months, successful. In what Iraqis call the Great Iraqi Revolution of 1920 and the British call the Iraqi Revolt, British Royal Air Force bombers and reinforcements from India killed some 8,450 rebels with a loss of over 400 British and Indian troops killed. The British public soon disliked the cost of men and money in Iraq.

The San Remo Conference followed British desires in uniting the Ottoman provinces of Mosul, Baghdad, and most of Basra into the new country of Iraq. A small portion of Basra province that had not been under direct Ottoman control, the Emirate of Kuwait, was left outside the new entity, although Iraq always claimed it belonged to Iraq. The Europeans had created Iraq, but the Iraqi revolt of 1920 showed that its inhabitants did not want European rule. Since the British had ruled out Abdallah as king (he was chosen by the people without British prior consent), they had to devise another way to run the country.

G : *Geography*

SAN REMO CONFERENCE

This conference of victors, held April 19–26, 1920, is not as famous as some of the postwar conferences because most of its decisions were ratified in August in the Treaty of Sèvres (which as you recall from Chapter 7, the new Turkish Republic repudiated). The purpose of the meeting in San Remo, Italy, was to abolish the Ottoman Empire and to divide up its lands. The countries at the conference to decide the fate of the Middle East for the next century were Britain, France, Italy, Belgium, Japan, and Greece. The United States was not in attendance, so there was no voice urging a settlement based on Wilson's Fourteen Points, which stressed self-determination. Similarly, neither Turkish nor Arab delegations were present. The people whose future was being decided were not just silent but absent from the table. Imperialists did those kinds of things.

The conference awarded Syria and Lebanon to France, which had interests in the area dating back to the Crusades. It gave Palestine (including Transjordan) and Iraq to the British. Sykes-Picot originally indicated a French role in the oil region of Mosul, but the British decided to keep it for themselves. To buy off French objections to the British getting the Iraqi oil fields, the conference also awarded France 25 percent of Iraqi oil. Most of these deals were ratified as new League of Nations "mandates" two years later. (For more on mandates, see Chapter 4.)

A meeting of British government and colonial administrators in Cairo in March 1921 switched kings. It made Abdallah the king of Transjordan and made Faisal, whom the French had kicked out of Syria, king of Iraq. In those days, Britain invented countries and kings. In Iraq, the British held a plebiscite on the choice of Faisal. Before the vote, the British arrested and deported General Sayyid Talib, a rival claimant to the throne. With no other candidates to oppose him, Faisal received 96 percent of the vote.

Iraqi nationalists by now hated the British; they wanted full independence. Then, as now, Iraq was hard to pacify. Young Saddam Hussein was raised by his uncle in an atmosphere of intense anti-British hatred. The king, put on the throne by Britain and with no family roots in Iraq, found it hard to crack down on Iraqi nationalists. He could not risk losing his standing as an authentic Arab war hero by being perceived as too close to his British colonial masters.

Britain decided to forego the mandate it had been promised and protected its interests in Iraq by a treaty. The treaty provided for the same role that Britain would have played under a mandate; that is, Britain provided advisors at all levels of the Iraqi government, and Iraq agreed to sign no treaties without British consent. Iraqi nationalists realized this was indirect British control but took solace in the thought that they had prevented the British from imposing a formal mandate. Indeed, these fledgling steps toward independence culminated in 1932, when Iraq was admitted as a full member of the League of Nations. Through the local ruling elite, Britain was still influential in Iraq.

K ⫶ *Key Concepts*

ANALOGIES

Most of our reasoning, especially in the social sciences, is by **analogy**, but such reasoning is often flawed and misleading, as no two cases are ever exactly alike. Looking at unruly Iraq after the 2003 war, some journalists eagerly seized on the 1920 Iraq Revolt against the British as an analogy and warning. There were points of comparison. In both, new victors proclaimed their intention of liberating Iraq but stayed as occupiers. Local nationalists disliked the previous regime (respectively, Ottoman and Saddam) but also disliked Western occupiers. In the interests of speedy restoration of order, both British and Americans brought in outside administrators and attempted to name outsiders as leaders, and this fostered even more nationalistic anger. In both cases, irregular guerrilla-type raids were met with tough retaliations, mass arrests, and searches of homes.

But there are several elements of **dysanalogy**. The United States sought no mandate, colony, or prolonged occupation of Iraq. All Americans, especially soldiers, wished to be out as quickly as possible. The Pentagon had a friendly exile, Ahmad Chalabi, in mind as interim leader but named him as one among many in the face of Iraqi rejection. In 1920 the Kurds, hoping for their own country, opposed the British. In 2003, the Kurds, insisting on autonomy, supported the Americans. One element that holds up is the persistence of Iraqi nationalism in the face of foreign occupation. Beware of overly facile analogies. Every time we see two historical events compared we must ask, "Do the elements of analogy outweigh the elements of dysanalogy?"

POST-FAISAL IRAQ

King Faisal's personal reputation kept Iraq's factions together. In 1933, however, Faisal died and was succeeded by his inexperienced twenty-one-year-old son, King Ghazi. The new king lacked the leadership skills (and interest) of his father, so the political forces in the kingdom split into pro- and anti-British camps. The pro-British camp was led by the most famous of the pre-war politicians, General (later Prime Minister) Nuri al-Said.

The country acquired new importance to the British as World War II loomed. Iraq was strategic, and in 1930 the Iraqi government signed a treaty granting the British access to air bases in the south, and basing rights for ground forces in the north. In the same year, Iraq began producing oil in commercial quantities. Soon a small (12-inch) pipeline carried some of this oil from Iraq through Transjordan to the port of Haifa in Palestine, all of it under British control. As the British pushed to increase their role in the Baghdad government, the anti-British camp pushed harder as well.

The tension led to a series of five coups from 1936 to 1941. The king continued to reign unopposed; the coups were aimed at the cabinet and the political rulers of the country. The monarchy changed hands in 1939 when King Ghazi died in an automobile accident and left the throne to his four-year-old son, Faisal II.

---

analogy   Finding that one case is like another.

dysanalogy   Finding that one case differs from another.

G : *Geography*

THE PEOPLES OF IRAQ

Iraq is mentioned in the *hadiths* of the Prophet as an area near the southern Tigris and Euphrates, so Arabs have, since the seventh century, called it Iraq. But British colonial administrators in Cairo invented Iraq's modern borders in 1921. In so doing, they united groups of people under one government that had little in common, Iraq's weakness ever since.

The three Ottoman provinces had reported to three different governors; there had been no geographic unity among the units for hundreds of years. The people within the provinces were also quite different from one another: Ethnically, about 80 percent of the people of Iraq today are Arab and 20 percent Kurds. From a religious viewpoint, an estimated 60 percent of Iraq is Shi'a, while some 38 percent are Sunni. Less than 20 percent of the population is Sunni Arab, but they have always held political power, whether under Ottomans, British, Hashemite kings (who were Sunni), or Saddam Hussein.

The population is divided roughly along the lines of the old provinces: The Shi'a Arabs are concentrated in the former province of Basra (although many live in Baghdad as well), the Sunni Arabs live in the former province of Baghdad, and the Sunni Kurds live in the former province of Mosul, but there is a good deal of overlap and mixing.

There is also a scattering of Greeks, Iranians, Assyrians, Turkomans, Orthodox Christians, Jacobite Christians, Jews, and even devil worshippers to make the mix more interesting. Finally, about one-sixth of the country is tribal, whose followers owe their allegiance to a tribal chieftain—usually a distant relative as tribes are large, extended families that united for self-protection over the years.

Iraqi histories often talk of "the nationalist movement." Such movements in the Middle East always start among intellectuals; mass actions come later when the educated classes incite the people to follow them. With so many different claims to loyalty, one has to ask whose nationalism the Iraqi nationalist movement was espousing? In the past, it has mostly meant that of the Sunni Arab minority.

WORLD WAR II

In 1941, pro-German former Prime Minister Rashid Ali al-Gailani returned to power in a military coup. He had already shown his colors by welcoming such prominent pro-Nazi leaders as Hajj Amin al-Husayni (see page 72) to take refuge from the British authorities in Palestine. The British could not countenance an Iraq aligned with Germany and invaded the country. In the early stages of the invasion, Rashid Ali's army tried to attack a British military base that had been established under the Anglo-Iraqi Treaty of 1930. The Iraqis were unsuccessful. After brief fighting, they returned Faisal II to the throne, and he ruled the country until the revolution of 1958. Because he was so young, his uncle Abdallah ruled as regent until 1953.

The first Arab-Israeli war had an impact on Iraq, as it did on all the countries of the Middle East. The Iraqi people responded to Israeli independence with anti-Western riots and anti-Jewish pogroms. Most of Baghdad's ancient Jewish community, some two and a half millennia old, left. The Iraqi government also cut the oil pipeline that connected northern Iraqi oilfields with Haifa, costing the Iraqi treasury millions in lost revenues until alternative export routes could be developed.

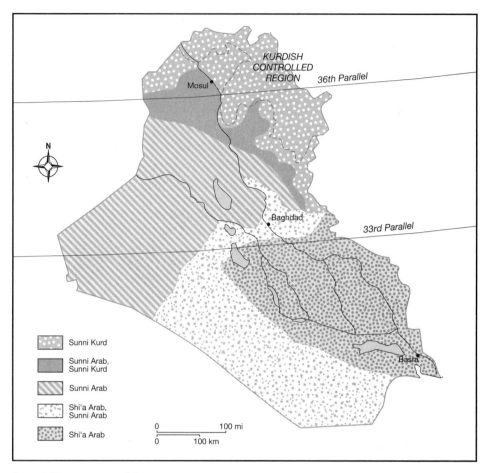

Iraqi Demographics

Much as they had done in Greece, Turkey, and Iran, the Soviet Union took advantage of the unrest in Iraq. The Soviet embassy ran a series of operations designed to increase the prominence of its proxy, the Iraqi Communist party. The arrest of a number of Communist leaders reinforced in the eyes of the palace the need for strong ties with Britain, even though the rise in Iraqi nationalism caused by the first Arab-Israeli war made the British position untenable. To avoid running afoul of Iraqi public opinion, in 1947 the British withdrew all their troops in the country that were left over from World War II, leaving their only presence at two air bases.

Control of the Baghdad government fluctuated between the pro- and anti-British forces throughout the early 1950s. By 1955, Britain's ally Nuri al-Said was back in power, and Nuri agreed to join the Baghdad Pact (see page 196). He made Britain pay a price, however. In return for joining the Baghdad Pact, Nuri got cancellation of the Anglo-Iraqi Treaty that kept Iraqi foreign policy hostage to Britain's approval. The Arab League, under the sway of Egypt's Nasser, condemned Nuri's agreement to cooperate with the British, and most Arab countries sought to isolate Iraq.

In 1956, Nasser became the hero of the Arab world (and on the streets of Baghdad) because of his successful opposition to the British, French, and Israeli invasion of the Suez Canal. In 1957, Crown Prince Abdullah and four former Iraqi prime ministers met with King Saud ibn Abdul Aziz during the latter's visit to Washington. The two sides agreed to bury the generations-old enmity between the Hashemites and the Saudis, so that they could work together to defeat Nasser's popularity among their own populations. Iraq then sought to federate with the other Hashemite monarchy in the region, Jordan, to create a counterbalance to the United Arab Republic of Egypt and Syria. The Hashemite federation was even shorter than the Egypt-Syria union; the Iraqi Revolution ended it in 1958.

THE RISE OF THE BAATH

On July 14, 1958, Brigadier General Abdul Karim Qasim (sometimes spelled *Kassem*) overthrew the Iraqi government. The young King Faisal II, Crown Prince Abdullah, Prime Minister Nuri al Said, and all members of the royal family that could be caught were executed. The new deputy prime minister, Colonel Abdul Salam Muhammad Arif, traveled to Damascus to sign a cooperation agreement with Nasser, ending Iraq's role in the anti-Nasser coalition. Premier Qasim also signed a treaty with Nasser's superpower patron, the Soviet Union, thus cutting Iraq's long ties with its founding power, Britain. Shortly thereafter, Qasim threw Colonel Arif into prison on charges of plotting a coup.

Iraq divided between supporters and opponents of Nasserism. The Communists took advantage of the stalemate between the two forces to increase their influence. The government of Premier Qasim allowed the Communists as a counterweight to the Nasserists. When a group of Communists marched on the northern city of Mosul in March 1959, however, the garrison, manned by Kurds, took advantage of the unrest and revolted. It was a brief fight, and the garrison was soon defeated by a combined force of government troops and armed Kurdish tribes. The Communists then tried to take advantage of the situation themselves and launched a pogrom against the middle class in the city.

The Communist forces of Iraq were strengthened further by the arrival the following month of Mullah Mustafa Barzani in the north (see Chapter 8). He and his followers had been living in the Soviet Union ever since fleeing there following the collapse of the Mahabad Republic in 1946. Following their success in terrorizing Mosul, the Communists moved on Kirkuk in July of 1959. It was their high-water mark.

Qasim realized that the Communists were too great a danger to be used against the Nasserists, and he brought them under control before they could seize power. He arrested the leadership, purged popular organizations and unions of Communist members, and turned back toward the West. He made an arms purchase from Britain in 1959 and signed cultural agreements with the United States in 1960.

D : *Domestic Structures*

WHAT IS THE BAATH?

Like its more famous contemporary, Nasser's Egyptian Arab nationalism, the **Baath** party advanced a socialistic, pan-Arab philosophy. Sorbonne-educated Syrian intellectuals founded the movement in the 1940s. The two most famous were a Sunni Muslim, Salah al-Din al-Bitar, and a Greek Orthodox Christian, Michel Aflaq. At a time when fascism was riding high in Europe and World War II renewed European intervention in the Middle East, these and other thinkers proposed a party that combined nationalism with socialism. (Aflaq had learned Marxism while in Paris.) They believed that the only way for Arabs to control their own lives was the rebirth (*Baath* means "rebirth" or "renaissance" in Arabic) of a united Arab nation.

Baathis eventually seized control in Syria and Iraq. Since there could only be one Arab nation that included both countries, the governments of these countries were referred to as "regional commands." Nationalist rivalries continued even in the pan-nationalist movement: The Baath party in each of the states claimed that they were the National Command, and the other state was a regional command. They established competing claims for leadership of the movement.

Baath has a secular ideology, seeking to unite Arabs of all religions. (This was probably the influence of the Christian Aflaq, who would have had no place in a movement based on Islam.) Despite its secular principles, it accepted Islam as the highest manifestation of the Arab culture. Some see Baathism as a kind of Arab fascism, at least as it was expressed by Saddam Hussein. Baathis organized themselves into clandestine cells until they seized power through military coups in both countries. At present, Baathism stands for nothing clear.

Qasim had few supporters in the country except the military. On the international front, he soon isolated himself just as he had done domestically. He nationalized most of the assets of the Iraqi Petroleum Corporation, which was British controlled and operated. In retaliation, the oil multinationals moved their investments to other countries in the region and denied Iraq the benefits of any increases in oil revenue. Qasim then took on the rest of the Arab world by laying claim to Kuwait. Britain sent forces to defend the newly independent country. Saudi troops later replaced British troops there. When the Arab League welcomed Kuwait as a full member, a combined unit of the Arab League replaced the Saudi contingent.

On February 8, 1963, the Baath party in Iraq overthrew the Qasim regime and took power for the first time. They shot Qasim and proudly displayed his corpse on television. The Baath in Syria seized power a month later. The two commands of the Baath party tried to negotiate unity with Egypt, since all three countries were now supposedly committed to Arab unity. But Nasser believed the Syrians had deceived him during the aborted United Arab Republic. He supplemented his negotiations with attempts to overthrow the Baathists and replace them with his own

---

Baath   Arab Socialist Renaissance party; came to power in Syria and Iraq.

people, and the negotiations fell apart. Arab unity, much commented upon in the Arab press from the 1930s to the present day, had been shown to be unfeasible in 1961 and again in 1963. The fiction would continue a number of years, however, as the three countries continued to periodically negotiate and sign various bilateral and multilateral unity agreements. None ever came to fruition. The trouble with Arab unity is that several countries want to lead it.

The leader of the Iraqi coup was Colonel Abdul Salam Arif, the same individual who had helped Qasim achieve power and who was imprisoned as his reward. Arif ruled as both president and chairman of the Baath Revolutionary Command Council (RCC). Arif did not like having to rule by committee, and he staged a second coup in November 1963 to eliminate the RCC. The only tie to the party in the new government was the powerless vice president, Baath party member General Hassan al-Bakr. The vice president kept his honorary title three months before resigning.

THE JUNE 1967 WAR

President Arif died in a helicopter crash on April 13, 1966. His brother, General Abdul Rahman Arif, promptly succeeded him and presided over a period of relative peace and prosperity. The Six Day War with Israel in June 1967 shattered the calm. Although the war did not last long enough for Iraqi troops to actually engage in battle, Israeli preemptive strikes wiped out the entire Iraqi air force. This provided the Soviet Union with an opportunity to expand its influence in the area, as Moscow promptly replaced all the destroyed aircraft with newer models. This act of friendship was followed by a number of economic, political, and military agreements between the two countries, and visits by high-level Soviet and Iraqi officials to each other's capitals.

On July 17, 1968, the Baath returned to power through another coup. Washington was briefly reassured by the overthrow of the Arif regime that had become so friendly with the Soviets. American discomfort increased, however, when two weeks later all pro-Western members of the coup were dismissed. The RCC transformed the country into a single-party state and rapidly solidified their hold over the instruments of power. The leader was General Hassan al-Bakr, the former vice president. Al-Bakr, in turn, appointed a distant cousin to be his vice premier, a Baathi enforcer named Saddam Husayn (spelled in the media as *Hussein*).

The new government's foreign policy was guided by a desire to improve Iraq's regional position rather than by an ideological compass. It fought with the Baath government in Syria over the Syrian construction of a dam, which reduced the flow of Euphrates river water into Iraq. Iraq also alienated Syria by building a pipeline through Turkey that, in effect, recognized Turkish control of Iskenderun—an area Syria still claimed was part of the Syrian homeland under its old name of Alexandretta.

The Baathis completed the break with Britain by nationalizing the rest of the Iraqi Petroleum Company. It also joined the Rejectionist Front along with other hard-line countries such as Syria and Libya, which were allies of the Palestine

C : Cultures

THE ETERNAL SALADIN

The Muslim, specifically Arab, world seems to need a Saladin from time to time. As we considered in Chapter 3, Saladin was the chivalrous twelfth-century Kurdish general who beat the Crusaders and ruled Egypt. Saladin, although of Kurdish origin, is an icon among Arabs: the hero who unified us and kicked out the Europeans. Because the Arab world continued to suffer the same problems—fragmentation and foreign dominance—a charismatic Saladin figure has been an intermittent phenomenon.

Nasser of Egypt seemed to have had a Saladin image of himself even before he led the 1952 coup that eventually made him Egypt's permanent president. Through the 1950s and 1960s, he used heroic references to himself as the man who would unify the Arabs and expel the foreigners. He saw his mission as the Arab world searching for the right man to liberate it—him. Most of the Arab world hero-worshipped him. Notice how even conservative Arab regimes—such as Saudi Arabia's discussed in Chapter 10—were initially drawn to him even though he represented a threat to their monarchies. They liked the way he stood up to the West, although they did not want to be overthrown.

Saddam Hussein of Iraq played the Saladin role. He proudly noted that he and Saladin were both born in Tikrit. Rationally, many Arabs knew Saddam was a brutal dictator, but emotionally they could not help admiring the way he stood up to the United States. Almost all Arabs favored Saddam in the 2003 Iraq War; hardly anyone spoke against his tyranny. Saddam played the same themes as had Nasser: Unify the Arabs and kick out the West. Across the culture gap, we had trouble understanding the overwhelming Arab support for Saddam. To us, he was a tinhorn dictator. To Arabs, he was the latest manifestation of the spirit of Saladin. We were not just fighting Saddam; we were fighting history.

The most recent Saladin-like figure is Shaykh Nasrallah, the leader of Hezballah in Lebanon. Nasrallah is the leader of a Shi'a sect, but his opposition to the Israeli invasion of Lebanon in 2006 led traditional Sunni leaders such as King Abdallah of Saudi Arabia and Egypt's Hosni Mubarak to praise him as a defender of Muslim land. Even the bitterly anti-Shi'a al Qaeda supported Nasrallah's efforts.

Another historical pattern showed up recently. Egypt and Mesopotamia have always been rivals, in competition to dominate the Middle East. They may have the same goals, but each wants to lead. Nasser made Egypt the leader; then Saddam Hussein tried to do the same for Iraq. With America watching Iraq, where will the next Saladin figure emerge? Osama or a follower in Saudi Arabia? We can be sure of two things about him: He will claim to be unifying the Arabs, and he will be anti-United States.

Liberation Organization. The Front opposed any recognition of Israel or negotiating peace with it. Iraq hosted the Baghdad summit of 1978, which condemned Egypt for negotiating a separate peace with Israel. As a leading source of instability in the Middle East and a leader in the movement opposed to Western influence, Iraq continued to deepen its ties with the Soviet Union. Iraq and the United States had no diplomatic ties from 1967 to 1984.

As for relations with Iran, Iraq had been fighting a low-intensity conflict with Iranian surrogates (the Kurds) from 1970 to 1975 (see Chapter 9). Saddam Hussein estimated that the Iraqi army lost 16,000 in the fighting and another 60,000 wounded. Under pressure, he signed the 1975 Algiers accords bringing stability to Iraq's northern territories and eastern border. The southern border remained a point of contention, however, as Baathists renewed Iraq's claims to parts of Kuwait. This time, Baghdad did not seek to justify its claims on history but on Iraq's strategic needs, since the lands it coveted controlled the approaches to the strategic Iraqi port of Umm Qasr.

On July 17, 1979, President al-Bakr stepped down after eleven years in office and appointed his cousin Saddam to succeed him. The new president ruled over a country that many economists judged was so advanced that it might soon surpass the economies of such European countries as Spain and Italy. Economic growth was not Saddam's primary ambition.

KUWAIT

Kuwait has a short history, as it has existed as an independent state for only about forty years. The current aristocracy (known as the *Utub* or "wanderers") arrived in Kuwait via Basra around 1750, having been previously driven out of Qatar. At the time, the area was considered part of the Ottoman Empire. There were two wealthy tribes among the migrants: the al-Khalifa, who controlled the lucrative pearl industry, and the al-Jalahima who owned the boats. The economics of the situation made conflict between the two tribes inevitable. To arbitrate competing claims, tribal chieftains elevated a third tribe to run the government, the al-Sabah, who have ruled (and mostly owned) Kuwait ever since. The al-Khalifa migrated out of Kuwait in the 1760s, and eventually became the ruling family in Bahrain. The al-Jalahima left at the same time, but remained a threat to the al-Sabah for a number of years.

KUWAIT'S BRITISH CONNECTION

The British East India Company traditionally used the Ottoman port of Basra as a transshipment point in the northern part of the Gulf, but they frequently turned to Kuwait as an alternative when politics kept them out of Basra. When Persians besieged Basra in 1775–1779, for example, the British used Kuwait as an alternative. They returned to Kuwait in 1793–1795 when local anti-British sentiment heated up in Basra. Again in 1821, when the British were in a dispute with Ottoman authorities, they removed themselves to Kuwait.

While the various members of the al-Sabah valued their British connection, they were not willing to surrender their independence to maintain it. Instead, the family played the British off against the Ottomans. In 1838, Shaykh Jabir I accepted to his court a representative of the Egyptian Pasha, Muhammad Ali, who was on the Arabian peninsula to reestablish Ottoman control of the area that had been conquered by the al-Saud. The Egyptians withdrew in 1840, but the shaykh's willingness to accept the caliph's Egyptian representative cemented his good relations with the Ottoman Empire.

In 1856, the British offered to switch their port permanently from Basra to Kuwait; Kuwait would gain shipping fees but would have to sign the usual British treaty surrendering rights of the shaykh to make foreign treaties or to cede any land without prior British approval. The shaykh refused the terms and in 1862, when British merchants began using Kuwait as a port of call, he closed the harbor to them. This allowed the traditional Kuwaiti merchant class to maintain their monopoly on shipping in Kuwait and was perceived favorably by Ottoman authorities in Basra.

In the 1860s the Ottomans insisted that Kuwait was a part of Basra province and tried to enforce their claims. Istanbul even dispatched naval vessels to impose its will. In reply, the shaykh notified Istanbul that the inhabitants were prepared to abandon Kuwait and migrate elsewhere rather than accept Ottoman supremacy. The governor of Basra supported the al-Sabah, and the Ottomans dropped their efforts to enforce their claims.

As the Ottomans moved against the second Saudi kingdom, Kuwait's Shaykh Abdallah II realized the two warring powers were squeezing him. To protect his de facto independence, in 1871 he accepted the Ottoman title of governor of the subprovince of Kuwait. Abdallah II had preserved his ability to operate, but at the cost of formally recognizing his position as an official of Basra province of the Ottoman Empire. Iraq later used Kuwait's Ottoman connection to demonstrate that Kuwait rightfully belongs to Iraq. Kuwait emphasizes that it was never Ottoman-ruled or part of Ottoman-administered Iraq, and thus Iraq has no historic claim to it.

Mubarak

Mubarak I founded the modern al-Sabah dynasty in 1896 with the help of two of his sons, Jabir and Salim. Since Mubarak's death, rule of Kuwait has alternated between the descendants of these two sons. Mubarak did not come to power cleanly. After his eldest brother Abdallah II died, the second in line was Muhammad I. Muhammad and younger brother Jarrah teamed up to run the country, and appointed Mubarak head of the military, keeping Mubarak with the troops in the desert, far from the palace. There are reports that Mubarak traveled that year to Bushehr in Persia and met with a British political agent. Whether this unconfirmed report is true or not, Mubarak went to the palace and, with the help of his two sons, assassinated Shaykh Muhammad and his brother Jarrah. He then seized control of the government.

Mubarak I presided over Kuwait during its most defining moments. In 1897, the Ottomans renewed the title it had bestowed on Mubarak's brother, governor of the subprovince of Kuwait. They insisted on Turkish rule of the subprovince, and Mubarak I turned to the British to act as a counterweight. In a secret agreement in 1899, the British finally got the Kuwaiti shaykh to sign the usual trucial agreement, cementing Kuwait's position into the British colonial system.

Armed with British defense guarantees, Mubarak launched a campaign against the al-Rashidis, who were closely aligned with the Ottomans. Mubarak lost the battle but won the war. Even though he was militarily defeated in 1901, Mubarak earned an alliance with the al-Saud family, who also opposed the Rashidis. (The al-Saud were living in exile in Kuwait, and they launched their third conquest of the peninsula from Mubarak's palace.)

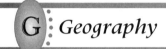

Geography

IS COLONIALISM ONLY EUROPEAN?

Anything that goes wrong in the Middle East is often blamed on colonialism. Many Algerian intellectuals, for example, blame their country's murderous political strife on French colonialists, who robbed and ruined Algeria. Intellectuals throughout the Middle East repeat the simplified story, often substituting British for French.

Is colonialism only a European phenomenon? A Turkish royal house hundreds of miles away controlled the coasts of the Arabian peninsula. Turks, ethnically very different from Arabs, sent governors from Istanbul, collected taxes, and kept the peace. Some Turks even settled in Arab lands. Ottomans ruled for the benefit of the **metropole** rather than for the benefit of the local population. The Ottoman Empire was a colonial empire but it was a Muslim empire, and that often justifies it in the Middle East.

WORLD WAR I AND KUWAIT

In 1913, the British betrayed their Kuwaiti allies in an effort to keep the Ottomans from joining the German side in the upcoming war. They acknowledged the Ottomans' claim that Kuwait was part of the Ottoman Empire and agreed to allow an Ottoman political officer to be assigned to Kuwait. Before the official could reach his new post, however, World War I broke out and the Ottomans joined it alongside the Central Powers.

Britain declared Kuwait an independent shaykhdom under British protection. Kuwait was unable to take advantage of its new status, however, because Mubarak I died in 1915, and his successor supported the Ottomans. As a result, the British blockaded Kuwait for the length of the war. At the same time, the Kuwaitis were fighting off the Saudi Ikhwan who advanced from the desert.

At the end of the war, the British Resident responsible for the Persian Gulf, Sir Percy Cox, convened a conference in 1923 that established the borders of modern Kuwait. Because no exact border could be created in the desert between Kuwait and Saudi Arabia, the parties agreed to the establishment of a neutral zone. Should any natural resources ever be discovered in the large, empty land of the zone, it would be divided between the Saudis and the al Sabah. With peace restored, the British then defended the Kuwaitis against the continuing raids of the Ikhwan.

In December 1934, the Gulf Oil Corporation and the Anglo-Iranian Oil Corporation signed a joint agreement with Kuwait establishing the Kuwaiti Oil Company. In 1935, this new entity discovered oil, guaranteeing that Kuwait would become one of the richest countries in the world and holder of the world's fourth-largest oil reserves. The oil company began exporting crude in 1946. Kuwait followed the lead of other Arab oil-exporting states and nationalized the industry by 1977.

---

metropole   The home or central country of an empire.

In 1938, Kuwait became the first country on the Arabian peninsula to convene a legislative assembly. The British Political Officer and Kuwaiti reformists forced the shaykh to accept this innovation. The fourteen-man Assembly elected the future Shaykh Abdallah III as its leader, but the ruling Shaykh Ahmad I assembled his supporters and closed the legislature after only six months.

The 1956 Suez Canal crisis inflamed anti-British emotion among young Kuwaitis. In 1958, Britain's major allies in the region, the Iraqi royal family, were overthrown and executed. Kuwaiti nationalists began to agitate against Britain's preferential status in the shaykhdom. To appease the critics, in June 1961 Shaykh Abdallah III ended the Anglo-Kuwaiti Defense Treaty of 1899. He declared Kuwait an independent country and joined the Arab League.

The ink had barely dried on the declaration when Iraqi President Qasim renewed the old Ottoman claims. Qasim said that since Kuwait had been a sub-province of Basra, and Basra was now part of Iraq, Kuwait was also legally a part of Iraq. Qasim's attempts to subvert Abdallah III's independence, however, had the opposite effect; by providing an outside enemy to rally against, it solidified the role of the al-Sabah family as defender of the country's independence.

First British, then Saudi, and finally an Arab League military force deployed to Kuwait to protect its sovereignty. Iraq never agreed to delineate its border with Kuwait, and in the 1970s renewed its claims on two areas of Kuwait that controlled the access to the Iraqi port of Umm Qasr, the island of Warba, and the Bubiyan peninsula.

In 1962, Abdallah III approved a constitution that limited the powers of the royal family, established a National Assembly that opened in January 1963, and guaranteed equality to all Kuwaiti citizens. (One catch: Kuwaiti citizenship is limited to its original families. Most of the people who work in Kuwait are descended from more recent immigrants and cannot become Kuwaiti citizens.) The elections produced a bloc of strongly anti-Western nationalists that kept the country in political turmoil. By 1967, there had been a strong backlash against the oppositions, and elections brought a solid, pro-government grouping into the Assembly. By 1976 however, Abdallah's successor, Shaykh Jabir III, decided that the Assembly was producing results contrary to the country's national interest, and he ordered the body closed. It was reconvened in 1981, with a number of religious conservatives among its members.

As the oil revenues continued to expand the country's production capabilities, the Kuwaiti population proved too small to run the country. The government accepted massive waves of immigrants, the majority Palestinian, to live and work in the country. These new inhabitants had no rights to remain in the country and no chance of ever obtaining citizenship, but they had the ability to make excellent money they would never earn in refugee camps. By 1990, the original Kuwaiti population was a minority in the country.

In foreign policy, once Britain announced its withdrawal from the Persian Gulf, the Kuwaitis tried to straddle the Cold War divide. It sold its oil to, and made most of its purchases from, the West. At the same time, however, it opened diplomatic relations in 1970 with the Soviet Union and with the People's Republic of China.

CONCLUSIONS

Iran, Saudi Arabia, Iraq, and Kuwait assumed their current forms in the early twentieth century. Their previous histories were, for the most part, a succession of murders, coups, and military conquests. What unites four disparate countries are oil, the Persian Gulf, oil, Islam, and oil. Did we mention oil?

With the exception of Iran, which has a history and civilization stretching back thousands of years, none of the countries would have been anything more than minor tribal principalities without the black gold. Once the countries produced commercial quantities of petroleum, they were integrated into the world economy and became strategic interests first of Britain and soon of the United States. As the British lion lost strength in its old age, the Americans assumed more of the responsibility of maintaining the peace in the Gulf. All the countries have a history of achieving their current borders through armed clashes. It is thus no surprise that fighting in the region continues into the twenty-first century.

KEY TERMS

analogy (p. 208)   dysanalogy (p. 208)
Baath (p. 212)   metropole (p. 217)

FURTHER REFERENCE

Abdullah, Thabit A. J. *Dictatorship, Imperialism, and Chaos: Iraq since 1989*. New York: Palgrave, 2006.

Batatu, Hanna. *The Old Social Classes and the Revolutionary Movements of Iraq*. Boulder, CO: Westview, 1992.

Crystal, Jill. *Kuwait: The Transformation of an Oil State*. Boulder, CO: Westview, 1992.

Dodge, Toby. *Inventing Iraq: The Failure of Nation Building and a History Denied*. New York: Columbia University Press, 2005.

Farouk-Sluglett, Marion, and Peter Sluglett. *Iraq since 1958: From Revolution to Dictatorship*, rev. ed. New York: Palgrave, 2001.

Khadduri, Majid. *Independent Iraq, 1932–1958: A Study in Iraqi Politics*. New York: Oxford, 1960.

———. *Republican Iraq: A Study in Iraqi Politics since the Revolution of 1958*. New York: Oxford, 1969.

———. *Socialist Iraq: A Study in Iraqi Politics since 1968*. Washington, D.C.: Middle East Institute, 1978.

Marr, Phebe. *History of Modern Iraq*, 2nd ed. Boulder, CO: Westview, 2003.

Miller, Judith, and Laurie Mylroie. *Saddam Hussein and the Crisis in the Gulf*. New York: Times Books, 1990.

Pavis, Timothy J. *Britain, the Hashemites, and Arab Rule, 1920–1925: The Sherifian Solution*. Portland, OR: Frank Cass, 2003.

Polk, William R. *Understanding Iraq: The Whole Sweep of Iraqi History, from Genghis Khan's Mongols to the Ottoman Turks to the British Mandate to the American Occupation*. New York: HarperCollins, 2005.

Rush, Alan. *Al-Sabah: History and Genealogy of Kuwait's Ruling Family, 1752–1987*. Atlantic Highlands, NJ: Ithaca Press, 1987.

Simon, Reeva Spector, and Eleanor H. Tejirian, eds. *The Creation of Iraq, 1914–1921*. New York: Columbia University Press, 2005.

Tripp, Charles. *A History of Iraq*, 2nd ed. New York: Cambridge University Press, 2002.

12   *The Iranian Revolution and War with Iraq*

Points to Ponder

- Was the Iranian Revolution bound to happen?
  - Would Iran have been better or worse if Mossadeq had stayed in power in the 1950s?
    - Could the right reforms have headed off Iran's revolution?
  - Did President Carter hasten the Iranian Revolution?
  - How could a country dependent on a superpower break away from it?
  - Is Iran a theocratic state, a democratic one, or a hybrid of the two?
  - What is the role of the United States in Iran today? What should it be?
  - Who is now in charge in Iran?
- Could Iran have another revolution?

THE PRESSURE COOKER

The United States was distracted in the 1970s by the resignations of the vice president and president, the unhappy end of Vietnam, and the 1973 October War. Nixon had posited the shah as the gendarme of the Gulf and had sold him over $10 billion of advanced weaponry paid for with increased oil wealth from the price run-up of the 1973–1974 oil embargo (see Chapter 10).

In January 1977 Jimmy Carter began his presidency with an evangelical Christian streak that proclaimed human rights a pillar of U.S. foreign policy. Some argue that foreign policy has to be amoral and pay little attention to human rights; trying to make it moral opens cans of worms. Oblivious to such perspectives and his own blind eye to numerous countries with humans rights abuses as bad as or worse than Iran's, Carter named Iran as a country that had to improve. Some Iranians took heart from Carter's emphasis on human rights. Iran was indeed a dictatorship that crushed opposition and dissent, often physically through its security service, the dread SAVAK. Deeply Islamic Iranians hated the secularization, and *bazaaris* hated being pushed out by larger modern firms. Furthermore, the big oil revenues ignited an inflation that melted salaries.

Some say that Carter persuaded the shah to relax his repression, and that caused all that followed. Others say the shah was reforming anyway to secure his son's succession to the throne. Either way, in May 1977 Washington signaled its approval of these changes by selling the shah F-16s and AWACS planes. Congressional criticism of the sale sent the shah a different signal: that some elements of the U.S. government were reconsidering its support of him.

In November 1977 the shah visited the White House. Sixty thousand Iranian students demonstrated in Lafayette Park across from the White House. As President Carter welcomed his royal visitor, police fired tear gas to disperse the demonstrators. The fumes drifted over the White House lawn and both leaders retreated into the White House with tears in their eyes. The television image was of two world leaders fleeing from the wrath of their people. Six weeks later Carter visited the shah in Tehran where he toasted the country (and by extension the monarch) as an island of stability. American Ambassador William Sullivan reported that the shah was elated by what seemed to be Carter's renewed support.

Opposition to the shah among secular groups grew in 1977. Groups such as the Tudeh (Communist) party and old supporters of Muhammad Mossadeq revitalized their networks. The real revolution began, however, in the opening days of 1978.

THE BEGINNING OF THE REVOLUTION

Specifically, on January 7, 1978, the government-run *Etella'at* newspaper condemned the Ayatollah Ruhallah Khomeini, then in exile in Iraq, and all clerics who opposed the shah. The accusations were extreme, and Khomeini's students, friends, and followers in the seminary city of Qom were horrified. On January 9, 1978, the clerics organized a demonstration march in Qom. Police opened fire, killing several. Iran's leading cleric, who had not been opposed to the monarchy, Ayatollah Kazem Shari'atmaderi, condemned the Pahlavis as anti-Islamic.

Following Shi'a custom, one mourning ceremony takes place at the burial and another forty days later. At that time demonstrators in Tabriz attacked theaters, bars, and anything that could be considered a symbol of the shah's new Iran. Some demonstrators were killed, producing renewed violence every forty days that continued until February 1979.

On August 19, 1978, a fire broke out at the Rex cinema in the southern oil town of Abadan, killing almost 500 people. It was Ramadan and the shah's supporters immediately blamed the religious opposition who had been setting fires to movie theaters throughout the country. The opposition called it a "Reichstag fire" set by the regime itself to place blame on its critics. In early September the religious opposition organized two demonstrations to celebrate the end of Ramadan, the Muslim month of daytime fasting. Under the shah's ban on all public gatherings, these demonstrations were technically illegal but police did not interfere. Emboldened by the regime's timidity in the face of civil disobedience, the opposition called for a general strike. The shah imposed martial law, in spite of the liberalization he had been promising. The next day, September 7, 1978, thousands gathered in Tehran's Jaleh Square and refused to disperse. Troops opened fire, killing from 100 to 1,000. The country was now racked with daily protests and strikes.

Iranian intelligence reported that the mastermind behind the opposition was Ayatollah Khomeini, whom the shah had exiled to Turkey in 1964. Khomeini had been living in the Iraqi Shi'a shrine city of Najaf where he used Shi'a pilgrims to smuggle his sermons into Iran. The shah had had enough and asked the Iraqis to expel Khomeini. France gave the ayatollah refuge in a Paris suburb.

KHOMEINI IN PARIS

The shah thought he had won a victory, but he was wrong. Paris's distance did not hurt Khomeini's ability to communicate. He simply recorded his anti-shah sermons and phoned them to Iran, where his followers recorded them on cheap cassettes and played them in mosques nationwide. Simple technology eluded the shah's communications monopoly.

The shah's plan was to work with the secular opposition of former Mossad-eqists in the National Front, sharing some power with them and breaking them away from Khomeini. Then, he believed, moderate religious leaders would support the new government. Front leaders went to Paris for Khomeini's consent to the shah's offer. The implacable ayatollah rejected the compromise, and the secularists stayed with him. The incident showed that the secularists had already subordinated themselves to the religious fanatics. Many later regretted it.

To restore order in the rapidly deteriorating situation, the shah established a military government on November 6, 1978. Each province got a military governor, and demonstrators retreated in fear. At the same time, the shah arrested leaders of his intelligence service and some of his political allies in order to try to appease the angry crowds. (These officials were still in jail when the revolution delivered them to the executioners.) He also continued to try to negotiate with the National Front. Khomeini and his followers interpreted these moves as acts of desperation—they were—and ordered the opposition to redouble its efforts.

THE LAST IMPERIAL GOVERNMENT

The shah finally convinced Shahpour Bakhtiar, French-educated and a longtime member of the National Front who had served as a member of Mossadeq's cabinet in the 1950s, to lead a civilian government. Bakhtiar assumed power as the last imperial prime minister on December 27, 1978. In his New Year's address he promised the creation of a social-democratic society. Bakhtiar did what he could. He dissolved the hated SAVAK and appointed secular nationalists to head the ministries. He was naive in failing to understand that as a secularist appointee of the shah he would soon be dumped by the Islamists.

K Key Concepts

WHAT WENT WRONG IN IRAN?

Twenty-five years after the revolution the shah's supporters still debate whom to blame for his fall. Some use the 1953 CIA-sponsored ouster of Mossadeq as a model and argue that another U.S. intervention could have saved the shah. Others look at the Huyser mission and see a deep U.S. conspiracy to dump the shah. Western analysts point to the shah's inability to meet the basic economic needs of the people, educational change, and rising expectations. Others claim that Iranians just wanted a change in government, especially in light of the regime's repressive techniques against dissent of any kind. Deprived of democratic means to voice their grievances, they turned to revolution.

More puzzling is why the shah equivocated in his response to this challenge. Early on, he saw he would either have to crack down by military means or liberalize to survive in power. Instead of sticking with one strategy, he vacillated between the two. We now know that the shah was dying of cancer, but no one in Washington was aware of it. Fatigue, mood swings, and weakened cognitive abilities from medications may have hurt his ability to make firm decisions.

The shah still relied on his American ally for guidance but did not know that Washington was deeply divided between the National Security Council and the State Department as to what to do. Secretary of State Cyrus (a Persian name) Vance would applaud the shah's plans to liberalize while National Security Advisor Zbigniew Brzezinski would call him and tell him to be firm. The shah's policies depended on whom he had last heard from. (For more on "no one in charge" of U.S. foreign policy, see Chapter 17.)

U.S. General Robert Huyser then visited Iran and possibly made things worse. Soon Iranians realized that it was Huyser and not Ambassador Sullivan who had Carter's ear. Huyser tried to convince the Iranian military that their longstanding ties with the Pentagon remained intact regardless of what events transpired in Iran. Acting on orders, Huyser encouraged Iran's military to support the new government and not rebel or flee. Since then, many monarchists claimed that Huyser had been sent to convince the military to side with the opposition, thereby guaranteeing the return of Khomeini. Huyser did encourage the military to open communication with Khomeini—something Washington had not done itself until it was too late.

On January 16, 1979, the shah left Iran. The night before, he went to the imperial cemetery and dug up the remains of his father, Reza I. He boarded the royal jet accompanied by his entire family, untold millions in cash, and his father's remains, indicating he did not expect to ever return.

Headlines screamed *Shah Raft* ("The shah has gone"). Everyone anticipated the return of Ayatollah Khomeini. Bakhtiar, fearing what would happen if Khomeini returned, closed the airports. Khomeini ordered his followers into the streets until Bakhtiar reopened the airports. On February 1, 1979, Ayatollah al-Ozma Ruhallah Khomeini returned to Iran aboard a chartered Air France jet to rule Iran, not as king but as Imam or Supreme Leader.

K : *Key Concepts*

CRANE BRINTON'S THEORY OF REVOLUTION

In 1938 Harvard historian Crane Brinton explained how revolutions unroll in a similar pattern. *The Anatomy of Revolution* has stood the test of time and closely fits the Iranian Revolution. Brinton saw the following stages:

1. The old regime loses legitimacy. Intellectuals especially lose faith in it. Curiously, this often happens when the economy is *improving*, a point made a century earlier by Tocqueville on the French Revolution.

2. Antiregime groups coalesce. Some political problems cannot be solved, such as forming a new government. Rioting breaks out, but troops cannot quell it. The old regime departs because it knows it is finished.

3. At first, moderates take over and institute reforms, but they have neither the power nor the guts to crush the real revolutionaries, who hold them in contempt.

4. Extremists push the moderates aside and bring the revolution to a frenzied high, punishing enemies and "immoral" people in a reign of terror. Purity becomes the law of the land. France had Robespierre, Iran Khomeini.

5. People cannot stand the revolutionary purity for long; they get fed up with rule by extremists. Brinton called this stage **Thermidor** after the French revolutionary month in which Robespierre was guillotined. Brinton likened it to a cooling down after a fever. It indicates the revolution is over.

In 1938 Brinton virtually predicted how the 1979 Iranian Revolution would unroll. He found a logic to revolutions that is still valid.

THE FIRST REVOLUTIONARY GOVERNMENT

Bakhtiar's opposition credentials were impeccable, but accepting a post from the shah doomed him in the eyes of Khomeini. The ayatollah ignored Bakhtiar, and soon fighting broke out between noncommissioned air force officers loyal to Khomeini and the Imperial Guard. The generals ordered the army into the barracks and declared their neutrality in the political struggle taking place. Bakhtiar and his cabinet had no choice but to resign because no one would listen to them. Bakhtiar hid and then fled into exile to promote resistance to Iran's Islamist regime. For that he was stabbed to death in 1991 in his suburban Paris home.

Khomeini appointed another old National Front hand, Mehdi Bazargan, a French-educated engineer, as his prime minister. Khomeini's victory was almost complete, and the monarchy was officially declared overthrown on February 11, 1979. Each year Iran commemorates the eleven days from Khomeini's arrival on February 1 to the abolition of the monarchy on February 11 as the "Days of the Dawn."

Thermidor   A calming down after a revolutionary high.

R ⦙ *Religions*

CAN THERE BE AN ISLAMIC REPUBLIC?

Is there such a thing as an Islamic Republic? Islam holds that sovereignty belongs to God alone, but in a republic sovereignty resides in the people. The Iranian Constitution tried to make these two concepts work together. The result is a mishmash that, with complex additional screening bodies, keeps the Iranian government incoherent.

Iran's constitution says that power comes from God and resides in God's chosen one, the Imam. But laws are made by a parliament that is elected by the people. But the Assembly of Experts can overturn the laws if they are deemed un-Islamic. But if a law is declared un-Islamic and the parliament wants it anyway, then the issue is resolved by the Expediency Council. So, at that point, is the law the will of the people? Is the law Islamic? What is the law?

IRAN'S ISLAMIC CONSTITUTION

The United States had little influence on the Iranian Revolution. Iranians were determined to master their own destiny and repudiate American influence. Khomeini played the Tehran political scene like the clever revolutionary he was. Lenin had nothing on Khomeini. For example, secular intellectuals liked Western thought and supposed religious revolutionaries could not run Iran. In February 1979, Bazargan picked a cabinet of secular oppositionists much like himself. They congratulated themselves on cleverly manipulating Khomeini's supporters into putting right-thinking people like themselves into power instead of people they considered clerical reactionaries.

Nothing was further than the truth. Revolutionaries, as they often do, created structures parallel to those of the state, working around Bazargan's official government. Revolutionary committees sprang up next to the police, and the Revolutionary Guard competed with the military. Revolutionary courts condemned monarchists to death and seized the properties of those who fled. The clerical supporters organized the Islamic Republic party (IRP) and prepared for electoral battle.

Under orders from the ruling Revolutionary Council, Bazargan organized a referendum on March 31, 1979, in which 98 percent of the voters supported establishing an Islamic Republic. Bazargan then appointed a committee of his fellow moderates to draft a new constitution along West European social-democratic lines. Under Khomeini's guidance, hard-liners reworked the document, making the key office the *Velayat-e Faqih* ("Rule of the Islamic Jurist"; see page 182), a role intended for its author, Ayatollah Khomeini. The constitution centralized power in this Supreme Leader and made the directly elected president much weaker. Supreme Leader Khomeini was entitled to these powers because of his unique qualifications as the religious and political leader of the country.

THE HOSTAGE CRISIS

After more than twenty-five years there is still no hard evidence that Ayatollah Khomeini or members of the government instructed radical students to seize the U.S. Embassy or knew about it in advance. It really doesn't matter, as once the students seized the embassy, Khomeini embraced the hostage taking and made it a cornerstone of his policy. Now he could dump the moderate Bazargan and break all ties with Washington.

The embassy had been taken before. Three days after the monarchy had been abolished students overran the embassy, taking the ambassador and other diplomats hostage. On that occasion Khomeini sent representatives to convince the students to let the diplomats go. So ingrained was the belief that the embassy was a "nest of spies" planning a counterrevolution that the students never left the embassy compound. For the next nine months American diplomats had to enter their own embassy through checkpoints manned by armed revolutionaries.

The revolutionaries believed that the Americans would repeat their 1953 covert action that had brought the shah back. They feared any American contacts with the shah. In fact, such contacts were not going well. Tehran had warned Washington that there would be serious problems if the shah or his family were admitted to the United States, and President Carter feared for the safety of Americans still in Iran. As a result, the contacts usually consisted of the shah's people reminding the Americans that he was an invited guest and the Americans responding that this was not the right time.

Only in October 1979 did the shah tell Washington that he had been battling cancer for five years and needed treatment in the United States. President Carter felt he could not deny medical treatment to an old U.S. ally. The shah flew to New York for medical treatment. Many feared it was only a matter of time before the embassy was seized again.

On November 1, 1979, demonstrators massed around the embassy to protest America's support for the shah. Iranian police protected the compound and brought the protest under control. The diplomats inside breathed a sigh of relief, believing the worst was over. On November 4, students who followed a revolutionary cleric, Hojjatollah Islam Mohammed Musavi-Khoeniha, attacked the embassy again, and the police let them in. It appears that the students did not plan to take the diplomats hostage or hold the embassy for long. They saw their actions as preventing the United States from overthrowing the revolution and as an expression of anger at America admitting the shah. They did not attempt an Islamic justification, as the Muslim tradition since the time of the Prophet was to protect the emissaries of foreign lands to the House of Islam. Basically, they poured out all their hatred of the shah on the country that had helped him for decades.

Once the press swarmed around the embassy, the militants realized they had a good thing. They found documents describing contacts between the embassy and moderate Iranian officials. This gave them power to denounce their political opponents as spies. Ayatollah Khomeini embraced the militants as "Children of the Revolution" and the hostage crisis was on.

The crisis caused the downfall of two governments. Unable to convince the militants to honor international law and release the Americans, after two days the Bazargan government resigned. For 444 days America watched nightly as the militants humbled its self-image and reputation. In the end it cost Jimmy Carter re-election. The militants treated the fifty-two hostages badly and tortured some. Most were jailed in the embassy basement and fed only bread and water.

THE FAILED HOSTAGE RESCUE

The shah completed his treatment and returned to Mexico in December 1979. The Americans asked for the hostages' release since the original reason for the seizure no longer existed: The shah was not in the United States. The militants replied the crisis would continue until the United States delivered the shah and his rumored wealth to Iran. Even when the shah died in 1980 in Cairo, the hostage crisis continued. The militants added demands for apologies and for refunds on loan payments. Clearly diplomacy was not the answer.

Carter, worried about the hostages' lives, in April 1980 ordered a daring hostage rescue of the kind that works in movies. The secretive Delta team was to helicopter into the middle of Iran and snatch the hostages. One thing after another went wrong. A helicopter rotor ripped a cargo plane, killing eight, and the mission was aborted. Some feared that if Delta had actually got into Tehran, the hostages would have been killed. The militants claimed that God himself had intervened to stop the American invasion and protect His Islamic Republic.

Secretary of State Cyrus Vance was kept out of planning the operation because he never would have approved. When he learned of it, he told Carter he would stay in office until the April 24 rescue operation but would resign immediately afterward. He was replaced by Senator Edmund Muskie. Now Carter was politically wounded and was voted out of office in November 1980. The conservative former governor of California and movie star Ronald Reagan won and was not shy about using military force. Khomeini saw the hostages no longer did him any good and released them precisely as Reagan was being inaugurated. Iran broke every rule in the diplomatic book and suffered when Iraq invaded later in 1980, for now it had no powerful friends or protectors.

BANI SADR: THE LAST OF THE LIBERALS

In January 1980, during the hostage crisis, Iranians elected a president. The clerics in the Islamic Republic party chose the ideologically pure Jalal ad-Din Farsi, but he was disqualified from running only weeks before the election. The IRP rushed a substitute candidate onto the lists but not in time. Moderate forces supported Abol Hasan Bani Sadr, a Sorbonne-trained economist and the son of an ayatollah. He had returned to Iran aboard the same jet as the ayatollah. Bani Sadr won with 70 percent of the vote. The educated moderates again congratulated themselves for controlling the direction of the revolution.

The United States in the Middle East

IRAN'S MUJAHIDIN

Mujahidin means "Holy Warriors" and has been used by Islamist guerrilla groups from Morocco to Afghanistan. In Iran, however, the Mujahidin-e Khalq (or People's Warriors) are violent leftists. The former head of the KGB in Tehran said the group was a major information source on Iranian affairs throughout the Cold War. Michael Rubin reports that the group murdered five American military technicians working with the Iranian army, and tried to kidnap the U.S. ambassador to Iran, Douglas MacArthur III. When this effort failed, the leader, Masoud Rajavi, escaped execution only after Soviet President Nikolai Podgorny personally appealed for clemency. One of the authors worked with American diplomats assigned to the Tehran embassy in the 1970s who were under heavy surveillance by the Mujahidin.

When the Iranian Revolution broke out, the Mujahidin supported the revolutionaries and tried to work with Khomeini's forces for the first year. Soon, however, Rajavi decided the new regime was not sufficiently revolutionary and would need to be replaced. Once the group began its efforts to take over, the full forces of the Islamic Republic were turned on it. The roughly 15,000 armed followers of Rajavi and his wife Maryam (former wife of Rajavi's top commander whom Rajavi ordered to divorce so he could have the wife as co-commander) fled across the border into Iraq. During the Iran-Iraq war, the Mujahidin cooperated with Saddam Hussein against their own country.

The Mujahidin assassinated a number of Iranian officials and were branded a terrorist group by President Clinton and the European Union. Most consider them a crazy cult, but many American neoconservatives see them as freedom fighters who could liberate Iran. They ignore their role in the terrorist attacks on Americans in the 1970s and the loathing of their own people for having cooperated with Iraq in the 1980s. Based in Paris, Mujahidin representatives lobby the U.S. Congress; their "army" is interned in Camp Ashraf in Iraq.

Despite the constitutional limits on his position, Bani Sadr believed his electoral margin gave him the authority to govern. He pledged to eliminate the revolutionary bodies. Khomeini swore in the new president two months before the first parliament was elected; he also gave Bani Sadr other duties such as commander in chief of the armed forces and head of the Revolutionary Committee. The ayatollah seemed to realize that authority was escaping his control and planned to get it back.

President Abol Hassan Bani Sadr was the last of the secular moderates in office. When the Bazargan cabinet resigned over the hostage crisis, Bani Sadr's status was not affected. He was protected because he had worked with Khomeini in Paris, and Khomeini had personal affection for him. Bani Sadr, however, was determined to reassert his authority over that of the revolutionary institutions and ran afoul of the IRP and its clerical supporters. He tried to resolve the hostage crisis because it hurt Iranian diplomacy, but this cost him Khomeini's backing.

The parliament controlled by the IRP thwarted his every move. Cabinet nominees were rejected and policy proposals turned down. After the Iraqi invasion, he retreated into his role as commander in chief, which gave him a platform to attack his critics. He criticized revolutionary figures for corruption, torture, misuse of power, and violating the constitution. These liberal positions won Bani Sadr the support of the Mujahidin-e Khalq, a strange Islamic-Marxist cult that had served the revolution but was being pushed out. In June 1981, parliament impeached Bani Sadr by a vote of 177 to 1 with 13 abstentions. Bani Sadr and the head of the Mujahidin, Masoud Rajavi, fled for their lives to Paris. The last of the liberal secularists had left the Iranian political scene.

Days later the Mujahidin bombed the headquarters of the IRP. Two months later they destroyed the prime minister's offices, killing the president, prime minister, head of the National Police, and others. This was the closest the Mujahidin ever came to power. In the resulting crackdown, the Mujahidin and the Tudeh (the old communist party) were crushed or fled into Iraq. Iran had essentially no more domestic opposition.

THE IRAN-IRAQ WAR

The Islamic Revolution declared that it was not only against the shah but also against "global arrogance," "corruption on earth," and "world-devouring imperialism," all meaning the United States. For several years they encouraged Shi'a communities to overthrow their "illegitimate" rulers. Shi'a opposition groups in southern Iraq, Bahrain, Kuwait, and Lebanon were supported by Iran, as were many fundamentalist Sunni groups, especially Palestinian.

Saddam Hussein in Iraq was enraged at Iranians telling his subjects to revolt. He also had some old scores to settle with Iran: the thousand-year Arab-Iranian conflict, Iranian support for Iraqi Kurdish groups, and the Shatt al-Arab border, which was forced on Iraq in 1975 (see page 156). Saddam was also greedy; the southwest of Iran is inhabited by ethnic Arabs and has much oil. Saddam believed that the Iranian military had been destroyed by the revolution, leaving "Arabistan" (the province of *Khuzestan* in Persian) easy pickings.

Iraq attacked Iran on September 22, 1980, and advanced rapidly. Iran's clergy unleashed their ideology and promised hundreds of thousands of youths eternal paradise for defending Islam. Untrained and unarmed, they charged Iraqi lines in waves. Bearing plastic keys symbolizing admission to heaven, they rushed willingly into mine fields. The clerics emptied Iranian jails of the shah's military commanders, promising them freedom for their military service. Losses were staggering. By May of 1982 the Iranians had repelled the Iraqi invasion, but Khomeini ordered the army to invade Iraq. He said he would settle for nothing less than the overthrow of Saddam Hussein.

By mid-1983 Iran had made some inroads. Iraq retaliated by launching a "war of the cities" in which Saddam lobbed SCUD missiles at Tehran. By 1987 the Iranians besieged Basra. In the north, Iran encouraged the Barzani Kurds to rebel. Saddam responded with the al-Anfal campaign: genocide of Kurds by poison gas (see Chapter 8).

THE AMERICAN TILT

No one in Washington liked Saddam, but believing the old Arab dictum that "the enemy of my enemy is my friend," America tilted toward Iraq in the hope of stopping Iran, a dangerous revolutionary power that held our diplomats hostage. We let rage dominate instead of clear thinking. In 1982 the United States removed Iraq from the list of state sponsors of terrorism despite the fact that Saddam sheltered Abu Abbas and numerous other Palestinian terrorists. We lent Iraq money and shared intelligence. In 1984 Washington restored diplomatic relations with Baghdad, a move we later regretted. Soon there were American diplomats and advisors in Baghdad. Some American officials were proud that we were weaning Iraq away from its dependency on the Soviet Union.

U.S. NAVAL INVOLVEMENT

Gulf Arab states, especially Kuwait and Saudi Arabia, gave Iraq generous loans, making them belligerents in Iran's eyes. Iran fired missiles at Kuwait City and hunted Kuwaiti oil tankers, many of them carrying Iraqi crude. Actually, Iraq had been attacking ships calling on Iranian ports for months. In early 1987 Kuwait sought international protection for its shipping fleet and Washington let them fly the stars and stripes. Soon the U.S. Navy protected the "American" ships by escorting them in armed convoys from the Gulf of Oman outside the Strait of Hormuz and then across the Gulf. Mines—some of them 1908 models sold to Iran by tsarist Russia—were the biggest worry. They were simple, cheap, and effective, and the U.S. Navy, intent on high-tech, had little mine-sweeping capability.

SADDAM TAKES THE OFFENSIVE

In 1986 Iraq turned to chemical weapons. With Iranian troops threatening Basra, Iraq's second-largest city, Saddam ordered gas to push the Iranians back. Iran may also have used some chemical weapons, but not as many. Thus did **weapons of mass destruction** debut into modern warfare.

During four months in 1988 Iraq won four major battles. Their chemical weapons unnerved the Iranians who fled en masse. Ayatollah Khomeini finally recognized that his dream of overthrowing Saddam would destroy his revolution, so he accepted a UN cease-fire resolution, stating he would rather drink poison. Khomeini never spoke in public again and died in June 1989 at age 89.

The Iran-Iraq war ended August 20, 1988, after almost eight years. Conservatively, about 233,000 died; ideological estimates range as high as a million, two-thirds of them Iranians. A huge Tehran cemetery, with a blood-red fountain,

---

weapons of mass destruction   The NBC weapons—nuclear, bacteriological, chemical, or "nukes, bugs, gas."

The United States in the Middle East

THE IRAN-CONTRA FIASCO

In 1983, the Iranian-backed Shi'a Hezbollah seized six American hostages in Lebanon. The Reagan White House, hoping to get them back and improve relations with Iran, offered Iran U.S. TOW anti-tank missiles through Iranian and Israeli middlemen. The hefty markup would then secretly fund the Nicaraguan *contras,* who were supposed to be fighting communism. Congress, suspicious of the contras' human rights abuses, had ended U.S. funding. By law, all funds taken in by the federal government must go to the Treasury, and none can be expended without Congressional appropriation. Anything else is an illegal "slush fund." Iran-Contra broke several laws. Although Reagan did not plan the operation, he approved of it retroactively in a Presidential Finding in January 1986.

It was a risky scheme that career professionals would have warned them against. Instead, the White House used dubious middlemen who claimed to have connections in Tehran but could not pass a lie-detector test. The 1986 operation was run by the National Security Council, which is not supposed to run any operations. Marine Lt. Col. Oliver North, enthusiastic but naive, was in charge. By the time the middlemen skimmed off their percentages, the contras got little.

Much worse from the Reagan administration's point of view, in October 1986 Iranian officials who were opposed to cooperation with America leaked news of the deal to a Lebanese newspaper. The president pleaded with the press not to pursue their investigation into the matter, arguing "American lives are at stake." The White House was embarrassed; it had broken its own law against trading with the enemy. If the United States could do it, why not the French or Japanese? One U.S. gift brought with the U.S. arms: a bible with an inscription from the president. Apparently no area expert explained to the NSC that Muslim fanatics do not much care for Christian bibles. Another American president looked foolish because he had tried to improve relations with Iran.

The U.S. hostages in Lebanon were finally released when neither Hezbollah nor Iran got any further benefit from holding them. The last, AP newsman Terry Anderson, was released in December 1991 after six and a half years.

commemorates the fallen, many of them teenagers. The war ended with the troops at nearly the original border. A horrible war had ended in the **status quo ante bellum**.

CONSTITUTIONAL CRISIS

In January 1988, with the war still on, Ayatollah Khomeini reversed fourteen hundred years of Shi'a jurisprudence with a statement that the Velayat-e Faqih was so important that its protection was a higher duty than any other. Since the Velayat-e Faqih ruled over a true Islamic State, and everything such a state did was correct, then the Islamic state could overrule any aspect of Islamic law that stood in its way. Only Khomeini had the power to make such an un-Islamic statement.

status quo ante bellum   Latin for the "situation before the war."

The United States in the Middle East

THE DOWNING OF IRAN AIR 655

On May 17, 1987, an Iraqi jet fired a French-made Exocet missile into the frigate USS *Stark* in the Gulf, killing thirty-seven American sailors. Baghdad claimed it was a mistake and the Reagan administration quietly accepted Iraq's apology, although many questioned if the attack was truly an accident. Slowly the United States was drawn into a naval war in the Gulf. One cannot be a little bit involved in the Gulf any more than one can be a little bit pregnant.

Increasingly U.S. and Iranian gunboats shot at each other. We were in a low-level but escalating war with each other. After an Iranian missile hit a reflagged Kuwaiti tanker, Navy SEALs blew up an Iranian oil platform in the Gulf that was rumored to be a launching point for raids.

On July 3, 1988, a scheduled civilian Iranian jetliner was flying across the Gulf over cruiser USS *Vincennes*, which thought it was another attack like the *Stark*. Misreading all signals that showed Iran Air 655 looked nothing like a warplane, panicked *Vincennes* crewmen shot it down with a missile, killing all 290 aboard. In dangerous situations, your mind plays tricks with you. The United States apologized and offered compensation to the families, but there was no way diplomatically to pass the money since Iran and the United States had no official diplomatic relations. Many Iranians believed the shootdown had been deliberate, a U.S. signal that the war would increasingly hurt Iran. It was not, but it may have persuaded Iran to end the war.

Khomeini used his new power in February 1988 to create the Expediency Council. The Islamic Republic had long been paralyzed; the conservative Council of Guardians vetoed laws from the more liberal parliament as contrary to Shari'a. Khomeini declared that an Expediency Council would resolve disagreements between the two bodies.

Khomeini's death the next year put the country into a constitutional crisis. The constitution said that the Supreme Leader had to be a preeminent theologian; if no individual possessed all the qualities for leadership then the position should be held by a council. No single theologian was found acceptable in 1989. President Ali Khamenei was considered an ayatollah but the Qom Theological Seminary had never approved his dissertation. The regime found a hundred-year-old cleric in Qom, Ayatollah Araki. The Council of Experts declared that Araki was the country's new *marja'*, "source of emulation," whom Iranians were to obey. Araki said to continue to follow the teachings of Khomeini and accept Ali Khamenei as the Supreme Leader.

Khamenei took Khomeini's old position but lacked Khomeini's status. The Speaker of the parliament, Ali Akbar Hashemi Rafsanjani, was elected the new president. Over the next eight years Iran underwent an ideological battle largely ignored in the West. Many prominent lay thinkers and clerics began to second-guess the revolutionary leadership; in their opinions the ruling clerics had usurped the rights of the people. They did not challenge the Islamic Republic but claimed they wanted to put the revolution back on the right course. This group's leader, Ayatollah Husayn Ali Montazeri, once Khomenei's likely successor, was stripped of his position and placed under house arrest for expressing doubts. These relative liberals supported the 1997 election of Muhammad Khatami as president.

U.S. *The United States in the Middle East*

MIXED SIGNALS

Positive and negative signals between Washington and Tehran alternate, first giving hope for normalization of relations and then dashing such hopes. First consider the positive signals. In 1990–1991 Iran remained neutral in the first Gulf War and even kept many Iraqi aircraft sent to Iran for safekeeping. Iran could have made some mischief but did not.

In 1998 President Khatami told an American television reporter that he supported cultural exchanges, and Secretary of State Madeline Albright invited the Iranians to seek normal relations. In 2006, now out of office, Khatami visited the United States as a private citizen and made similar suggestions.

In 1999 the United States eased sanctions on Iran. Now American companies would be able to sell food and medical items to Iran. In 2000 Washington allowed importation of Iranian caviar, pistachios, and carpets, albeit with high tariffs. In May 2000 the World Bank approved its first loan to Iran in seven years. The United States did not veto it.

In September 2001 the Iranian people held candlelight vigils in sympathy for 9/11. In October, when the United States began its retaliation against Afghanistan, Iran said it would help U.S. pilots who came down in Iran. President Khatami condemned Osama bin Ladin and the 9/11 murders. Iran stayed neutral while the United States drove the Taliban from power. (To be sure, Iran had always disliked the Sunni Taliban, who persecuted Afghan Shi'a.)

In 2001 at the UN General Assembly the Iranian foreign minister and U.S. secretary of state met and shook hands, a symbolic step.

In 2002 U.S. Senator Joseph Biden (D-Delaware) proposed the Senate Foreign Relations Committee meet with Iranian parliamentarians. Tehran did not oppose it.

In 2003 Iran remained neutral in the second Gulf War. President Khatami suggested renewed ties with the United States, and Tehran's foreign ministry quietly proposed negotiations that could, it hinted, include Iran's nuclear program.

But positive signals have always been followed by negative ones: Iran was neutral in the 1991 and 2003 Gulf Wars but condemned U.S. attacks on a Muslim country and wants American forces out of the

THE RAFSANJANI YEARS

For many years Hashemi Rafsanjani was considered the most powerful man in Iran. A pragmatist and deal maker, he got cooperation among competing factions when he was Speaker of parliament. He was in the middle of the Iran-Contra dealings with America but kept on good terms with conservatives. In 1989 he was elected president. His economic policies were a disaster. Khomeini had come out of the war without having borrowed a single penny from any foreign power; Rafsanjani now sought to buy some popularity and stimulate the economy through deficit spending. The country went on a consumer spending binge that led to inflation and big international debts.

Rafsanjani also presided over the solidification of conservatives in power. In his second term parliamentary elections returned a conservative majority, although party identification is not permitted. After the presidency, Rafsanjani became head region. In 1993 newly elected U.S. President Clinton announced a policy of "dual containment" of both Iran and Iraq. In 1995 he signed an executive order banning trade with Iran.

In June 1996 Saudi Hezbollah truck-bombed Khobar Towers, an American barracks in Saudi Arabia, killing nineteen U.S. soldiers. Iran was suspected immediately, and although some support the idea that there was an al Qaeda connection, in June 2001 a federal grand jury confirmed the bombers had Iranian support. (The two are not necessarily mutually exclusive.)

In August 1996 Congress passed the Iran-Libya Sanctions Act, punishing any company doing business with the terrorist countries. Europeans denounced and ignored the U.S. law. Net impact: Europeans and Japanese make money trading with Iran while U.S. firms are frozen out.

In March 2000 Iranian hard-liners heard a speech by Secretary Albright as an admission of U.S. guilt but demanded a formal U.S. apology.

In October 2001 Supreme Leader Ali Khamenei condemned U.S. air strikes on Afghanistan as part of America's plan to dominate the Middle East. After the Taliban's fall, Iran began to support groups opposed to the U.S.-backed Afghan interim government.

The same month Iran resumed purchase of Russian arms. Russia had ceased the sales during the Yeltsin era because of American pressure.

In January 2002 President George W. Bush (43) in his first State of the Union Address condemned Iran as one of the "axis of evil." This shocked Iranians, especially reformers, who had hoped to improve relations.

In January 2002 Israel captured the *Karine A* carrying fifty tons of weapons from Iran's Revolutionary Guard to the Palestinian Authority.

In May 2002 and in May 2003 Supreme Leader Ali Khamenei condemned the foreign ministry's proposal that Iran negotiate with the United States.

Since the March 2003 U.S. and British invasion of Iraq, Iran has spread its influence into Iraq by supporting Shi'a militias, particularly those of Muqtada al-Sadr, a young firebrand cleric.

In May 2003 Washington accused Iran of harboring al Qaeda militants who planted bombs in Saudi Arabia. American accusations that Iran is building nuclear weapons have increased over the years. In sum, hints of improvement have not changed the underlying hostilities of hard-liners on both sides.

of the Expediency Council. Unpopular, in 2000 he placed thirtieth out of thirty seats from Tehran in the parliament. Rafsanjani refused the seat and stayed in the Expediency Council. In 2005 he was one of two candidates to win in the first round of balloting for president. Widely believed to be corrupt—his friends and family became very wealthy—he won only 38 percent in the second round and lost to the mayor of Tehran, the clean but fanatic Mahmoud Ahmadinejad.

THE URGE TO REFORM

Muhammad Khatami was elected by mistake; had the Council of Guardians known that they were getting a relative liberal—by Iranian standards—they would never have allowed him to run. They have the power to bar candidates who are not sufficiently Islamic and used this to keep anyone out of the political scene who did not support a hard line. In 1992 the Council unseated forty-five incumbent members of parliament, including government ministers, for insufficient revolutionary fervor.

In 1997 the hard-liners' man was Ali Akbar Nateq-Nuri. The system was fixed to guarantee Nateq-Nuri victory. To maintain a facade of legitimacy and to split any opposition vote, the Guardian Council approved three other candidates to also appear on the ballot. Two of them had close ties to the hard-liners. The third was a weakling cleric, a former minister of culture who left to run the National Library: Muhammad Khatami. The hard-liners did not care for Khatami's moderate politics, but he had revolutionary credentials, was a family friend of Supreme Leader Khamenei, and was a direct descendent of the Prophet, entitled to wear a black turban.

Tapping a growing desire for reform, Khatami came from out of nowhere to become the leading candidate. He never was a liberal; "cautious reformer" is more accurate. The regime's bully boys, the Ansar-e Hizballah, tried to halt the Khatami express. These groups of youths—misrepresented as students or as spontaneous defenders of the revolution—traveled in government buses to harass pro-Khatami rallies. Pro-Khatami newspapers were shut down and Khatami campaign offices closed. Khatami was even denied permission to campaign in some cities. Khatami followers tried to work as poll watchers but were blocked by the police. It all made Khatami more popular.

Iranians flocked to the polls, believing they had been offered a choice for the first time since the revolution. Khatami won two-thirds of the votes. Two years later, 70 percent voted for Khatami allies in parliament. It looked like the beginning of moderation and reform. In 2001 Khatami was reelected with 70 percent.

REFORMISTS BLOCKED

Khatami should have known that he could not get even mild reforms. Ever since the attempts of Bani Sadr, it was obvious that the president had no real power. Hard-liners controlled the judiciary and the key ministries, and had the Supreme Leader on their side. Khatami's initial election brought a brief flurry of political and press freedoms. Numerous intellectuals took advantage of the opening to begin newspapers and magazines attacking the regime from different angles. Some published details of the 1998 murders of political dissidents by the intelligence ministry, probably with the approval of the highest levels of government. The Supreme Leader dismissed the minister of intelligence and declared the killings were a rogue operation. Khamenei ordered the arrest and trial of the lead perpetrator, who allegedly committed suicide in jail, but there was no way to confirm it.

Soon the judiciary closed all the newspapers and imprisoned editors and writers. President Khatami could not stop the imprisonment of his closest political ally, the mayor of Tehran, Gholam Hossein Karbaschi. People hoped that parliament would support the new president, but when it formed a committee to investigate abuses in government, Supreme Leader Khamenei declared the targeted offices were direct extensions of his own and outside the purview of parliament. Khatami, whatever reformist intentions he may have had, was blocked at every turn.

D : *Domestic Structures*

THE AHMEDINEJAD GOVERNMENT

In 2005, the populist mayor of Tehran, Mahmoud Ahmadinejad, was elected president of Iran. Supreme Leader Ali Khamenei's oldest son ran his campaign, which enjoyed the support of the clerical establishment. The Pasdaran revolutionary guards and the fanatic Basij militia turned out en masse; Ahmadinejad had been a member of both. The election was not free or fair, as the Council of Guardians screened out most candidates and silenced any critical media. Ahmadinejad may have been involved in the planning of the 1979 U.S. embassy seizure.

Elected mayor of Tehran in 2003, Ahmadinejad fought corruption and poverty, the populist themes that won him the presidency. He is a good politician, visiting many of the outer provinces that are usually ignored by the central government.

Ahmadinejad says he has been chosen by God for his office. He follows Ayatollah Mesbah Yazdi, leader of an ultraconservative religious movement. Ahmadinejad frequently visits the well where the twelfth Imam is reportedly located until his return into time, and he reported a "heavenly light" about him when he addressed the United Nations.

Once elected to the presidency, Ahmadinejad returned to the revolutionary rhetoric of 1979. He said Israel should be "wiped off the map" and denied the Holocaust ever took place, words that heightened Israel's insecurity and further isolated Iran. Iran's efforts to acquire weapons of mass destruction did not help. Opposed to any ties with the West, he recalled numerous Iranian ambassadors and purged the foreign ministry of those with Western thoughts.

Ahmadinejad's fanaticism forced the rest of the Iranian power hierarchy to rein him in. In August 2005, parliament rejected four of his proposed cabinet members as incompetent. Supreme Leader Khamenei emphasized that foreign policy is not the responsibility of the president but of the Supreme National Security Council that reports directly to him. This council is headed by none other than former President Ali Akbar Hashemi Rafsanjani, the candidate Ahmadinejad defeated in the second round in 2005. The pragmatic loser is now running foreign policy.

Iran's clerical establishment now has to pay the price for picking a true believer.

Khatami drew much of his support from young Iranians. Voting age is sixteen. After a spurt of births (now curbed), over half of Iranians are under twenty-five. Most Iranians today have little or no memory of the shah, the Islamic Revolution, or the battles of the older generation. Now they are fed up with Islamic fanatics telling them how to run every aspect of their lives. They like democracy and the United States. Iranians showed a mass outpouring of spontaneous sympathy for America after 9/11. They are Muslim but want the mullahs in mosques, not in government. Increasingly, mullahs agree. Mullahs who run Muslim economic foundations called *bunyads* have become corrupt and rich. Anything can touch off a student protest, for example, the closing of newspapers or arrest of critics. The regime immediately attacks with toughs who beat them and police who arrest them, often on campus. This does nothing to quiet discontent, which may someday boil over into revolt.

In his second term, Khatami was a defeated man. Iranians despaired that he or anyone else could give them freer, happier lives. The ballot having done them no good, they stopped voting as an act of protest, and turnout plunged. Half in jest, some urged the United States to liberate Iran. With all their efforts at reform blocked, some parliamentarians threatened mass walkouts, and Khatami threatened to resign the presidency. Either would severely damage the already shaky **legitimacy** of the political system.

THE IRANIAN NUCLEAR CRISIS

Iran's attempts to obtain nuclear technology stretch back to the 1950s. After the Iranian Revolution, the government quickly resumed efforts to develop nuclear technology. The Bushehr nuclear reactor was bombed repeatedly in the Iran-Iraq war, so Iran dispersed its projects throughout the country and continued in secret. Iran claims its nuclear technology is for peaceful uses only, citing a *fatwa* from Ayatollah Khamenei forbidding the use of nuclear weapons. Iran argues it is entitled to develop the technology under Article 4 of the Nonproliferation Treaty, which allows "peaceful purposes without discrimination." Iran originally allowed the IAEA to inspect its facilities but ceased cooperation, claiming the IAEA was a tool of the United States.

The Bush administration reacted with alarm in 2002 upon learning of Iranian nuclear developments. Why should an oil exporter need an alternative energy source? Washington assumed the program was a cover for building a bomb. The technology for the first leads into the second. Once you have a fair amount of enriched uranium for power plants, you can cook it into weapons-grade plutonium.

In April 2006, the IAEA voted to refer Iran to the United Nations for failure to allow inspections. Four days later, Ahmadinejad announced that Iran had mastered the enrichment cycle and had thus joined the nuclear club, an ominous hint at nuclear weapons. Diplomatic initiatives tried to halt further Iranian development. The United States and Europe backed a Russian proposal to provide Iran with access to enriched uranium for a light-water reactor; the Russians would then retrieve the uranium after its use. Tehran remained defiant. Washington charged Iran with delaying tactics and pushed for immediate international steps against the Tehran government. The UN Security Council can move only with the combined political will of its five permanent members—tough to achieve, as France and Russia seek markets for their nuclear technology, and China opposes anything that infringes on a country's sovereignty.

At the same time, in 2006, the Iranian-sponsored Hezbollah, composed of Lebanese Shi'a militants, infiltrated Israel, killed eight Israeli soldiers, and kidnapped two. An enraged Israel invaded the south of Lebanon for a month and inflicted terrible damage, killing more than a thousand Lebanese, most of them civilians. This boosted Hezbollah's prestige as the only force that could stand up to Israel. Then

---

legitimacy   Feeling among people that the regime's rule is rightful.

Hezbollah dispensed plentiful Iranian cash to help Lebanese rebuild, another public relations coup. All this aroused Sunni worry that Iran was spreading its influence, boosted by mammoth oil revenues, to lead a Shi'a revival and make Iran the top power in the Middle East. The Sunni-Shi'a violence of Iraq could spread.

Conclusions

In 1978 Iran was America's closest ally in the Middle East; a year later Iran was America's greatest enemy. A group of clerics and secular liberals overthrew the monarchy, but the Islamists outsmarted the secularists and established an Islamic Republic under the charismatic rule of Ayatollah Khomeini.

Since Khomeini's death, many Iranians want freedom and democracy, but they are constantly blocked by an Islamist elite, which holds effective power even if reformists are elected to high office. An Islamist fanatic, Ahmedinejad, won the 2005 presidential election, pulling the United States and Iran even further apart. Iran's efforts to acquire nuclear technology and support of Hezbollah in Lebanon make matters worse.

Key Terms

legitimacy (p. 238)   Thermidor (p. 225)

status quo ante bellum (p. 232)   weapons of mass destruction (p. 231)

Further Reference

Abdo, Geneive, and Jonathan Lyons. *Answering Only to God: Faith and Freedom in Twenty-First Century Iran.* New York: Henry Holt, 2003.

Alexander, Yonah, and Milton Hoenig. *The New Iranian Leadership: Ahmedinejad, Nuclear Ambition, and the Middle East.* Westport, CT: Praeger, 2007.

Al-Suwaidi, Jamal S. *Iran and the Gulf: A Search for Stability.* London: I. B. Tauris, 2002.

Ansari, Ali M. *Confronting Iran: The Failure of American Foreign Policy and the Next Great Crisis in the Middle East.* New York: Basic Books, 2006.

Bakhash, Shaul. *The Reign of the Ayatollahs: Iran and the Islamic Revolution.* New York: Basic Books, 1984.

Bill, James A. *The Eagle and the Lion: The Tragedy of American-Iranian Relations.* New Haven, CT: Yale University Press, 1988.

Chubin, Shahram. *Iran's Nuclear Ambitions.* Washington, D.C.: Brookings, 2006.

Ganji, Manouchehr. *Defying the Iranian Revolution: From a Minister to the Shah to a Leader of Resistance.* Westport, CT: Praeger, 2002.

Hiro, Dilip. *Iranian Labyrinth: Journeys through Theocratic Iran and Its Furies.* New York: Avalon, 2005.

Hoveyda, Fereydoun. *The Shah and the Ayatollah: Iranian Mythology and Islamic Revolution.* Westport, CT: Praeger, 2003.

Keddie, Nikki R. *Modern Iran: Roots and Results of Revolution,* 2nd ed. New Haven, CT: Yale University Press, 2006.

Nasr, Vali. *The Shia Revival: How Conflicts within Islam Will Shape the Future.* New York: W. W. Norton, 2005.

Sick, Gary. *All Fall Down: America's Tragic Encounter with Iran.* Harrisonburg, VA: Penguin Press, 1987.

Takeyh, Ray. *Hidden Iran: Paradox and Power in the Islamic Republic.* New York: Times Books, 2006.

13 The First Gulf War

Points to Ponder

- Can Americans and Middle Easterners understand each other?
- Is there any validity to Iraq's claims to Kuwait?
- Why did the United States leave the 1991 war unfinished?
- Was Saddam deterred in 1991?
- Should the United States have finished off Saddam in 1991?
- How effective were UN resolutions in curbing Iraq?
- Did U.S. intervention in the Gulf bring democracy to any Gulf state?

With the long Iran-Iraq war over, the United States maintained its watch on the threat of Iranian-sponsored Islamic fundamentalism. Some in Washington hoped that Iran and Iraq would be so busy watching each other they would not bother anyone else, but Saddam Hussein had other ideas. For the Arab Gulf states, Iraq had been their "Defender against Persian Aggression," and they had loaned him vast sums. Now the oil shaykhdoms wanted to get back to making money and began to pump oil to pay for the last war. Both Kuwait and Iraq exceeded their OPEC quotas, driving down oil prices. Arab potentates also demanded that Saddam begin to repay his war loans.

Willie Sutton once said he robbed banks because that's where the money is. Saddam eyed his neighbor Kuwait for the same reason. Iraq had some unclear historical claims to Kuwait, but the stronger draw was the multibillion dollar Kuwait Development Fund. With considerable forethought, the rulers of Kuwait had planned for the day the country no longer had oil and had been depositing a portion of their oil revenues into the fund for future generations. Just as American corporations eye a company with liquid assets for takeover, Saddam eyed Kuwait.

He prepared the way with a series of excuses. First, he demanded that the Arabs forgive his war debt, which Iraq had paid with the blood of its soldiers. Next, he accused Kuwait of cheating on its OPEC quota, pretending Iraq had not. Kuwait naturally denied the charges and continued to produce as before. Finally, Saddam accused Kuwait of stealing Iraqi oil by "slant drilling" in the Rumaila oilfield, which is split by their boundary. He said that oil wells on Kuwait's side of the border were drilling diagonally and taking the oil from Iraqi soil. In 1990 he threatened military action if Kuwait did not cease its activities and reasserted Iraq's old claims that Kuwait was a province of Iraq. He began massing Iraqi army troops along the Kuwaiti border.

THE WEAK AMERICAN RESPONSE

The United States was never close to Saddam even during the 1980s when they co-operated against Iran. Saddam distrusted every offer of help from the Americans, convinced it was a Trojan horse that would lead to his destruction. Similarly, Americans could not warm to a merciless dictator who made his way to the top by murdering political opponents. They could work with such a man, but he never got an invitation to the White House. Mistrust breeds miscommunication, and that leads to misunderstanding.

When the Bush 41 administration took office in January 1989, policymakers realized that Iraq had emerged from the recent war as the most powerful country in the Persian Gulf region. They sought a working relationship with Saddam through "constructive engagement," a policy that mixes cooperation with suggestions for change that Washington also used with the Soviet Union and South Africa. By the end of the year the administration concluded the policy was not working— Saddam would not budge—and Washington discussed how to reverse course and reduce contacts with Iraq.

By July 1990, U.S. intelligence had noticed the Iraqi troop movements. Washington was split as to whether this was merely a bargaining tactic with the Kuwaitis or if it was a military exercise. They checked with their Middle East allies: Egyptian President Hosni Mubarak, Turkish President Turgut Özal, Saudi ambassador to Washington Prince Bandar, and many other regional leaders. They were unanimous that the troops were a part of Saddam's bargaining strategy. No one believed Saddam was preparing to invade.

On July 25, 1990, U.S. Ambassador April Glaspie met with Saddam personally. Ambassador Glaspie, a career foreign service officer, was fluent in Arabic and schooled in diplomatic compromise and making harsh messages palatable. Like the State Department as a whole, she thought Saddam was angling for a better oil-drilling arrangement with Kuwait and did not comprehend that he intended to seize Kuwait. She told Saddam that U.S. interests in the region were important, and we would not stand by if Saddam threatened those interests. Unfortunately, Saddam heard her mild wording as a message that issues between Iraq and Kuwait were an inter-Arab affair that should be solved by the countries involved. Then she left on vacation.

The United States in the Middle East

CENTCOM

When the first Gulf War crisis began, CENTCOM was a paper holding company headquartered in Tampa, Florida—thousands of miles from its operational area. At that time CENTCOM was a joint-forces headquarters that upon mobilization could command major subordinate forces. Still, until the balloon went up, there was not a single combat soldier assigned to it. Contingency plans called for CENTCOM to borrow previously identified combat units from other theaters of operation, once the National Command Authority had redirected priorities. Many felt that in light of the Iran-Iraq war, the general instability of CENTCOM's area of operation, and the Carter doctrine that the Persian Gulf is a vital interest to the United States, CENTCOM deserved a robust standing force. CENTCOM's commander, General Norman Schwarzkopf, was a blustery old warrior who had been given a preretirement job in Florida. Few liked working for him because of his mercurial personality.

In 1980 President Jimmy Carter created the Rapid Deployment Joint Task Force in response to the Iran hostage crisis. The Pentagon signed a basing agreement with the Sultanate of Oman and the local headquarters for the task force was established there. At the beginning of 1983, with the Soviet occupation of nearby Afghanistan and the continuing Iran-Iraq war, President Ronald Reagan replaced the task force with the more permanent CENTCOM. The command had to be situated in Florida because none of the Gulf countries were willing to allow their territory to be used as an American military base. It was—and still is—a peculiar situation in which we were trying to defend countries that did not wish to be defended.

Saddam should have reversed his mobilization, but he did not take the American warning seriously. The United States had never before deployed troops in the Middle East in sufficient number to stop his invasion, and no major U.S. forces were in the Gulf now anyway. A credible deterrence would have required many U.S. troops and ships in the Gulf. Otherwise a warning sounds like a bluff. In addition, Kuwait was not a close U.S. ally. It had always been stubbornly independent and hosted the largest Soviet legation in the area. Kuwaiti princes frequently opposed U.S policies and were highly critical of the Saudis for being so close to the Americans. To Saddam, it was not credible that the United States would put its forces in harm's way to protect one of its loudest critics.

Another explanation is that Saddam believed he had U.S. approval to invade Kuwait. When Saddam tried to engage Ambassador Glaspie with his complaints about Kuwaiti violation of Iraqi borders with slant drilling, Glaspie replied that the United States had no opinion on inter-Arab conflicts such as Iraq's border disagreement with Kuwait. This was completely in accord with the State Department's position. In Washington, spokeswoman Margaret Tutweiller told the press that the United States had no defense treaty or security commitment to Kuwait. Diplomatically, Tutweiller and Glaspie gave the correct answer, that the United States did not want to be the hegemonic power in the Gulf and would rely on Iraq and Kuwait to negotiate between themselves without U.S. supervision.

 *Cultures*

A FEMALE AMBASSADOR TO AN ARAB STATE?

The U.S. ambassador to Baghdad in 1990, April Glaspie, was bright, tough, and an expert on the Middle East. But Arab culture does not accord women equality. Men do the work of the world; women stay home and raise children. Out of politeness, many Arab states agree to a female ambassador from America, but do they respect her? A special problem comes with a cold-blooded murderer like Saddam Hussein. Could any female ambassador deliver a tough warning that he would understand?

The American answer has been that diplomats and soldiers overseas are images of America, which gradually and with much struggle has moved toward racial and gender equality. We must show the world a true picture of America, not an America of white male supremacy. Such a picture also encourages gender equality in the host country. Female U.S. soldiers in Saudi Arabia in 1990–1991—driving vehicles, working with men, even giving orders—were noticed by Saudi women despite Saudi efforts to hide them. Some Saudi women subsequently broke the law and started driving. They were responding to years of personal restrictions on their lives, but the timing of their protest was hardly coincidental. Saudi authorities soon put a stop to that.

If a host country tells us that they do not want our female soldiers or diplomats, should we give in to them? This is not a simple problem. American and Arab cultures are very different. Should we be sensitive to Arab culture and send no women, or should we stay true to what America stands for? Would Saddam have listened more carefully in 1990 if an American male ambassador had delivered a warning? How about someone like tough, barrel-chested Deputy Secretary of State Richard Armitage, a former Navy officer and high Pentagon official? Different jobs require different types of people.

Saddam heard a different message because he was asking a question the American diplomats had not heard: Do you really care if I take Kuwait? Saddam came away from the meeting understanding that the United States would really not care. Glaspie returned to the embassy convinced that she had defused an international crisis, and she cabled Washington that tensions would now be reduced.

To be on the safe side, the United States offered to send fighter planes to the Gulf to show Saddam that American allies also were capable of marshalling forces. Unfortunately, none of the Arab countries except the United Arab Emirates (UAE) would accept an American military presence. The root of the problem was that there was no U.S. military presence in the Gulf to deter Saddam because the Arab governments of the region refused to invite the Americans in. No credible forces, no deterrence.

By July 28, the Pentagon changed its mind when it realized that there were too many Iraqi troops for a bluff, and they did not seem to be exercising. To make matters worse, Iraqi armored carriers and missile launchers were being taken out of storage and sent to the border. Chairman of the U.S. Joint Chiefs of Staff Gen. Colin Powell contacted Gen. Norman Schwarzkopf at CENTCOM and told him to review and update the contingency plans for the defense of Kuwait.

THE INVASION OF KUWAIT

Saddam concentrated 100,000 troops on the Kuwait border and on August 2, 1990, ordered them to seize Kuwait. Within hours they had taken Kuwait City and were approaching the border of Saudi Arabia. Saddam announced that his occupation of Kuwait was temporary and that he would soon withdraw. It was only later in the crisis that he announced that Kuwait had returned to the Iraqi motherland forever.

Washington was worried on a variety of fronts, but the most serious concern was for the free world's supply of petroleum. Since World War II, every American president had acknowledged that unfettered access to Gulf oil was an important U.S. interest. Saddam had owned 20 percent of the world's known oil reserves before the invasion; now he had Kuwait's reserves. He had also shown his willingness to use Iraqi military might to influence and possibly crush any Arab country that opposed him. Many feared that, with Iraq controlling so much oil directly and threatening Saudi Arabia's oil rich Eastern province, OPEC would become an extension of Iraqi policy.

There were other American concerns. President Bush said a primary concern was that an aggressor should not invade a neighboring country and grab its natural resources. He thought of Munich in 1938 and how appeasement of Hitler had led to World War II in 1939. Arabs in the region, by contrast, pointed to Israel's occupation of the West Bank. They believed American concern about international law was spurious. Why, they asked, did the United States not support nonaggression in the case of Israel?

The Saudis were equally concerned but from a different perspective. After talking to American officials and reviewing U.S.-supplied intelligence, the king and his council feared that Saddam would not be content with his seizure of Kuwait and might order his troops to invade Saudi Arabia. The Kingdom's oil fields, after all, were not that far from Kuwait's.

Not wanting to create a panic, Bush maintained his normal schedule and flew to Aspen, Colorado, to give a speech with British Prime Minister Margaret Thatcher while Washington worked on the problem. A first step was to go to the United Nations and obtain support from the international community for any actions they would take. The UN condemned the aggression and ordered an embargo on Iraqi oil. Turkey cut its pipeline, and the American navy blockaded the Gulf. Saddam was cut off from his buyers except through Jordan, where 60 percent of the population was of Palestinian origin and considered Saddam a hero for defying the West. The anger of the street allowed Jordan's King Hussein no choice except to align his small kingdom with Iraq.

Bush and Thatcher discussed options in Aspen. Some reports say the Iron Lady persuaded the president to oppose the Iraqi invasion, but more likely she merely reinforced decisions Bush had already tentatively made. When he returned from Aspen, Bush told the press that he would not allow the invasion to stand.

General Powell met with the Saudi ambassador, Prince Bandar, in Secretary of Defense Dick Cheney's office to request Saudi permission to base American troops there. Bandar said the Kingdom would welcome the intervention but only if they could count on America staying the course. After America's withdrawal

U.S. *The United States in the Middle East*

WOBBLY GEORGE

Saddam Hussein decided early on to test whether UN sanctions meant anything. On August 26, 1990, an Iraqi tanker approached U.S. Navy ships in the Gulf. To determine if the tanker was carrying oil, the Americans would have to stop it and board it for inspection. If the Iraqis resisted a shooting war would have commenced on the spot.

The Bush team wavered and recommended the American cordon pull back to give diplomacy time to work. Maybe one of our Arab allies could convince Saddam to turn the ship around. Or maybe we would determine that the ship had no oil. Or maybe we could follow the ship until after it left the Gulf because boarding there would be easier.

Bush spoke with Prime Minister Thatcher to get her consent to move the blockade. The Iron Lady of Downing Street told the president, "Look, George, this is no time to go wobbly. We'll do it this time, but we can't fall at the first fence." The allies stopped the ship, but the story, in amplified form, made Thatcher appear as the real spine in the alliance.

---

from Vietnam and Lebanon, the Saudis did not want to align against their powerful northern neighbor and then be left stranded. The American team outlined their plan to place 100,000 soldiers in the Kingdom, and Bandar saw it was a commitment that could not be easily reversed. After consulting with his uncle the king, Bandar said that if the Bush administration sent a delegation to Saudi Arabia the king would agree to America's planning. Cheney was immediately dispatched, and the next day King Fahd formally requested American assistance to defend his kingdom. Operation Desert Shield was born.

The Army flew the 82nd Airborne Division to the Kingdom, but it was just a trip wire, telling Saddam that if he invaded he would be fighting the American army. Its presence demonstrated U.S. commitment to stop further Iraqi advances, as well as a firm American military commitment. The American military had played the same trip-wire role in Europe, guaranteeing American involvement in the defense of the continent if the Soviet Union ever attacked.

In reality, despite U.S. Army Rapid Response doctrine, the 82nd would have had a hard time single-handedly fighting the fourth largest army in the world. Military analysts have long pondered the efficacy of sending paratrooper/infantry against armor if actual combat had broken out. It gave the Americans time, however, to build up their forces in the Gulf, ultimately reaching a half-million men and women with heavy weapons.

A number of people tried to mediate the crisis, including Soviet President Mikhail Gorbachev. At the same time, President Bush began building a coalition against Saddam. Before it was over, Arab countries such as Saudi Arabia, Egypt, and even Syria would join the Americans against a fellow Arab land. Egyptian President Mubarak commented that the world that he had known and worked for all his life, that of Arab unity, had ended.

KUWAITI LOBBYING

The Kuwaiti government, now in exile but still in control of billions of dollars, worked to sway American public opinion. Under the deceptive title "Citizens for a Free Kuwait," Kuwaiti officials hired the blue-chip public relations firm Hill and Knowlton for $11 million. As part of the effort, the daughter of the Kuwaiti ambassador to Washington appeared before Congress, claiming to be a refugee who had personally observed Iraqi soldiers throwing babies onto hospital floors to steal their incubators. It was a fabrication, but Kuwait later justified its actions by stating that the big picture was correct. What was the problem with a little embellishment? Lying and wars are natural twins.

Kuwait need not have gone to such extremes. Saddam's actions were bad enough. He seized thousands of civilians in Kuwait and in Iraq and moved them to strategic sites as human shields. He finally released the helpless noncombatants when he realized their presence would not stop the United States and his holding them was hurting rather than helping his international image.

FROM DESERT SHIELD TO DESERT STORM

By mid-October 1990, U.S. deployments to the Gulf had reached the level that the Pentagon had projected was needed to protect Saudi Arabia from attack. General Powell traveled to Riyadh to outline plans for an offensive against the Iraqi occupiers of Kuwait. Upon Powell's return, President Bush ordered the Pentagon to double the number of U.S. forces in Saudi Arabia. The White House had made its decision to remove the Iraqi army from Kuwait. They began negotiations at the UN, and the Security Council in November authorized "all means necessary" to remove Iraq from Kuwait.

But no one had asked Congress. While Secretary of State James Baker flew to Geneva in early January for a meeting with Iraqi Foreign Minister Tariq Aziz, Bush realized that politically he could not order troops into combat without congressional approval. The War Powers Act of 1973 said that if he committed troops without Congressional approval, he could only keep them in theater sixty days unless Congress subsequently authorized a longer stay. But no president has ever acknowledged the constitutionality of the act; additionally, no one knew how long Americans would have to be deployed. Bush wanted the American people on his side, and so he decided to seek the formal approval of the people's elected representatives before he acted further. Bush did not seek a declaration of war, and Congress, which was split on the issue, would likely not have passed it. On January 12, 1991, the Congress narrowly gave the President the authorization he was looking for—a joint resolution authorizing the president to use U.S. combat troops to eject the Iraqis from Kuwait.

The UN-imposed deadline of January 15 came and went as world tension climbed. On January 17, 1991, U.S. jets began attacks on Iraq. Bombs and cruise missiles rained on Baghdad and other high-value targets for more than a month. Saddam responded with SCUD missile attacks on Americans in Saudi Arabia and

∪S The United States in the Middle East

THE UNITED STATES AND UN RESOLUTIONS

The UN was on America's side in the first Gulf Crisis. The Security Council passed a number of resolutions condemning Iraq and detailing what the international community expected. When the First Gulf War finally broke out, Washington said it was acting in fulfillment of UN Resolutions. Even though there were numerous countries around the world in violation of UN resolutions, the world community agreed to enforce these. In the second Gulf War of 2003, Washington made the same claims—and none of the resolutions on Iraq had been revoked—but many European powers condemned U.S. actions. These are some of the seventeen UN Security Council resolutions dealing with Iraq:

August 2, 1990—SC660—Condemns invasion of Kuwait and demands Iraq withdraw.

August 6, 1990—SC661—Imposes economic sanctions on Iraq.

November 11, 1990—SC678—Gives Iraq until January 1991 to withdraw and authorizes "all necessary means" to implement SC660.

April 3, 1991—SC687—Calls for destruction of all chemical and biological weapons and all missiles with a range greater than 150 kilometers and creates **UNSCOM** to inspect for these weapons.

April 5, 1991—SC688—Condemns Iraq's repression of civilians.

August 15, 1991—SC707—Asks for unfettered UNSCOM and International Atomic Energy Agency (IAEA) inspections

October 11, 1991—SC715—Demands that Iraq accept UNSCOM and IAEA inspectors unconditionally.

October 15, 1994—SC949—Demands Iraq cooperate fully with UNSCOM and withdraw troops it deployed to Kuwaiti border.

June 12, 1996—SC1060—Condemns Iraq's refusal to cooperate with UNSCOM inspectors.

June 21, 1997—SC1115—Condemns Iraq's menacing actions against UNSCOM helicopters.

November 12, 1997—SC1137—Condemns Iraq's violations of previous resolutions.

December 17, 1999—SC1284—Orders Iran to grant immediate and unconditional access to new **UNMOVIC** inspection teams (replacing UNSCOM).

November 13, 2002—SC1441—Declares Iraq "in material breach" of previous resolutions.

Did SC 1441 authorize the United States to invade Iraq in 2003? It depends on which legal expert you consult. Europeans believed that while 1441 condemned Saddam, it did not authorize the use of force. No authorization of force under Chapter 7 had been passed since SC678 in 1990. American government lawyers, however, pointed out that the legal concept of material breach meant that infractions of a contract were so great that the contract itself was null and void. From this legal analysis, there was no second Gulf war in 2003, which just continued the 1991 war because Iraq's material breach negated the 1991 cease-fire. SC678 still applied. Which analysis is correct? History is written by the victors.

UNSCOM   UN Special Commission to inspect Iraq for WMD following the 1991 Gulf War.
UNMOVIC   UN Monitoring, Verification, and Inspection Commission, 1999–2003.

Conflicts

JOINT RESOLUTIONS FOR WAR

Congress has not passed or seriously entertained a declaration of war since December 1941. Indeed, very few countries have. Declarations of war may be passé in the modern world, where presidents move fast and need flexibility. Instead of declarations of war, presidents get Congress to pass joint resolutions, bills of identical wording passed by both houses allowing the president to take specified military steps overseas. Although milder than a declaration of war, a joint congressional resolution, when signed by the president, has force of law. They do not require the president to go to war; they merely let him if he thinks the situation warrants it.

The Cold War saw several joint congressional resolutions, but the 1964 Tonkin Gulf Resolution came back to haunt Congress. President Lyndon Baines Johnson (LBJ) asserted that North Vietnam had attacked U.S. destroyers in the Tonkin Gulf, which was not the whole story. Congress quickly and obediently passed a joint resolution authorizing LBJ to use the military in Southeast Asia, thinking he would not really go to war. It was just a warning to North Vietnam. But LBJ used it to take America to war. It was perfectly legal but infuriated Congress.

Until 9/11, Congress was cautious, understanding that a joint resolution was the functional equivalent of a declaration of war: You pass it, you got yourself a war. In October 2002, Congress debated a joint resolution with some care and passed it, knowing it would take us to war. Just as the Gulf of Tonkin Resolution eventually met with fierce criticism for providing the president with a blank check, however, the 2002 resolution has led to numerous court battles. It states: "The President is authorized to use the Armed Forces of the United States as he determines to be necessary and appropriate in order to defend the national security of the United States against the continuing threat posed by Iraq." War critics believe giving the president the ability to decide unilaterally what is necessary and appropriate was an unintended delegation of congressional power to the executive branch. The Supreme Court ruled in *Hamdan v. Rumsfeld* that, contrary to Bush administration arguments, there were limits to this delegation and the government could not imprison U.S. citizens as "enemy combatants" without due process of law.

on nonbelligerent Israel. Saddam hoped that Israel would respond by jumping into the fray, thereby alienating the Arab members of the coalition. He believed that if the Arabs withdrew support from the United States, the Iraqi army could sustain a war of attrition until the United States tired of conflict and withdrew.

Saddam's plan could have worked too well. Most Israelis (and CNN) expected poison gas. A flight of three Israeli jets appeared on U.S. radar headed for Baghdad. The American government requested Israel to call them back, promising we would take care of the problem and defeat one of Israel's greatest enemies without Israeli intervention. The Bush administration also promised an aid package and rushed Patriot missiles to Israel to shoot down incoming SCUDs. The Patriots were ineffective but a psychological boost. An important U.S. persuader: denial of the electronic Friend or Foe Indicator (FFI). Without the proper FFI, an Israeli jet stood an excellent chance of being shot down by the allies as an Iraqi warplane. Israel decided to wait out the conflict.

Conflicts

DID DETERRENCE WORK?

Many analysts believe the Cold War did not explode because of mutual **deterrence**. With both sides loaded with nuclear weapons, neither dared use them. Does deterrence work after the Cold War? Some say it did work in the 1991 Gulf War. Saddam had weapons of mass destruction (namely, chemical) but did not use them on Israel or on U.S. forces because he believed neither country would hesitate to nuke him.

Saddam tried to goad Israel into entering the Gulf War, thinking it would break up the alliance. He fired forty conventional-explosive warheads at Israel. Many missed and none did much damage. Why did he not shoot chemical warheads at Israel? He was capable of it, but he thought he knew how Israel would react: with nuclear weapons, of which Israel reportedly has as many as 300. Saddam wanted Israel in the war, but not in that way. Deterrence worked. Some say we should have considered the possibilities of deterrence against Iraq in 2003.

For the only time since World War II the United States and Soviet Union were on the same side of an international conflict. There are many reasons why the Soviets were willing to cooperate in an American attack against a Soviet ally. The Berlin Wall fell in 1989, signaling the end of the Soviet empire, and the United States was emerging as the sole superpower. It was in Moscow's interest to cooperate with the new **hegemon**. Soviet leader Mikhail Gorbachev was also piqued by Saddam's unwillingness to accept Soviet advice. James Baker was in Siberia with Soviet Foreign Minister Eduard Shevardnazde when Iraq attacked Kuwait. With the two already sitting at the same table, it was relatively easy to issue joint statements condemning aggression.

GROUND ATTACK

On February 24, 1991, after thirty-eight days of air attacks, the allied ground attack began. Within four days the Iraqis were defeated and fleeing Kuwait. Troops on the sole road north, the "Highway of Death," became sitting targets for U.S. airpower. General Powell grew uneasy at the slaughter and convinced the president and General Schwarzkopf to offer a cease-fire. Powell noted that with the liberation of Kuwait the United States had met its and the UN's war aims. Saudi Arabia and other U.S. allies did not want a wider war. A unilateral U.S. conquest of Iraq may have saved the world much trouble later. Fully 60 percent of Saddam's

deterrence   Preventing an attack by inducing fear of retaliation.
hegemon   Leading or dominant power.

Republican Guard, his best units, escaped, and his real pillar of support, his security police, were intact. *Bellum interruptum* again. When the magnitude of the mistake sank in, Washington vowed to never let Saddam off the hook again.

Withdrawing from Kuwait, Saddam's army, full of hatred, set fire to Kuwait's oil fields and befouled Gulf waters by opening the oil taps. There was little or no military purpose to this wanton ecological destruction, which actually changed the weather for a time.

The generals from the allied and Iraqi sides met at Safwan inside Iraq and negotiated a cease-fire. Not wishing to humiliate the Iraqis further, there was no demand that Saddam personally sign the cease-fire accords. This mistake gave Saddam the ability in later years to say he had never agreed to the arrangements. As a defensive measure, the allies forbade the Iraqis the use of aircraft over the country. The Iraqi generals pointed to the destruction of the country's infrastructure and asked the allies for permission to use helicopters so that they could administer distant provinces. Schwarzkopf soft-heartedly agreed, leading to mass slaughters.

THE FAILED REBELLIONS

President Bush 41 urged the people of Iraq to rise up and overthrow their brutal government. Thinking that the humiliated and weakened Saddam would soon be overthrown by his own people was one reason Bush did not press the war further. But the Americans were not in contact with members of the various ethnic and religious groups in Iraq, and U.S. troops were under orders to not assist them.

In the south of Iraq, the Shi'a majority rebelled; in the north the Kurds pursued their age-old demands for an independent homeland. The Iraqi army, commanded by Sunnis, with air support from the Schwarzkopf-approved helicopters, brutally put down the uprising in the south. Tens of thousands died while American troops in the area did nothing.

The Americans were in a peculiar position. The Shi'a were harkening to the U.S. president's call, but the American soldiers abided by the cease-fire their commanders had just signed. Since the Iraqi army was attacking its own citizens and not allied troops, they were not violating the cease-fire, and the Americans' hands were tied. Some American help for the Shi'a might well have gotten Saddam overthrown.

Saddam next turned to the rebellious Kurds, but they did not wait for extermination; after all, they had survived Saddam's attempted genocide in the 1988 al-Anfal campaign. Many fled across the border into the mountainous wastelands of Turkey, causing serious discomfort for the Turkish government, which realized it was now responsible for humanitarian aid. The refugees had no food, clothing, or shelter; they would die if Turkey did not give costly assistance. Turkey was losing millions in transit fees because of the closed Iraqi pipeline and other trade. Worse, Turkey was in the middle of putting down an insurgency by its own Kurds; the Turkish general staff feared the refugees included guerrilla fighters who would join the Turkish conflict. The Turks demanded that the international community help.

Conflicts

GULF WAR SYNDROME

Thousands of American soldiers returned home from the 1991 war complaining of blinding headaches, rashes, and nerve problems. The symptoms were more than psychological, such as posttraumatic stress disorder; they were physical.

A number of theories tried to explain the malady: exposure to depleted uranium in U.S. antitank rounds, smoke from oil fires, immunizations against biological agents such as anthrax, or desert mites. One interesting possibility: Saddam may have ordered chemical and biological weapons buried along the lines of expected allied advances. As allies destroyed enemy fortifications they would unknowingly release the toxic materials. After much analysis, no single explanation is accepted as solid.

Britain's new prime minister, John Major, proposed a safe haven in northern Iraq, and the UN did establish such a safety zone north of the thirty-sixth parallel. The United States added its support, ordering Iraq to withdraw its military from the area. Protected by American guns, the Kurds reversed the flow and returned home. Eventually the United States and Britain created "no-fly" zones over the northern and southern thirds of Iraq.

THE WAR OVER WEAPONS OF MASS DESTRUCTION

For the next decade Saddam delayed and obfuscated in a desperate attempt both to stay in power and to preserve his military capabilities. The crown jewels in his arsenal were his weapons of mass destruction (WMD), especially gas. His long record of deceit and constant dissembling suggested that he still had WMD in 2003.

Following the creation of UNSCOM to supervise destruction of Iraqi WMD, Saddam ordered his scientists to hide anything pertaining to the WMD program. He then declared some of his chemical weapons to the UN and denied having a biological program. Later, when confronted with proof that he was lying, Saddam said the research was for defensive military purposes.

By June 1991 Saddam's troops fired into the air to prevent UNSCOM inspectors from examining Iraqi trucks carrying nuclear-related equipment. In September inspectors from the UN's International Atomic Energy Agency (IAEA) discovered files documenting the Iraqi nuclear weapons development program, leading to a four-day standoff as Iraq tried to prevent the inspectors from taking a copy of the documents with them.

In March 1992 Iraq confirmed it had some ballistic missiles and chemical weapons, but the numbers declared were suspiciously low. Saddam said the Iraqi military had destroyed most of the materials themselves the previous summer, instead of turning them over to the UN.

In July 1992 an inspection team tried to enter the Iraqi agriculture ministry in search of archives on the banned weapons programs. The Iraqis prevented the inspectors from entering for seventeen days until they gave up.

Iraq also denied UNSCOM permission to fly into the country using its own aircraft. Had Saddam won this point, UNSCOM would have needed to fly in Iraqi airplanes, effectively ending the "no-fly" zones. Instead of agreeing to the Iraqi demands on his last full day in the White House, President Bush launched Tomahawk missiles into Baghdad. Iraq relented, and the inspections continued.

THE CLINTON YEARS

Bill Clinton was elected on a platform that emphasized domestic politics. He accused outgoing President Bush of being too involved with international affairs. Every new American president who announces he is giving priority to domestic problems is destined to be deeply involved in foreign affairs. (It happened to both Clinton and Bush 43.) For the next eight years Clinton tried to avoid taking decisive action in Iraq, but sometimes he had no choice in the matter.

Saddam was a vindictive ruler, and in the Middle East all politics is personal. When former President Bush visited Kuwait in April 1993, Saddam tried to take revenge by sending a hit team to Kuwait to kill Bush, but the Kuwaiti security service arrested the would-be assassins. In response, Clinton ordered a cruise-missile attack on Iraqi intelligence headquarters in Baghdad. He had the attack take place at night when the headquarters building was empty, thereby limiting its impact in favor of a symbolic statement.

Meanwhile skirmishes with weapons inspectors continued. Saddam refused to allow them to install cameras at missile engine test grounds until the inspectors threatened to leave the country. Saddam tested Clinton's resolve by again marshalling his forces on the Kuwait border but backed down when the UN Security Council demanded it. Then, in July 1995, Saddam admitted he had an offensive biological weapons program but denied he had weaponized any materials.

In November 1995 UNSCOM intercepted a shipment of Russian gyroscopes headed for Iraq. Likely use: missile guidance. In December UNSCOM drained the Tigris and uncovered additional missile components. In May 1996 UNSCOM destroyed Iraq's main biological weapons production complex.

Saddam then ended the limited cooperation he had been providing. When inspectors wanted to search a sensitive site, Iraqi troops prevented them. When an inspector tried to take pictures out of a helicopter, an Iraqi military officer assaulted him. UNSCOM later videotaped Iraqi officials burning documents and dumping materials into a river while they sat at the front gate of a facility waiting for permission to enter.

In September 1997 UNSCOM was again denied permission to visit a "food laboratory." One of the inspectors sneaked in through a rear entrance and observed several men running out with suitcases. The inspector grabbed one of the suitcases from the fleeing men and found it full of logbooks documenting Iraqi efforts to

Cultures

THE IN-LAW PROBLEM

Husayn Kamil and his brother were married to Saddam's daughters and knew about Saddam's weapons programs. Trying to make new lives for themselves, in August 1995 they fled to Jordan with their families. There Husayn Kamil gave UN inspectors directions to his farm in southern Iraq where the inspectors exhumed details of the Iraqi military and nuclear weapons programs. The UN was startled to find that Iraq was less than a year from the development of a working nuclear device. It was a major black eye for Saddam.

Kamil was the toast of Amman for several months, but when his brief fame was over he realized he had no future outside Iraq. He tried to join the Iraqi opposition, but they said he had blood on his hands and would not take him into their ranks. In February 1996 Kamil received a message from Baghdad that all was forgiven. Saddam invited him to come home and promised no punishment. Against everyone's advice, Husayn Kamil trusted his father-in-law and he returned to Baghdad.

That same night members of the Kamil clan surrounded the home where Husayn was staying. Saddam's daughters were seized and whisked away to a presidential compound, never to be seen in public again until the Americans captured Baghdad in 2003. Husayn and his brother were tortured and beaten to death. Saddam said it was an honor killing by the family that he had nothing to do with. Actually, honor killings are part of Muslim culture, but it was clear that Saddam ordered them murdered. From that time on, no one believed an "all was forgiven" message from Baghdad. Like his model Stalin, whom Saddam carefully emulated, personal cruelty went with tyranny.

create illegal bacteria and chemical compounds. The books came from the Special Security Office, so the inspectors headed to that facility for a surprise inspection. Iraq refused them entry. Following additional UN pressure, Iraq admitted it had been producing VX nerve gas as recently as May 1997.

Saddam worked to split the allied coalition. Countries such as France, Germany, and Russia were interested in establishing commercial relationships, so Saddam reasoned it wouldn't take much to strip these countries away from the United States. His first gambit was to pledge total cooperation with weapons inspectors but only if the UN no longer sent any Americans as members of the teams. Rather than comply, in November 1997 UNSCOM withdrew from Iraq. When they returned two weeks later, Saddam refused to allow them to inspect his many presidential palaces.

By 1998 the Gulf was again on the verge of war. After six years of Saddam's antics, Britain and the United States began plans for military intervention. Faced with such resolve, Saddam resumed cooperation with weapons inspectors, even opening up several of the presidential palaces. In August Tariq Aziz certified that Iraq was now free of weapons of mass destruction and demanded the inspections cease. In light of the U.S. inability to find evidence of WMD in the 2003 war, Aziz may have been telling the truth. But after all the lies, no one believed him. Iraq then expelled the teams on October 31, 1998.

Clinton had to do something no matter how much he wanted to avoid a Middle East war. He ordered air strikes on Iraq but cancelled the order when Iraq agreed to allow UNSCOM to return. Actually Britain and the United States waged a low-scale bombing campaign against the Iraqi air defense system throughout the entire decade. New planned air strikes were to have been more extensive than the "routine" bombings Iraq had been absorbing. A month after the UNSCOM inspectors returned to Iraq, they pulled out again because of Iraqi noncooperation. The UN evacuated its other aid workers and the United States and Britain launched four days of bombings.

Rather than pretending to cooperate as Iraq had previously done countless times, this time Iraqi Vice President Taha Yassin Ramadan announced it would no longer cooperate with UNSCOM. Saddam had picked his time perfectly. Three of the five permanent members of the UN Security Council called to lift the oil embargo on Iraq. Instead of punishing Iraq for failing to cooperate, Russia, France, and China wanted to reward Saddam. The UN created UNMOVIC as a replacement for UNSCOM, but Saddam refused to cooperate. The stage was set for the arrival of George W. Bush, who finished what his father started.

CONCLUSIONS

Writers often refer to the Iraqi conflict of 1990 and 1991 as the First Gulf War. It might be more appropriate to consider the conflict to be the opening skirmishes in a thirteen-year war that only ended when America took the whole country in 2003. We will call 1991 the Gulf War and 2003 the Iraq War for the sake of clarity.

There were good reasons to defend Kuwait from Iraqi aggression, not least of all Kuwait's oil reserves. There were morally compelling reasons for the United States to intervene in the Balkans earlier than it did, or in Rwanda, but in the case of the Gulf, American security interests were at stake; they were not in the other conflicts.

The United States won the 1991 war but allowed it to end halfway through, not wanting to lose American lives to invade Iraq and overthrow Saddam with little help from allies or the UN. Besides, Washington figured that Saddam would soon be overthrown. Instead, his security police shot tens of thousands who tried. Both Republicans and Democrats have engaged in wishful thinking regarding Iraq.

Saddam Hussein actively developed chemical, biological, and nuclear weapons, constantly deceiving UN inspectors. He had no compunctions about using such weapons, as he showed in the Iran-Iraq war. In many ways, whether we found evidence of these programs was immaterial: Saddam's behavior throughout the 1990s clearly demonstrated that once the United States let up the pressure and the international inspectors went away, he would have resumed his programs. It did not seem possible to deal with Saddam in any humane, rational way.

KEY TERMS

deterrence (p. 250)   UNMOVIC (p. 248)

hegemon (p. 250)   UNSCOM (p. 248)

FURTHER REFERENCE

Coughlin, Con. *Saddam: King of Terror.* New York: Ecco, 2004.

Fürtig, Henner. *Iran's Rivalry with Saudi Arabia between the Gulf Wars.* Reading, UK: Ithaca Press, 2002.

Hamza, Khidhir, with Jeff Stein. *Saddam's Bombmaker.* New York: Simon & Schuster, 2000.

Khadduri, Majid, and Edmund Ghareeb. *War in the Gulf, 1990–1991: The Iraq-Kuwait Conflict and Its Implications.* New York: Oxford, 1997.

Little, Douglas. *American Orientalism: The United States and the Middle East since 1945.* Chapel Hill, NC: University of North Carolina Press, 2002.

Malone, David M. *The International Struggle over Iraq: Politics in the UN Security Council, 1980–2005.* New York: Oxford University Press, 2007.

Mottale, Morris M. *The Origins of the Gulf Wars.* Lanham, MD: University Press of America, 2001.

Public Broadcasting System. *Frontline: The Gulf War. Oral History.* <www.pbs.org/wgbh/pages/frontline/gulf/oral.html>.

14 The 2003 Iraq War and Aftermath

The horrifying attacks of 9/11 triggered two American invasions, of Afghanistan in 2001 and of Iraq in 2003. The terrorism of 2001 unleashed a torrent of American emotion eager for retribution. President George W. Bush, with Texas twang and simple sentence structure, connected with mass emotions in a way that more intellectual leaders seldom do. With this, an enraged public and Congress asked few questions and followed Bush to war. Complexities and doubts came later.

The Iraq War is hotly controversial. The Bush administration, **conflating** Osama with Saddam, used four points to sell it to the American people and Congress: (1) Iraq had WMD, (2) Iraq supported al Qaeda, (3) Saddam Hussein was brutal, and (4) we could make Iraq and the region democratic. The first two points were flatly wrong, the product of false intelligence reports. No one disputed the third point, but many questioned if Iraq was a threat to us. As for democracy, there were some elections in Iraq and other Middle Eastern lands, but they did not lead to moderation or stability. The Bush administration then added a fifth point: We had to fight terrorists in Iraq before they came here. Many Americans believed it.

---

conflate   To meld or confuse distinct entities.

COVERT WAR IN AFGHANISTAN

Afghans, still tribal in organization, do not like being ruled by anybody, especially foreigners. In 1747, Afghanistan broke from the Persian empire and became independent. Afghans tolerated a weak, traditional monarchy because it left them alone. The long reign of King Muhammad Zahir (1933–1973) is remembered as a time of peace and prosperity. Modernization changed Afghan society, producing a class of educated young Afghans impatient for reform. A coup overthrew the king in 1973, and Afghanistan has been in turmoil ever since. In 1978, Communists took power in a coup and then sought help from Moscow. Most Afghans hated the Communists and started an insurrection against them; by 1979 the insurrection was nationwide and getting covert U.S. aid. The Soviets knew the situation was bad but could not let a dependent Communist regime go down the drain, so they intervened directly and massively in Afghanistan. It turned out to be a major mistake, contributing to their own demise.

In late December 1979, Soviet troops landed at Kabul airport, immediately shot the president (a Communist, but from the wrong faction) and his family, and installed a Communist president more to their liking. Soviet troops soon numbered 120,000 (15,000 were killed), and many returned embittered and drug-addicted. They could not subdue the Afghan *dushmani* (bandits), as they called them, even with exceedingly brutal tactics that wiped out whole villages. Some 3 million Afghans fled to Pakistan and another 2 million to Iran. From camps in Pakistan, mujahedin with equipment supplied by the U.S. Central Intelligence Agency, training by Pakistan's ISI (Inter-Services Intelligence agency), and money from Saudi Arabia made forays back into Afghanistan to mercilessly harass the Soviets and their unenthusiastic Afghan troops. Volunteers came from all over the Muslim world, especially from Saudi Arabia. Encouraging them with money and guidance was a quietly charismatic Saudi fundamentalist, Osama bin Laden.

Tipping the balance, in 1986 the rebels got American shoulder-fired Stinger missiles. Soviet helicopters fell at the rate of one a day and soon learned to keep their distance. From then on, the Soviets were on the defensive and pulled out entirely by early 1989, the same year they cut loose their East European satellites. The Soviet Union collapsed at the end of 1991. The Afghan war cost the Soviet Union friends and influence, especially in the Muslim world. Moscow's attempts at relaxing tensions with the United States were wrecked by the invasion. U.S. President Jimmy Carter declared he "learned more about the Soviets in one week" than he had in all previous years. He began a U.S. arms buildup (often attributed to Reagan), cancelled grain sales to the Soviet Union, and pulled the U.S. team out of the 1980 Moscow Olympics. U.S. aid flowed to the Afghan rebels. The Soviets had gotten themselves into a vulnerable situation, and we made it worse, draining them and getting back at them for their help to North Vietnam. In international relations, turnabout is fair play.

The Bush 41 administration vaguely promised aid to the victorious mujahedin, but when their several tribes started fighting among themselves Washington walked away from and forgot Afghanistan, which seemed remote and unimportant as the Cold War ended. These problems do not solve themselves, however, and

G *Geography*

THE "GAME OF NATIONS"

In the nineteenth century, Britain and Russia played what came to be known as the Great Game of Nations in the lands between the tsarist empire and the British Raj of India. The Russians aimed to push south, enrolling Persia, Afghanistan, and Tibet in their **sphere of influence**. The British in India aimed to stop them by keeping these borderlands at least neutral buffer zones if not in the British sphere. Decades of treaties, intrigues, espionage, and armed expeditions by the Russians and British gave Kipling the setting for *Kim*.

In the First Afghan War (1839–1842), the British in India, fearful of anarchy and Russian influence in Afghanistan, marched in with 12,000 troops to install a pro-British king in Kabul. The old king, though, in 1841 led an uprising of outraged Afghans, and in early 1842 the British agreed to leave. The Khyber Pass, the gate to India, was just 90 miles away, but they never made it. Afghan tribesmen picked them off in the rugged terrain. According to legend, only one British survivor, a surgeon, staggered back through the Khyber alive. Britain tried to subdue Afghanistan twice more, in the Second Afghan War (1878–1880), and the Third (1919), at which point Afghanistan achieved full independence, and Britain, badly burned, left it alone. Wrote Kipling of the British fighting in Afghanistan:

> When you're wounded and left on Afghanistan's plains,
> And the women come out to cut up your remains,
> Just roll on your rifle and blow out your brains,
> And go to your Gawd like a soldier.

In 1907, Britain and Russia agreed to let each other establish spheres of influence in Persia, the Russians in the north and the British in the south. Afghanistan was to remain neutral, in neither sphere, and it did until the Communists took over in 1978. The Soviets in the 1980s and Americans in the 2000s might have learned something from the earlier British experience: Afghanistan is not hard to get into, but it can be impossible to tame or rule.

Afghanistan descended into complete chaos presided over by local "warlords," who obeyed no central authority.

In late 1994 the **Taliban** movement of students trained in Saudi-financed *Wahhabi* (see page 187) schools in Pakistan and supplied by the ISI moved into the chaos and took over most of Afghanistan. The Taliban were mostly Pushtuns of the south, and other Afghan commanders fought them, slowly retreating back into the northeast corner of Afghanistan. Basically, Pakistan's military invented the Taliban to stabilize their northern neighbor. No one likes chaos on their borders. Another reason: A stable Afghanistan could be a corridor for a natural-gas pipeline from Central Asia to Pakistan.

---

sphere of influence   Area where imperial power holds sway.
Taliban   Persian for students; fundamentalist movement that took over Afghanistan in the 1990s.

Geography

Afghanistan and the Gulf

Bound Afghanistan:

Afghanistan is bounded on the north by Turkmenistan,
Uzbekistan, and Tajikistan;
on the east by China and Pakistan;
on the south by Pakistan;
and on the west by Iran.

In 1979 Washington saw that the Persian Gulf region could soon be in very hostile hands. The anti-U.S. Islamists of Ayatollah Khomeini in Iran were bad enough. The Soviet takeover of Afghanistan late that year made things worse. Soviet bases in the south of Afghanistan put Soviet air power a mere 300 miles from the Strait of Hormuz, a strategic waterway through which flows much of the world's oil. Washington feared that Moscow's thumb was, or soon could be, on the world's petroleum throat, and the United States could not let this happen. Geography rather than ideology explains both Soviet and U.S. motives.

Afghanistan is important for another geographical reason. It bordered the Soviet Union (now it borders the ex-Soviet **Central Asian** republics of Turkmenistan, Uzbekistan, and Tajikistan), where Muslims live who are related to the peoples of Afghanistan. If the **mujahedin** beat the new Communist regime, they would spread their militant Islam into the rapidly growing and not completely reliable Soviet Muslim population. The successor republics have this same problem today. This explains why Russian and Central Asian governments helped the United States knock out the Taliban in 2001. Geography sometimes produces common—if temporary—interests between hostile countries.

The United States did not much care about Afghanistan until terrorists hit American targets. The same Osama bin Laden who had fought the Communists in Afghanistan turned bitterly anti-American by 1991. In 1990, Saudi Arabia had invited U.S. forces onto its soil to mass for the 1991 Gulf War. Attacking a brother Arab country was bad enough for bin Laden, but allowing U.S. troops to remain on sacred Muslim ground after the war was unforgivable. Osama aimed his jihad against Americans and anyone cooperating with them, namely, the House of Saud. Osama had never been a U.S. ally and had no contact with Americans in the Afghan struggle.

Bin Laden, expelled from Saudi Arabia in 1991, set up shop in Khartoum, Sudan, where he helped a Muslim fundamentalist regime consolidate power. Accusing him of anti-U.S. terrorism, the United States pressured Sudan to expel him in 1996. Osama went to Afghanistan where he helped the Taliban take over most of the country. Al Qaeda fighters became the most effective element of the Taliban

Central Asia   Ex-Soviet region between Caspian Sea and China.
mujahedin   Muslim holy warriors.

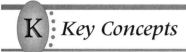

Key Concepts

BLOWBACK

The term "blowback" comes from the use of poison gas in World War I. If used carelessly, it could blow back in the user's face. The term later broadened to mean "negative unanticipated consequences," for example, aiding a group or country that then turns against their benefactors. You may think you have similar or compatible interests with the group and could use them to achieve your goals, but they accept your help only on a temporary and opportunistic basis. Their agenda is power for themselves, not the promotion of your interests. "Blowback" describes the Middle East quite well.

A prime example is U.S. aid to the Afghan militias who fought the 1979 Soviet occupation of their country. We were delighted to get the Soviets bogged down in an unwinnable war. But the Afghan freedom fighters fought each other. Some were anti-American. None said thanks. Out of the chaos the Taliban seized most of Afghanistan and instituted a hostile, repressive regime, supported by and home to Osama bin Laden. Afghanistan blew back in our face. U.S. help to Iraq in the 1980s also blew back in our face. Careful whom you help in the Middle East.

armed forces. On August 7, 1998, al Qaeda bombers simultaneously blew up the U.S. embassies in Kenya and Tanzania. U.S. Navy cruise missiles hit one of Osama's training camps in Afghanistan, but he had already departed. You cannot do everything with air power.

Instantly, 9/11 was pegged as an al Qaeda project, and Washington demanded that the Taliban turn over Osama and his top lieutenants. The Taliban head of Afghanistan, Mullah Muhammad Omar, refused, claiming to be innocent of any wrongdoing. The Taliban had a weak spot: They had not taken all of Afghanistan. In the mountainous northeast of the country, anti-Taliban forces, the Northern Alliance, held out under the command of the charismatic Ahmad Shah Massoud. As a favor to Mullah Omar, shortly before 9/11, Osama sent two al Qaeda suicide bombers posing as television journalists to kill Massoud, supposing that would end the Northern Alliance. Instead, it energized it.

U.S. Special Forces used this opening brilliantly, and within days were inside Afghanistan, working with local anti-Taliban fighters. Their chief weapons were radios and global positioning systems, with which they could pinpoint Taliban positions for air strikes launched from U.S. bases and aircraft carriers in the Gulf. Many Afghans had grown to detest the fanatic Taliban—who forbade music, radio, television, and flying kites, while forcing women to wear head-to-toe chadors and men to grow beards—and soon other groups joined in (some changed sides). By December, the Taliban were defeated. The bold operation involved few U.S. forces or casualties. Unfortunately, follow-up was weak, and most al Qaeda and Taliban leaders—including Osama and his second-in-command, Egyptian physician Ayman Zawahiri—slipped across the border to the mountain wilds of Pakistan's Northwest Frontier Province, a tribal area where government writ does not run and Westerners are not permitted.

Most of the world supported U.S. actions in Afghanistan, and antiwar protests were few. Sympathy for 9/11 was genuine, and no one had a good word for the Taliban, who had made themselves isolated and detested. They had just blown up ancient statues of gigantic Buddhas carved into a mountainside, a UNESCO-designated World Heritage Site. (Before Islam, Buddhism had been prominent in Afghanistan.) Pakistan and Saudi Arabia, the sponsors of the Taliban, broke relations with them. Even Iran approved, as the Sunni Taliban and Shi'a Iranians have no love for each other, and the Taliban had killed Shi'a Afghans and Iranian diplomats. Iran offered to help downed American fliers. Russia, facing its own problems with a Muslim breakaway movement in Chechnya, arranged for U.S.-bases in Uzbekistan and Tajikistan. The UN accepted America's actions in Afghanistan.

Afghanistan, still lawless and untamed, is again a job half-done. The Taliban regrouped in Pakistan and fight again in Afghanistan's south. The Afghan warlords are as bad as ever, corrupt mini-tyrants who rob and repress their provinces. A U.S.-approved president, Hamid Karzai, educated in India and English-speaking, took office, but few outside of Kabul answer to him. Opium-poppy cultivation, suppressed by the Taliban, is again Afghanistan's top moneymaker. Afghanistan needs far more foreign help. Along with 18,000 U.S. soldiers, America's NATO allies—Canada and Britain provide the largest contingents—have some 22,000 troops in Afghanistan, not nearly enough. Critics charge we should have concentrated on Afghanistan and stayed out of Iraq.

THE IRAQ WAR

According to several accounts, Bush listened to hawkish Vice President Dick Cheney and Defense Secretary Donald Rumsfeld and their **neo-conservative** deputies, who within days of 9/11 pointed to Iraq as a source of terrorism as bad as Afghanistan. And Iraq had weapons of mass destruction, they claimed. They also argued that eliminating Saddam would restart Israel-Palestine peace talks and establish Iraq as a regional model of democracy.

Former Treasury Secretary Paul H. O'Neill and others say that Bush 43 came to the White House already intent on removing Saddam Hussein, who had sent a hit team to kill his father on a visit to Kuwait in 1993. Bush may have decided on war with Iraq with little or no help from neo-conservatives, making 9/11 the occasion but not the cause of the war. Bush 43 decided on war with Iraq in late 2001 but kept his plans vague until mid-2002.

One week after 9/11, mysterious letters containing anthrax were mailed to various parts of the United States, including Capitol Hill. Five died. Rumor had it that the Egyptian leader of the 9/11 hijackers, Muhammad Atta, met in Prague that summer with a senior Iraqi intelligence official. Did Iraq supply Atta with a sample pack of anthrax to try out in America? U.S. and Czech intelligence officials

---

neo-conservative   Rediscovery of tough-minded foreign policies, including use of force, often by ex-liberals.

dismissed the claim, but at the time it added to U.S. suspicions of Iraq. (The FBI named an American scientist as a "person of interest" in the case.)

In December 2001, White House speechwriter David Frum was instructed to incorporate a justification for war with Iraq in the president's State of the Union address, and on January 29, 2002, President Bush called Iraq, Iran, and North Korea the "axis of evil," his first public indication that he was preparing for war. In contrast to Afghanistan, most of the world did not support Washington on Iraq. Many felt the U.S. accusations of major, ongoing Iraqi programs of WMD or Iraqi sponsorship of terrorism were exaggerated and unproved, certainly not a valid basis for war. World sympathy and support for America largely dried up because of Iraq, but Bush was unbothered. Always inclined to unilateralism, Bush 43 made it clear that, unless Saddam came clean fast on his WMD, we would go to war with a "coalition of the willing," meaning mostly Britain, where Prime Minister Tony Blair supported Bush despite British public opinion that, like all of West Europe, strongly opposed the war.

Moderate and internationalist Secretary of State Colin Powell—once the Army's top general who had also urged caution on Bush 41 before the 1991 war with Iraq—urged that we first make the case in the United Nations to gain multilateral support. Powell was one of the few top Bush appointees who fought in Vietnam, an experience that convinced him the case for any war must first be overwhelming, and then the war must be pursued with overwhelming force. In Vietnam, we failed to do both. Generals, who have to actually deliver their soldiers' lives, are among the most cautious about going to war. The administration neo-cons were all civilians, few with military service. None knew Iraq or the Arab world or spoke Arabic.

The UN had set up a new program, UNMOVIC, to make sure Iraq had gotten rid of its WMD (see Chapter 13). In the early 1990s, after the Gulf War, UNSCOM had supervised the destruction of Iraqi weapons, and Iraq claimed it had not re-activated these programs and had no weapons of mass destruction. By 1998, however, UNSCOM, frustrated by non-cooperation and deception by Baghdad, left Iraq, and suspicions remained of secret and mobile weapons labs. Baghdad's continual lying led almost everyone—including UN inspectors, most intelligence agencies around the world, the Clinton administration, and congressional Democrats—to believe that it still had WMD.

Why did Saddam not give in at the last minute and permit full inspections? Some analysts argue that he never thought the United States would actually attack. U.S. policy for years had been to preserve Iraq in order to contain Iran. We established relations with Iraq and helped it in its war with Iran in the 1980s. In 1991, we refrained from finishing off Saddam because we wanted to preserve Iraq against Iranian expansion. Saddam did not believe Washington would overturn its long-standing policy of keeping Iraq together. Based on previous experience with U.S. policy, Saddam's actions were rational.

The UN debated whether the United States could legally go to war without further UN sanction. The UN **Security Council** had passed seventeen resolutions

---

Security Council   Fifteen-member UN body assigned to keep the peace. (Do not confuse with *National Security Council.*)

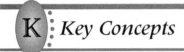

Key Concepts

BUREAUCRATIC POLITICS

Studying foreign-policy decisions as the result of bureaucratic politics enjoyed brief vogue in the early 1970s. One influential article claimed that squabbling among agencies led to the U.S naval blockade of Cuba in 1962. (More recent research shows that President Kennedy was in command at all times and that bureaucratic infighting had little to do with his decision.) The 2003 Iraq War recalled some of the bureaucratic-politics theory. The war did bring friction between the State and Defense Departments, but President Bush directed policy.

The conduct of foreign relations used to be in the hands of the secretary of state, but during the Cold War the initiative drifted to the **National Security Council** (NSC), a 1947 creation that has as much power as the president wants to give it. Under Nixon, national security advisor Henry Kissinger built the NSC into the center of foreign policy, easily eclipsing State. The Department of Defense (DOD) also took on foreign-policy functions. Indeed, it is difficult to separate security policy from foreign policy. DOD gives crisp, clear answers while State voices doubts and ambiguities. Another factor: DOD has billions of defense dollars to spend, millions in almost every Congressional district. State has little to spend, and that is in Washington and overseas. State has no natural domestic constituency; Defense has a big one. Since Eisenhower's strong-willed Secretary of State John Foster Dulles, that office has shrunk in importance and influence compared to DOD and the NSC.

Colin Powell looked like an effective secretary of state, and he did his best to keep foreign-policy primacy in State, where many foreign-service officers know the complexities of the Middle East and so tend to be cautious. Defense, especially under forceful and blunt-spoken Donald Rumsfeld, preferred simplicity to complexity, a style suited to President Bush. Rumsfeld and his neo-con deputies took the initiative on Iraq policy. The best Powell could do was delay the war a bit until he could place the matter before the UN and our allies. He had little success, and Defense proceeded with a brilliant war but a terrible aftermath. State was the clear loser in 2003, and Powell retired at the end of Bush's first term. Powell said little about the Iraq War, but his former deputy denounced it.

Rumsfeld thought Defense could handle postwar Iraq on the cheap and on its own. State Department officials predicted accurately what could go wrong and planned in detail how to run Iraq after the war, but DOD ignored the plans. State argued that its Agency for International Development, with experience in disaster relief in coordination with charitable non-governmental organizations (NGOs), should play a major role. State Department officials believe Iraq's postwar chaos was in part the result of DOD taking over Iraq policy.

over twelve years on Iraq, starting with Resolution 660 condemning Iraq for invading Kuwait in 1990. One resolution after another demanded that Iraq cease building and eliminate its WMD, but Iraq evaded, lied, and misled UN weapons inspectors. No UN resolution authorized war with Iraq. In November 2002, it passed Resolution 1441 declaring that "Iraq has been and remains in material breach" of the previous resolutions. That is all we need, declared the Bush administration. Others—including France, Russia, and China, who sought to balance U.S. power—

National Security Council   White House body to coordinate and oversee defense and foreign policies.

Conflicts

PRE-EMPTIVE OR PREVENTIVE WAR?

One of the minor debates on the Iraq War was whether it was a pre-emptive or preventive war. The difference is one of time pressure. If war is nigh and you are sure the other country is ready to strike you, then you may wish to pre-empt them by striking first, as Israel did in 1967 (see page 93). Much of the world sees this as a legitimate use of force.

Preventive war has no legitimacy. It implies a longer time frame. You see a problem coming up with a hostile country, but it is not an urgent threat. You decide to attack anyway, on the theory that you are heading off a worse war later. Launching a war to prevent a war is dubious and wins no world sympathy. It may start precisely the big war you wished to prevent. Bismarck, Germany's nineteenth-century unifier, called preventive war "suicide from fear of death." The Bush administration stopped calling the war pre-emptive, as Iraq had been in no condition to attack anybody.

have veto rights on the Security Council and claimed 1441 did not give Washington legal authority to go to war. War resolutions have been rare over the life of the UN: Korea in 1950, Iraq in 1991, and Afghanistan in 2001. Bush, part of the Republican isolationist tradition that never liked the UN, said the UN could not block U.S. military action that, he argued, was pre-emptive self-defense.

THE QUICK WAR

Neither Saudi Arabia nor Turkey, who had been helpful in the 1991 Gulf War, would let us launch the 2003 invasion from their soil. Saudi and Turkish opinion strongly opposed it. Washington offered Turkey $6 billion in aid, but Ankara demanded $32 billion. It was perhaps fortunate that the whole aid/bribery process failed, as it demeaned both countries. Two small Gulf states, Kuwait and Qatar, allowed use of their territories to mount an invasion of Iraq. U.S. and British ground forces massed and trained in little Kuwait in late 2002 and early 2003.

The U.S. plan of commanding General Tommy Franks was bold but risky. Starting with the first bombing of Baghdad on March 19, U.S. mechanized forces, both Army and Marines, moved rapidly up the Euphrates valley, taking out Iraqi troops who wished to do battle but not delaying to secure cities or even their **lines of communication**. The British took Basra, the largest city of the south. U.S. forces reached the ring of Iraqi Republican Guards around Baghdad in two weeks. "We executed faster than they could react," said a U.S. officer. Only the need to refuel slowed U.S. columns as they sped up highways and across desert.

lines of communication   Routes along which an army moves, supplies itself, and communicates.

There were two risks to this strategy. This long LOC, little defended, would be easy prey for Iraqi fighters—both army and civilian militias—that had been by-passed but were still intact. They could cut off our rapidly moving spearhead. Most military commanders are cautious about overextending and thus inclined to go slow to make sure their LOC are secure. Franks gambled that Iraqi guerrilla forces—chiefly the Saddam Fedayeen, who threw their lives away in attacks on U.S. columns—would not stop us. He was right in the short term but wrong in the long term, for precisely these fighters formed the core of the resistance that made Iraq ungovernable for years. Franks nearly fired an American commander who urged that we mop up these Fedayeen before streaking on to Baghdad. Several generals grumbled that leaving the guerrillas alive and free meant insurrection later.

The second risk, widely predicted, was that Saddam would order urban warfare in Baghdad, a sprawling metropolis of 5 million. He did not. Some suggest that Saddam feared soldiers would desert in the big city or carry out a coup. The U.S. advance was so swift that Iraqi generals did not have time to adjust their defenses. The taking of Baghdad only three weeks after the war began was almost unopposed. On April 9, 2003, a U.S. Marine tank pulled down a big statue of Saddam Hussein in the center of Baghdad before a cheering Iraqi crowd. After that, it was just mopping up. The main-unit fighting part of the war lasted less than a month, and on May 1, 2003, President Bush proclaimed "mission accomplished" from the deck of an aircraft carrier. The Pentagon planned to have all but 30,000 U.S. troops out of Iraq by September 2003.

Attempts to kill Saddam Hussein with smart bombs missed. He sneaked out as the Americans took Baghdad, after his sons (killed in a firefight in Mosul in July) fetched $1 billion dollars from the national bank. Several of Saddam's relatives made it to Syria. Saddam avoided the elaborate bunkers under his numerous palaces in favor of his native Tikrit. U.S. soldiers found the great dictator in a "spider hole" at a farm in December of 2003; he surrendered without a fight. The Iraqi government tried Saddam, who contemptuously turned the courtroom into a pulpit to justify himself. An international tribunal—he had invaded both Iran and Kuwait—would have been a better venue to try Saddam. At his 2006 hanging, Saddam's Shi'a executioners taunted him, and he spat back, "Persians!"

After a long and thorough search, no WMD were found in Iraq, refuting the chief U.S. reason for the war. One top official told the Senate: "We were all wrong." Intelligence officials said the administration had leaned on them to report as fact rumors and fabrications supplied by self-seeking Iraqi exiles. The administration claimed that Iraq had purchased uranium from Niger, but it was based on a bogus document that had been discredited for months. To make a case for war, a special Defense Department team "cherry picked" intelligence and ignored evidence to the contrary. Some recalled the 1964 Tonkin Gulf incident, when President Johnson used ambiguous reports that North Vietnamese boats had attacked U.S. destroyers to get Congress to quickly authorize war. The absence of Iraqi WMD made many Americans feel they had been lied to.

What had happened to Iraq's WMD? It now seems they really were destroyed in the 1990s. But then why did Baghdad behave so deceptively? Top Iraqi officials,

Conflicts

REVOLUTION IN MILITARY AFFAIRS

For some years U.S. defense thinkers had discussed the electronic **revolution in military affairs** (RMA) that was supposedly changing the art of war, mostly to our benefit. Command, control, communications plus intelligence (C3I) added computers to become C4I. Spy satellites, signal intercepts, instant radio and e-mail communication, global positioning, and **precision guided munitions** (PGMs) had given U.S. armed forces a big lead. Other armies, even those of NATO allies, lagged twenty or more years behind us. PGMs enable us to knock out much of the enemy's brain in the first hours of a war, leaving him blind and confused. In the 1991 Gulf War, only one U.S. jet in five could bomb a target sighted by laser; twelve years later, all could. In 1991 only 9 percent of our bombs were "smart"; in 2003 two-thirds were. Front-line U.S. combat vehicles now have computers.

RMA helps explain the quick U.S. victories over Iraq in both 1991 and 2003 but does not give us an advantage in all situations. Anywhere an enemy can hide—in forests, mountains, cities, or among friendly populations—can negate PGMs. Low-tech opponents can sometimes bypass high-tech armies. Al Qaeda hid in caves in the Tora Bora Mountains and crossed undetected into Pakistan at night. (They likely bribed soldiers on both sides of the border.) The Saddam Fedayeen attacked U.S. convoys with small pickup trucks, although they did little damage and were quickly destroyed. The fact that they were willing to die should have suggested that they would not soon give up.

interrogated after the war, said they focused on deterring Iran, not on the United States. Saddam, always intent on puffing up his power, wanted Iran to think that he still had gas. Saddam's bluff led straight to the U.S. invasion. Other Iraqi officials said that Saddam had ordered new WMD programs, and his scientists told him they were under way. Instead, crooked scientists pocketed the money for their bogus programs. Dictatorships are notoriously corrupt.

FROM TYRANNY TO ANARCHY

Overthrowing Saddam was easy, but after him came chaos that the Bush administration had not anticipated or planned for. U.S. military might was impressive, but armed forces do nation-destroying, not nation-building. Critics, including active and retired U.S. generals and diplomats (such as George F. Kennan, founder of the Cold War "containment" policy), warned of a chaotic aftermath but were ignored. Several retired generals publicly urged Rumsfeld to resign, which he did after the 2006 Republican electoral defeat.

revolution in military affairs War becoming high-tech.
precision guided munitions Smart bombs.

The self-assured Rumsfeld assumed that occupation would be easy and short, and a federal democracy would be quickly set up. Eric Shinseki, the U.S. Army's top general, told Congress we would need several hundred thousand American troops to pacify Iraq. Rumsfeld scoffed at the notion, but it proved accurate. Cost estimates were also far too low. White House economic advisor Lawrence Lindsey estimated in September 2002 that a war with Iraq could cost from $100 billion to $200 billion. The White House said that was much too high and fired him. It soon turned out to be much too low. Deputy Defense Secretary Paul Wolfowitz (a prominent neo-conservative) told Congress that, figuring oil revenues, Iraqi reconstruction might cost nothing. In 2006 the full costs of the Iraq War—including veterans' health care, all salaries and construction projects, and increased interest payments on the national debt—were estimated as topping $1 trillion in a few years.

Two important specialties were not in the Pentagon's combat plans: military police and civil affairs, what you need to run a country. These units are almost entirely in the reserves, to be mobilized only when needed. The Pentagon focuses on its combat branches, as it must; MPs and civil affairs were an afterthought. In actuality, they should have arrived one day behind our combat troops, who are not trained and should not be used for police duty. To do so invites catastrophe. MPs, civil affairs, and certain engineering units could have immediately imposed law and order, got local administration running, and restored water and electricity. Instead, only a few arrived and weeks later, after the situation had deteriorated. The Pentagon named retired U.S. General Jay Garner—respected by Kurds for helping them in the early 1990s—temporary administrator, but with little money or staff, things quickly fell apart. Garner followed the initial U.S. military plan to retain most of the Iraqi army to let it restore order.

U.S. diplomat L. Paul Bremer soon replaced Garner and set up the Coalition Provisional Authority (CPA) in May 2003, an occupation government. A CPA staff was quickly cobbled together from miscellaneous U.S. sources—federal, state, and local governments, think tanks, and Republican loyalists. Inexperienced but arrogant, they planned to redo Iraqi society according to the neo-conservative blueprint. The CPA fired all Iraqi Baath party members—including military, police, teachers, and health workers—leaving no one to get Iraq's infrastructure working and putting the entire pacification burden on overstretched U.S. forces. It took years to train a new Iraqi army and police force, and they were unreliable. Bremer and the CPA staff continually overrode experienced U.S. military officers, and many of them blame the Iraq mess on mistaken CPA policies.

The U.S. administration of Iraq was uncoordinated and dysfunctional. Bricks of $100 bills were passed out with little accounting, and contractors skimmed millions in U.S. aid from reconstruction projects. Critics say Bremer botched the job, but the whole thing may have been inherently infeasible, no matter what administrators, methods, or policies were put in place.

Iraqis refer to the 2003 war as the *suqut* (collapse) as it left a vacuum where there should be government. Electric, water, and sewage systems were not working. The civilian infrastructure, highly centralized and under the tight control of Saddam's Baath party, evaporated. Monumental looting broke out, initially by angry and impoverished citizens, soon by criminal gangs, and later as deliberate sabotage.

U.S. soldiers, with no plans and underestimating the situation, guarded only a few buildings. Most other sites nationwide—including the national museum housing priceless ancient artifacts, hospitals, even a radioactive nuclear storehouse—were looted and left in ruins. Some 3 million tons of Iraqi weapons, ammunition, and explosives, dispersed in thousands of caches, were not destroyed or guarded. Baathists and jihadis helped themselves to them and turned artillery shells into deadly "improvised explosive devices" (IEDs).

Many Iraqis, to be sure, were delighted to be liberated. They had cowered in fear for decades. Crowds bashed the toppled statues of Saddam and cheered the Americans. Within a month, though, complaints replaced cheers. Used to the government providing everything—jobs, food, medical care, pensions, schooling, police—Iraqis expected the Americans to provide everything. That was not possible and not our intention. Americans, with their strong sense of self-reliance, thought Iraqis were being unreasonable. Iraqis, with no other means of support, felt they had been made desperate by the American takeover. Many disliked Saddam, but he had built their world, which we had just demolished, producing terrible insecurity. Iraqis fear getting killed just walking down the street. Neither the Americans nor new Iraqi forces make their lives even halfway secure. No security, no legitimacy.

Soon a Baathist insurgency broke out among the Sunni, first against American troops, then against Shi'a. There was not one single organization or brain behind the uprising but dozens of shadowy groups, many descended from the Baath, Saddam's secular ruling party, or his Fedayeen militia. Their motives were largely nationalistic and pro-Sunni. Some, however, were Islamic jihadis, including hundreds from neighboring countries. Dozens of shadowy groups, mostly Sunni, melded nationalism and Islam. The most dangerous group—which carried out numerous car suicide bombings—called itself al Qaeda in Mesopotamia and was headed by an elusive Jordanian Wahhabi fanatic, Abu Musab al-Zarqawi, who was finally killed in 2006. Much of the U.S. effort in Iraq was in catching insurgents and training Iraqi police and soldiers to catch them. The United States was reluctant to leave Iraq in a state of chaos, although many charged the U.S. presence fueled and prolonged the insurgency. It was the classic dilemma of fighting guerrillas: Strong measures to defeat them also harm civilians, who then aid the insurgents.

The Americans named an Iraqi Governing Council in 2003, composed of highly educated Iraqis (some returned from exile) from all Iraq's population groups, but because it was named by foreigners it enjoyed no legitimacy. Amidst civil disorder the handover of sovereignty to an interim Iraqi government was postponed until mid-2004, and we became unloved occupiers. Many Iraqis said the U.S. presence made things worse.

In 2004 a U.S. soldier e-mailed out shocking digital photos of Army guards abusing naked Iraqi prisoners at Abu Ghraib prison in Baghdad. The guards were untrained and unsupervised reservists; a few enlisted soldiers were convicted but no officers. The Bush administration said harsh interrogation techniques were legal. The methods—including desecrating Qur'ans—started in Afghanistan and Guantánamo on combatants captured in Afghanistan. Abu Ghraib, the killing of Iraqi civilians, and rape of a young girl and murder of her entire family deepened Islamic hatred worldwide and dampened U.S. public and congressional support for the war.

The United States in the Middle East

IRAQ AND VIETNAM

As the Iraq War dragged on, American critics compared it to Vietnam, claiming we were "bogged down" in Iraq. The Bush administration replied hotly that there was no comparison and we were not bogged down. There was some truth to both views.

First, the terrain was vastly different. Iraq was nearly perfect for our kind of conventional war. Recalling Vietnam, American officers joked: "We do deserts; we don't do jungles." Vietnam used mostly draftees but no reservists; Iraq used no draftees but many reservists (at one point, 50 percent of U.S. forces there). Iraq has lots of oil, Vietnam none.

The strongest difference was the nature of the enemy. Both wars were fought at least partly by guerrillas, but the Communists in Vietnam were united and under Hanoi's central control. Iraqi insurgents, drawn from the Sunni Arab fifth of the population, are fragmented with no one in overall control. The Vietcong could sell their nationalist ideology to other Vietnamese. Sunni fighters cannot sell Sunni supremacy to Shi'a or Kurds, who will never again accept Sunni rule. This is the ultimate weakness of the Sunni cause: They can start a civil war but not win it.

There were some similarities. Both Iraq, invented by the British in the 1920s, and South Vietnam, invented by the Americans in the 1950s, were artificial countries whose regimes had little legitimacy. The chief weaknesses in both were political, not military, namely, how to rally the people to, respectively, the corrupt and inept Baghdad and Saigon governments. Both wars were sold to the U.S. Congress in panic mode over, respectively, 9/11 and the Tonkin Gulf incident, and passed as joint resolutions, not as declarations of war. With no end in sight in either case, Congress, even members of his own party, started abandoning the president. In both wars the United States had few allies and faced much international criticism.

The greatest similarity was in U.S. public opinion, which declined in both wars over time and in response to U.S. casualties. Support for both wars started at around 70 percent but fell by half after three years. Americans dislike long, inconclusive wars. (Actually, Sun Tzu said 2,500 years ago: "No one ever benefits from a long war.") Arguments widely accepted early in the wars—"stopping communism" and "war on terror"—persuaded fewer and fewer Americans. At the end of 2006, U.S. war dead in Iraq passed 3,000 (along with some 100,000 Iraqis).

In both Vietnam and Iraq there were no nice ways to exit. Both wars reduced the president's party to minority status. Nixon won in 1968 vowing "peace with honor" but brought neither. Leaving Iraq quickly could bring complete chaos and regional war, but staying in a worsening situation was leading to the same. In late 2006, a distinguished bipartisan committee called the Iraq situation "grave and deteriorating" and urged withdrawal. Bush rejected the idea and even increased U.S. troop strength. He saw progress and swore we would stay until "victory." He deemed our training of Iraqi police and army successful. The goal of Iraqi democracy was forgotten. As Vermont Republican Senator George Akin urged for Vietnam: "Declare victory and get out."

The great difficulty, not seriously considered in prewar Pentagon planning, was that Iraq had never jelled as one country. Conflict among Sunni, Shi'a, and Kurds was murderous. Many Sunni did not believe they were only a fifth of Iraq's population; they thought they were about half and deserved to rule Iraq, as they always had. Saddam gave all important jobs to Sunni Arabs, especially those from his own clan. The 2003 war dethroned them, and the 2005 elections (see page 289) gave ruling power to the Shi'a, 62 percent of the population, whom the Sunni despise. Most violence in Iraq is caused by Sunni car bombs against the Shi'a, who now own the police and army and retaliate by murdering Sunni at random. Sunni are routinely kidnapped and killed by security police in official uniforms and vehicles. By 2004 Iraq was in a low-level civil war that kept getting worse. The Sunni bombing of a major Shi'a shrine in Samara in February 2006 marked a major escalation. Americans were not happy at being in the middle of someone else's civil war, but many Americans and Iraqis agreed that the United States had to stay until things calmed, an optimistic notion.

IRAQ'S KURDS

Iraqi Kurds do not call themselves Iraqis, and no Iraqi flags fly in Iraqi Kurdistan. They were never happy about being included in Iraq after World War I and asked the new League of Nations to give them their own country (see Chapter 8). Britain and the new Republic of Turkey put a quick stop to that. Making up about 20 percent of Iraq's population, at times Kurds have revolted and fought running civil wars with Baghdad (and with neighboring Turkey). Fearing that the Kurds favored Iran in the Iran-Iraq war, Saddam gassed forty-nine Kurdish villages in 1988. Mothers died trying to shield their children from the toxic fumes. By gas and executions, Saddam killed some 100,000 Kurds in 1988. Thundered the Iraqi general in charge: "I will kill them all with chemical weapons! Who is going to say anything? The international community?" U.S. officials soon learned of the gas attacks but said little and did nothing to stop them. Both Iran and Iraq used poison gas in their war in the 1980s.

After the 1991 Gulf War, Iraq's Kurdish area became de facto independent. Saddam's army moved in to kill Kurds after U.S. policy let him survive in power but warned him to keep out of the mountainous area in the northeast of the country where most Kurds lived. In fear of their lives, Kurds fled their homes in the mostly Kurdish cities of Mosul and Kirkuk, which Saddam had been repopulating for years with Sunni Arabs who would be loyal and grateful. In harsh conditions, Kurds survived only with U.S. air cover and aid shipments. Saddam's army learned to keep back and send no aircraft into the "no-fly zone" north of Kirkuk.

The hardy Kurds adjusted to their unfortunate circumstances and even prospered and enjoyed their autonomy. With considerable oil fields and astride the main highway from Iraq into Turkey, Kurds made money from the trucks smuggling oil north and merchandise going south. The area's two main parties—the Kurdish Democratic party (KDP) and Patriotic Union of Kurdistan (PUK), who fought each other in the 1990s—now run and rule as a combined slate under party strongmen who tolerate no opposition. During the 2003 war, U.S. airborne dropped in to help the Kurds liberate Mosul and Kirkuk. Iraq's Kurds are pro-American, figuring that the U.S. presence protects them. If the U.S. position in Iraq becomes untenable, some suggest we pull back to Kurdistan.

G Geography

FEDERAL IRAQ?

Americans like **federalism** and think it is the natural solution to many political problems. There is nothing natural or easy about federalism. To work, it must be carefully crafted and balanced. A federal system may contain **particularistic** cultures, but they cannot be totally different from one another. Major differences in language, religion, or economics often lead to breakaway movements, as in Quebec, India's Punjab, and Croatia. All three Communist federal systems collapsed after their respective dictatorships were lifted: the Soviet Union, Yugoslavia, and Czechoslovakia. Even the United States split in two in the 1860s.

A successful federal system requires loyalties and responsibilities divided and balanced between the subunits and the central capital. If the subunits have too much autonomy, the system turns into a **confederation** and usually then falls apart, the fate of Yugoslavia. If the center has too much power, the system turns **unitary** with the subunits as little more than administrative conveniences, as in Stalin's Soviet Union. Federal institutions, such as the U.S. Senate or German Bundesrat, must give neither too much nor too little representation to states. There is one federal Arab state, the United Arab Emirates (UAE), formed in 1971 out of six quarrelsome principalities on the southeast shore of the Persian Gulf (a seventh joined later). It works rather well but has few ethnic or religious divisions and a big Sunni majority.

Can federalism work in Iraq? Considering its particularistic differences—Kurds in the north, Sunnis in the center, and Shi'a in the south—federalism sounds like a solution. But their differences may be too great. Few are Iraqi patriots, loyal to Iraq as a whole. Sunni Arabs claim to be Iraqi patriots because they view Iraq as "their thing," with themselves its natural leading element. Their western region of Iraq has little oil, so they demand a unitary system that guarantees them a share of Iraq's oil revenues. The Kurdish north and Shi'a south have Iraq's oil fields and plan on keeping most of the oil revenues for themselves. The Kurds might go along with a confederal system that left them alone. Shi'a parties are already building an Iranian-style Islamic republic in their region. A federal Iraq could fall apart. Too much power in Baghdad, however, could ignite **center-periphery tensions** that have plagued Iraq for all its existence. There will be no easy federal solution for Iraq.

How then to merge an autonomous Kurdistan into Iraq? In a free election, most Iraqi Kurds would vote for independence, but Kurdish leaders say that they could live within a federal Iraq, provided that they governed themselves and kept their own army, the tough *peshmerga*. The 2005 constitution granted most

---

federalism   Division and balancing of powers between central government and autonomous divisions, such as U.S. states and German *Länder*.

particularism   Regional feeling that its culture is distinct and must be preserved, as in Texas and Bavaria.

confederation   Extreme form of federalism with subunits able to override the central government, as in the U.S. Articles of Confederation or the southern Confederacy.

unitary   System that concentrates most power in the nation's capital with little autonomy left to territorial divisions.

center-periphery tensions   Resentment of outlying areas against rule by the nation's capital.

Kurdish demands. With control of the cities of Mosul and Kirkuk and oil fields, the Kurdish economy boomed. Turkey will not stand for an independent Kurdistan in Iraq, as it would encourage Turkish Kurds to demand autonomy or even union of the southeast quarter of Turkey with the Iraqi portion to make a large Kurdistan. (Iran fears the same thing among its Kurds.) Turkey fought a gruesome fifteen-year civil war that cost over 30,000 lives to crush the PKK, the Kurdish Workers party, which sought to separate from Turkey. Fear of Turkish invasion persuades most Iraqi Kurdish leaders to pretend to be part of Iraq while practicing near-independence.

THE SHI'A PROBLEM

The other problem is in roughly the southern half of Iraq, occupied mostly by Shi'a, a majority of Iraq's population but one always shortchanged in political power and wealth. Many Shi'a hated and feared Saddam, and some now copy the Shi'a fundamentalist government in neighboring Iran. Shi'a clerics found refuge from Saddam in Iran, but for 1,300 years the historical and religious heart of Shi'a has been not the holy city of Qum, Iran, but the holy Iraqi cities of Najaf and Karbala, which see Qum as a rival and upstart.

After the 1991 war, Iraq's Shi'a rose up and might have won with a little U.S. help. U.S. and other coalition forces had liberated much of their territory, and President Bush 41 at first encouraged Iraq's Shi'a (and Kurds) to overthrow the brutal Saddam, which many were glad to do. Bush was mistaken in thinking that the weakened Saddam would soon be ousted with no help from us. Saddam had lost part of his army, but his great strength was his security police and Baath party, which were intact and kept him in power. Washington had second thoughts about the uprising when Iran-based Shi'a fighters infiltrated the south of Iraq to spread Islamic revolution. Opposed to Iran as much as to Iraq, we did not attempt to stop Saddam's Baath party members and security services from executing some 30,000 Shi'a, including top clerics, on suspicion of disloyalty. After the 2003 war, mass graves of Saddam's Shi'a victims—bound, blindfolded, and shot in the head, some of them children—were found in several places. It is for this reason that Iraqi Shi'a now mistrust the Americans and want us to leave. Never tell people to revolt against tyranny unless you are prepared to help them all the way, a lesson we should have learned from the Hungarian Revolution of 1956.

Iraq's Shi'a follow their imams, especially Grand Ayatollah Ali al-Sistani, who was born and raised in Iran. Unlike Khomeini in Iran, Sistani followed the Shi'a tradition of no direct role in politics. A word from Sistani, however, to vote for the constitution or the Supreme Council for the Islamic Revolution in Iraq (SCIRI) turned out millions of Shi'a voters. SCIRI was founded in 1982 in Iran; its Badr Corps made raids from Iran into Iraq. Now the Badr Corps—with Iranian money, arms, and agents—has set up an Iranian-style Islamist republic in Basra, where women are veiled and alcohol is illegal. Iran was the only winner of the 2003 war. It got rid of a terrible enemy to its west (Saddam) and gained a Shi'a-dominated Iraq, in which it had great influence.

Becoming part of Iran or splitting away from Iraq is not the Shi'a goal. Unlike the Kurds, they do not want a separate state but want to run a federal Islamist Iraq, and they feel entitled to do so based on their numbers and their cruel mistreatment at the hands of Sunni: "Now it's our turn!" One project Shi'a sought and got was to reflood the vast marshes where the Tigris and Euphrates flow together and where many of their ancestors, the so-called "Marsh Arabs," had lived for centuries. Saddam, to crush the Shi'a revolt, drained these marshes, turning them into desert. Iraqi Shi'a swear they will never again live under Sunni Arab rule. In 2005 they had the votes to get a Shi'a government, whereas angry Sunni claimed they had been shortchanged. It will be hard reconciling these very different visions of Iraq.

THE FUTURE OF IRAQ

Iraq could easily slide into either of two bad outcomes. It could fall apart into three separate countries—Kurds in the north, Sunni in the west, and Shi'a in the south. Some advocated letting Iraq divide into its "natural" countries as a way to settle things. They argue that Iraq was a mistaken, fake entity to begin with, a British imperial construct.

The breakup solution is tempting but dangerous. Iraq would not break apart peacefully. Sunni bombers target Shi'a mosques, funerals, and holy sites trying to start a civil war. Shi'a militia inside the police form death squads to take revenge on Sunni. Both Sunni and Shi'a practice "ethnic cleansing" to rid their neighborhoods of the other group. In a full-scale civil war, Sunni would call for help from brother Sunni countries such as Saudi Arabia, Jordan, and Egypt, who might come to the rescue. Iran would come to the aid of its Shi'a brethren and, with a bigger and better army, likely defeat Sunni Arab intervention. Iraq's oilfields would be shut or ablaze, depriving the world of 2 million barrels of oil a day. World oil prices would top $100 a barrel, leading to a global depression. A civil war would quickly escalate into a regional war into which the United States would be drawn in fear that Iran would annex or dominate Iraq. The breakup of Iraq could lead to a U.S.-Iran war.

The other scenario—perhaps slightly less bad—is the rise of a new Iraqi dictatorship, this time in Shi'a hands. Saddam was no accident; countries like Iraq slide easily into *praetorianism* (see page 46). As we saw in Turkey, when civilian rule breaks down amid chaos, the military takes over to "save" the country. Dictatorship is one of the few ways to govern a fragmented, unruly country. Rulers who try to be nice in countries like Iraq are soon overthrown by ruthless types like Saddam, who preemptively murder all possible opponents. Democracy does not take root everywhere (see Chapter 15).

The mechanism for a new Iraqi dictatorship is already visible. We are training it: the Iraqi army. The more we build a cohesive, powerful Iraqi army, the more likely its generals will use it to seize power. This may produce stability but not democracy. The United States has experience in manufacturing praetorianism. In the interwar years, U.S. Marines landed in several Caribbean and Central American republics to restore order. As part of this, they trained a local national guard, which then took over the country and ran it for decades (example: the Somoza dynasty that ruled Nicaragua from 1934 to 1979).

CONCLUSIONS

9/11 propelled a vengeful United States into two wars, in Afghanistan in 2001 and Iraq in 2003. Al Qaeda was headquartered in Afghanistan, whose fundamentalist Taliban regime refused to turn its leaders over to us. America had great world support in overthrowing the Taliban, which was done quickly and cheaply by Special Forces helping local anti-Taliban fighters. The Taliban, based in Pakistan, have regrouped, and Afghanistan is untamed.

In late 2001 Bush 43, bolstered by neoconservatives, decided to also take out the tyrannical regime of Saddam Hussein in Iraq. During 2002, as his plans became clearer, most of the world parted company with the United States. Many did not believe that Iraq's alleged WMD or ties to terrorism warranted a war. The UN Security Council had condemned Iraq many times but refused to authorize war, so Bush proceeded unilaterally. After the war, no gas or bugs were found.

The 2003 war itself was brilliant and quick, but the too-few U.S. troops could not control the chaotic aftermath. All authority collapsed, and massive civil strife broke out. American enthusiasm for the occupation of Iraq declined over time and with mounting casualties. Under U.S. supervision, Iraqis struggled to found a democracy, but Sunni, Kurds, and Shi'a (a majority of Iraqis) have conflicting expectations of a federal Iraq. (For more on Iraqi democracy, see Chapter 15.) There is no nice U.S. exit from Iraq.

KEY TERMS

center-periphery tensions (p. 272)　　neo-conservative (p. 262)
Central Asia (p. 260)　　particularism (p. 272)
confederation (p. 272)　　precision guided munitions (p. 267)
conflate (p. 257)　　revolution in military affairs (p. 267)
federalism (p. 272)　　Security Council (p. 263)
lines of communication (p. 265)　　sphere of influence (p. 259)
mujahedin (p. 260)　　Taliban (p. 259)
National Security Council (p. 264)　　unitary (p. 272)

FURTHER REFERENCE

Ajami, Fouad. *The Foreigners' Gift: The Americans, the Arabs, and the Iraqis in Iraq.* New York: Free Press, 2006.
Allawi, Ali A. *The Occupation of Iraq: Winning the War, Losing the Peace.* New Haven, CT: Yale University Press, 2007.

Beeman, William O. *Iraq, a State in Search of a Nation*. Westport, CT: Praeger, 2005.

Blix, Hans. *Disarming Iraq*. New York: Knopf, 2004.

Bremer, L. Paul. *My Year in Iraq: The Struggle to Build a Future of Hope*. New York: Simon & Schuster, 2006.

Brigham, Robert K. *Is Iraq Another Vietnam?* New York: PublicAffairs, 2007.

Campbell, Kenneth J. *A Tale of Two Quagmires: Iraq, Vietnam, and the Hard Lessons of War*. Boulder, CO: Paradigm, 2007.

Cordesman, Anthony H. *The Iraq War*. Westport, CT: Praeger, 2003.

Diamond, Larry. *Squandered Victory: The American Occupation and the Bungled Effort to Bring Democracy to Iraq*. New York: Times Books, 2005.

Fawn, Rick, and Raymond Hinnebusch, eds. *The Iraq War: Causes and Consequences*. Boulder, CO: Lynne Rienner, 2006.

Galbraith, Peter W. *The End of Iraq: How American Incompetence Created a War without End*. New York: Simon & Schuster, 2006.

Gordon, Michael R., and Bernard E. Trainor. *Cobra II: The Inside Story of the Invasion and Occupation of Iraq*. New York: Pantheon, 2006.

Hashim, Ahmed S. *Insurgency and Counter-Insurgency in Iraq*. Ithaca, NY: Cornell University Press, 2006.

Hersh, Seymour M. *Chain of Command: The Road from 9/11 to Abu Ghraib*. New York: HarperCollins, 2004.

Malone, David M., Ben Rowswell, and Markus E. Bouillon, eds. *Iraq: Preventing a New Generation of Conflict*. Boulder, CO: Lynne Rienner, 2007.

Packer, George. *The Assassin's Gate: America in Iraq*. New York: Farrar, Straus and Giroux, 2005.

Phillips, David L. *Losing Iraq: Inside the Postwar Reconstruction Fiasco*. Boulder, CO: Westview, 2005.

Record, Jeffrey. *Dark Victory: America's Second War against Iraq*. Annapolis, MD: Naval Institute Press, 2004.

Ricks, Thomas F. *Fiasco: The American Military Adventure in Iraq*. New York: Penguin, 2006.

Shadid, Anthony. *Night Draws Near: Iraq's People in the Shadow of America's War*. New York: Henry Holt, 2005.

Stewart, Rory. *The Prince of the Marshes, and Other Occupational Hazards of a Year in Iraq*. San Diego, CA: Harcourt, 2006.

Woodward, Bob. *State of Denial: Bush at War, Part III*. New York: Simon & Schuster, 2006.

15 Middle Eastern Modernization and Democratization

The topics of these final three chapters are interrelated; one subject feeds logically into the other. *Modernization* sets the stage for a country's *democratization*. Modernization, however, is the difficult transition between traditional and modern, during which much can go wrong. Most of the Middle East is now undergoing rapid modernization; it is a work in progress. We cover these two topics in this chapter.

Democratization in the Middle East, however, leads to the emergence of *political Islam;* they are, after all, Muslim countries in which religion has always loomed large. A politicized Islamic faith can lead down either moderate or extremist paths, the latter to *terrorism.* We cover these topics in Chapter 16. Altogether, these four topics pose major questions for U.S. foreign policy in the Middle East, which we discuss in Chapter 17: What, if anything, can we do about all this?

FAILURE OF MODERNIZATION?

Modernization is inevitable and happening at an accelerating rate. The question is how the Middle East will become modern. It will not emerge as identical to the West; it will keep much of its traditional values. The rapid exchange of products,

Traditional Arab transport plods past an Israeli kibbutz, an outpost of modern farming methods. Israeli culture, essentially European, moves quickly. Arab culture moves slowly. (*Michael G. Roskin*)

people, and ideas make societies modern whether or not they wish to be. Population growth and massive unemployment make economic modernization imperative. Even Islamists who decry Western (especially U.S.) cultural imperialism use television and the Web to preach their views.

Many analysts of the Middle East see its present crisis as a failure of modernization, a view that has been around for centuries and is voiced today by both Western and Muslim intellectuals. A thousand years ago, Muslims were far ahead of Christian Europe, but about five hundred years ago the balance began to shift. Europe was rapidly modernizing and the Ottoman Empire was not. The 1571 naval battle of Lepanto, in which a joint Venetian, Spanish, and Austrian fleet defeated an Ottoman fleet, was a sign that power was shifting. At the time, when the Ottoman Empire was at its peak, the Ottomans dismissed Lepanto as a minor setback. The Turks dominated the Mediterranean and Black Seas, the Middle East and Balkans, and twice besieged Vienna.

More decisive pushbacks of Ottoman power came in 1683 when they failed to take Vienna for the second time and the 1699 Treaty of Karlowitz, which freed Hungary and Transylvania from Ottoman rule. By 1878, Russia had pushed the Turks out of Romania and Bulgaria and neared Istanbul. By the time World War I began, the Ottomans held only a little corner of Europe (still part of Turkey).

Why could the Turks not respond to these defeats by modernizing their society and beating the Europeans at their own game? Increasingly, Ottomans themselves asked this question, and demands for reform stirred the Empire in the

K : Key Concepts

MODERNIZATION THEORY

Modernization theory, a broad-brush term that traces back at least to Hegel, argues that all facets of a society hang together as a package. If you change one important element, you soon change everything else. For example, when you bring manufacturing into an agricultural society, you also bring urbanization, education, higher standards of living, and mass communications, as well as shifts in customs, tastes, and expectations. After some decades of such changes and much turmoil, the traditional society becomes modern. The transition phase is called **modernization**, and it is a tumultuous and risky time when nations frequently break down into authoritarianism.

Modernization theorists, drawing heavily on Max Weber and perhaps too focused on Europe and Asia, also expected that modernization would diminish the role of religion. But in the Middle East, secularization did not accompany modernization, and some societies, in reaction to the strains of rapid change, became more religious than ever and resist modernization. (For more on this, see Chapter 16.)

At a certain point during the modernization process, demands for democratization rise. Countries with **per capita GDPs** below $5,000 have trouble establishing democracies, but ones with per capita GDP of $6,000 or higher ("middle-income countries") can usually establish democracies. Attempts at democracy in poor lands tend to fail as populist **demagogues** or military officers turn themselves into authoritarian rulers. Democracy seldom takes hold in poor countries. India is an interesting exception; neighboring Pakistan with its alternating civilian and military rulers is more typical of the Third World. Middle-income countries, however, have large and educated middle classes, and they form the bases of democracy. Demagogues do not fool middle-class citizens, who reject demagogic promises and vote for moderate politicians with feasible programs. Most middle-income and richer countries are stable democracies. As Taiwan, South Korea, Brazil, and Mexico achieved middle-income status, they turned from authoritarian to democratic.

But, warn modernization theorists, if you push this process too fast, before the system is ready for democracy, it can break down into authoritarianism (example: Russia under Putin). How can you tell when small children are ready to walk? When they get up and start walking. Pushed too soon, they simply fall down.

late nineteenth century. In 1908 the Young Turk movement of military officers (one of them: Mustafa Kemal, later known as Atatürk) attempted to reform and modernize the Empire. They were only partially successful because key elements of the Empire did not wish to become like Europe. The Ottoman Empire was old, complex, carefully balanced, and based on an Islamic legitimacy in which the temporal ruler, the sultan, was also the spiritual ruler, the caliph (successor to the Prophet). Serious modernization would rip this structure apart.

modernization   The process of shifting from traditional to modern.

per capita GDP   Sum total of what is produced in a country in a year, divided by population; a measure of prosperity.

demagogue   Politician, often *charismatic,* who manipulates masses with deceptive promises.

Key Concepts

THE HUNTINGTON CHALLENGE

Harvard political scientist Samuel P. Huntington jolted both academics and policy makers with his 1993 article in *Foreign Affairs,* "The Clash of **Civilizations**," later expanded into a book. Huntington saw several civilizations, most of them based on religion, which is a major component of culture:

Western—Formed from Western Christianity (Catholic or Protestant), with European and North American branches.

Slavic/Orthodox—Formed from Eastern Christianity, such as Russia and Serbia.

Islamic

Sinic—East Asia countries of Confucian background, such as China and Korea.

Hindu—India as a separate civilization.

Japanese—Borrowed much from the Sinic and the Western but a separate civilization because it bent everything it borrowed.

Latin American—Mostly Catholic, but an odd blend of European, native American, and North American influences.

African

Huntington sometimes included Buddhist, such as Sri Lanka and Thailand, as a civilization, but it consists of few countries and they show little solidarity among themselves.

Within a civilization, countries can generally understand and get along with each other. Between civilizations, though, misunderstanding is frequent and sometimes hostile. Huntington argued that the Cold War had covered over these tensions, but with the Cold War over they had come out with renewed vigor and were now the main dynamic of world politics. Not all civilizations clash; Latin American civilization gets along with all the others. Huntington's theory explained why Poland, the Czech Republic, and Hungary turned quickly to democracy and market economies while Russia, Ukraine, and Bulgaria did not. The former, mostly Catholic, were returning to their roots in Western civilization while the latter, mostly Eastern Orthodox, resisted adopting Western patterns.

Instead, the Ottomans embarked on halfway and half-hearted modernization. "We will copy the Europeans in some things," decided the Ottoman elite, "but preserve our overall traditional system." This was not possible, as partial modernization leaves the job undone. The Ottomans, for example, could modernize their military with Western-type weapons and uniforms. But a modern army needs an industrial base to make the weapons. This means factories, workers, entrepreneurs, engineers, and transportation networks. You need an educated officer corps to organize and train the army. You need modern universities and military academies. In short, you cannot become just a little bit modern; you have to go all the way, which the Ottomans refused to do.

---

civilization   In Huntington's theory, a large area of shared culture based mostly on religion.

The real problem, wrote Huntington, is Islamic civilization, which clashes with most of the others: "Islam has bloody borders." As he was writing, a three-sided civil war in ex-Yugoslavia set Catholic Croats, Orthodox Serbs, and Bosnian Muslims against each other, a perfect illustration of Huntington's theory, which fit many other areas: Russians against Chechens, Indians against Pakistanis, Israelis against Palestinians, and Americans against Islamic fundamentalists.

Not everything fit Huntington's theory. Muslim countries also fought each other, as did Iraq and Iran through the 1980s. In 1990 and 1991, the West made common cause with several Muslim countries to expel Iraq from Kuwait. Even in 2003, America got cooperation from some Persian Gulf countries. Increasingly, Europe and the United States quarrel over everything from the Iraq War to beef imports and capital punishment. NATO was hollowed out until it became a paper alliance. American thinkers had long explained U.S. culture as a repudiation of Europe, not an extension of it.

Huntington's challenge was to the sometimes glib assumptions that after the Cold War a single, happy world would emerge. Francis Fukuyama (perhaps trying to be provocative) wrote of the "end of history": After communism there are no ideological alternatives to capitalist democracy. Thomas Friedman of *The New York Times* became a prophet of **globalization**, proclaiming as inevitable and wonderful the free flow of goods, capital, and information that would uplift poor countries and unify the globe. Fukuyama and Friedman foresaw a "universal" culture that is a lot like America. Actually, globalization is an old vision, going back to at least the optimistic Victorians of the nineteenth century, a vision that collapsed in World War I.

Huntington's challenge was also to the sometimes glib "nation builders" of both the Clinton and Bush 43 administrations, who supposed democracy could be set up just about anywhere, even in Iraq. Those who are culturally at odds with the West do not strive to become like the West; they reject the West: "We are not like you and do not wish to become like you." As American and British forces liberated Iraq, many political views appeared among Iraqis. Only a few intellectuals, some of them returning from exile in the West, proposed secular democracy. The biggest single political current was among the Shi'a majority of Iraq, many of whom embraced an Islamic republic modeled on Iran's. The Kurds of the north of Iraq, who had been autonomous for more than a decade, had a sort of democracy, although it was dominated by clan loyalties and strong leaders. And more than a few Iraqis harkened to the stability of the brutal Saddam regime. "At least then we had jobs and electricity," was their cry. Growing a democracy in Iraqi soil was difficult. Huntington warned us in advance.

By way of contrast, starting with the 1868 Meiji Restoration Japan embraced thorough modernization. So secure are Japanese in their Japaneseness (*nihonjinron*) that they did not fear Western ways. In one generation, Japan went from traditional to modern, copying the West in everything from industry and education to medical care and naval warfare. Why could the Japanese do it and the Turks not? The answer in part is cultural. Japan had long imported foreign culture—for example, Buddhism and Confucianism from China—but always bent and shaped it to suit Japanese needs. Japanese religions are vague, flexible, and no barrier to modernization, the opposite of the rigidities of Islam. Shintoism and Buddhism have no single book or doctrine and can mutate without limit. Japan's emperor was a living god

globalization   The world becoming one big, capitalist market.

for Japanese, but he was largely a figurehead and neither a sultan nor a caliph. Japanese did not fear that modernization would erase their culture; indeed, it was only by modernizing that Japan could preserve itself. Japan's ability to modernize is rare, however. Adaptability and flexibility like that is so far found only in East Asia.

Many Arab intellectuals agree that the underlying problem is an Arab cultural antipathy to modernization that urgently needs to be overcome. Several of them coauthored a series of UN studies, *The Arab Human Development Reports,* which found corruption, declining economies, lagging science and technology, widespread illiteracy, suppression of women, poor governance, and no political freedoms, elections, or media. The *Reports* jolted the Arab world and encouraged some regimes to reform a little.

READY FOR DEMOCRACY?

As the clouds of the Iraq War gathered in 2002, some of the hawkish neo-conservatives who supported war included among their reasons a chance to democratize the Middle East. Knocking out the Saddam regime, they argued, would not only curb weapons of mass destruction and terrorism but allow the United States to set up a democracy that would in turn encourage democracy in other Middle Eastern countries. Iraq would be a demonstration project for the entire region. America would reform the Middle East. President Bush 43 asserted that all people crave democracy, and Americans would help them achieve it.

In 2004 the Bush administration floated a "Greater Middle East initiative" to bring democracy to the entire region but did not consult in advance with any of its leaders. Egypt's President Hosni Mubark summed up the region's chilly rejection: "Whoever imagines that it is possible to impose solutions or reform from abroad is delusional. All peoples by their nature reject whoever tries to impose ideas on them." Nothing more was heard of the Greater Middle East initiative. The Iraqi and Egyptian elections of 2005 and Palestinian elections of 2006 did not lead to democratic governance. Elections do not equal democracy.

Most experts on the Middle East and on democracy saw little chance of it. Iraq, and indeed most of the region, is far from ready for democracy, critics claimed. The Republicans themselves had scoffed at the Clinton administration's policies of "enlargement of democracy" and "nation-building" as muddle-headed "international social work." Indeed, the long-standing conservative view is that societies change themselves; efforts to speed up or guide this process are dangerous meddling, whether practiced by liberals or Leninists. But the proponents of democracy for Iraq were not conservatives; they were neo-conservatives, people from liberal backgrounds who rejected the **relativism** and pacifism they claimed had taken over the American intellectual left. Traditional conservatives are skeptical of activism; neo-conservatives like muscular intervention. The two strands at first coexisted uneasily within the Bush 43 administration but broke apart over Iraq.

---

relativism   View that there is no absolute morality and that social and political questions are complex and ambiguous.

Cultures

WOMEN AND DEMOCRACY

The treatment of women is connected to democratization, although it is hard to tell which causes which. Often the two improve simultaneously. Islam traditionally consigned women to an inferior role, although there are many regional variations. They got little or no education and were expected to stay home and bear children. Women's testimony in court was worth half that of men, and women were entitled to only a half share in wills. Husbands could shed wives by the simple declamation, "I divorce thee." Women had to go through elaborate Shari'a procedures.

Things are changing rapidly. The Arab **fertility rate** has fallen by half in two decades. The average woman in Oman bore ten children twenty years ago but now bears under four (still quite high). There are several reasons for this. Over a generation, the age of marriage has risen markedly. Unemployed young men cannot afford brides, and apartments are expensive. Arab women are getting far more education. Saudi girls were allowed to go to school only in 1964; now more than half of Saudi university students are women (70 percent in Qatar and Kuwait). More education means fewer babies and more pressure for women's rights.

Could the Middle East eventually turn democratic? You have to **disaggregate**, as each country is different. Most are still poor. Some oil kingdoms enjoy high per capita GDPs, but they are based on an accident of nature, not on the slow and arduous growth of industry. Their incomes are badly distributed, with few rich and many poor people. They have a sort of fake middle class that depends on government jobs and handouts but lacks the autonomy and interest groups of a real middle class. Non-economic factors also work against Middle Eastern democracy. Regional, ethnic, and religious differences rend many lands in the region. But some have a growing, educated middle class that could handle democracy.

Some cultures resist becoming modern or democratic. Their religions may reject both. And under certain circumstances modernization might lead not to democracy but to vicious and well-armed dictatorships. Some modernize but resist becoming democratic. Malaysia, 60 percent Muslim, enjoyed rapid economic growth—from poverty in the 1960s to a middle-income $9,000 per cap by 2000—but grew *less* democratic, declining in the FH rating from "free" to "partly free." Those who crossed Malaysia's president got in bad trouble. (If modernization theory is correct, Malaysia could soon become a democracy.) Fareed Zakaria reminds us that elections can produce **illiberal democracy**, where a majority votes for regimes that silence dissent, repress others, or march to war. Hezbollah won seats in Lebanon's parliament and two cabinet ministries but did not give up its arms and

---

fertility rate   Number of children average woman bears (not same as *birth rate*).

disaggregate   To break apart or unbundle.

illiberal democracy   Free elections that produce extremist or intolerant governments.

even incited a new war with Israel in 2006. Americans tend to equate elections with democracy, but democracy is far more complex than just elections.

Free elections in the Middle East could bring radical Islamists to power, and they would not be democratic or peace-loving: one man, one vote, one time. Said a Jordanian intelligence official: "For the Islamic fundamentalists, democratic reform is like toilet paper. You use it once and throw it away." The best we can hope for, some say, are moderate and rational authoritarian regimes that stress stability and economic growth. But others point to non-fanatic Islamic parties that could lead to democracy. A moderate Islamist party governs Turkey.

Much depends on how the transition is carried out. In Brazil, a well-managed period of "decompression" made opposition parties legal and elections clean, and eased the way to stable democracy. If we persist in supporting dictatorial regimes, some liberals charge, moderates will give up and turn to revolution. The shah of Iran never decompressed his dictatorial rule; he had no plans to relinquish power. The result was his violent overthrow and the takeover by extremists, who shot the moderates. Iranian democracy never had a chance because the shah made sure there would be no transition. Will Egypt and Saudi Arabia make the same mistake of waiting until it is too late? As President Kennedy said: "Those who make peaceful revolution impossible, make violent revolution inevitable."

Are the countries of the region sufficiently advanced in economic terms to make a transition to democracy? It is hard to tell. The countries of the **Gulf Cooperation Council** (GCC)—Kuwait, Saudi Arabia, Bahrain, Qatar, United Arab Emirates, and Oman—enjoyed spectacular growth since World War II, based either on oil or servicing the oil and shipping industries. Current projections give the Gulf states about a hundred years as major oil producers. Within living memory, they went from camels and kerosene lamps to glittering high-rises and e-trading. Since 1960, GCC population has risen sixfold, the fastest growth in the world, partly through the world's highest birth rates and partly through massive immigration from poorer countries bordering the Indian Ocean. The net effect of this has been to keep per capita GDP stagnant—in some places declining—as population growth eats up economic growth.

Political, social, and religious modernization did not keep pace with economic growth. There is nothing automatic about modernization. Derided earlier as "tribes with flags," the GCC countries are all hereditary monarchies, some of them (Kuwait and Bahrain) moving cautiously toward democracy. All of these monarchies claim to be in touch with their people through the *majlis,* local receptions open to all men in which the visiting prince dispenses advice and money to individual pleaders. Charming, but hardly democracy.

The GDP of Spain exceeds that of all twenty-two Arab countries combined, including oil producers. These Arab states currently have a combined population of 300 million (the same as the United States), but by 2020 it is projected to reach between 410 and 459 million. Many will be jobless and angry. Arab thinkers recognize that something must be done, and soon.

Gulf Cooperation Council   Loose grouping of monarchies on southern shore of Persian Gulf.

K ⋮ *Key Concepts*

CIVIL SOCIETY

Philosophers have recognized for centuries that what makes any society work is only partly government institutions such as kings, parliaments, and officials. Much depends on the associations that form in the large area between family and government: clubs, religions, businesses, even informal networks of neighbors and coworkers talking with one another. British philosopher Edmund Burke called them "the little platoons of society." This **civil society** is widely believed to be the foundation of stability and democracy. Pluralistic habits grow out of associations not controlled by government. Can the United States promote civil society, or is it something that each country must develop itself?

If civil society is undeveloped or has been deliberately crushed by a dictatorship, order and democracy will have rough going. Totalitarian systems, such as Stalin's, extend state power over civil society and carefully control it. No church, club, or business is free; all are run or supervised by the single ruling party and its dictator. It was neglect of this factor that tripped up reform in post-Soviet Russia. We supposed that once the Communist regime was ousted, a happy, prosperous, and democratic Russia would quickly emerge. Instead, lawlessness and decline led to the authoritarian regime of President Putin. In contrast, Poland, which had a civil society—much of it centered on its defiant Roman Catholic Church—emerged quickly from communism to a market economy and democracy.

Saddam, who modeled himself after Stalin, likewise stomped out civil society in Iraq. All religions were controlled, most of the economy was state-owned, and his Baath party supervised everything. Saddam's regime even penetrated the family and neighborhood. Relatives and neighbors learned to say nothing political; the other person might be an informer. Iraqis learned to trust no one, an attitude still present. When the Saddam regime collapsed, it left behind little civil society to promote order and democracy. It left a vacuum partly filled by the Shi'a clergy. In several cities, including Shi'a areas of Baghdad, mullahs, exuding natural authority and organizational skills, took over and ran hospitals, charities, and city cleanup. They also instituted Iranian-style Islamist controls.

In Middle East countries the space between family and government is dominated by mosques and mullahs. Nothing else has a fraction of their influence. Churches are important in the West (especially in America), but so are corporations, labor unions, and affinity groups. Most Muslim countries have little of these. When you overthrow an authoritarian regime in the Middle East in the expectation that civil society will form the basis for democracy, you soon discover organized Islam filling the vacuum. (We will explore political Islam at greater length in the next chapter.)

You cannot fill anarchy with democracy. Efforts to do so will be tumultuous, unstable, and soon taken over by an authoritarian regime, some of them worse than others. Washington was mistaken about post-Saddam Iraq, just as it had been about Russia. Americans supposed that law, order, and democracy spring up spontaneously once you remove a totalitarian regime. They need first the patient cultivation of civil society. Pollsters can actually measure this by asking a cross section of citizens if they think most people can be trusted. Where high, it indicates a civil society. Civil society is likely to take some decades, as it tends to grow with rule of law and the economy. If neither grow, stable democracy is unlikely.

civil society Associations, some informal, between family and state and the pluralistic values that come with them.

Key Concepts

MIDDLE EAST REGIMES

Nothing is simple in the Middle East, and descriptions of the region's regimes require many qualifications. First, we should distinguish between "loose" and "tight" authoritarian regimes. The former permit a little freedom; the latter are control freaks, run by the *mukhabarat,* earning them the title "security states" based largely on the police. A good example was Saddam Hussein's Iraq, which was also a **totalitarian** regime, because his Baath party attempted to control everything, aided by the brutal security police. Nominally, Syria is also run by a Baathist party, but it is little more than a vehicle for personalistic rule, currently by the son of the previous dictator. Israel and Turkey are both parliamentary democracies, but Israel's is stable and Turkey's has at times been unstable.

Iran's regime is the hardest to classify. It has some of the institutions of democracy and some of **theocracy**. Its parliament and president are elected, but from a limited slate supervised by top Muslim clerics, who also veto efforts at liberalization. Iran probably has the greatest democratic potential of the region. The emir (prince) of Qatar has embarked on democratization by permitting an elected assembly and freer media.

Freedom House in New York annually rates countries for both "political rights" and "civil liberties" by giving 1 for most free and 7 for least. The average of these two are shown for 2006 along with FH's classification of "free" (1.0–2.5), "partly free" (3.0–5.0), and "not free" (5.5–7.0). Several countries of the region have improved in recent years. Among FH's worst for 2006 were Iran, Libya, Saudi Arabia, and Sudan.

The prevalence of authoritarian regimes should not be surprising or mysterious. The great German sociologist Max Weber, a century ago, explained **charismatic** authoritarian systems as characteristic of the painful transition from traditional to modern societies. At this in-between stage, traditional **legitimacy**, such as those of monarchs, has broken down, but modern "rational-legal" legitimacy, such as those of democracies, is not yet established. In this time of weakness, powerful personalities seize power by coup and keep power by their security police, control of mass media, and rigged elections.

Democracy-building became a hot topic among American analysts and academics. Is it feasible? Can the United States implant democracy in Iraq or anywhere else? Those in favor point to Germany and Japan after World War II as examples of successful democratization. This is a false analogy; Germany and Japan were industrialized countries with educated populations who had some democratic experience between the two world wars. The Nazis and Japanese militarists had discredited themselves; many citizens hated them and welcomed democracy. In

---

totalitarian   Regime that attempts to control everything and remake society, more thorough than *authoritarian.*

theocracy   Rule by priests.

charismatic   Ability to sway masses by strong personality.

legitimacy   Mass feeling that regime's rule is rightful.

Country	Type	Executive	2006 FH Rating
Afghanistan	attempting democracy	weak president	5.0 partly free
Algeria	military dictatorship	permanent president	5.5 not free
Bahrain	traditional monarchy	hereditary prince	5.0 partly free
Egypt	loose authoritarian	permanent president	5.5 not free
Iran	Islamist semi-democracy	theocrat	6.0 not free
Iraq	attempting democracy	weak PM	5.5 not free
Israel	parliamentary democracy	elected PM	1.5 free
Jordan	traditional monarchy	hereditary king	4.5 partly free
Kuwait	traditional monarchy	hereditary king	4.5 partly free
Lebanon	consociation	president	4.5 partly free
Libya	tight authoritarian	permanent president	7.0 not free
Morocco	traditional monarchy	hereditary king	4.5 partly free
Oman	traditional monarchy	hereditary prince	5.5 not free
Pakistan	military dictatorship	changeable president	5.5 not free
Qatar	modernizing monarchy	hereditary prince	5.5 not free
Saudi Arabia	traditional monarchy	hereditary king	6.5 not free
Sudan	Islamist dictatorship	permanent president	7.0 not free
Syria	tight authoritarian	hereditary president	7.0 not free
Tunisia	one-party dominance	permanent president	5.5 not free
Turkey	parliamentary democracy	elected PM	3.0 partly free
United Arab Emirates	traditional monarchy	hereditary princes	6.0 not free
Yemen	authoritarian	permanent president	5.0 partly free

postwar Germany and Japan, democracy did not start from scratch. In Russia, where it did start from scratch, it failed.

The Middle East has come late to democracy. In the middle of the past century, British General Sir John Bagot Glubb, an old-fashioned imperialist and commander of the Jordanian Arab Legion (see page 82), groused: "We have given them self-government for which they are totally unsuited. They veer naturally toward dictatorship. Democratic institutions are promptly twisted into engines of intrigue." True, Middle East governments have been **authoritarian**, either traditional monarchies or personalistic dictatorships, but are they natural or fostered by foreign powers?

Outside influences have been important. The British, French, Americans, and Soviets never supported democracy in the region. During the Cold War,

authoritarian   Non-democratic governance.

Washington feared Communist or other radical influence and was content to have friendly dictators in power. American support for democracy in the Middle East came only after 9/11. In 2005 Secretary of State Condoleezza Rice told a Cairo university audience: "For sixty years my country—the United States— pursued stability at the expense of democracy in this region, here in the Middle East. And we achieved neither. Now, we are taking a different course. We are supporting the democratic aspirations of all people."

Only Israel is a stable democracy, but it was brought from Europe by Jewish settlers with a democratic political culture and did not apply fully to Israeli Arabs, much less to those in the occupied territories. Turkey has had an unstable democracy; its elected governments operate under an implied military veto. Turkey has had three military coups since World War II and one change of government to avoid a military takeover. Lebanon looked like a democracy for much of the post-war period, but it was a contrived system based on a set allocation of political positions among its many religions, *consociation* (see page 98). The Middle East looked unready to grow democracy.

THE ROCKY IRAQI ROAD

Democracy did not fall automatically into place in Iraq after the 2003 war. The process was longer and harder than the neo-cons had supposed. A democratic structure emerged in 2005, when Iraq held three elections, all of them carried out with reasonable fairness, although the Sunni protested they had been cheated. The first, early in 2005, was for a preliminary parliament to draft a new constitution. No Iraqi census could accurately set the number of seats for each of Iraq's eighteen provinces, so the entire country served as one big electoral district. Many election experts think this is a bad idea. Sunni leaders, who distrusted the whole process, ordered their tribes and clans not to vote, so Sunnis were underrepresented in the new assembly. (If each province had gotten seats based on population, Sunni would have gotten their fair share of seats even with a low turnout.) As expected, a Shi'a coalition took a majority of seats, but to get a constitution all would accept, additional Sunni were invited to participate. It took a half year of wrangling to form a government (see page 289).

Drafting a new constitution was laborious, especially regarding issues of federalism and religion. Some saw excessive Shi'a fundamentalist influence in it. While it does not make the *Shari'a* (see page 33) Iraq's legal system, it specifies that no law may contradict the "established rulings" of Islam. Feminists feared that this could be used to end equal rights for women. The constitution was approved by **referendum** in October 2005, but it was a close call. If a majority in three of Iraq's eighteen provinces had voted no, it would have failed nationwide. And four of Iraq's provinces are predominantly Sunni Arab, the group with the biggest grudge.

---

referendum   Mass vote on an issue rather than for candidates.

D : *Domestic Structures*

IRAQI DEMOCRACY

On paper, Iraqi democracy is an example of a parliamentary system chosen by proportional representation. It resembles European systems but does not function as smoothly. Each of Iraq's eighteen governorates (provinces) gets seats in a 275-member assembly in proportion to number of registered voters (based on population would be fairer), ranging from five seats for desert Muthanna in the south to fifty-nine for giant Baghdad. In each province, parties publish a list of their candidates; voters choose one list. Every party that wins over 5 percent in that province gets seats in proportion to its percentage. A party that wins 25 percent in a province entitled to sixteen seats gets four seats, the first four names on its list. That accounts for 230 seats. The remaining forty-five "compensatory" seats are used to even up numerical discrepancies at the national level, as in Sweden. The December 2005 Iraqi elections saw an impressive 80 percent turnout with the following results:

Party	Representing	Percent of Vote	Seats
United Iraqi Alliance	several Shi'a parties	41.2	128
Democratic Patriotic Alliance of Kurdistan	two main Kurdish parties	21.7	53
Iraqi Accord Front	Sunni Islamic parties	15.1	44
Iraqi National List	secular, all groups	8.0	25
Iraqi National Dialogue Front	moderate Sunni and others	4.1	11

Several other parties won a few seats.

Six agonizing months of negotiations produced a coalition government (or "cabinet") of the four largest parties. Negotiations were intense over who—Shi'a, Sunni, and Kurds—got which of the thirty-seven ministries in the cabinet. With 250 out of 275 seats, this coalition is actually an emergency government of all important parties with essentially no opposition in parliament. Such governments, sometimes useful in time of war, typically do not last. In Baghdad, Sunnis were constantly suspicious that Shi'a ministers allowed Shi'a hit squads in the police and army to kill Sunnis with impunity. Shi'a, on the other hand, were suspicious that Sunni leaders were shielding Sunni terrorists.

The parties settled on a compromise prime minister, Nuri Kamal al-Maliki, 56, a leader of the second-largest Shi'a party, Dawa ("the Call" to Islam). Maliki was always anti-Saddam and fled a death sentence in 1980 for exile in Iran and Syria. He vowed to end the sectarian killings and pull Iraq together, but the warring parties did not cooperate. The parliament also elected a president, a Kurd, and Sunni and Shi'a deputy presidents. Iraq also has a federal Supreme Court, whose justices are named by the president and approved by the parliament. The Iraqi political structure looked democratic on paper but could not stop the violence.

Finally, at the end of 2005, Iraq held its first regular elections for parliament. This time it was by province, and Sunni leaders, realizing that their boycott of the earlier elections was a mistake, urged their people to turn out. Most Iraqis vote not as Iraqis but as Shi'a, Sunni, or Kurds. This ensured that the winner was the

United Iraqi Alliance (UIA), an alliance of two main Shi'a Islamist parties and others. Washington's favorites, secular parties that aimed to draw Sunni and Shi'a together, fared poorly. Americans had trouble understanding the depth of **primordial** feelings in the Middle East, a factor that limits democracy in many countries (see *communalism*, page 12).

The fact that the Shi'a alliance won only a minority of parliamentary seats may have been a lucky break, for it meant that Shi'a politicians would have to negotiate with Kurds and Sunni Arabs to form a cabinet and pass laws. If the Shia's United Iraqi Alliance had won a majority, it would have run the Baghdad government by itself and left Kurds and Sunni disgruntled and alienated.

The negative side of this was that it took six months of haggling to form a government, and that government could fall apart. In such cabinets, as we saw in Israel (page 85), coalition parties often disagree over policy and threaten to quit, paralyzing the government's ability to make decisions. The Kurdish and Sunni parties in the Iraqi coalition were often unhappy over Shi'a power and policies. The root of the problem is that Iraq had never become a single country. One way to govern such fragmented countries is through *consociation*, the sharing of executive power among several groups, as in Lebanon. The 2005 Baghdad government did this; it gave the presidency and eight ministries to Kurds, seven ministries to Sunni, and nineteen ministries, including prime minister, to Shi'a. This system is not majority rule—it deliberately blocks majority rule—but could be one of the few ways to govern Iraq. Iraq could easily slide into full-scale civil war, making its try at democracy an historical footnote.

CAN SAUDI ARABIA DEMOCRATIZE?

Saudi Arabia is currently supervising a cautious, incremental, and partial democratization, clearly a better plan than sudden democratization. Oil wealth, especially the price jumps of 1973 and 1979, had enabled the House of al-Saud to buy off threats and problems. Saudi youths got sinecure jobs, but now there are not enough such jobs; you cannot put everyone on the government payroll. Manual labor is done by imported workers from Egypt, Pakistan, even the Philippines, at one-third the cost of Saudi labor. Some 60 percent of the Saudi workforce is foreigners, which the regime is trying to limit by the "Saudization" of jobs.

One of the world's highest rates of population growth—an amazing 4.1 percent a year from 1960 to 2000—rapidly tripled the Saudi population to the current 27 million. Young Saudis, a majority of the population, are mostly unemployed and bored. The outlets available to American youths—girls, drinking, rock music, and movies—are forbidden in the Kingdom. Radical Islamism grows because it is one of the few things to do. An estimated 2,500 young Saudis have gone to Iraq for jihad, where many have been killed, some in martyr operations.

---

primordial   Groups you are born into, such as tribes and religions.

Saudi per capita GDP plunged from a peak of $24,000 in 1980 to $10,000 in 2000 (thanks to oil prices, recovered to $15,000 in 2006) and it is distributed very unequally. Especially favored are the 7,000 or so princes, the product of multiple and rotating wives, each of whom gets an allowance of a least several thousand dollars a month; some get millions a year. Many get huge commissions on business deals and government contracts; corruption is rife. The royal family passes out wealth in the form of jobs and charity to supporters and petitioners. Such **clientelism** is found throughout the Third World. Little noticed are the large numbers of poor people in Saudi Arabia; the oil boom passed them by.

As Samuel Huntington pointed out in his magisterial 1968 *Political Order in Changing Societies,* modernizing monarchs create hatred against themselves and doom their own regimes. The educational and economic improvements they foster make them utterly out of date. Generously handing out money, a traditional form of power in the Middle East going back centuries, no longer buys loyalty. Young Saudis feel little gratitude to the royal house that has funded their college educations; they feel resentment and bitterness at those who have all the wealth and power of the country. How could an educated person remain loyal to a corrupt and secretive medieval regime? Properly channeled, these relatively recent demands for greater political and economic equality could form the basis of a democratic transition. Left to fester, they feed only revolution—in the Saudi case, Islamist rage of the sort that ripped Iran apart.

No Middle Eastern monarchy has made the transition to democracy, although the emir of Qatar may be attempting it now. Instead, some have already been overthrown with a variety of bloody and dictatorial results. Since the 1950s, Huntington noted, monarchy has been overthrown in Egypt, Iraq, Libya, Ethiopia, and elsewhere. He virtually predicted the fall of the shah of Iran. Is the Saudi court, ensconced in palaces and Spanish villas and surrounded by obsequious courtiers, immune to this logic?

In 2003 the Saudi Council of Ministers announced low-level elections. The cautious steps seemed well thought-out and calculated to slowly bring Saudi citizens into political participation. On a staggered basis in the spring of 2005, Saudi men voted for half the members of 178 municipal councils, none of which has much power. The other half and the mayors continued to be appointed. Registration and turnout were not massive, but some Saudis were happy at being able to vote for the first time. "The steps have to come slowly so the society can accept it," said the mayor of Riyadh, who is also a royal prince. The big question: Can such small steps adapt an essentially medieval kingdom to the modern world before revolution hits?

Contradictions tear at Saudi Arabia. Some political speech is permitted but nothing that offends the Wahhabi clergy or attacks the House of Saud. Newspapers may discuss modernization and democratization but not criticize Islam in any form. Some editors are fired. Saudi television carries little but Wahhabi preachers, one reason Al Jazeera and other satellite channels are so popular. Even mild protests are punished by lashing and long jail terms. Education has grown but instills Islamic

---

clientelism   Money and favors the rich and powerful distribute to gain support.

D ⁝ *Domestic Structures*

MODERATE ISLAMISM?

Not all political Islam is militant or dangerous, argue some scholars of the Middle East. Increasingly, there are moderate forms of Islamism compatible with democracy. Turkey's current ruling Justice and Development party had its roots in long-standing efforts to roll back Atatürk's secular reforms. Now in power, however, Prime Minister Erdogan (remember, it's pronounced "Erdowan") has mellowed. He no longer writes fiery Islamist poetry but seeks Turkey's entrance into the European Union.

The original Islamist organization, the Muslim Brotherhood, was founded in Egypt in 1928 by Hasan al-Banna, who proclaimed, "The Qur'an is our constitution." It served as the model for political Islam throughout the Sunni world and now has many branches—such as Hamas—some of them moderate, or at least not violent. The Al Jazeera satellite television network (see box on page 293), for example, is described as voicing a modernized Muslim Brotherhood line: anti-tyranny, anti-corruption, and anti-United States, but not pro-jihad. As the rigged 2005 Egyptian elections showed, "independent" candidates known to represent the Brotherhood got many votes by promising clean government and social services.

Some thinkers argue that America's best bet could be moderate Islamists. They alone have the (mostly underground) organization and voter appeal to democratize authoritarian dictatorships and monarchies before they explode and fall into the hands of Islamist revolutionaries of the Osama stripe. When we see an "Islamic" or "Islamist" party or movement, we must first analyze it before we condemn it. Some of them we may be able to work with.

correctness and minimizes modern subjects. Saudi women attend all-female universities but still cannot drive.

The king and many Saudi princes know they must modernize but are not willing to take on conservative forces, which have much to lose from modernization. Democratizing amid discontent is perilous, like opening the lid of a hot pressure cooker: it blows off. "We're the most conservative country in the world," said one prince, but they do seem smart enough to give way gradually to the forces of modernity.

CAN EGYPT DEMOCRATIZE?

Saudi Arabia is the oil and money leader of the Middle East, but Egypt is its population and intellectual leader. The Arab soul may be in Mecca, but the brains are in Cairo. Books, journals, and higher education have long flowed from Egypt to the rest of the Arab world. Egypt was a monarchy until it was overthrown in a coup in 1952. Since then, its president has been a general (Nasser, Sadat, Mubarak) who served until death. They were all "elected," but no one was allowed to seriously oppose them.

Modernity impinged on Egypt. Sadat changed the economy away from import substitution and in favor of boosting exports. One of the biggest changes was

K ⋮ *Key Concepts*

THE COMMUNICATIONS REVOLUTION

A new and highly influential mass medium marked the 2003 war that was not present for the 1991 war: Al Jazeera ("The Island"), the most popular of some 150 Arab-language satellite television channels. Heretofore, Arab mass media—all television and radio, most newspapers—had been rigorously state controlled, delivering only what reinforced the regime, often by deflecting discontent onto the United States and Israel. Regime brutality and corruption were never mentioned. In 1996 Al Jazeera, based in Qatar and funded by its emir, went on the air with critical news and views controlled by no government. Satellite technology overleaps ground stations and goes right into homes via a little dish antenna. Al Jazeera's frank, modern news coverage resembles that of an American network; many of its staff learned their trade with the BBC Arabic service. Ideologically, Al Jazeera is said to reflect a Muslim Brotherhood line.

Washington detests Al Jazeera for its anti-U.S. slant, especially after 9/11, when it aired Osama bin Laden's taped appeals for jihad. Like most Arabs, Al Jazeera was pro-Iraq in the 2003 war; Washington and many Arab governments charge that they distort reporting. Al Jazeera says it covers the news professionally, everything from Israeli repression in the West Bank to the toppling of the Saddam statue in Baghdad with cheering Iraqis kicking it. Some 40 to 50 million Arabs regularly watch Al Jazeera, one of the few free Arab media and by far the region's favorite news source.

Al Jazeera's criticism of U.S. policy aside, what will be its long-term impact? Communications are an important factor in modernization and democratization. Informing viewers and listeners of a better, freer life undermines authoritarian regimes. The United States supported Radio Free Europe and Radio Liberty, CIA fronts that broadcast accurate news into, respectively, East Europe and the Soviet Union. Today, we still support Television Martí, which does the same for Cuba. The East German Communist regime could never gain full legitimacy with most of its citizens able to receive uncensored television broadcasts from West Germany and West Berlin.

Al Jazeera helps by pushing corrupt, dictatorial regimes to clean up their administration and open up to democracy, but it also carries extremist preachers. Like most Arab intellectuals, Al Jazeera criticizes the United States. Get used to it. If Washington persuaded Qatar to close or control Al Jazeera, what kind of a statement would that make about U.S. support for press freedom? America has no way to stop the critical coverage and comments of Al Jazeera, but it is also a catalyst for the kind of changes we want in the region. Nobody promised that a free press would report only nice news.

---

that now most Egyptians get their news from Al Jazeera and ignore state television. In his 2005 State of the Union address, President Bush urged Egypt to "show the way to democracy in the Middle East." A wide variety of Egyptian political currents stirred, and pro-democracy demonstrations, led by the Movement for Change, or *Kifaya* ("enough"), broke out in 2005. Egyptian President Hosni Mubarak gave way and authorized opposition involvement in a presidential election, but it was neither free nor fair.

The leading opposition candidate, a liberal 41-year old lawyer, Ayman Nour, founder of the Tomorrow party, was jailed in early 2005. U.S. pressure got him released, but regime thugs harassed his campaign. Turnout was low. Mubarak won with 88.6 percent for his fifth six-year term as president. Nour officially got 7.3 percent, but no outside election observers were allowed. Nour, protesting the election was rigged, was arrested and sentenced to five years on trumped-up charges. The U.S. State Department called the election a "historic departure" and "positive first step." State has to say nice things.

Parliamentary elections in December 2005 for the rubber-stamp People's Assembly were no better. They were run in three rounds over five weeks. Candidates who did not win a majority in the first round went to runoffs later. The main opposition, the feared and famous Muslim Brotherhood, was as usual not allowed to run openly. Nasser banned it in 1954—it really was fanatic and dangerous—and hanged many of its leaders. The Brotherhood now claims to reject violence but is still technically illegal for advocating Islamic rule. Its naive but effective slogan "Islam is the Solution" promised to solve all problems, from hunger and economic development to getting rid of the Americans and the Israelis. The Brotherhood is well organized and helps the poor with food, medical care, and community problems the regime neglects. Many Egyptians see the Muslim Brotherhood as the only hope for change.

In the 2005 elections, 150 Brothers ran as "independents" and won 86 seats in the 454-seat parliament; Mubarak's National Democratic party (NDP) won 314 seats. The Brotherhood ran in only a third of the contests to avoid alarming the regime; otherwise the Brotherhood might have won a majority. As it was, police killed more than a dozen Brotherhood supporters, arrested hundreds, and blocked access to polling stations in pro-Brotherhood areas. NDP thugs attacked Brotherhood voters and organizers and stuffed ballot boxes. The Brotherhood's effective message: Egyptians are outraged at the crooked Mubarak government and at poverty. The regime answers chronic unrest and terrorism with massive jailings. Egypt is unstable.

Did the two Egyptian elections of 2005 show democracy was coming, or were they fake exercises to please Washington? Egypt gets $2 billion a year (Israel gets $3 billion) in U.S. aid and does not wish to lose it. Egyptians ask if a Muslim Brotherhood government would be moderate or extremist. No one could tell, but it is likely we will find out.

CONCLUSIONS

The 2003 war was supposed to establish democracy in Iraq and encourage it throughout the Middle East, but this was infeasible. The region has known little democracy and currently ranks low in Freedom House's ratings. Some see the problem as a cultural failure to modernize. Even Turkey has not been able to overcome Islamic resistance to modernization. Democracy needs a large, educated middle class, lacking in the Middle East. Islam has never had a reformation, which could contribute to modernization and democratization; instead it has emphasized rigidity and salafiyya (see next chapter). Huntington's "civilizational theory," which sees an Islam hostile to most other civilizations, rejects optimistic predictions of globalization and democratization.

Independent television such as Al Jazeera, with criticism of Arab regimes and the United States, has brought a communications revolution. Saudi Arabia used to be able to buy off discontent, but an exploding population and great income inequality have persuaded the House of Saud to undertake a slow, cautious democratization to head off an Islamist upheaval. Egypt, ruled by a general since 1952, held two rigged elections in 2005. The Muslim Brotherhood, founded in and still powerful in Egypt, could eventually take over. Optimists see moderate forms of Islamism emerging, ones we can work with.

KEY TERMS

authoritarian (p. 287)

charismatic (p. 286)

civil society (p. 285)

civilization (p. 280)

clientelism (p. 291)

demagogue (p. 279)

disaggregate (p. 283)

fertility rate (p. 283)

globalization (p. 281)

Gulf Cooperation Council (p. 284)

illiberal democracy (p. 283)

legitimacy (p. 286)

modernization (p. 279)

per capita GDP (p. 279)

primordial (p. 290)

referendum (p. 288)

relativism (p. 282)

theocracy (p. 286)

totalitarian (p. 286)

FURTHER REFERENCE

Carothers, Thomas, and Marina Ottaway, eds. *Uncharted Journey: Promoting Democracy in the Middle East.* Washington D.C.: Carnegie Endowment, 2005.

Ernst, Carl W. *Following Muhammad: Rethinking Islam in the Contemporary World.* Chapel Hill, NC: University of North Carolina Press, 2005.

Feldman, Noah. *After Jihad: America and the Struggle for Islamic Democracy.* New York: Farrar, Straus & Giroux, 2004.

Gerner, Deborah J., and Jilian Schwedler, eds. *Understanding the Contemporary Middle East,* 2nd ed. Boulder, CO: Lynne Rienner, 2004.

Hunter, Shireen T., and Huma Malik, eds. *Modernization, Democracy, and Islam.* Westport, CT: Praeger, 2004.

Huntington, Samuel P. *The Clash of Civilizations and the Remaking of World Order.* New York: Touchstone, 1997.

Kassem, Maye. *Egyptian Politics: The Dynamics of Authoritarian Rule.* Boulder, CO: Lynne Rienner, 2004.

Lynch, Marc. *Voices of the New Arab Public: Iraq, Al-Jazeera, and Middle East Politics Today.* New York: Columbia University Press, 2006.

Owen, Roger. *State, Power, and Politics in the Making of the Modern Middle East,* 3rd ed. New York: Routledge, 2004.

Perthes, Volker, ed. *Arab Elites: Negotiating the Politics of Change.* Boulder, CO: Lynne Rienner, 2004.

Pratt, Nicola. *Democracy and Authoritarianism in the Arab World.* Boulder, CO: Lynne Rienner, 2006.

Rabasa, Angel M., ed. *The Muslim World after 9/11.* Santa Monica, CA: RAND, 2004.

Rugh, William A. *Arab Mass Media: Newspapers, Radio, and Television in Arab Politics.* Westport, CT: Praeger, 2004.

Thompson, Michael, ed. *Islam and the West: Critical Perspectives on Modernity.* Lanham, MD: Rowman Littlefield, 2003.

16 Political Islam and Terrorism

Points to Ponder

- Is political Islam inevitable? Must it be extremist?
- Could Islam undergo a reformation?
- What is *salafiyya* and why is it enjoying an upsurge?
- Do Muslim immigrants in Europe become culturally European?
- Why is terrorism difficult to define?
- Can conventional military force stop terrorism?
- What are the origins and goals of al Qaeda?
- Who was Sayyid Qutb and what was his influence?
- What are the "micro" and "macro" levels of analysis?

Political Islam is inevitable. As we discussed in Chapter 2, Islam was born intertwined with government; the two were never supposed to be separate. Europeans brought secularism relatively recently into the Middle East along with the concept of nation as distinct from the community of believers. Neither secularism nor nationalism displaced the much older and deeper value of an Islamic realm ruled by Qur'an and caliph. Secularism and nationalism took centuries to develop in Europe.

For much of the twentieth century, both Europeans and local rulers tended to accept the European notion that nation holds first place while religion is cultural, personal, and secondary. Atatürk exemplifies this approach (see Chapter 7), but the House of Saud may have had a shrewder appreciation of how much Islam matters in governance (see Chapter 10). Minimizing or suppressing Islam, as in Turkey, Egypt, Syria, Iran, and other lands, never worked on a long-term basis. Islamic movements continually rumbled underneath such systems, ready to erupt, as we saw with the Muslim Brotherhood in Egypt (see Chapter 15). In free 2006 Palestinian elections, the Islamist Hamas bumped aside the secular PLO (see Chapter 6).

R ⠿ *Religions*

A MUSLIM REFORMATION?

Islam has never undergone a **reformation**. Instead, it has undergone a series of re-affirmations and for a millennium has been essentially frozen. Groups have branched off from Islam (Druze, Alawites, Baha'is), but they have not influenced mainstream Islam. The two great branches of Islam, Sunni and Shi'a, have no quarrel over the Qur'an but over who was the legitimate successor to the Prophet.

Originally Islam permitted independent, rational interpretations of the Qur'an (*ijtihad*), but between the ninth and eleventh centuries these were eliminated in favor of a single, orthodox interpretation (*taqlid,* literally "emulation"). With this, intellectual rigidity blanketed the Muslim world. The Arab inheritors of the philosophy and science of ancient Greece failed to develop it further. The brilliant Islamic civilization—whose architecture is still magnificent—that was far ahead of Europe in A.D. 1000 found itself overtaken by 1600, although it did not know it.

How important was the Protestant Reformation to the history of the West? Most thinkers rank it high; Max Weber posited it as the underlying element of Western modernization. While it is hard to prove which caused which, Luther's nailing of his ninety-five theses to the church door came closely in time with capitalism, absolutism, scientific and technological innovation, and the strong state. One of the elements that contributed to the Reformation was printing—Gutenberg's Bible (in German) appeared in 1455—which enabled large numbers of Europeans to read Scripture for themselves. Hitherto, reading the Bible (in Latin) was generally reserved for Roman Catholic priests. With Scripture newly available through printing, readers could quickly see that much of what they had been taught as sacred was not found in the Bible. Parts of Catholic practice could thus be discarded, and worshippers felt they were reaching a Christianity that was truer to its written sources.

Many Middle Eastern intellectuals tried Western ideologies and found them wanting. During the 1930s and World War II, some found fascism attractive. The Baath parties of Syria and Iraq were modeled on the fascism then riding high in Europe (see page 212). Young Egyptian army officers such as Nasser and Sadat belonged to the fascist-tinged Young Egypt movement and looked forward to a German victory in North Africa that would kick out their British occupiers. After the war, straight nationalism took over, as Egyptians, Syrians, Iraqis, Libyans, and others cheered the ouster of their colonial masters.

That accomplished, many turned to socialism, helped along by Soviet aid, propaganda, and scholarships. An older generation of Arab intellectuals and leaders successively tried fascism, nationalism, and socialism (example: Nasser). Since at least the 1970s, these Western movements have been dead or irrelevant in the Middle East. Increasingly, educated Middle Easterners proclaim, as does the Egyptian Muslim Brotherhood, "Islam is the solution." They tried Western ideologies (but not free-market liberalism) and found them inapplicable and unsatisfying. Now they are returning to their Muslim roots. Modernization did not make Islam obsolete; it made it newly relevant.

reformation   The modernization of a religion, often based on original texts.

When a Middle Eastern regime opens the door even a crack to democracy, the first parties through it will be politicized forms of Islam. An Islamic role in governance may be inevitable, but what kind of Islam? The issue is far from settled. Important currents of change and moderation compete and mingle with attempts to return to a mythical Islamic past. How this is resolved will determine the evolution of the Middle East for the twenty-first century. Some argue that much depends on the ability of Islam to adapt to the modern world.

There are signs that an Islamic reformation is brewing. Muslim philosophers in several countries suggest interpretations of the Qur'an that are not anti-modern. Ironically, this may have gone farthest in Iran, where having to live under an Islamist regime provokes doubt and resentment: Is this corrupt dictatorship what the Prophet had in mind? A potent force is educated women, most advanced in Iran, where female university students outnumber male university students. Almost axiomatically, educated women do not gladly submit to male domination, and they find no justification for it in the Qur'an. They find, instead, that male domination comes from old and local traditions that were assimilated into Islam but bear no necessary relationship to the faith. To get back to the original, pure Islam, therefore, these primitive traditions must be discarded.

Another source of Islamic rethinking is Muslims living in West Europe and the United States, who could serve as agents of modernization and moderation back in their home countries. This, unfortunately, turns out to be a double-edged sword. Islam in the West can also turn extremist when Muslims cannot or will not adopt Western culture. First, Muslims are not supposed to live outside the *dar es salam*, the "house of peace," meaning the great community of Islam. The outside world, the *dar al harb*, "the house of war," is ignorant and dangerous. Historically, Muslims might visit it for business but not stay. Muslims residing in Europe came only when European empires brought them in as sailors, students, and workers from their colonies in the nineteenth century. Large numbers came only in the twentieth century, especially after World War II. If they had jobs and good money at home, few Muslims would settle in Europe.

Some religious rethinking among Muslims in West Europe must take place. How else can you live there without making some accommodation to the prevalent secular culture? Muslims in Europe and America have to emphasize tolerance for themselves and this has introduced the broader notion of tolerance for all. Iran's former President Muhammad Khatami, for example, served earlier in Hamburg's Islamic Center; he professed to be open to Western ideas of freedom. Some Muslim clerics in West Europe have started to articulate new ideas that could contribute to an Islamic reformation.

Some young Muslims in Europe, however, show signs of a **bounce-back effect**, becoming more Islamic than their parents ever were. Anthropologist Ernest Gellner, who taught in London, was among the first to explicate the trend, which occurs almost automatically among people brought into a new and very different culture. It is a psychologically confusing ordeal; those undergoing it lose their sense of identity: Who am I? Uprooted from their Islamic culture back

---

bounce-back effect   Reversal of views and values from those held previously.

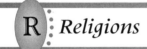

Religions

SALAFIYYA

Under stress—such as the Mongol invasion and more recent Western pressure—Islamic society tends to seek salvation by returning to a strict interpretation of the Qur'an. For centuries, certain Sunni Muslim thinkers have articulated the doctrine of **salafiyya**, and it has continued as a puritanical criticism of many Muslim rulers. (Salafiyya is not present in Shi'a Islam, which has its own brand of fundamentalism. Salafis despise Shi'a as pagan renegades.) Wahhabism and al Qaeda are salafi movements.

Salafis emphasize that Islam, starting with the Prophet, has always had to fight both idolatry and hypocrisy. Muhammad faced pagan beliefs and false Muslims from the beginning. Worship of anything but Allah—such as pre-Islamic practices, the modern nation-state, or material possessions—is idolatry. Those who claim to be Muslims but just use Islam to gain or retain wealth and power are hypocrites. (See discussion of Taimiyya in Chapter 2.) This includes most current Muslim governments. And these twin dangers constantly beset Islam, so salafis must be forever on guard against them and willing to engage in jihad to stop them.

Salafis such as bin Laden ideologically despised Saddam Hussein's Iraq, for it was the most secular Arab state and preached nationalism, which is a form of idolatry. Neither do salafis really like Palestinian nationalism, for it tends to worship Palestine rather than Allah. This religious divide does not prevent salafis and nationalists from cooperating opportunistically with each other when both benefit. Destruction of Israel and liberation for Palestine were not at the top of Osama's list; he included them more recently as devices to mobilize angry Muslims. Accordingly, al Qaeda can make temporary and ad hoc alliances with a variety of Muslim movements that it really does not approve of. Once salafiyya wins, it will break and discard these idolatrous nationalisms and construct a single community of Islam, as the Prophet intended.

Modern salafi extremists argue that the West is attacking Islam—the 2003 conquest of Iraq seemed to prove it—and all good Muslims must defend their faith and lands against crusaders, Zionists, and Americans. Even worse are Muslim rulers who go along with and seek favor from the Americans, such as Egypt's Sadat (assassinated in 1981) and the House of Saud, which only pretends to be pure. Actually, the founding doctrine of Saudi Arabia was the 1744 alliance of the Saud family with the Wahhabi branch of salafiyya, an alliance that eventually unified the Kingdom in 1932. In return for Wahhabi support, the Kingdom teaches salafiyya in its own schools and funds Wahhabi schools in other Muslim lands, especially in Pakistan. True salafis such as Osama bin Laden are not fooled by this outward show of piety, however, and struggle to bring down the hypocritical House of Saud.

home, they have not joined European culture. Many Europeans dislike and discriminate against them. They cannot feel whole-heartedly British or French even if they are educated and employed, and many are not. Muslims in Britain have three to four times the jobless rate of white Britons. America has an easier time of integrating Muslims, as we are all descended from immigrants and generally tolerate diverse cultures. Until recently, Europe has been a source of emigrants, not a goal of immigrants.

---

salafiyya   "The way of the forefathers"; reactionary doctrine of alleged pure Islam; basis of current Islamic extremism. Adjective: *salafi.*

P ⋮ *Personalities*

THE PHILOSOPHER OF ISLAMISM

Little known outside the Arab world, Egyptian writer Sayyid Qutb (1906–1966) has a hypnotic influence on Islamic fundamentalists. A thinker in the salafi mold (see box on page 300), Qutb (pronounced CUT-eb) is credited with devising the intellectual basis of **Islamism**, at least among Sunnis. Born in Cairo, he had memorized the Qur'an by age ten but then went to a modern college. He knew both traditional Islam and Western socialism and tried to synthesize them. Only Islam, he wrote in the 1940s, can deliver social justice. In the late 1940s he earned a master's degree at the Colorado State College of Education in Greeley but hated America for its sexual permissiveness. So much for understanding through student exchanges.

A brilliant intellectual and powerful writer, Qutb was reacting against the encroachment of Western thought in the Muslim world. He emphasized that Western wealth, philosophy, and science had only made humans unhappy. Only by fusing these ideas with traditional Qur'anic teaching would humans find happiness. The splitting of faith and reason, God and science, was a Christian error the West had inflicted on the world, leading to confusion and madness. The solution was to return to the Qur'an, reconstitute the Muslim caliphate that Atatürk had terminated in 1924, and restore Shari'a as the legal system. Martyrdom was a perfectly acceptable method for this end.

Qutb was the leading theorist of Egypt's important Muslim Brotherhood (see page 292), who found Nasser a dangerous secularist and tried to assassinate him. In retaliation, Nasser outlawed the Brotherhood and jailed its members, including Qutb, whom Nasser had hanged in 1966. Qutb's brother fled to Saudi Arabia where he taught Islamism to a student named Osama bin Laden.

The result has been that some young Muslims in West Europe identify as Muslims first and only and throw themselves into the Islamic fundamentalism preached in several mosques throughout Europe. One can find the children of Pakistani immigrants in Britain, clothed and educated exactly like other young Britons, who suddenly around college age become super-Muslims—bearded, clothed in body-length shirts, learning Arabic, and plotting to kill Westerners, especially Jews. The leader of the Pakistani Islamist gang that slit the throat of *Wall Street Journal* reporter Daniel Pearl (and distributed a video of it) in 2002 was born and educated in Britain, as were those who bombed London subway trains in 2005 and plotted to blow up jetliners in 2006. In England one can attend celebrations of 9/11. Said one Muslim youth in England: "We should all get together and kill all the Jews." All of the recruitment and planning for 9/11 took place in Germany among Arab (chiefly Saudi) students, who became fundamentalists *after* living in Germany for some time, not before. As French scholar Olivier Roy observed, much Islamist terror incubates in Europe and targets Europeans.

Accordingly, do not count on cross-cultural familiarization to lead to understanding and toleration. People from Muslim cultures are both intrigued and shocked at Western culture. They recognize its economic and technological superiority, but

---

Islamism   Islam turned into a political ideology.

Conflicts

THE "RESISTANCE" MOVEMENT

The current popular word in the Middle East is "resistance," which several groups use in their title or statements. Hamas, for example, is the Arabic acronym for Islamic Resistance Movement. Islamists see a Western attempt to take over their culture, religion, territory, and oil, and they claim to be resisting it. Throughout the Muslim world, Hezbollah leader Hassan Nasrallah and Iranian President Ahmadinejad are celebrated for resisting Israel and the United States.

"Resistance" has a nice ring to it in Arab ears. It helps legitimate extremist causes, as it indicates Muslims are simply defending themselves. Chief targets are Israel, which seizes Arab land, and the United States, which resistors say aims to redo the entire Middle East to suit itself. Arab regimes cooperating with the Americans, such as Egypt and Saudi Arabia, are also targets. With this mindset, almost anything the West does—from invading Iraq to opposing Iran's nuclear efforts to stopping genocide in Darfur—seems to prove the need for Muslims to resist, by violence if need be.

There is no one single resistance movement. Iran and Syria, by some estimates, have formed an "axis of resistance," but it has trouble leading because no Sunni regimes will follow Shi'a Iran or Alawite-governed Syria. (The Alawites are an offshoot of Shi'a.) Salafi movements such as al Qaeda and the Islamic Brotherhood claim the title of "resistance" for themselves, but they too form no cohesive whole. The chief use of the word is as a motivator and rallying cry.

they deplore its lack of humane and spiritual values. Where we see freedom and individualism, they see materialism and sexual debauchery. In Muslim eyes, we are immoral. Muslims in Europe or America may like their higher incomes but deplore the erosion of the family and religious values that anchor their lives. Getting to know you does not necessarily mean getting to like you.

ISLAMIST TERRORISM

Not all forms of political Islam turn into or produce Islamist terrorism. True, once the mystical pursuit of true Islam is uncorked, it may drive those who imbibe to the extreme of Osama bin Laden and al Qaeda. But it may also mellow and synthesize with Western thought. In the Middle East non-state fighters are usually grouped into three categories: Palestinian, Hezbollah, and al Qaeda.

Palestinian groups include Hamas, Palestinian Islamic Jihad, the Al Aksa Martyrs Brigade, Black September, Popular Front for the Liberation of Palestine, and others. The first two of these are Islamist, the others secular. These groups are of vital importance to Israel since they are fighting to wipe out the Jewish state. They have killed a number of Israeli soldiers and more Israeli civilians.

To the United States, the Palestinian groups are important largely because they threaten Israel. They have not often targeted citizens of Western states, but some fear they will turn to attacks against Westerners. Some already have. Black

September attacked Israeli athletes at the 1972 Munich Olympics and did not ask if the security guards were German citizens. Six months later, the same Black September, an offshoot of Yassir Arafat's Palestine Liberation Front (PLO), assassinated the U.S. ambassador in Khartoum, Sudan. PLO terrorists threw Leon Klinghofer (in his wheelchair) off a cruise ship in 1985, knowing he was an American. In 1997 a Palestinian gunman opened fire on people on the top of the Empire State Building in New York City. We may not be immune from Palestinian terrorism. Al Qaeda began its anti-American crusade over U.S. support of the group's true target, Saudi Arabia. The same logic could lead Hamas or Palestinian Jihad into targeting any country supporting Israel.

Lebanese Shi'a, the largest and poorest of Lebanon's many population groups, formed Hezbollah (the Party of God) in 1982, with Iranian help. Until September 11, 2001, Hezbollah had killed more Americans than any other terrorist group. Hezbollah destroyed the American embassy in Beirut, used truck bombs on the U.S. Marine and French barracks in Beirut, and kidnapped and tortured U.S. and U.K. citizens throughout the 1980s. Ronald Reagan pulled U.S. forces out of Lebanon. Then in the Iran-Contra scandal (see Chapter 12), we provided Hezbollah's principal supporters (Iran) with some weapons to fight Iraq. After that, Hezbollah had no reason to target westerners.

Hezbollah maintains a terrorist arm sometimes called the Islamic Resistance and a military structure in the south of Lebanon, where most Shi'a live. Hezbollah members sit in the Lebanese parliament, and Hezbollah hospitals and clinics aid the Shi'a population. Hezbollah politicians insist they are not terrorists but Lebanese patriots resisting Israeli occupation. Israel unilaterally withdrew from Lebanon in 2000, but this did not satisfy Hezbollah's clever chief, Sheikh Hassan Nasrullah. In 2006, Hezbollah infiltrated Israel, killed eight Israeli soldiers and kidnapped two. Predictably, Israel retaliated with air strikes and an invasion that killed over a thousand Lebanese, mostly civilians. Hezbollah resistance boosted its popularity. Even Sunni cheered Hezbollah, which became the most powerful group in Lebanon.

AL QAEDA

The "Mother of all Islamist Terrorist Groups" is al Qaeda or "the Base," founded in Afghanistan. Islamists from around the world converged on the Soviet-occupied Afghanistan to wage holy war against the infidel. Osama bin Laden paid for many of the warriors' travels. He intended the Base to be the military basis of a new and pure Islamic caliphate. The term also refers to the computer database he compiled of his fighters.

When the Soviets withdrew from Afghanistan in 1989, the jihadis claimed they had single-handedly defeated one of the two world superpowers. They never accorded any importance to U.S.-supplied Stinger missiles, Chinese military support, or the collapse of the Warsaw Pact. Instead, they spun the Soviet withdrawal into their founding mythology. Beating one superpower, they argued, showed they could make the other, the United States, retreat from Muslim lands.

K: *Key Concepts*

DEFINING TERRORISM

It is often said that one man's terrorist is another man's freedom fighter. Terrorism is a currently popular subject but can be hard to define. In 1942 the leader of the Irgun, Menachem Begin, joined with remnants of the Stern gang who had escaped from prison to launch a series of attacks against the British in Palestine. The Stern remnants, now called Lehi, included Yitzak Shamir. They assassinated British officials and in 1946 bombed Jerusalem's King David Hotel, where the British had a headquarters, killing ninety-one, including fellow Jews. Shamir, at one time under a death sentence, ordered the killing of British policemen. Begin and Shamir eventually became prime ministers of Israel. Were they terrorists or freedom fighters?

If the Jewish leaders were freedom fighters struggling for an independent Israel and were forced to use unconventional tactics against a larger occupying force, how were they different from Palestinians who launch attacks against Israeli targets today? If Begin and Shamir were terrorists, does their involvement in legitimate politics afterward remove the terrorist label? If so, are Hezbollah officials who have been elected to the Lebanese parliament no longer terrorists? Does it matter to the United States that their diplomatic partners did or did not engage in terrorist acts fifty years ago?

Terrorism is hard to define, although many try. All the UN documents of the last thirty years dealing with the issue would total over 1,800 pages and not produce a single definition. The U.S. government defines terrorism in Title 22 of the U.S. Code Section 2565f(d): Terrorism is the "premeditated politically motivated violence perpetrated against noncombatant targets by sub-national groups of clandestine agents, usually intended to influence an audience." International terrorism involves citizens or the territory of more than one country; a terrorist group is any group practicing international terrorism or that has significant subgroups that practice international terrorism.

Let us examine each aspect of the definition. There is little controversy over what constitutes violence, although one could argue whether psychological violence qualifies. If Palestinian demonstrators at the federal building in downtown Los Angeles counter-demonstrate against Jewish demonstrators and they raise their arms in imitation of suicide bombers on the West Bank, have they engaged in terrorism?

The violence has to be premeditated and politically motivated. Thus an impulsive action by a lone gunman to commit "suicide by cop" by spraying the El Al counter at Los Angeles International Airport was not considered terrorism. His motive was personal rather than political. But what about the Palestinian bomber who seeks revenge for the killing of a family member? His motive is also personal and not political. Is it terrorism?

To count as terrorism, the violence must be perpetrated on non-combatants. If perpetrated on soldiers in wartime, it resembles war. This raises the question of whether a state of war exists. The French Resistance in World War II quickly learned to avoid taking on the German army; they concentrated on "spreading a thin film of terror" (in the words of Bernard Fall, who aided them) between French citizens and the

With the Soviets out, the Islamists largely left Afghanistan and Pakistan and returned home to Algeria, Libya, Egypt, Saudi Arabia, Yemen, and other countries. Some retired from military activities but most spread the Islamist message in their homelands. In some cases, they infiltrated and took over pre-existing groups; in others they organized from scratch. These "Afghan Arabs" formed a transnational group and stayed in touch with one another, shared training and techniques, and counted on one another when traveling. Whenever an Afghan Arab landed in a

Germans and their Vichy puppet government so as to make France ungovernable. As such, they mostly killed French civilians who collaborated with the Germans. After the 2003 war Baathis and jihadis did the same to Iraqis who cooperated with the Americans. When Hezbollah blew up the U.S. Marine barracks in Beirut in 1983, killing 241, were they attacking combatants or non-combatants? The Marines were originally there for peacekeeping but soon slid into supporting the Christian side. When supporters of al Qaeda drove a boat full of explosives into the USS *Cole,* was the American warship a combatant or non-combatant? It was not on war duty, and we were in no war at the time.

The violence is perpetrated by sub-national groups, usually by clandestine agents. This does not include the military forces of nation-states. When Iraq dispatched clandestine agents to assassinate former President Bush in Kuwait in 1993, was it terrorism? Or was it simply an act of war? (For terrorism as a type of warfare, see box on page 310.) When a sub-national group such as the Kurdish Democratic party sent clandestine agents to sabotage Iraqi military facilities in the 1970s, was it terrorism? If so, how is it different when the same group committed the same sabotage in 2003 in support of U.S. Operation Enduring Freedom?

The violence is almost always designed to influence an audience, what the old Russian anarchists called "propaganda of the deed." Killing one tsarist official may be unimportant except to arouse the masses. Terrorists above all want to be noticed, to rally others to their cause. A terrorist strike that draws no media attention is almost worthless.

Terrorism often resembles crime, but the former is intensely political and the latter not. The goal of a terrorist is the overthrow of a hated political authority. The criminal just wants money. To be sure, in Colombia crime and politics overlap. The leftist rebels and right-wing paramilitaries may have started with political motives, but now both profit so much from the drug trade that the political goals take second place. Both sides call each other terrorists. The United States sees the drug traffic as crime but quickly got involved in fighting Communist-type guerrillas. The for-profit war in Colombia will be difficult to end; there is simply too much money to be made.

An international terrorist group is one that strikes citizens or territory of another country. According to this definition, American militia groups, the reclusive Unabomber, and the Ku Klux Klan do not qualify as international terrorist groups because their activities stayed inside one country. When Syrian Muslim Brothers launched attacks against the government of Hafez al-Asad, it consisted of Syrians fighting in Syria. He called it terrorism and brutally crushed it, but it was not international terrorism.

Some commentators have tried to avoid the definitional problems, quoting Supreme Court Justice Potter Stuart on pornography: "I know it when I see it." Terrorism is an action that a government decides to label as terrorism. Once the action carries the label it can be condemned outright and participants can receive extra punishment when they are caught. Terrorism is not a legal concept but an emotional one—regardless of Title 22 or its equivalent in other countries.

country he had the names of fellow jihadis who would give him food, shelter, and operational assistance.

Osama bin Laden's ideas are set in the fundamentalist Islamist interpretation of Islam, *salafiyya* (see page 300). Originally he concentrated on removing the Soviet Union from Afghanistan. His theory was that the atheist Soviets were infidels who had taken Muslim lands by force. Since the Dar al Islam (House of Islam) was under attack, it was the individual duty of all Muslims to oppose the Soviet occupation.

P: *Personalities*

OSAMA BIN LADEN

The quietly charismatic Osama bin Laden (also spelled Usama bin Ladin) was a scary figure to the West. Osama was born in 1957, the seventeenth son (of over fifty children) of a poor Yemeni immigrant to Saudi Arbia who became a construction billionaire and died when Osama was ten. Osama was tall, skinny, and quiet but pious. He knows modern Western thought, having earned degrees in civil engineering and economics, but also studied Sayyid Qutb (see box on page 301) and other salafi thinkers. Osama has had five wives and two dozen children.

When the Soviets invaded Afghanistan in 1979, bin Laden found his life's work. He encouraged, organized, and funded with his own money Arab fighters in Afghanistan in the early 1980s. Osama set up guesthouses throughout Pakistan where his recruits were indoctrinated with his interpretation of Islam. He moved to Peshawar, Pakistan, permanently in 1986. In Afghanistan, his forces won some and lost some, but he portrayed all their actions as major and victorious. Bin Laden was always good at spinning the media to enhance his prestige. The U.S. government never worked with bin Laden during this period. American support was funneled through Pakistan's Inter-Services Intelligence agency (ISI) with no U.S. say where its money and weapons went.

On August 1, 1990, the "godless regime" of Iraq's Saddam Hussein invaded Kuwait and threatened Saudi Arabia. Bin Laden flew to Riyadh to offer to defend the kingdom with his jihadis, so the king would not need Western help. After defeating the Soviet Union, Osama thought it would not be hard to beat Iraq. Instead, the al-Saud turned to the long-time guarantor of their security, the United States. Bin Laden was appalled at inviting infidels into the Kingdom; according to tradition, the last words of the Prophet before he died were: "No two religions in the land of the two holy places" of Mecca and Medina, now taken to mean the entire Saudi peninsula. Now the royal family that pledged to uphold Islam in the Kingdom was violating the Prophet's dying edict. Dissident clerics in the Kingdom agreed with this view. Spurned by a royal family he now perceived as hypocritical puppets of the West, he openly encouraged opposition to them. He left the Kingdom for Sudan before he could be arrested.

In Sudan he invested his millions in a variety of businesses and opened terrorist training camps. Saudi Arabia stripped him of his citizenship and cut off his funds. The bin Laden family, whose fortune depended on Saudi royalty, disowned him. Under U.S. pressure, Sudan expelled their guest. In May 1996 bin Laden returned to the familiar territory of Afghanistan, where he provided training and assistance to jihadis in fifty-five countries and began a careful campaign to bomb U.S., Saudi, and other targets.

After Afghanistan, Osama's ire fell on the House of Saud and other Islamic rulers who were not sufficiently pious. He called them the "near enemy." Osama applied two tests: the personal piety of the ruler and his efforts to implement Shari'a law. Most, in his eyes, flunked. Bin Laden believed Saudi rulers were impious personally and a danger to Islam for inviting a non-Muslim army into the Kingdom. He vowed to overthrow the House of Saud as part of his goal of making Muslim countries truly Islamic.

Soon he turned his attention to the United States—which he called the "far enemy"—because of America's presence in the Middle East and support for Israel and heretic Arab governments. Remove the U.S. prop, and the House of Saud will fall. It was just a short step to see the United States as the principal threat to

Cultures

THIEVES IN THE NIGHT

A remarkable 1943 novel by Arthur Koestler—better known for *Darkness at Noon*—gives keen insight into the making of a terrorist. In *Thieves in the Night* an idealistic Jewish leftist, under the pressure of Arab attacks on his kibbutz and British indifference, logically concludes that armed Jewish resistance is the only path open. Koestler, a man who tried about everything the twentieth century had to offer, had worked in Palestine and saw such attitudes take shape in the minds of Lehi gunmen. He does not justify terrorism, but he explains it well. Ironically, the pattern fits Palestinian Arabs too: Under extreme pressure and frustration, terrorism seems logical. Koestler's title is actually from the New Testament ("The Lord shall come as a thief in the night," 1 Thessalonians 5:2).

Muslims worldwide. In 1998 he declared it was all Muslims' duty to kill Americans anywhere they could be found.

Originally bin Laden did not show much interest in the Israel-Palestinian conflict. In 1998, however, he merged his al Qaeda organization with the Egyptian fundamentalist groups Gama'at Islami (sometimes spelled Jamaat Islami) and Egyptian Islamic Jihad. Their leader, Egyptian physician Ayman al-Zawahiri, soon became Osama's second in command. Zawahiri brought with him the Egyptian opposition to Israel. Bin Laden subsequently declared Muslims had to fight against the United States and Israel both to rid the world of the heretic regimes and to defend their faith.

Neither bin Laden nor Zawahiri are Islamic clerics; they do not hold the title of *mufti* and are therefore not entitled to issue binding religious edicts, *fatwas*. For religious justification, bin Laden relied on radical clerics on the fringe of Islamic thought to issue *fatwas* supporting his positions. By 2000 he had the leader of the Afghan Taliban, a religiously undereducated activist, Mullah Omar, to provide the legitimating religious rulings. In return, bin Laden encouraged his followers to accept Omar as the Caliph for Muslims worldwide. Religious justification, blind hatred, and access to technology, money, and weapons were a potent mixture.

TERRORIST ATTACKS

In 1992 al Qaeda conducted three bombings in Yemen, targeting American servicemen attempting to bring aid to Muslims suffering from hunger and deprivation in Somalia. When American intervention in Somalia deepened, bin Laden sent trainers to teach Somalis how to shoot the tail assembly of helicopters. The result, as shown in the book and movie *Black Hawk Down,* was the death and capture of American servicemen. Weeks later President Clinton ordered U.S. troops out of Somalia. Bin Laden had learned that military opposition could make the Soviets withdraw from Muslim lands and that the same tactics could make the United States withdraw as well.

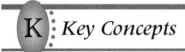

Key Concepts

ESSENTIALISTS VERSUS SPECIFISTS

Several schools of thought emerged to explain radical and violent Islamism, especially suicide bombing. Many proclaimed they had the right answer, but their theories seldom explained all cases of this complex phenomenon. They may be divided into two broad approaches, *essentialist* and *specifist.*

We call the first essentialist because it aims to get at the essence of militant Islam. As such, it is home to those who analyze religion and culture on a broad scale. Some commentators note *suras* (sections) of the Qur'an urge true Muslims to expand by the sword and slaughter infidels until the entire world is Muslim. This, they claim, is the true essence of Islam, but it is not supported by the long periods of calm and tolerance of several Muslim caliphates. To be sure, the periods of calm were punctuated by occasional outbursts of intolerance, but on the whole Christian Europe was much less tolerant.

Samuel Huntington (see pages 280–281) sees Islam as a civilization that almost reflexively clashes with Western, Slavic/Orthodox, and Hindu civilizations. Huntington's famous phrase: "Islam has bloody borders." (Huntington opposed the Iraq War, thinking it foolish to try to "fix" a different culture.) For those who seek an essence, the ultimate cause of Islamist terrorism is Islam.

Some thinkers deny there is an "essence" and claim the search for one is illusory. Essentialist analyses are much too general and depart from reality, protest those we call specifists, of which there are several varieties. In the shock of 9/11, many immediately advanced a poverty explanation. Only desperately poor people do such things, so the long-term solution is alleviation of poverty. Neo-cons dismissed this notion as typical of liberals who suppose that more "programs" will cure malignant evil. They pointed out that most of the 9/11 murderers were middle-class and educated. True, but most terrorists come from situations of high unemployment. The Middle East and North Africa have the world's highest rates of unemployment.

Demographics provides another specific explanation. High birth rates have produced a population bulge of young Muslims. Young men, especially unemployed ones, frustrated and angry, often turn to militant causes, a problem now hitting Saudi Arabia. French expert Olivier Roy notes that West Europe, where there are millions of Muslim immigrants, produces many terrorists. Not assimilated into European culture, they become alienated and easy prey for fiery Islamist preachers. This would explain the young British Muslims who blew themselves up on London subway trains and a bus in 2005 and immigrant Moroccans who blew up Madrid trains in 2004. It would not explain the 2005 suicide bombing of three hotels in Amman, Jordan, which killed Arabs.

In the United States followers of the blind Egyptian Sheikh Abdul Rahman plotted to blow up the World Trade Center in New York City in 1993 with a van bomb. The blast killed six people and injured a thousand. The bombers' leader, Ramzi Yusef, was a nephew of leading al Qaeda organizer Khalid Shaykh Muhammad. The same group also had plans to destroy the Statue of Liberty, the Empire State Building, and the tunnels connecting Manhattan to New Jersey.

Ramzi escaped to the South Pacific where he continued his terrorist plans. In 1994 and 1995 he planned the assassination of Pope John Paul II during his visit to Manila, bombings of U.S. and Israeli embassies in the area, midair bombings of trans-Pacific jetliners, and the assassination of President Clinton during a visit to the Philippines. According to press reports, police captured him when he accidentally set fire to his kitchen while mixing ingredients for a bomb.

University of Chicago political scientist Robert Pape's studies of suicide bombers worldwide found little religious influence. The originators and chief perpetrators of the technique are the Tamil Tigers, Marxist separatists who demand a Tamil state in the north and east of Sri Lanka. The commonality in suicide bombings in many lands, found Pape, was the desire to rid a country of foreign occupiers, be they Soviets, Americans, Israelis, or Sinhalese (the main nationality of Sri Lanka). The solution, then, is for the foreigners to get out. Pape's theory explains suicide bombings of Americans in Iraq, but the most victims by far are Iraqi Shi'a, and they are not foreign occupiers. It does not explain the 2004 Bali bombings unless you count Australian tourists as an occupying force. It is also a stretch to say the young Muslims in Europe blow up trains to protest the Iraq situation. And how would one explain British converts to Islam, some of whom are also eager to plant bombs? If Muslims anywhere, even converts, can commit such acts in support of distant co-religionists we return to an essentialist explanation: The whole culture is to blame.

Another specific explanation notes that bombers aim at the corrupt and dictatorial regimes that dominate the Middle East. Egyptian and Saudi youth, helped by Islamist preaching, attack hated political authorities. The solution: democratize the Middle East. Neo-cons push this approach, but there is little evidence that it will work. Lebanon held free elections that put Hezbollah deputies into parliament and the cabinet. Then Hezbollah started a new war with Israel. A freer country may simply offer more opportunities for rebellion. Saddam Hussein, with his brutal security police, was untroubled by radical Islamists.

Huntington would not dispute the specific points offered to explain Islamist terrorism but would note that, taken together, they form an overall pattern of an angry and violent civilization. Accumulate enough specific reasons and you reach an essentialist conclusion.

For sound analysis of the motives of suicide bombers and other terrorists, at least two things need to be sorted out. First, the "level of analysis" has to be settled. Are we talking about the **micro** level, which looks at individuals, or the **macro** level, which looks at whole countries or even the world? We cannot assume that individual behavior and attitudes explain the behavior of millions of people, and vice-versa.

The next analytical problem is the bundling together of unlike cases. Palestinian, Lebanese, Saudi, Egyptian, Iraqi, and other killers have different motives and socioeconomic and psychological profiles. Interviews of Palestinian "martyrs" do not explain the 9/11 terrorists, who in turn do not explain Iraqi suicide bombers. In contrast to the 9/11 Saudi killers, Moroccan bombers in 2003 were poor and uneducated. One size does not fit all. Different political situations create extremists with different motives. Beneath the several factors that could lead to terrorism, the one consistent point they have in common is the passionate embrace of Islam.

In 1995 a car bomb destroyed the front of the Saudi National Guard building in Riyadh, killing five Americans and two Indians. The Saudis arrested and beheaded four of their fellow countrymen for the crime. Three of the four admitted to having fought in Afghanistan, one in bin Laden's own group. On August 7, 1998, suicide bombers blew up trucks full of explosives at U.S. embassies in Nairobi, Kenya, and Dar-es-Salaam, Tanzania, within nine minutes of each other. Planning for the bombings had taken five years. The bombs killed 224 and injured thousands, most of them local Muslim Africans.

micro   Looking at the close-up picture of individuals.
macro   Looking at the big picture, a whole country or the world.

K ⋮ *Key Concepts*

Low-Intensity Warfare

One way to define terrorism that avoids some of the complexities and ambiguities is simply to see it as a type of low-intensity warfare. We can array warfare on a spectrum or scale. At the top is all-out warfare between countries, with uniformed soldiers, much equipment, massive destruction, and essentially no limits. World Wars I and II are examples. Not all wars are total; some are confined to one area. The United States and China fought in Korea but not outside of Korea. Some wars have only a little at stake. Argentina and Britain fought a brief, undeclared war over the Falklands (Malvinas, if you prefer) in 1982 but did not attack each other's homelands. It simply would not have been worth it.

Smaller is **guerrilla** warfare. Guerrilla is simply Spanish for "little war" and was first used in the early nineteenth century as Spanish patriots, civilian "partisans," strove to expel Napoleon's legions. Faced with a much stronger occupying power, the partisans (with British help) resorted to irregular tactics. The opening stages of guerrilla struggles are often insurgencies, a group trying to overthrow a hated political authority. The Pentagon calls this "low-intensity warfare" and instituted "counterinsurgency" tactics to oppose it. The Green Berets in Vietnam are examples.

It is here that we get to terrorism. Typically, an insurgency starts with and continues to commit acts of terrorism. A small group of believers robs a bank, shoots police, or bombs a main street. They hope the hated political authority overreacts by arresting, torturing, or bombing many people. The more they do, the more recruits for the insurgents' cause. Hezbollah played this card brilliantly in 2006. They deliberately provoked Israeli attacks knowing that the great destruction and loss of innocent Lebanese lives would rally world Muslim opinion to their cause. Even Sunni extremists who hate Shi'a, such as al Qaeda, supported Hezbollah, at least temporarily. The terrorist practices a kind of jujitsu, using the larger mass of the opponent to trip him. We might see terrorism as entry-level warfare. Once the terrorists' political commitments become rooted in a population, they are hard to root out. Hezbollah illustrates the progression of an angry group from terrorism to guerrilla warfare to conventional warfare with rockets.

On January 1, 2000, al Qaeda tried to bring in the new millennium with simultaneous attacks on tourist sites in Jordan and at the Los Angeles International Airport. Law enforcement authorities foiled the attacks before they could take place. An alert U.S. Customs official spotted the nervous driver on a ferry from British Columbia to Washington State. Two days later in Yemen, jihadis tried to pilot a rubber boat full of explosives into the side of the USS *The Sullivans,* but the overloaded boat sank. The Americans never knew that they had been targeted. Ten months later, the same fanatics drove their boat into the USS *Cole,* killing seventeen American sailors and almost sinking the warship. After that attack, the Pentagon ceased using Aden as a refueling port. Bin Laden had won again.

---

guerrilla   Irregular small-unit, hit-and-run warfare.

9/11

On September 11, 2001, America finally saw al Qaeda as a major threat. Al Qaeda terrorists armed with box cutters and led by Egyptian Muhammad Atta hijacked four American airliners. They did not try to smuggle weapons or explosives on board but used the planes' fuel as bombs. Two planes destroyed the World Trade Center, killing almost 3,000 and causing billions in damage. Citizens of eighty countries, many of them Muslim, died in the attack. It was Britain's greatest terrorist tragedy as well as America's. A third plane crashed into the Pentagon, killing 180. The fourth plane, high over Pennsylvania, turned toward Washington, D.C. Passengers who heard on their cell phones of the other attacks rushed the hijackers. The plane crashed and all died. Their sacrifice prevented the plane from killing possibly hundreds or thousands more had it reached its target in the nation's capital.

In retaliation, an angry America invaded Afghanistan, deposed the Taliban government, and killed hundreds of al Qaeda supporters (see Chapter 14). Many of the leading members of al Qaeda were killed or captured. The two at the top, bin Laden and al-Zawahiri, escaped to hide in the tribal territories in Pakistan's lawless Northwest Province.

On May 12, 2003, al Qaeda launched a wave of bombings inside Saudi Arabia. Three car bombs detonated simultaneously inside residential compounds where foreign workers stayed. At least twenty-nine foreigners were killed, including seven Americans. Bin Laden's actions delivered three messages simultaneously: They had not been defeated, they could operate inside the capital city of their enemies, and they had not abandoned their goal of driving Americans out of the Kingdom. One of the compounds was the residence of Vinnell corporation employees who trained the Saudi National Guard. Four days later, fourteen suicide bombers killed twenty-nine people in five explosions in Casablanca, Morocco. The targets included a Jewish center and the Belgian consulate. Moroccans associated with al Qaeda had attacked the foreign presence in a distant corner of the Dar al-Islam.

Over the past fifteen years there have been hundreds of terrorist attacks and attempts. Some, such as shoe-bomber Richard Reid and Jose Badillo, were al Qaeda associates who were stopped. Others had nothing to do with this international terrorist conspiracy but were motivated by their own causes. Clearly the United States and Western Europe remain targets of bin Laden's wrath.

LESSONS LEARNED

There are a number of lessons to be learned from the terrorist attacks, most importantly that al Qaeda does not give up. Agents affiliated with it tried to take down the World Trade Center in 1993; others finished the job in 2001. Al Qaeda tried to sink a U.S. warship in Yemen in January 2000; it succeeded in October. It tried to stop Americans from supporting the Saudi National Guard in

1995 and returned to the target in 2003. It likes to show its reach by organizing simultaneous attacks on multiple targets. The targets themselves are usually symbolic but may also have some economic importance. Finally, al Qaeda has no compunction about shedding Muslim blood—as it did in bombing three Jordanian hotels in 2005. Still, 8 percent of the world's Muslims strongly support anti-U.S. terrorism.

The United States may have the most powerful army in the history of the world, but its military prowess has been unsuccessful in removing the terrorist threat of Osama bin Laden and his supporters. The country is currently engaged in a long twilight struggle with the terrorists, employing the country's law-enforcement and intelligence organizations. Numerous arrests of al Qaeda supporters throughout Europe show that in the War on Terror the United States still can count on allies that opposed its 2003 invasion of Iraq.

The arrests are a good sign: We have had a number of successes in the War on Terror. They are also a bad sign: Despite the arrests, al Qaeda seems to have little trouble recruiting. "The Base" no longer has its safe haven in Afghanistan, and in many ways the organization has been decapitated. While this may hurt the organization's ability to coordinate, it also makes it harder to root out its component parts. Al Qaeda is more a mood than an organization. It is like a charitable foundation to which like-minded groups come for ideas and money. Take away the headquarters as the allies did in Afghanistan and the many affiliates still function. It has no formal structure, headquarters, or membership (roughly estimated at 18,000). Searching for al Qaeda's links to any particular country—Afghanistan or Iraq—is frustrating. Even if some connections are found—and nothing significant was found in Iraq—al Qaeda has already vanished like the mist. But it is always ready to regroup and try again.

Al Qaeda is motivated by a number of grievances, some reasonable, some not. There is poverty and suffering in the Islamic world. Israel exists and is at war with elements in the Palestinian territories. Many Islamic rulers pay little attention to the needs of their people or the precepts of their faith. American troops are posted in more Islamic lands than ever. Even changing these conditions cannot guarantee an end to terrorist attacks. The demographic bulge in Muslim lands produces millions of angry young men, who can easily fall into salafi fanaticism. An estimated 70,000 to 100,000 young Muslim men have undergone Islamist training of some sort. One current fear is that Iraq now serves as a terrorist training ground, as Afghanistan did earlier. We could be inadvertently replenishing al Qaeda's ranks. Now training also takes place in Pakistan.

Western governments actively support many of the conditions opposed by al Qaeda for what they deem reasons of national interest, such as U.S. support for Saudi Arabia. Bin Laden and his people hope that terrorist attacks will convince the West that the price they pay to pursue these interests is higher than the benefits received. When that happens, they reason, the West will withdraw, as it did in Vietnam, Beirut, Somalia, and Yemen. The questions for policy makers: How important is the Middle East to Western interests? Is the occasional terrorist attack (no matter how horrific) a price we are willing to pay? Further terrorist attacks are likely.

CONCLUSIONS

Political Islam is inevitable and appears immediately with democratization in the Middle East. It does not necessarily produce extremism or terrorism. Some see evolving and moderating forms of Islam, possibly an Islamic reformation, pushed along by thinkers and educated women.

One man's terrorist is another's freedom fighter, especially in the Middle East, where people who have committed "terrorist" acts later became national leaders. For the United States the most serious form of international terrorism is Islamist terrorism as practiced by al Qaeda, which got its start in the Islamic struggle against the Soviets in Afghanistan. While al Qaeda received no direct U.S. support, America must take some blame for creating the climate that encouraged jihadis. Similarly, the Saudi royal family protests that they are victims of Islamist terrorism, but they have to take some blame for allowing an extremist interpretation of Islam to spread.

There will be no victory in the War on Terror, no parade when the troops come home. This war is fought in the shadows and will continue as long as there is Islamist hatred. For that hatred to subside, Islam may have to undergo a reformation that makes its values compatible with the modern, democratic values of the West.

KEY TERMS

bounce-back effect (p. 299)

guerrilla (p. 310)

Islamism (p. 301)

macro (p. 309)

micro (p. 309)

reformation (p. 298)

salafiyya (p. 300)

FURTHER REFERENCE

DeLong-Bas, Natana J. *Wahhabi Islam: From Revival and Reform to Global Jihad*. New York: Oxford University Press, 2004.

Donohue, John J., and John L. Esposito, eds. *Islam in Transition: Muslim Perspectives*, 2nd ed. New York: Oxford University Press, 2006.

Farmer, Brian R. *Understanding Radical Islam: Medieval Ideology in the Twenty-First Century*. New York: Peter Lang, 2007.

Fattah, Moataz A. *Democratic Values in the Muslim World*. Boulder, CO: Lynne Rienner, 2006.

Forest, James J. F., ed. *The Making of a Terrorist: Recruitment, Training, and Root Causes*, 3 vols. Westport, CT: Praeger, 2005.

Gerges, Fawaz A. *The Far Enemy: Why Jihad Went Global*. New York: Cambridge University Press, 2005.

Hafez, Mohammed M. *Why Muslims Rebel: Repression and Resistance in the Islamic World.* Boulder, CO: Lynne Rienner, 2004.

Hoffman, Bruce. *Inside Terrorism,* rev. ed. New York: Columbia University Press, 2006.

Jenkins, Brian M. *Unconquerable Nation: Knowing Our Enemy, Strengthening Ourselves.* Santa Monica, CA: RAND, 2006.

Kepel, Gilles. *The War for Muslim Minds: Islam and the West.* Cambridge, MA: Harvard University Press, 2004.

Klausen, Jytte. *The Islamic Challenge: Politics and Religion in Western Europe.* New York: Oxford University Press, 2005.

Lawrence, Bruce, ed. *Messages to the World: The Statements of Osama bin Laden.* London: Verso, 2005.

Mickolus, Edward F., with Susan L. Simmons. *Terrorism, 2002–2004: A Chronology,* 2 vols. Westport, CT: Praeger, 2005.

Musalam, Adnan A. *From Secularism to Jihad: Sayyid Qutb and the Foundations of Radical Islamism.* Westport, CT: Praeger, 2005.

Norton, Augustus Richard. *Hezbollah: A Short History.* Princeton, NJ: Princeton University Press, 2007.

Pape, Robert A. *Dying to Win: The Strategic Logic of Suicide Terrorism.* New York: Random House, 2005.

Randal, Jonathan. *Osama: The Making of a Terrorist.* New York: Vintage, 2006.

Roy, Olivier. *Globalized Islam: The Search for a New Ummah.* New York: Columbia University Press, 2006.

Scheuer, Michael. *Through Our Enemies' Eyes.* Dulles, VA: Potomac Books, 2006.

Takeyh, Ray, and Nikolas K. Gvosdev. *The Receding Shadow of the Prophet: The Rise and Fall of Radical Political Islam.* Westport, CT: Praeger, 2004.

Wright, Lawrence. *The Looming Tower: Al-Qaeda and the Road to 9/11.* New York: Knopf, 2006.

17 *The United States and the Middle East*

Points to Ponder

- Since when has the United States been deeply involved in the Middle East?
- What did the Soviets try to do in the Middle East? Did they succeed?
- How and why did Lebanon twice draw in U.S. Marines?
- When did U.S. policy shift from even-handed to pro-Israel?
- How did Kissinger rig the results of the 1973 war?
- Is Jerusalem widely recognized as Israel's capital?
- What is the influence of the religious right on U.S. policy on the Arab-Israeli dispute?
- Is the U.S.-Saudi relationship stable and reliable?
- Is war with Iran possible? Under what circumstances?
- Can America steer clear of the Middle East?

The United States has long had contact with the Middle East, but until World War II the connection was weak and intermittent. Europe, Latin America, and Asia mattered far more. President Jefferson sent America's first overseas military expedition "to the shores of Tripoli" in 1805 to stop piracy against U.S. merchant ships in the Mediterranean. (It did not stop.) Tripoli, in present-day Libya (there is another Tripoli in Lebanon), was then nominally part of the slowly decaying Ottoman Empire, with which the United States developed trade relations. The Ottomans permitted American missionary activity, but only among the Christians of the empire. Muslims are not permitted to exit the faith; **apostasy** is punished by stoning to death. American schools and colleges in Istanbul, Beirut, and Cairo educated many future leaders of the region, all of whom stayed Muslim. (The Mormons, who proselytize almost everywhere, do not send missionaries to Islamic countries.)

U.S. interest in the region grew with World War II, and for several reasons. The British had oil contracts with Iraq and Iran sewn up decades earlier, but the

---

apostasy   Abandoning a religion.

immensity of the Saudi oil fields became clear during the war, and here the United States was in on the ground floor, establishing a close relationship with the ruling House of Saud even under President Franklin D. Roosevelt. As soon as Germany invaded the Soviet Union in 1941, Britain and Russia acted on their 1907 agreement (which Iranians always hated) to chop Iran in three, Russia in the north and Britain in the south with an unoccupied belt in the middle. The United States soon took over from the British and turned Iran into a major supply corridor for the beleaguered Soviet Union. After the war, the United States made Iran and Saudi Arabia the pillars of its anti-Communist containment policy in the region.

U.S. EVEN-HANDEDNESS

The Holocaust and birth of Israel also forced the United States to pay attention to the Middle East. Before World War II, it had been British and French spheres of influence. Troubled by guilt over having done little to save Jews from the Holocaust, America firmly supported the new Jewish state, even to the point of antagonizing Britain, by mobilizing votes in the UN in 1947 and by Truman's instant recognition of Israel in 1948. The United States also sold surplus World War II tanks and trucks that Israel used for decades. Israel's standard tank in 1973 was a U.S.-made Sherman, first produced in 1942 but refitted by the Israelis with a bigger gun (105mm) and engine into a "Super-Sherman."

Truman, however, upon the advice of the Arab-leaning State Department, kept a polite even-handedness in the Arab-Israeli dispute. Eisenhower was cool toward Israel as he tried to minimize Soviet influence in the Middle East. The Cold War and fear of losing the Arabs to communism kept U.S. policy in rough balance; we could not be especially pro-Israel. Eisenhower was angry at the 1956 British-French-Israeli attack on Egypt and told them to clear out. Johnson was sympathetic to Israel in the 1967 war but too bogged down in Vietnam to take much of an interest.

At its birth, Israel defined itself as neutral in the Cold War. Israel was founded by socialists—or at least they thought they were—and many still harbored warm feelings toward the Soviets as brothers in arms against the Nazis. Moscow recognized Israel just a few minutes after Washington did. Stalin was not pro-Israel but merely saw a way to get the British out of the Middle East. The paranoid Stalin did not trust Jews—he called them "rootless cosmopolitans"—and unleashed a wave of anti-Semitism in the Soviet Union and its East European satellites, where Jews were sent to prison or the gallows, making Israelis doubt and then oppose the Soviet Union.

After Stalin died in 1953, his flamboyant successor, Nikita Khrushchev, began courting the **Third World**. In 1955 he signed up Egypt as a client state, the first of several in the Arab world, and Israel rethought its neutralism, by then seriously at odds with reality. The neutrals of the Cold War—led by Nehru of India, Sukarno of Indonesia, and Nasser of Egypt—declared solidarity with the Arabs and

Third World   Asia, Africa, and Latin America.

The United States in the Middle East

MARINES IN BEIRUT, 1958

The U.S. Marines blown up in their barracks in Beirut, Lebanon, in 1983 (see box on page 320) marked the second time they had been there. Almost forgotten was the Marines' first visit in 1958. Eisenhower had hoped to improve relations with Nasser by opposing the 1956 Israeli-British-French invasion of Egypt, but Nasser did not reciprocate. Instead, Nasser became more radical, expansionist, and pro-Soviet. To some American specialists, it looked like Nasser was helping the Soviets gain control of the Middle East. This was not the case—communism and Nasserism were two very different things—but the Cold War led to great oversimplifications.

In 1958, Lebanon experienced a constitutional crisis and major breakdown, a harbinger of the total breakdown that was to come in the 1970s. Lebanon had gained its freedom from France in 1943 on the basis of power balancing among a dozen religions in what was called the National Pact, with Christians having more power than Muslims. The presidency, for example, was always in the hands of a Maronite Christian (a local branch of Catholicism, independent of but tied to Rome). The basis of the National Pact was an out-of-date census that had counted more Christians than Muslims. By the late 1950s, with the Muslim birth rate far exceeding that of Christians, Muslims were probably in the majority, and they demanded a bigger slice of power.

In 1958, a rivalry among Christians initially triggered conflict. President Camille Chamoun sought to amend the Lebanese constitution to allow him to serve a second term. A rival for the presidency, General Chehab, controlled the military and had the support of Muslims who were angry with Chamoun for not breaking relations with Britain and France after the 1956 Suez crisis. As civil war neared, Chamoun called for help, citing the Eisenhower doctrine. There was no threat of communism, but Washington wanted to show resolve following Nasser's union with Syria and the loss of Iraq to the West in 1958. U.S. Marines landed in Beirut in 1958, but only after a tense standoff on the beach with General Chehab's army. Nothing special happened, the Marines soon left, Chamoun stepped down, and Chehab succeeded him. The National Pact remained in effect. The relatively minor incident marked the first U.S. intervention with troops in the Middle East and the beginning of deeper U.S. involvement.

---

accepted the Arab line that Israel was an outpost of Western imperialism. In 1967 the Soviet Union—which helped start the Six Day War (see page 91)—and its satellites (plus Yugoslavia) all broke diplomatic relations with Israel, and Israel turned staunchly anti-Soviet.

THE NIXON TILT

President Richard Nixon greatly deepened U.S. involvement in the region, and on Israel's side. Previously, Washington had been rather hands-off in Arab-Israeli wars; now it was hands-on. Nixon warned Moscow not to intervene in the 1973 October War and backed it up by putting U.S. forces on heightened status. Nixon delivered a credible deterrence threat in 1973, and the Soviets heeded it. He also sent U.S. warships to the Eastern Mediterranean.

G: *Geography*

RECOGNITION OF JERUSALEM

The United States, like most nations, does not officially recognize Jerusalem as Israel's capital, even though it houses Israel's parliament and chief executive offices. (But not its defense ministry, which remains in Tel Aviv, farther from potential attackers. Germany for the same reason left its defense ministry in Bonn when it moved its capital to Berlin in 1991.) Only Costa Rica and El Salvador have their embassies in Jerusalem.

The U.S. **embassy**, like most, is in Tel Aviv, although a **consulate general** in Jerusalem handles many contacts. Officially, the United States still designates its consulate general there as "Jerusalem, Palestine," perhaps the last remnant of the 1947 UN partition plan. In order to avoid recognizing Israel as sovereign in Jerusalem, American staffers in the consulate general are accredited to no host government, an unusual situation. The United States has many agreements with Israel but no formal defense alliance, although many refer to Israel as a U.S. ally. Security relations are close but have never been formalized into a treaty.

Modern warfare consumes munitions at an incredible rate, making logistics extremely important. Israel in 1973 soon ran short but was resupplied by rapid U.S. airlifts. Defense Minister Moshe Dayan told the Knesset, "We are firing shells this afternoon that we didn't even have in the country this morning."

But Nixon and his national security advisor Henry Kissinger, who had just become secretary of state, played a trickier game than merely supporting Israel. When Israel was in trouble, U.S. munitions flowed quickly to Israel, some from U.S. stores in Germany, others from stateside, in massive airlifts. But when the tide of battle reversed and Israel was winning, U.S. munitions dried up. Using a "good-cop-tough-cop" routine, Kissinger told Jerusalem he was trying to get more airlifts while Defense Secretary James Schlessinger said that we had no more to spare. It was a gimmick to restrain Israel from another victory.

Kissinger was no expert on the Middle East (he specialized in the Soviet nuclear threat), but he had a fine feel for power, as shown in his Harvard dissertation on post-Napoleon Europe and its manipulation by Austrian Prince Metternich. You do not reach peace directly (the pacifist mistake), but by first balancing power so the two sides have an incentive to talk. If Israel simply wins again, Kissinger believed in 1973, it will be 1967 all over again—total Arab rejection of any talks. So, in 1973 neither side could totally win nor totally lose; there had to be a psychological balance. This allowed Kissinger to shuttle (on Air Force One) between Cairo, Jerusalem, and Damascus, hammering out cease-fires that separated the parties

---

embassy   Diplomatic representation of one country to another, usually a house in the host country's capital.

consulate general   A diplomatic post of lesser status and more limited functions than an *embassy*.

𝖴𝖲 : *The United States in the Middle East*

THE CARTER DOCTRINE

Faced with growing instability in the Persian Gulf, President Jimmy Carter publicly acknowledged on January 23, 1980, a reality that dated back to at least World War II. "Let our position be absolutely clear: An attempt by any outside force to gain control of the Persian Gulf region will be regarded as an assault on the vital interests of the United States of America, and such an assault will be repelled by any means necessary, including military force." Although aimed at the Soviet Union, later presidents expanded the Carter Doctrine to include Iraq and Iran.

by demilitarized zones. These formed the basis of subsequent Egyptian-Israeli talks that led to peace.

The 1973 war also marked an open split between the United States and its European allies on the Middle East. As the United States got deeply involved, Europe emphatically stayed out. In 1973 Germany objected to the use of U.S. bases and munitions in Germany to resupply Israel. These bases were strictly for NATO purposes and the United States had no right to use them for anything else, claimed Bonn. By the same token, Portugal objected to the use of U.S. bases in the Azores to refuel the U.S. aircraft carrying munitions to Israel. The 1973 war thus marks an issue that came to a head in the 2003 war. The 1949 North Atlantic Treaty does not extend to the Middle East, although Washington wishes it did. NATO'S inability to expand its role from European defense to a Western security community that speaks with one voice outside of Europe made NATO irrelevant in the twenty-first century.

With the 1973 U.S. tilt toward Israel, the United States and Israel recognized their mutual interest in opposing Soviet power, which at that time looked quite threatening. The shift also marked a partial reversal of alliances in domestic U.S. politics. At least since Franklin D. Roosevelt, most American Jews had been Democrats, a constituent block of the Democratic party. With Nixon, however, some American Jews turned Republican. (During the nineteenth century, most Jews had been Republicans; things change.) Many were turned off by ultraliberals in the Democratic party. They feared the growth of Soviet power and worried about Israel's security. Some Jewish intellectuals became neo-conservatives and served Republicans in Washington.

Bush 41, with diplomatic experience and contacts with Arab leaders, was rather evenhanded and could speak firmly to Israel. Not so Bush 43, who is by far the most pro-Israel U.S. president. The religious right, a large portion of the Republican electorate, turned pro-Israel. Fundamentalists read the Bible literally, and it states that God gave this land to the Jews for eternity. Starting in the 1960s, fundamentalist authors (often citing the Books of Daniel and Revelation) wrote that the rebirth of Israel heralded Christ's second coming, and this view, encouraged by Israel, took over the religious right, who are now more pro-Israel than some Jewish Americans.

The United States in the Middle East

BLOWN UP IN BEIRUT, 1983

President Reagan's Secretary of State George Shultz, new to the job and with little knowledge of the Middle East, thought he understood the region and believed the United States could play a constructive peacemaking role. By 1982, Lebanon was in ruins, its territory rent by a dozen politico-religious militias and occupied by Syria and Israel. Along with France and Italy, the United States sent peacekeeping forces to try to calm Beirut. U.S. Marines went ashore, backed up by a battleship. Congress in effect rescinded its **War Powers Act** by giving Reagan eighteen months to use these forces, because they were "not involved in hostilities." But they were.

The trouble with trying to keep peace in a civil war is that you are quickly driven to take sides. Then the other side hates you and shoots at you. In this case, the United States drew close to the Lebanese Christians and found itself the target of Lebanese Muslims. In retaliation, a U.S. battleship fired huge (but inaccurate) naval shells into Muslim positions. America was now involved in someone else's civil war but did not want to admit it. There were warnings. A widely respected (and pro-Arab) American scholar, Malcolm Kerr, president of the American University of Beirut, was gunned down outside his office. In April 1983 a car bomb demolished the U.S. embassy in Beirut, killing more than sixty.

Then, in October 1983, a Hezbollah suicide driver crashed a Mercedes truck loaded with dynamite into the barracks of sleeping U.S. Marines at Beirut airport, killing 241. (The French peacekeepers were likewise bombed.) America was shocked, and Reagan swore we would not "cut and run," but we did. Too late came the realization that you cannot play peacemaker in the midst of an ongoing civil war, a lesson that still was not learned when West Europeans attempted to do it in Bosnia a decade later.

As Texas governor, Bush visited Israel in 1988. Then-Foreign Minister Ariel Sharon gave him a personal helicopter tour and established a close relationship. Bush was impressed with how vulnerable Israel was, especially at its narrow neck. With 9/11, Bush identified the terrorist attack on America with terrorism against Israel; we were both victims of the same evil forces. Officials of previous administrations saw the U.S. role as broker and complained that Bush 43 was too close to Israel.

Should the United States strongly support Israel? Jerusalem likes Washington telling Israel's enemies that America will not permit Israel's destruction, so they should abandon such illusions and settle. Some U.S. analysts, however, worry that backing Israel too much lets it expand West Bank settlements and invade Lebanon. Arab rage against the United States mounts, fueling more terrorism and harming any honest-broker role America might play.

War Powers Act   1973 U.S. law to limit president's use of troops overseas.

D ⋮ *Domestic Structures*

THE ISRAEL LOBBY

Two American academics created a minor storm with a 2006 article criticizing the power of the "Israel lobby" in Washington. John Mearsheimer of the University of Chicago and Stephen Walt of Harvard voiced an undercurrent of complaint that had been around for decades: Jewish interest groups, well-organized and well-funded, have undue influence in U.S. Middle East policy, tilting it strongly toward Israel. Israel gets about $3 billion a year, making it the largest recipient of U.S. aid since World War II, and Israel is no longer a poor country. U.S. support allows Israel to forever delay a viable Palestinian state. The article's most damning accusation was that Jewish neo-conservatives pushed the United States into the 2003 Iraq War as a way to safeguard Israel. Any who criticize Israel, either on Capitol Hill or in academia, are accused of anti-Semitism, as were the two authors. The net impact, they charge, is an absence of free and open debate on U.S. Middle East policy.

Observers agree that the American Israel Public Affairs Committee (AIPAC) is one of the most influential lobbies in Washington, in the same league as AARP and the National Rifle Association. AIPAC delivers funds and votes to pro-Israel candidates. Several Washington think tanks put out pro-Israel analyses. Other views are little heard.

But this is what Washington is all about: immoderate lobbying aimed at obtaining undue influence. American democracy is highly pluralistic and places few curbs on interest groups. AIPAC simply does what pro-Arab, pro-Greek, pro-Taiwan, and many other groups do, but perhaps does it better. Big Oil is not shy about influencing policy. How can you limit them? And what is the "right" amount of influence any one group should have? Who should be in charge of U.S. Middle East policy? Exxon? State Department Arabists? No panel of disinterested experts could successfully define U.S. national interests in the Middle East.

Mearsheimer and Walt have a point but oversimplify. Israel does not get everything AIPAC wants. Washington has said no to Israeli settlements and moving the U.S. embassy to Jerusalem. Some Israelis criticize AIPAC for supporting hard-line Israeli parties and policies. Many American Jews favor peace. The biggest single influence on U.S. Middle East policy is not AIPAC but 9/11, which seemed to make Americans and Israelis brothers in arms against terrorism.

WHAT ROLE FOR AMERICA?

The Bush 43 administration—specifically, his first national security advisor (and secretary of state in his second term), Condoleezza Rice—entered the White House saying not much could be done about the Israel-Palestine struggle; Washington should just support Israel and advance no special peace initiatives. American diplomats and even presidents had worked long and hard on the "peace process" only to see it fail. We were too involved in the Middle East and should distance ourselves from it, argued the White House. We cannot fix it and should stop trying.

It was a plausible notion, but then came 9/11 and everything changed. America learned that the Muslim world was seething in anger at America, and one of its main complaints was U.S. support for Israel. Palestinian militants displayed pictures of Osama bin Laden and the World Trade Center. Bush proclaimed new interest in an Israel-Palestine settlement. A "Quartet" of America, the European Union, the UN, and Russia drew up a "road map" for a settlement, but it led nowhere and was quickly forgotten. Soon Bush's involvement in the Middle East resembled that of Clinton. In 2005 now Secretary of State Rice flew to the area to personally mediate a problem between Israel and the Palestine Authority over Gaza. It was exactly the kind of involvement she earlier eschewed, but she did a good job. Again in the 2006 Hezbollah War with Lebanon, Rice initially advocated hands off until Hezbollah was crushed. But pressure over the slaughter of civilians soon pushed her into seeking a cease-fire. In foreign policy, you do not always get to do what you wish.

THE MUSLIM WORLD AFTER THE WAR

The 2003 war cost America most of its Arab and Muslim friends. A late 2005 poll found that only 7 percent of Arabs supported al Qaeda's terrorism, but 36 percent liked how al Qaeda "confronts the United States." Arab intellectuals—some of whom studied in the United States and have relatives here—used to see a positive U.S. influence in moving their societies to freedom and democracy. With the Iraq War, they ceased defending America. The 2006 Israeli fight with Hezbollah made things worse. Actually, educated Arabs know and admire American freedom and democracy; they just oppose U.S. policy, especially support for Israel and for authoritarian regimes. Intellectuals are important; they gradually steer society by ideas and respected positions in law, education, science, and communications. The loss of Arab intellectuals is a long-lasting price America is paying.

As in 1991, the **Arab street** raged briefly at the U.S. invasion of a brother Arab country. After the 2003 war, however, this anger did not fade. Once again, Arabs and Muslims had been humiliated by the Christian West. Many Arabs felt that the Americans were arrogant, crowing at the ease and speed of their victory. Hundreds volunteered for a jihad against the Americans in Iraq. America sees itself as doing a difficult job for the good of the whole region and is disappointed that few say thanks.

Arabs feel that every time the West wins, they lose, a feeling that goes back to the *Reconquista* and Crusades. Arab regimes killing their own citizens is either ignored or excused. Hafez Assad, long Syria's brainy and brutal dictator, leveled Hama with artillery fire in 1982, killing some 20,000 Syrians, to crush the Muslim Brotherhood. Few Arabs said anything; Syria is hard to govern and needs a strong hand at the top, was the excuse. Saddam Hussein killed as many as 500,000 Muslim Iranians and 120,000 Muslim Iraqis, but few Muslims said anything; even Tehran condemned the U.S.-led attacks on Iraq in both 1991 and 2003. Now Sudan practices genocide against fellow Muslims in Darfur, but Arab governments take no notice. Facing the West, Islam displays a solidarity

---

Arab street   Short for public opinion in Arab countries.

that they ignore when facing each other. If we do it to ourselves, it is because the other side is not truly Muslim. If outsiders do it to us, they are the new crusaders trying to destroy Islam.

One moderate Arab intellectual said it was not the "Arab street" that worried him; it was the "Arab basement," the places out of sight where enraged youths concoct plots and bombs. Al Qaeda, very loose-knit, does not publish membership statistics, but groups following its ideology clearly got more volunteers after the Iraq War. Its terrorist activities did not disappear. Islamist bombings hit Saudi Arabia, Morocco, Spain, Indonesia, India, England, and Jordan.

Will the hostility of the Muslim world hurt the U.S.-led hunt for terrorists? Some countries, such as Saudi Arabia, suddenly discovered they had an incentive to join the hunt before al Qaeda overthrew them. But other Muslim countries quietly discovered that they could calm domestic unrest and gain respect in the Muslim world by dragging their feet in the hunt for terrorists. Yemen, an al Qaeda playground, promised cooperation with U.S. officials but let suspects in the *Cole* bombing escape. Some governments work both sides of the street, with one ministry cooperating with the United States while others help terrorists hide and ply their trade. Pakistan never thoroughly combed through its lawless northwest looking for Osama and his associates, who almost certainly were (or still are) there. Al Qaeda affiliates conduct a terror campaign in Kashmir to help Pakistan win it from India, and Pakistan does not want this shadowy relationship revealed. Cracking down on al Qaeda could cost Pakistan its best terrorists. Remember, Pakistan's ISI set up the Taliban and aided al Qaeda in Afghanistan. Al Qaeda is not despised everywhere.

The Bush about-faces raise the question of how involved we should be in the Middle East. Clearly, a hands-off policy begs for an explosion. The White House initially did not try to stop Israel's 2006 war against Hezbollah, arguing that a cease-fire would simply delay a solution to Iranian-backed terrorism. Lebanese civilian casualties, however, were so horrific that Washington found itself isolated and criticized and soon worked overtime on getting a cease-fire. Hands-off is not possible.

But a hands-on policy also begs for trouble. The two Beirut visits by U.S. Marines illustrate how we can get involved in other people's civil wars (see boxes on pages 317 and 320). A major American presence, especially military, angers local populations (which happens in South Korea and Japan as well).

WHAT NEXT FOR U.S. POLICY?

Is the 2003 Iraq War a template for further U.S. actions in the Middle East? Rumors swirled that after that war we would soon invade Syria and depose the sister Baathist regime that had ruled there for decades. By 2007 there were hints that we would go after Iran, which likely is building nuclear weapons. Would it be wise? It was perhaps good that we were too busy in Iraq to invade another country in the region.

The United States in the Middle East

GETTING NATO INTO THE MIDDLE EAST

NATO performed admirably for forty years (1949–1989). It first made Stalin less frightening and let European economies and self-confidence recover. NATO gave America the legal and moral structure with which to defend West Europe while giving West Europeans the excuse to avoid defending themselves. From its beginning, NATO was plagued by imbalance, with the United States spending more on the defense of Europe than the Europeans did. Starting with Truman, all presidents complained that our European partners had to do more in their own defense. NATO's failure to support the United States in the Middle East in 2003 was years in the making. The end of Communist regimes in East Europe in 1989 and demise of the Soviet Union in 1991 made explicit what had long been implicit: What good is this alliance?

It could be very good, if it could redefine itself, in Samuel Huntington's terms, as Western civilization with a sense of solidarity and mission to defend itself against barbarism. But Huntington erred, many now agree, in posing the West as a single civilization with European and North American branches. Seymour Martin Lipset, with much better empirical grounding, emphasized the cultural differences between Europe and the United States.

Europeans complain that American politicians are cowboys, too quick to see threats and charge out to run the world. But it is equally true that Europeans, with some exceptions, are too immersed in welfare-state pacifism to venture outside their Continent. A Swiss friend told one of the authors years ago, "You know, Europe is so drenched in blood from centuries of warfare that Europeans really won't fight again. They've had it with wars."

More importantly, the interests of the United States and West Europe were never identical—they were complementary—and in 2002 they rapidly diverged over the Middle East. Americans and Europeans simply did not see the Middle East in the same way. Washington sees a region on the brink of chaos that we must stabilize—to halt terrorism, to insure the flow of oil, to foster democratization, and to reach an Israel-Palestine compromise. Europeans see a dangerous region that outside intervention can only destabilize. They see Israeli intransigence as the barrier to peace. American public opinion is pro-Israel, European anti-Israel. Some suggest Europeans are burying their guilt over their World War II actions and inactions by denouncing Israelis as fascists. Americans see Israelis as fellow believers and fighters against terrorism. No amount of diplomacy can bridge these different perceptions.

According to some reports, the neo-cons in the Bush administration viewed war with Iraq as simply a first step to establishing a major and long-term presence in the region. We would set up semipermanent U.S. bases in Iraq and vacate our bases in unreliable Saudi Arabia. Then we would not have to ask anyone's permission for U.S. military action throughout the region. Extremists would know that U.S. power was just in the next country. That would also encourage Saudi Arabia, Syria, Iran, and other regimes to turn to democracy, argued the neo-cons.

Almost instinctively, few Americans liked that picture, and it quickly vanished as U.S. troops stayed to pacify an unruly Iraq, which might be the least secure place in the region for a U.S. base. America, born in a revolt against an empire, does not like to see itself playing empire. Empires are bad; free and independent peoples are good. The Cold War was one of the few times we kept U.S. forces overseas for decades, and that was to defend willing allies.

Ironically, the only time NATO invoked Article 5 of its 1949 founding treaty ("attack on one . . . attack on all") was when a tentacle of the Middle East reached out and wounded America on 9/11. A German AWACS plane took a few turns around the Northeast, a little photo op that may be the only time Europe will ever come to the defense of America. And Iraq was very much about 9/11, which changed the psychology of America. Americans suffered it; the Europeans did not. America was angry; Europe was not. America was deeply involved in the Middle East; Europe sees U.S. intervention as making things worse. Americans go to war; Europeans turn to diplomacy and international law. European NATO forces have contributed to peacekeeping in Afghanistan but see no similar role in Iraq.

Some analysts see the differences as naturally arising from the fact that America is now the most powerful nation on earth while Europe has only modest power. Powerful countries stride forth to remake the world to their liking; weak countries hunker down, hoping trouble passes them by and criticizing the strong nations for arrogance and misuse of power. For decades, especially since Vietnam, European intellectuals have criticized American foreign policy. A few just plain hate America, a hatred that came out again with the Iraq War in 2003. Official Washington used to take their criticisms with forbearance, determined not to let it harm the Atlantic alliance. A few sarcastic peeps about feckless Europeans came from Henry Kissinger, Zbigniew Brzezinski, William Cohen, and Capitol Hill. With the Iraq War, however, Washington criticized back, loudly and openly. What a few realists muttered for years in academic journals and op-ed pieces was now heard from the highest levels. Secretary of Defense Donald Rumsfeld was the most caustic, but the White House and State Department did not disavow his remarks.

Europe has been very cautious about involvement in the Middle East. Following the toppling of the Taliban in Afghanistan in late 2001, eventually 32,000 NATO forces (some of them U.S., British, and Canadian) are attempting to stabilize the country but face a major Taliban resurgence based in neighboring Pakistan. Europeans, led by an Italian *Carabinieri* general, monitor the border crossing between Egypt and the Gaza Strip. As part of getting Israel out of the south of Lebanon in 2006, Europe pledged to contribute 7,000 soldiers to the UN to help the Lebanese army occupy that area. They were not instructed to disarm or fight Hezbollah. The European approach to the Middle East is to send few soldiers and only for peacekeeping.

The problems of a U.S. empire emerged a century ago. We took the Philippines in 1898 but got a bad conscience when we had to crush an insurrection of Filipino patriots against us. The war officially ended in 1902, but conflict continued until 1913. We told the Filipinos we had come to liberate them from Spanish tyranny, but then we stayed. The Philippines, thought Teddy Roosevelt and his fellow imperialists (the neo-cons of their day), would be a splendid base for U.S. commerce and power in Asia. By 1907 even Roosevelt saw the mistake: First we had to fight to keep the Philippines, then we would have to defend the Philippines, and growing Japanese power already loomed on the horizon. We had acquired a vulnerability. Lightly garrisoned and nearly forgotten between the wars, the Philippines were easy pickings for the Japanese in 1942. Empires cost money, troops, and a shift of attention from domestic affairs to overseas affairs.

G ⦂ *Geography*

A UNIPOLAR WORLD?

How is power distributed around the world? Many political scientists described the Cold War as **bipolar**. After the demise of the Soviet Union in 1991, the situation is not so clear. Some see a **multipolar** world dominated by several blocs, including the United States, West Europe, China, and Japan.

But neo-conservatives (see page 282) see the world as **unipolar**: The United States has so much power that it can and must lead the world. Only we have the economic and military power to balance and stabilize a tumultuous and dangerous world. Historically, a stable world has required a stabilizer, such as Britain in the nineteenth century. If we do not lead, no one will. The unipolar view of the world underlies some of the *unilateralism* of the Bush 43 administration: Try to lead others, but act alone if need be. According to the neo-cons (and many others), the European Union and UN can be relied upon for nothing.

Many criticize the unipolar-unilateralist view. It is at odds with the much older conservatism of the Republican party, which tends to isolationism, not involvement in distant lands. As such, there were disagreements among Republicans over the unipolar view. It assumes America has enough power to stop aggression and rogue states throughout the world. This in turn assumes the American people and Congress have the money and patience to sustain major overseas military involvement.

U.S. public opinion is volatile, and isolationism can leap out. Fifty-nine percent told a 2006 poll the United States should *not* take the lead in solving international problems. A similar percent thought the war in Iraq had been a mistake. A short crusade rallies Americans, but a long war costs votes. Consider the effects of Korea on the 1952 U.S. election and Vietnam on the 1968 election.

The unipolar-unilateralist approach also minimizes the difficulties and complexities of areas like the Middle East. Do we have sufficient expertise and language skills in these areas? Are the experts listened to? The unipolar view also assumes most of the world will follow America's lead. The Iraq War made allies *less* willing to follow Washington and degraded America's image abroad, especially after revelations of torture. Unilateralists assume the United States can get along without allies or even sympathy from the rest of the world. This is a mistake. Going it alone really does leave America alone and isolated.

ISLAMIC RAGE AND U.S. RESPONSE

Muslims have been getting beaten by the West for centuries. The Moors were pushed back in Spain over eight centuries until expelled in 1492. The Turks were pushed back in the Balkans over two centuries until confined to their little corner of Europe in 1913. Defeat by the West in World War I led to the end of the Ottoman Empire and Caliphate. Osama bin Laden referred to this end of the last Muslim empire as a terrible tragedy the West had inflicted on the entire community of Islam. The British and French occupied Arab lands and treated them as colonies.

---

bipolar   World dominated by two major powers, the United States and Soviet Union.

multipolar   World divided among several power centers.

unipolar   World dominated by one superpower.

Peace

CAN DIPLOMACY WORK?

Diplomacy is widely misunderstood, both by its proponents and its detractors. Some urge, "Give diplomacy a chance!" They see it as a substitute for war. Others scoff at diplomacy as worthless. When necessary, they say, countries must be prepared to go to war. Both sides exaggerate.

At certain times, when two parties to a dispute are willing to compromise, diplomacy that is carried out well can prevent the dispute from getting worse and sometimes solve it. When the two sides have been exhausted by war, they may be ready for diplomacy. Europe after the Napoleonic wars was ready for diplomacy; this is why the 1815 Congress of Vienna worked and set up a Europe that avoided major wars until 1914. This is what happened with the peace treaties of 1979 between Israel and Egypt and of 1994 between Israel and Jordan. When the time is ripe, diplomacy can work.

But when two sides are far apart over basic issues—the case most of the time in the Israel-Palestine dispute—diplomacy can do little. No amount of smooth diplomacy can bridge the gap between the two on such difficult issues as Jewish settlements in the West Bank, the right of Palestinians to return to old homes in Israel, and Jerusalem as capital of a Palestinian state. Perhaps after some years of bashing each other silly, the two sides will decide it is time to compromise. This situation, however, cannot be wished into existence.

When the time is ripe, there are techniques of **third-party diplomacy** that can help: good offices, mediation, conciliation, arbitration, and adjudication. The first three have been tried for the Middle East, mostly sponsored by America, some by European countries.

Good offices are the most basic third-party diplomacy. A country not a party to the dispute provides a meeting place and security.

Mediation takes the process to the next level. Here the third party suggests compromises.

Conciliation is a more involved mediation in which the third party proposes solutions to the conflict.

Arbitration is much more difficult and happens rarely among nations, and then only on small matters. Here the disputants give their consent to the third party to actually decide the issue.

Adjudication is even harder, as it requires countries to put their fate in the hands of an international court. Sometimes boundary and trade details can be arbitrated or adjudicated between non-hostile countries, but in the Middle East the issues are the life or death of nations, and no country turns its existence over to a court. One cannot extrapolate domestic legal systems onto the world scene.

Then Israel, a branch of Europe in Muslim eyes, repeatedly beats Arab armies, occupies more and more Arab land, and crushes Palestinians who complain about it. And finally the United States twice makes quick work of Iraq, killing thousands of civilians as "collateral damage." Is there no end to the humiliation? This is the psychological self-portrait of Arabs and to a certain extent of Muslims as a whole: always the defenseless victim. Now, everything Muslims felt about Crusaders, Mongols, and British imperialists is focused against the United States. We do not really deserve it, but can America escape it?

diplomacy   Official contacts between countries.
third-party diplomacy   Neutral country helps settle dispute.

Some Muslims realize the fault is in their authoritarian regimes, soaring populations, and faltering economies. Other ex-colonial lands had similar grudges, but they faded. India had justifiable rage against British imperialists, which they transferred to the United States, the new English-speaking power that wished to arrange the world to suit its commerce and its values. As India gained self-confidence and self-respect through economic growth, this hostility faded. Now a newly capitalist India (big growth industry: computer operations) has excellent relations with the United States. An unspoken factor pulling the two together: both face Islamic terrorism.

Muslim lands could undergo a similar transformation. It will not happen easily or automatically. A thousand years ago, Islam was a vibrant, growing culture, far ahead of Christian Europe in science, medicine, commerce, architecture, and tolerance of other religions. Muslims have a proud past they could refer to. The narrow, bitter past offered by the salafis harkens back to the fourteenth century, after the Mongol conquest of Baghdad in 1258 wounded Islamic civilization.

Can the United States play any role in this process? Intervening with troops may be an occasional unfortunate necessity, but America must not make a habit of it. Every intervention reinforces the Muslim sense of humiliation and victimization, which leads to more rage. Economic examples are much better. Indeed, it was the incredible growth of Japan, South Korea, Taiwan, Hong Kong, and Singapore from poverty to world-class prosperity that chipped away at the self-confidence of Communist regimes. The ultimate weakness of Islamic extremism is that it cannot put food on the table. Many former Islamic revolutionaries in Iran now realize this.

One example of a Muslim country that modernizes into prosperity and democracy may be worth more than America's vast military strength. As economist Paul Krugman points out, no one has been able to predict the next lands of rapid economic growth; it is always a surprise. Famed Swedish economist Gunnar Myrdal penned his pessimistic *Asian Drama: An Inquiry into the Poverty of Nations* in the 1960s. Scarcely was the ink dry when several Asian countries began to take off. (He underrated the growth of manufacturing for the world market.) The Muslim world may surprise us.

If we are not careful, the current U.S.-Islamic antipathies could turn into a new Cold War. Already, some Americans speak of it as such: a long, bitter, ideological struggle in which Islam is the new Soviet Union. If that view ever gets planted—and some on both sides are busy planting it—your generation will know the fears and frustration of the Cold War, which our generation waged and eventually won. It was not a pleasant thing; it cost millions of lives in wars and squandered vast resources in weapons systems which, if used, could have destroyed the planet. Let us not go through anything like that again.

How to prevent it? Keep rage in check. The West is certain to be hit with more horrifying terrorist strikes. Al Qaeda will attempt many attacks, some small and some on the scale of 9/11. Furthermore, there are other Islamist organizations beyond al Qaeda that could follow in its footsteps. The Palestinian Hamas organization may expand its suicide bombings beyond Israel; the United States would be the natural target. America will have to be on guard for decades and must organize for it (see box on page 329). U.S. homeland security does not have nearly the funding to safeguard America. A major weakness: the thousands of containers that come in by ship every day.

D : *Domestic Structures*

CATCHING TERRORISTS: NO ONE IN CHARGE

Is the United States organized to effectively fight terrorism? Before 9/11, the U.S. government had terrorism on the far-back burner. There were many indications of a terrorist strike, but U.S. agencies were not talking to each other and had no plan to fight terrorism. The Federal Bureau of Investigation is legally not supposed to operate overseas, where it has no powers of arrest. (Some FBI agents representing the Justice Department are in embassies to coordinate activities against organized crime with host countries.) The FBI is generally unequipped with foreign-language and area skills to make sense of underground movements. Before 9/11, terrorism was a low FBI priority. It ignored its own field agents who urgently signaled that Arab visitors were taking flying lessons for dangerous purposes. As critics exclaimed after 9/11, the FBI catches bank robbers.

American intelligence agencies, on the other hand, are loaded with area and language expertise but have no legal power to arrest anyone or even to carry out operations inside the United States. One standard intelligence mission is to penetrate foreign organizations with its own informants. This is terribly difficult with al Qaeda because it recruits from kinfolk and neighbors who know each other personally. Immigration and Customs Enforcement (ICE, formerly INS) is our front line against terrorism, but it is underfunded and overburdened. Years after 9/11, there is still no single computer system or data base by which the FBI, intelligence agencies, ICE, and local police can share information.

The U.S. armed forces are superbly trained and equipped to destroy hostile countries but not to catch small groups of hostile characters. They too are not law-enforcement agencies, and using them as a heavily armed police force invites tragedy, like crushing a gnat with a bulldozer. Top civilian officials sometimes think that the Army or Marines can be used as police, but military officers, knowing what can go wrong, generally oppose such misuse. As of now, no U.S. department or agency is set up to catch terrorists, a task that falls between stools. Some coordination and centralization came with the new Department of Homeland Security, but the FBI and intelligence agencies are not part of it.

What is needed is a new, small agency—perhaps part of Homeland Security—that draws on the intelligence capabilities of all other agencies and has the policing capabilities to track down terrorists. It will have the weapons and training of Special Forces, area expertise, the detection capabilities of the FBI, and the law-enforcement powers of police. It will be a sort of international SWAT team with language skills. So far this is seen only in fanciful television dramas.

We will also need an important element that the Bush neo-cons have scorned: international law. What will give this imaginary SWAT team permission to operate on foreign soil? To send armed men into another country without permission is an act of war. The world urgently needs to develop a body of terrorism law that most countries accept. The United States must take the lead here, and, yes, even sign treaties that are binding on itself. The Bush administration rejected the International Criminal Court, claiming it would bring frivolous anti-U.S. charges against our soldiers. One administration neo-con argued that no treaty binds America, which may do as it wishes.

The problem here is that if the United States is not bound by a treaty on terrorism law, few other countries will be. Reciprocity is the basis of international law. Fortunately, precedents are at hand: centuries-old laws on piracy. As Israeli Attorney General Gideon Hausner pointed out in the 1961 Eichmann trial, pirates may be tried and hanged by whoever catches them. Their crimes are the concern of all, not just one country. In our day, terrorism equals piracy.

K : *Key Concepts*

FIVE STEPS TO DISBELIEF

Disbelief and disillusion over Iraq have grown among Americans in the same way they did over Vietnam (see page 270), not all at once but in logical steps that reality forces upon us. Attentive citizens during both wars tended to progress from supporters to critics in five stages:

1. Uncritical belief. No one likes war, but if we don't stop them there (Communists in Vietnam, al Qaeda in Iraq), we'll have to fight them elsewhere, possibly here. Washington knows what it's doing, and we must support the president and our troops. Our military effort is both moral and necessary.

2. Things aren't working quite right. Some of our weapons and tactics are not well suited to the situation; we should change them. The local government (in Saigon or in Baghdad) is corrupt, inept, and unpopular. It is unable to mount a cohesive, spirited campaign against insurgents. It must reform itself.

3. "If only" criticisms emerge that focus on particular techniques, policies, and personalities: "If only al Maliki (or Diem) could get a handle on the situation." In philosophy, "if only" claims are called "counterfactual," situations that do not actually exist and probably never could. Examples: "If only Sunni and Shi'a could cooperate." "If only we had sent more troops to establish order early." "If only Saigon could stop its revolving-door governments and get some stability."

4. A "new approach" stage logically follows when it becomes clear that the hoped-for changes of the "if only" stage are not going to happen. As the Baghdad or Saigon regimes appear incapable of reforming themselves, previous supporters mutter: "What we need is an entirely new approach." A pragmatic secretary of defense replaces a can-do enthusiast (Gates replaces Rumsfeld; Clifford replaces McNamara) and comes up with a new approach. U.S. forces are slowly withdrawn—Nixon's "Vietnamization"—to push the local regime to shape up and look after its own security. Success is defined downward: "Get out, but don't let it look like an American defeat. If Baghdad or Saigon lose, it's their fault." We thus distance ourselves from the problem.

5. Inherent infeasibility dawns on many: "Well, the whole thing was inherently infeasible from the beginning. We never should have gotten involved." Not all make it to this stage, as some are reluctant to admit they had been wrong in supporting the wars. Much criticism stalls at stages 3 and 4. Politicians prefer if-only critiques because they are easier to handle than inherent-infeasibility critiques, which imply they did not perform due diligence in voting for the war.

But America must not lapse into indiscriminate rage against Muslims, for that plays into the hands of the terrorists. Invading Muslim lands on suspicion of terrorism convinces more Muslim youths to join a jihad. Rage can be contagious: We catch it from Islamic extremists and sneeze it back to the whole region, which is exactly what the terrorists want. The extremists, following the revolutionary theory of "the worse, the better," try to create maximum chaos out of which they suppose they will be the net winners. They may be terribly mistaken and simply end up with a destroyed, impoverished region.

Conflicts

WAR WITH IRAN?

Bogged down in Iraq, America lost its appetite for any more wars in the region. But the United States and Israel are on collision courses with Iran, and war is possible. The election of fiery Mahmoud Ahmadinejad as Iran's president in 2005 (see page 237) increased tensions such as these:

- Hardliners in Washington believe Iran has made a client state out of the Shi'a south of Iraq and could eventually do the same with all of Iraq. Some think Tehran is trying for an Iranian-dominated "Shi'a crescent" through Iraq, Kuwait, Bahrain, and the Eastern Province of Saudi Arabia. Iraq's south is already a Shi'a Islamic republic. The growth of Iranian influence was inevitable with the destruction of the Saddam regime, something the Bush administration failed to anticipate.

- A full-scale Iraqi civil war could bring Iranian military intervention, which in turn could lead to regional war as Sunni countries (Saudi Arabia, Jordan, Egypt) come to the rescue of their Sunni correligionists. Iran, with a bigger and better army, would beat Arab forces. Would the United States stand for this or would it enter the conflict?

- Iranian sponsorship of Lebanon's Hezbollah gave Iran a role in the Arab-Israeli dispute. Iranian money, rockets, and training made Hezbollah an impressive fighting force, giving Tehran bragging rights that only Shi'a are gutsy enough to stand up to Israel.

- Iran's nuclear program, probably aimed at acquiring nuclear weapons, made Israel nervous. Quoting the late Ayatollah Khomeini, Ahmadinejad wanted Israel "wiped off the map." When Israel gets nervous, it preempts. In 1981, Israeli aircraft hit Iraq's Osirak reactor to damage its nuclear program. Israel's former chief of staff, Air Force General Dan Halutz (whose parents came from Iran) was asked how far he would go to prevent Iran from getting nukes. He replied: "2,000 kilometers."

- Washington is also totally against Iran getting nukes, which would make it the regional power. Pentagon officials worry Iran could also pass on a nuclear device to Hezbollahis or other extremists for another, bigger 9/11. The United States thus might conduct a preemptive strike against Iran or condone an Israeli one.

- Iran is eager to prove, contrary to Sunni disdain, that Shi'a are good Muslims, possibly the best Muslims. Iranian power, aided by vast oil revenues, is growing in what some call a "Shi'a revival" throughout the Muslim world.

Iran's expansion of its power and prestige, to be sure, do not necessarily lead to war, but they do set the stage for it. President Bush in 2007 voiced a tougher line on Iran, one resembling his 2002 line on Iraq. Iran's clerical rulers, illuminated by a few rays of pragmatism, understand that Ahmadinejad is not to be trusted with military functions and curtailed his powers.

America must be well-armed but remember that force of arms alone cannot settle this problem. Occasional military steps will be necessary, but they must be carried out calmly and always with an eye on the aftermath. Remember, the West won the Cold War not by fighting but by waiting. Eventually, the Soviet Union collapsed under pressure of its own faulty economic system. Many Americans were frightened of the Soviet Union during the long Cold War, but history was always on our side, and it is now. Our generation made it; yours will too.

CONCLUSIONS

World War II brought the United States into the Middle East in a major way. The region's oil—especially that of Saudi Arabia, with whom President Roosevelt established personal ties in 1945—and the founding of Israel pulled the United States into the affairs of the Middle East. We may wish to stay out but cannot. The United States consumes one-fourth of the world's oil, most of it imported.

U.S. policy toward Israel and the Arabs was more or less even-handed until Nixon, who resupplied Israel in the 1973 war, when Europe turned first neutral and then hostile toward Israel. Israel likewise abandoned its early neutrality between Moscow and Washington and turned sharply to America.

Bush 43, looking at the intense U.S. involvement in the Middle East of previous administrations, wished for a smaller U.S. role but soon put the United States more deeply into the region than ever. Neo-cons in the Bush administration especially favored U.S. involvement, but this led to U.S. unilateralism with few allies.

The United States faces major Middle East policy choices. How long should the United States keep troops there and how many? Can several U.S. agencies—which communicate little with each other—be melded into an effective antiterrorist force? Can America make and adhere to new international laws against terrorism? How to best handle Islamic rage directed against the West? If we turn to rage ourselves, we may be creating a new and long-lasting Cold War.

KEY TERMS

apostasy (p. 315)

Arab street (p. 322)

bipolar (p. 326)

consulate general (p. 318)

diplomacy (p. 327)

embassy (p. 318)

multipolar (p. 326)

third-party diplomacy (p. 327)

Third World (p. 316)

unipolar (p. 326)

War Powers Act (p. 320)

FURTHER REFERENCE

Beeman, William O. *The "Great Satan" vs. the "Mad Mullahs": How the United States and Iran Demonize Each Other.* Westport, CT: Praeger, 2005.

Benjamin, Daniel, and Steven Simon. *The Next Attack: The Failure of the War on Terror and a Strategy for Getting It Right.* New York: Henry Holt, 2006.

Clarke, Richard A. *Against All Enemies: Inside America's War on Terror.* New York: Simon & Schuster, 2004.

Daalder, Ivo H., Nicole Gnesotto, and Philip H. Gordon, eds. *Crescent of Crisis: U.S.-European Strategy for the Greater Middle East.* Washington, D.C.: Brookings, 2006.

Fawcett, Louise, ed. *International Relations of the Middle East.* New York: Oxford University Press, 2005.

Fouskas, Vassilis K., and Bülent Gökay. *The New American Imperialism: Bush's War on Terror and Blood for Oil.* Westport, CT: Praeger, 2005.

Halliday, Fred. *The Middle East in International Relations: Power, Politics and Ideology.* New York: Cambridge University Press, 2005.

Kashmeri, Sarwar A. *America and Europe after 9/11 and Iraq: The Great Divide.* Westport, CT: Praeger, 2006.

Kegley, Charles W., Jr., and Gregory A. Raymond. *After Iraq: The Imperiled American Imperium.* New York: Oxford University Press, 2006.

Khalidi, Rashid. *Resurrecting Empire: Western Footprints and America's Perilous Path in the Middle East.* Boston, MA: Beacon, 2005.

Klare, Michael T. *Blood and Oil: The Danger and Consequences of America's Growing Dependency on Imported Petroleum.* New York: Metropolitan Books, 2004.

Mueller, John. *Overblown: How Politicians and the Terrorism Industry Inflate National Security Threats, and Why We Believe Them.* New York: Free Press, 2006.

Potter, Lawrence G., and Gary G. Sick, eds. *Security in the Persian Gulf: Origins, Obstacles, and the Search for Consensus.* New York: Palgrave, 2002.

Quandt, William B. *Peace Process: American Diplomacy and the Arab-Israeli Conflict since 1967,* 3rd ed. Berkeley, CA: University of California Press, 2005.

Telhami, Shibley. *The Stakes: America in the Middle East.* Boulder, CO: Westview, 2003.

Youngs, Richard. *Europe and the Middle East: In the Shadow of September 11.* Boulder, CO: Lynne Rienner, 2006.

Index